D0206060

# CALIFORNIA & THE FICTIONS OF CAPITAL

# CALIFORNIA & THE FICTIONS OF CAPITAL

George L. Henderson

New York Oxford

Oxford University Press

1999

Oxford University Press

Oxford New York
Athens Auckland Bangkok Bogotá Buenos Aires Calcutta
Cape Town Chennai Dar es Salaam Delhi Florence Hong Kong Istanbul
Karachi Kuala Lumpur Madrid Melbourne Mexico City Mumbai
Nairobi Paris São Paulo Singapore Taipei Tokyo Toronto Warsaw

and associated companies in
Berlin Ibadan



Published by Oxford University Press, Inc.
198 Madison Avenue, New York, New York 10016

Oxford is a registered trademark of Oxford University Press



Library of Congress Cataloging-in-Publication Data
Henderson, George L., 1958–
California and the fictions of capital / George L. Henderson.
p. cm.
Includes bibliographical references and index.
ISBN 0-19-510890-6
1. American literature—California—History and criticism.
2. Capitalism and literature—California. 3. California—Historical geography. 4. California—Economic conditions. 5. Capital—California—History. I. Title.
PS283.C2H46 1999
810.9'32794—dc21 97-52308

1 3 5 7 9 8 6 4 2

Printed in the United States of America
on acid-free paper

# Contents

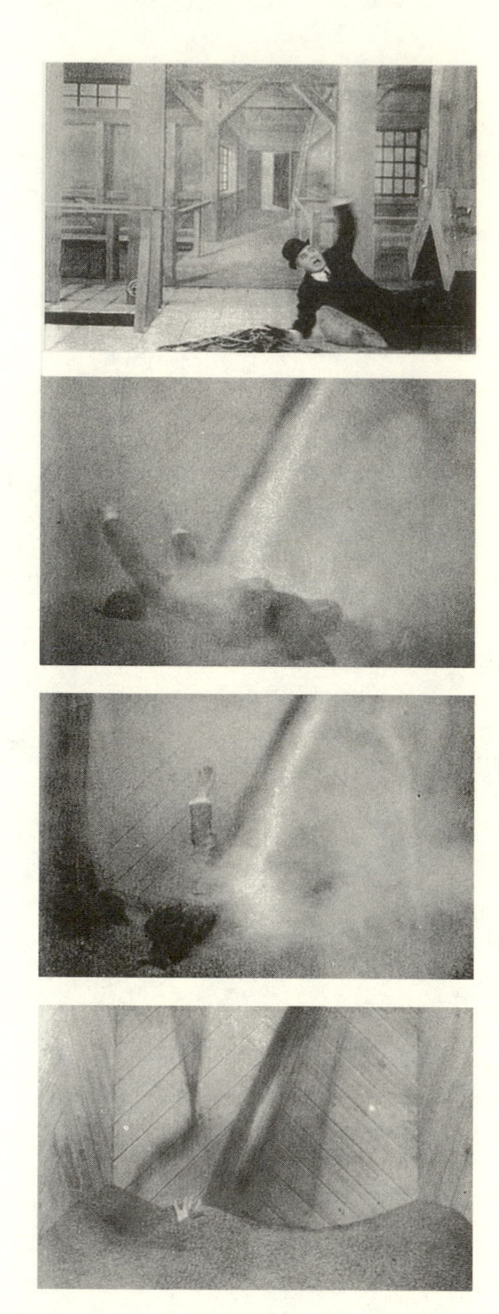

D. W. Griffith, "A Corner in Wheat" (1909). (Courtesy of Kino Film International Corporation.)

# Introduction

## *The Alchemy of Capital and Nature*

Though he was already dead, Frank Norris had a good year in 1909. His epic novel *The Octopus* (1901) was brought to the screen by visionary film artist D. W. Griffith—no other filmmaker has touched it since. Titled "A Corner in Wheat," the film is a confident, bare-bones distillation of the novel's hundreds of pages into fewer than fifteen minutes of viewing time. It is of course no substitute for the original, a point compounded by the fact that Griffith drew on a second Norris novel, *The Pit* (1903), also a rather long book. Griffith's work is such a treat for Norris's readers because it superbly confirms that Norris was an expert craftsmen of signature tableaux, devices that regularly punctuated his narratives and that allowed him to tie together the worlds of meaning he had been summoning up. Of several exemplary scenes that structure the two novels, one from *The Octopus* was perhaps guaranteed to be filmed. This was an especially macabre sequence involving a conniving grain speculator, who is destined for live burial under the tons of wheat he has amassed. Thrashing about in a pelting rain of wheat, choking on grain dust, and trying desperately to stay alive, he inevitably succumbs. The wheat continues to pile up around him, until only one hand is able to poke through in a final, gruesome salute. In Norris's hands, the speculator, also an urban sophisticate, has tumbled into the hull of a ship while the wheat was being loaded. In the film, he happened to have plummeted to the bottom of a grain silo. But no matter the difference in detail, the scene is a brilliant summation of the novel's back and forth movements between San Francisco and its startlingly productive hinterland, the San Joaquin Valley. As such, it establishes a host of disquieting themes and questions.

For one thing, here is a man who has been profiting without producing: What sort of economy could properly allow that? Who could call watching the ticker tape "work," and why, up to the point of the speculator's demise, should it have brought such riches? But assuming this man is actually a legitimate creation of his economic environment, and yet still he comes to an untimely end, what sort of economy would eat its own progeny? Does it need people like this, or want to do away with them? Perhaps both. Or first one and then the other. For the sake of the overall good of the economic machinery, perhaps the machine must kill a portion of itself in order to move on. But move on where? Where did it come from in the first place and what will be its wellspring in the future? The urban sophisticate, for example, apparently specialized in things "rural." Was he out of his element, or was the polis the uncontested master of a far-flung geography? Maybe the rural is best served by suffering the whims of urban capital and urban aspirations. Or, perhaps we have it reversed; it's the wheat that has its grasp on the speculator. It's rural economy, not urban whims, that make time and place endure, that create wealth, settle populations, and build cities. But what is it about rural economy that offers attractions to capital and its circuits? And on what basis would this appeal last?

The kicker is that all these seemingly disparate entities—the speculator versus his wheat, finance versus production, city versus country—are far more alike than one might think at first. Speculative profits tend toward the unpredictable, but so too does the rural economy. Agricultural production is notoriously sporadic. Bumper crops are followed by lean years, while, in any one year, late frosts or torrential storms may stunt the harvest: The inconsistencies are legion. Speculators are compulsive and so is nature. What initially seems like the clash of opposites in Norris's story, therefore, is better read as the complementary energies of regional political economy. Somehow, casualties aside, the rhythms of capital and the rhythms of nature find each other.

It is no stretch, then, to say that lurking behind the image of the speculator's death in the wheat, there is more than a hint that conditions transcend this one individual. The speculator is not just a speculator, nor the harvest just a pile of grain. When there are speculators, there must be something speculative about economy itself. And when this character drowns in the harvest, there must be something risky about nature that needs to be taken into account. (In fact, one truth behind the mass of grain is that the soil has been mined of its nutrients.) The point, it would seem, is that capital and nature are webs of constraint and confinement that must be carefully recast as fields of opportunity. To be sure, the resulting alchemy can be as volatile as it can be profitable.

In California, these are old and defining themes, nature and capital. Most famously, they began with gold. Or rather when the gold gave out—for post Gold Rush California clarifies what those few heady years were all about. When the placers grew scarce and the hoses that flushed the Sierra hillsides of their riches grew flaccid, the unity of money and nature in California (what gold most essentially *was)* was rent asunder, ensuring that desire for more of that unity held fast. This book focuses on the period during which pride of place and visions of alchemy next came to agriculture,[1] and did so by virtue of an enveloping capitalist economy. A major arena of emphasis here is how—as a desired end—the capitalist transformation of California was narrated and represented, by whom and through what rhetorical means. The result is a work of historical geography, political economy, and literary criticism.

Some of what I have written about here is taken for granted now, especially the explosive growth of irrigation and the fantastic levels of California's farm output. It is easy to forget, however, that a crop does not only spring from the soil. Since the 1850s, California agriculture has partaken of the dynamics of a capitalist economy whose circuits surrounded and supported, encroached and exploited. The result was not one countryside but many, each with its own trajectory but all shot through with the more general processes of capital circulation. It is deeply ingrained that America's agricultural regions are places that "settlers" made and less appreciated that at times money got there first. Then it was money, and labor, that had to be coordinated, cajoled, and disciplined. For whose benefit? It is doubtful that rentiers and grain kings, orchardists and engineers greeted quite the same dawns. And surely all (or a large part anyway) of the Arid West by now appreciates the hydrological feats of the last hundred-plus years. But to say that getting water from where it was wet to where it was dry presented problems is to venture a serious understatement.

My assumption is that none of those doings *had* to happen, but were instead the results of particular opportunities and constraints. I will argue here that a large part of California's development in the late nineteenth and early twentieth centuries was structured by the uneasy relations between capitalism and agriculture. An important theme here is that agriculture embodies capital and simultaneously resists it. In part one I examine the implications of this for California's economic history, as a history of capital, while in part two I do the same for certain aspects of bourgeois cultural production. (That at least is a convenient shorthand. In fact, both parts of the book are concerned with political-economic and cultural trajectories.) Pivotal to part two is an engagement with the California novel, a rich repository of geographical imaginations and a densely expressive outlet for the expression of alchemic desires. In the early 1880s, California writers began to turn in earnest to the subjects of rural land and water development and its financing. Along with promotional tracts and the production of certain archetypal landscape images, some of which are also treated here, their novels were efforts at theorizing bourgeois economy in ways sympathetic to bourgeois anxieties.

I have turned to this literature, then, not in search of illustrations with which to decorate the "real" doings of Californians, nor with the claim that literature "realistically" documents lived experience back then, but with a question: what did it mean that this fiction was written at all? The idea of turning nature into money was an ideology that had to be bolstered. And it didn't solve any problems so much as state what the problem was.

The framework I wish to propose for the study of these novels and of California is the very phenomenon with which the writings themselves are concerned: social and geographical processes of uneven development and the circulation of capital. For my purposes here, uneven development is understood as one of capitalism's calling cards; it is the hallmark of a system that periodically tends toward crisis.[2] A discussion of three manifestations of uneven development are woven into these pages. One is temporal—the tendency for capitalist development to be expressed through cycles of boom and bust, which various polities continually try to navigate. The second is social—capital develops differently in different sectors, say agriculture versus industry; it positions groups of people differentially with respect to the "benefits" of capitalism; and it positions individuals differently with respect to their relations to circulating capital.[3] The third aspect of uneven development is spatial—while capital needs a physical produced landscape for the perpetuation of its own operations, this is capital taken out of immediate circulation, often quite anxiously.[4] Such a landscape—sometimes rural and agricultural, sometimes urban and industrial, sometimes voiding distinctions between the two—becomes not only the solution for capitalism's survival but the source of some of its most dire problems.

## Why the Late Nineteenth-Century Countryside?

Uneven development is always instantiated locally (though it be a multiscaled process). It alerts us to capitalism as not just a mode of production but a mode of production that is also about place making. To prize it apart and to see it in economic, geographic, *and* cultural terms demands a sharp focus.

Social and economic historians of California have long recognized that the 1880s were a turning point. Convention holds that the departure away from the political and economic obsession with mining was definitive. As for a signal event, some historians prefer to focus on the collapse of the Comstock and the Bank of California in the mid 1870s, and others on the legal proscription of hydraulic mining in 1884. The important point is that after the decline of mining, agriculture picked up the slack in California's economic lifeline. (I review the basic developments in chapter 1, while in chapters 2 and 3 I isolate two themes for special treatment: respectively, the circulation of financial capital in agriculture, and the circulation of variable capital through migrant labor and the awkward social-cultural position this implied for farmers as what I call "capitalist laborers.") The reconstitution of the economy in the countryside, so clear in the 1880s, was manifest in multiple but related directions: in rising crop production, in the economies of rural real estate and land and water development, in bold manipulations of the physical environment, and in an elaborate migrant labor market. Hardly abstract forces, the events underlying what Frank Norris called the "new order of things" were riddled with social struggle. Money, too, defined the new order. Nor was money all an abstraction. Money's rearrangement in space and its investment in different economic sectors represented conscious (if sometimes self-deluded) acts. Investors in California's cities, primarily San Francisco and Los Angeles, plowed their profits into the fertile lands of the San Joaquin Valley, Southern California, and the Imperial Valley. But, in turn, each of these regions generated its own turnover and reinvested it locally. A portion of these investments, both local and not, were directed at the development of irrigated agriculture. Irrigation generated a font of wealth and valorized much subsequent diversification of California's regional economies. Water, like land, was an essential venue for the geographic circulation of capital. The hitch was that capital brought to the irrigated countryside a turbulence all its own.

In short, no account of California's experience in the late nineteenth century can ignore the rise of the "new" agriculture. Agriculture describes not what was fading from view but what lay, to a substantial degree, on California's horizons—and this, curiously enough, following a previous phase of industrialization. Although they were hailed as a panacea for unemployed miners, for out-of-work urban laborers—not to mention the financial big guns in search of a place to put their surplus—the state's farms were lashed to the fits and starts of capital, which they in fact embodied. And Californians, regularly on intimate terms with the jolts of boom and bust, came to know it.

If the declining incomes of the 1870s (a decade of mining speculation, failed banks, and ruination in the stock market) gave agriculture and irrigation their allure in the 1880s, too much production too soon raised problems again by the 1890s, until the willful formation of new commodity sectors, new markets, and improved production and distribution techniques brought California's producers into the limelight again. Caught in a classic cost-price squeeze in the 1920s, however, with the additional debt burden after years of rapid irrigation expansion, California agriculture, like that in much of the nation, again began a slide into depression (see the excellent overview in California Development Association 1924).

To the obvious fact that agricultural profits were not won overnight is the corollary that they were not made in one place. Rural California, as chapters 4 through 7 relate, was not an undifferentiated outback. (See the introduction to part II for an overview.) Revenues emerged from select locales, with capital shuttling between them. In their sometimes dramatic moves to plug the gaps of spatially uneven flows of capital, bankers, investors, and speculators tied these locales together—for example, San Francisco to the San Joaquin Valley or Southern California to the Imperial Valley—seeing to it that portions of the money that had been made in one time and place would appear in the form of credit or venture capital to help fund rural development somewhere else.

And to the successive historical and geographic "frontiers" of capital is an added corollary: these were sources of cultural meaning in their own right. There was a real catch here. Money was perceived to be a troubling and, ironically, meddling presence to bourgeois culture. I have said that money was not all that abstract, but, if a small anthropomorphism may be permitted, this ran counter to its furtiveness, that is, the apparently mysterious ease with which it appeared, disappeared, and fluctuated in value. This was an affront just as it was the *sine qua non* of bourgeois society. Rural smallholders ached for a steady stream of credit and then strained to master their growing indebtedness. Bankers, speculators, and railroad heads doled out funds only to wring their hands over payment schedules. The literati and the pulp writers, too, wondered how to map the elusive geography of money. Time and again what they thought would be perfectly transparent agrarian landscapes turned out to be dense and duplicitous thickets. One need look no further, perhaps, than to Norris's *The Octopus* or Harold Bell Wright's 1911 bestseller, *The Winning of Barbara Worth*, to realize that landscape for them explained little. Instead it had to be explained.

## The Discourse of Rural Realism

Land and irrigation development, as wedded to sources of financing and larger circuits of capital, were eagerly recruited as subjects for California fiction. (I hope readers will consider it a reasonable balance that while much of this fiction is today little known, it actually concerns reasonably well known [to historians at least] events—the Mussel Slough affair, the Southern California 1880s land boom, the Imperial Valley flood, and the San Francisco-Hetch Hetchy and Los Angeles-Owens Valley controversies.) In such fiction, novels for the most part, what I call the discourse of *rural realism* was concertedly invoked. There, in fiction, because it was embedded in narrative, rural realism was most seamlessly joined to other species of discourse, just as its fragility was most easily apparent.

Rural realism is, on the one hand, not unlike what Michael Schudson notes about the "capitalist realism" of advertising art—both realisms visually idealize capitalist production and spheres of consumption (Schudson 1984; see also Marchand 1985). It seems to me that something very like this idealization happened with a certain class of California novel. I am not summoning realism in the usual literary sense then (although I am concerned that the urban bias of historians and theorists of nineteenth-century literary realism be disturbed[5]). Instead, what I have in mind is the fabrication of a discourse that depicted, subserved, and responded to the rhythms of the circulation of capital through the countryside. Arising from that impulse, rural realism was the amalgamation of characters, plots, settings, and narrator voices mobilized for the purpose of totalizing the ideals of the liberal capitalist market. Rural realism was the desire to extend that market to its geographical conclusion, excluding no place and bypassing no one—save those upon whom "Anglo-Saxon" disfavor fell. It was one of the dream images of white (mostly) California that its outsized portion of western spoils would bring about that conclusion.

Apologia for capital though it was, rural realism was, conversely, Janus-faced. It was, for example, hostile to competing (read urban or eastern) capital formations. It was also a critique: instead of taking capitalism to task *prima facie*, it made an issue of how to make capital less crisis ridden (temporally, socially, spatially), or at least make it seem so. Rural realism was a discourse that could see through reasonably well to some of capital's repeating, and bound to be repeated, flaws, but was so *borne of* capital that its critique stopped short and safe. As such, rural realist discourse does not so much open a window onto California's political economy because it somehow "represented" or "documented" it, but because rural realist discourse was an aspect of bourgeois political economy.

By the same token it should be noted what rural realism was not. I am not arguing that it was a literary genre. Nonetheless, since the period covered here witnessed the production of what are commonly called the genres of realism, regionalism, and romance, I explore how rural realist discourse was refracted, aided, and abetted by those genres, such as I understand them.[6] The novels represented here (see the list of sources for an overview), I would want to add, are in no sense reducible to rural realist discourse. Many of them are equally Anglo-Saxon preoccupations with supposed racial superiority (at the expense of Latinos especially), nationalism, and gender. But such preoccupations were hardly inimical to fixations on the problems of money and class that underwrote rural realism. Quite the contrary, they helped to reproduce those fixations and counted heavily upon them.

From Frank Norris and Mary Austin to Harold Bell Wright, the writers who trained their eyes on the California countryside did not set their sights thus because the California farmscape was an exotic residual in an otherwise industrialized America. I see these authors as writers who understood what geographer Stephen Daniels calls the "duplicity of landscape" (Daniels 1987). That is, they were not taken in by the aesthetic pleasures of the rural to the extent of missing the fact that the rural was the scene of some of the most sophisticated (and for them, sublime) manipulations of capital. One ought not read, for example, Sarah Orne Jewett's Maine idyll, *The Country of the Pointed Firs*, and Mary Austin's cavil about Los Angeles rummaging around the Owens Valley in *The Ford* and assume they share the same sensibility, however rural the settings of both books. Or as Frank Norris's main character in *The Octopus* would discover, writers, bred on sentiment and local color, might gravitate to "pastoral" California, and, intending to romanticize its marginality, find that the rural was the very picture of everything that was contemporary and modern about the Far West. The economic status of the rural differed vastly from place to place in the post–Civil War decades. In the case of California, the rural was nowhere near being economically residual and represented futurity in many ways. Its appeal in California fiction was its economic primacy, rather than its romanticized marginalization, as was often the case with evocations of the former plantation South in the late nineteenth century. In California fiction, then, a new structure of feeling fixated on the countryside, not because the countryside was being left behind, but because it had become a dominant arena of accumulation.

## Why Rural Realism, Why the Novel?

Attention to texts as fully imbricated with the "world outside the text" is no longer much of a dare, except to those who think no such world exists or to those who assert that texts have no place in that world. Instead, the exact arrangements and the finer points are what stick in the craw. While I will not claim to have settled these imbrications, I will say that my way of thinking through them owes much to the sort of close readings of narrative and historicity (for me, a historical spatiality) performed by New Historicism (e.g., Veeser 1989), including its extraordinarily patient exegeses of the logics that undergird specific narratives (e.g., Michaels 1987).

For New Historicists, when it comes to meaning, plurality reigns. Meanings may be cultural, social, economic, or political, or some combination of these, but the point, or one point, is less to keep these domains separate than to expose their arbitrary boundaries and seek out the projects these boundaries serve in the first place. For a *New York Times* interviewer, Stephen Greenblatt summed up the New Historicism as folding the history of texts and the textuality of history into each other. Lest there be fears of a return to idealism therein, these words are not to be taken to mean that history (or geography) can be reduced to a set of representations but that theories of the world must be and have been built *with* representations. And it makes as little sense to deny the existence of these as it does to deny the existence of on-the-ground events. But I take the real critical move of New Historicism to be that it employs close readings as a mechanism for returning readers' attention to the material world. It has the intention of evoking the social and cultural density that gives birth to texts in the first place, looking to texts not with the expectation that they will clarify that density and afford a glimpse into the zeitgeist, but with the assumption that they will bear social and cultural relations out in language, narrative, and character. Any presumed social theoretical clarification *in* literature (let's say, the presumption that the novel is a diagnosis) is in the end really a player within those very relations (a socially, culturally bred diagnosis).

All of which does not necessarily make the task of interpretation any easier. New Historicism may, for example, make it rather difficult to decide what kind of "commentary" a given novel offers. It gives rise, for example, to the question of whether or not it is very meaningful for a novel to register ambivalence about capitalism when, as Michaels argues, the available array of ambivalences are constituted by one's position within capitalism. (I take this issue up in the introduction to part two.) I should say, however, that one poses this particular question to certain kinds of books and not others. Perhaps it is especially appropriate for that stream of late-nineteenth- and early-twentieth-century novel that engages the gritty, crushing realities of modern life (e.g., Bradbury and MacFarlane 1976). But, as the New Historicist approach will also allow us to recognize, other types of books would turn the question almost completely around: If writers actually did want to register their fondness for capitalist political economy, how would they do it?[7] (In the case of *The Octopus*, Norris at first takes a critical stance toward capitalism and then, famously, abandons it. This is less a contradiction than a rhetorical maneuver through which Norris produces his own version of rural realism.) What would they have to emphasize and what would they feel compelled to ignore? And if they were to hail capitalist political economy when *agriculture* had essentially *rescued* regional capital (a two-fold conundrum), how might matters be complicated?

At the surface, rural realist discourse applauds agriculture's importance for capital (and vice versa, for in the discourse each was good for the other) in the Far West. Deeper down, rural realism expresses a structural problem peculiar to agriculture's relationship to the capitalist mode of production. To wit, in the decades following the Civil War, industrial capitals increasingly took over aspects of production—such as implement making and milling—that had been historically relegated to on-farm manufacturing or small-scale, decentralized craft production (see Pudup 1987). But these ballooning industrial sectors could not replace natural processes per se (e.g., plant growth and reproduction). In blunt terms, factories could make a plough but they could not manufacture an ear of corn (see Goodman et al. 1987). Agriculture was a site that capital could not fully make its own and was yet that site which capital intently strove to capture—an irony for the mode of production whose origins were so intensely agrarian. In chapter 2, drawing upon work in rural sociology, Karl Marx's *Capital*, and the work of geographer David Harvey, I argue at length that this gap created an enormous opportunity for finance and rentier capitals to develop through American agriculture—California representing a special case, in that it represents both the westward tilt of finance capital and the development of some of the most sophisticated financial structures of the early-twentieth-century United States. That is, if nature posed an obstacle to one faction of capital, as rural sociologists Mann and Dickinson (1978) insist, other factions of capital, whose earnings were based on the appropriation of values through sale of farm credit and mortgages, were busy indeed.

The not-quite duality of capital and agriculture lent to rural realism the formidable energies of ambiguity: agriculture was of importance to and yet separate from capitalism proper, and here was a gap that was resoundingly productive for discourse. Because agriculture was not completely capitalist, in the industrial sense, but because it was clearly articulated with the circulation of capital in the wider sense, it could be a cultural site for thinking through—and worrying about—what was desirable in one kind of capitalist trajectory as opposed to another.[8]

Moreover, if the glare of industrialization was never quite outshone, neither was the cultural luminosity of a pre-capitalist rural past. Not quite "sunshine" and not quite "noir"—apologies to Mike Davis (1990)—the rural realist gambit could not be ventured lightly. It always signaled the potential displacement of the myth it competed against and thereby had to also keep alive. Agrarian and "middle landscape" images, redolent of the historical tensions between the countryside and the city or technology and nature, have long operated on European and Euro-American soil, as Leo Marx and Henry Nash Smith once told about. To California, such images, by simply focusing attention on the hinterland, constituted a readily available set of references through which the bourgeois ambivalences over, but ultimate desire for, intensified circulation of capital in the late nineteenth century could gain further expression. In ways that I hope to make clear, ruminations over the despoliation of older, simpler ways of life gave way in rural realism to the bourgeois desire for capital's own redemption by "going rural." Rural realism appropriated stock images—of fruited plains, embowered farmsteads, glistening rivulets—only to better assert that the "rural" in rural realism would be no refuge from capital but would be one of the most desired places for it. (Moreover, rural realism is more about the dynamics of capital itself, not just "machines in the garden" [Marx 1964].) More than once are the characters who bring rural realism to life led to the fields and orange groves *by* bankers and developers rather than running there to get away from them. Capital could *bring the rural into being and, recursively, would be the better for doing so.*

Let us say also that the discourse of rural realism was sustained specifically by the mode of representation which carried it. Chapter 3 will give a foretaste of this in its discussion of three short stories written in the early 1890s as a promotional campaign to encourage urban investment in California farmland. Part two extends the point: one does not only look for rural realism in novels; one looks through novels (or other representations) at rural realism. Much can be made of the novel as a distinct cultural form (e.g., Bakhtin 1981). While it is beyond the scope of this book to offer a theory of the novel, it is appropriate to say that "the novel" was a narrative vehicle in which rural realist discourse could be tested among other discourses. This testing could be prolonged (refuted and reasserted, and refuted and reasserted again). Rural realism could be developed as an organic, self-evident presence in characters' everyday lives; it could be the very mode of storytelling. It could make the transition from idea and assertion to a *sine qua non* of narrative and historical, geographical logic. I'm not sure that any form other than narrative fiction could hold rural realist discourse up in quite that way.

## Stalking the Interdisciplinary Wilds

This book, like any other, is the result of conscious selection—with a larger goal in mind. I want to better understand the practices of capitalism. These practices are insistent and many-branched, intentional but often not. While I am loathe to argue, grand narrative style, that these practices are all-constitutive of motive, identity, and outcome, it would be foolish to ignore that there was little they did not brush up against and that there is still much to be learned from tracing their circuitous pattern.

*California and the Fictions of Capital* is therefore by necessity a work of hybrid scholarship. That it has depended on the findings and insights of disciplines other than my own field of geography has made for a highly enjoyable venture, while of course suggesting to me many times the cumbersome nature of academic departmentalization in the first place. It must be said, however, that for all its rewards, working across disciplines imposes a double burden. By definition it requires navigating unfamiliar waters, which to me has meant plying the currents of cultural and literary studies and American history. Such a search for new insights and their subsequent translation into one's own project raise the possibility of vulgarizing the refinements in perspective that only accompany long familiarity with a particular field. So, while it has been my goal to produce a work that borrows less than it adds something new, I must acknowledge there is plenty of the former, my desire having been to not have to reinvent the wheel. In this regard, the economically inflected histories of California and the American West, written by William Cronon, Donald Worster, Donald Pisani, Gerald Nash, Mansel Blackford, and Richard Orsi, for example, have been essential. Kevin Starr's non-stop histories of California are also important touchstones, even if my sentiments are closer to those of Carey McWilliams.

Potentially riskier is undertaking the second burden, that interdisciplinarians enter into their labors ignorant of who their audience really is and will be. Sure, we make our guesses and plot our intentions, but the whole point is to be partly wrong. (But not too wrong.) We cast the net widely, hoping for a new and unsuspected audience, only to overshoot those whose interests dovetail most closely with our own—from them we learn of our most important sins of omission. Which is to say that fellow geographers have presented to me the best of guardrails: compass points that indicate room to move and musical notes when I have careened into the metal. I will never be able to thank Dick Walker and Don Mitchell enough for timely, thoughtful, and generous readings of these chapters. And this does not compare to what I have learned from each, both personally and in their published work, about capital, California style. Many other people have read this book in whole or in part. I thank them all for their criticism and encouragement: Susan Craddock, Lucy Jarosz, Mona Domosh, James McCarthy, Bernie Herman, Chandos Brown, Kirk Savage, Terry Whalen, Bob Gross, Chris LeLond, Sallie Marston, and Miranda Joseph.

Like many a first book, this owes its origins to a dissertation. Although that incarnation is quite different from the present one, I still have debts of gratitude to Dick Walker, Allan Pred, and Genaro Padilla for fostering my thought experiments on economy and culture. Berkeley Geography graduate seminars with Michael Watts, Allan Pred, and Dick Walker opened up what were the key questions for me, the ones I keep asking about capital, consciousness, representation, and the production of spaces where everything comes together and falls apart. But if seminar meetings had not been bolstered by the wonderfully intense conversations and friendships of fellow grad students, nothing would have made sense. Susan Craddock, Eric Hirsch, Rod Neumann, Lucy Jarosz, Jorge Lizárraga,

Alex Clapp, Brian Page, Marcia Levenson, Rick Schroeder, Liz Vasile, Katharyne Mitchell, and Susan Pomeroy will, I hope, see themselves in these pages.

I am grateful for financial support along the way. A Chancellor's Dissertation Year Fellowship at Berkeley gave me a push out the door, while a postdoctoral fellowship at the Commonwealth Center for the Study of American Culture, at The College of William and Mary, once again put me in rare company. Kirk Savage, Elizabeth Thomas, and Grey Gundaker opened their hearts and minds to me. Terry Whalen, Chandos Brown, and Bob Gross saw that the mind of a geographer could be a little messy, but they counseled me on this project in ways that I still reflect on. I am grateful to the Department of Geography at Colgate University for very generously allowing me use of an office and computing facilities. A Small Grant from the University of Arizona's Social and Behavioral Sciences Research Institute allowed one more summer research trip to California. Then and on many other occasions the staff of the Bancroft Library has been kind and gracious: I thank Terrie Rinnie for much needed use of a library carrel and Dave Rez for always being on the lookout for books that might interest me.

A round of graduate training at the University of Delaware convinced me quite early that geography, social and economic history, and cultural history belong together. Edmunds Bunkse, confidant and mentor, taught me things about place that truly changed my world forever. Lessons in American social and cultural history and historical geography taught by Yda Schreuder, David Allmendinger, and Richard Bushman are more durable than they know.

I have had a years-long conversation on economics and economic theory with Tom Bonomi and similarly protracted talks with Gray Brechin and Jorge Lizárraga on California history. Here at the University of Arizona, I have had the support of many colleagues and friends. In particular, my discussions with Marv Waterstone, Miranda Joseph, and Sallie Marston echo through these pages.

I wish to express my gratitude to family and friends whose encouragement (and patience) have been more important than anything else: Susan, companion and colleague for life; George, Sr., the two Suzannes, Tom and Mary Beth, Lane, Jean, Elaine, and Marsha—no families could be more supportive; and friends whose ears are warm from listening for too long, Dave, Jenny, Jeff, David, Peg, Sandy, Carl, Ted, Jane. . . .

Thomas LeBien, Susan Ferber, Lisa Stallings, and Brandon Trissler, all of Oxford University Press, were kind and judicious each step of the way. I am grateful for David Lott's meticulous copyediting, for the indexing skills of Dave Prytherch and Penny Waterstone, and for Mark Patterson's graphics know-how; I must also thank the anonymous reviewers who were in enough agreement about what needed doing to get me to do (most of) it. Any mistakes or oversights, factual or aesthetic are mine.

Finally, thanks to Penguin USA, publisher of Frank Norris's *The Octopus*, and to International Publishers Co., publisher of Karl Marx's *Capital*, volumes 1 and 2, for permission to reproduce extracts of these works. I thank *California Farmer* for permission to quote from back issues of the *Pacific Rural Press* and wish to acknowledge Edward Arnold, publisher of the journal *Ecumene*, which printed an early version of chapter 6 (1.3[1994]: 235–55). Kino International Corporation kindly allowed the use of its video version of D. W. Griffith's "A Corner in Wheat," while MOMA's Film Stills Archive supplied the Griffith still for the jacket.

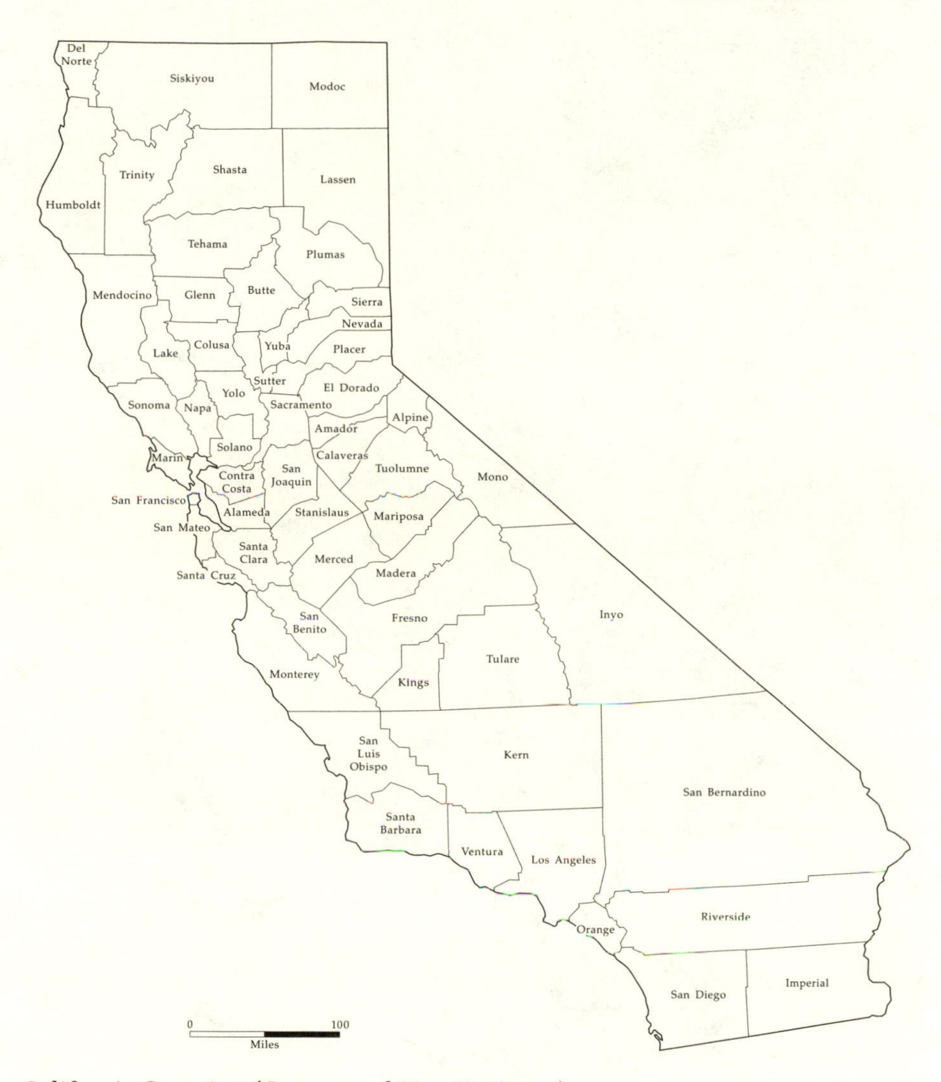


California Counties. (Courtesy of Tina Espinoza).

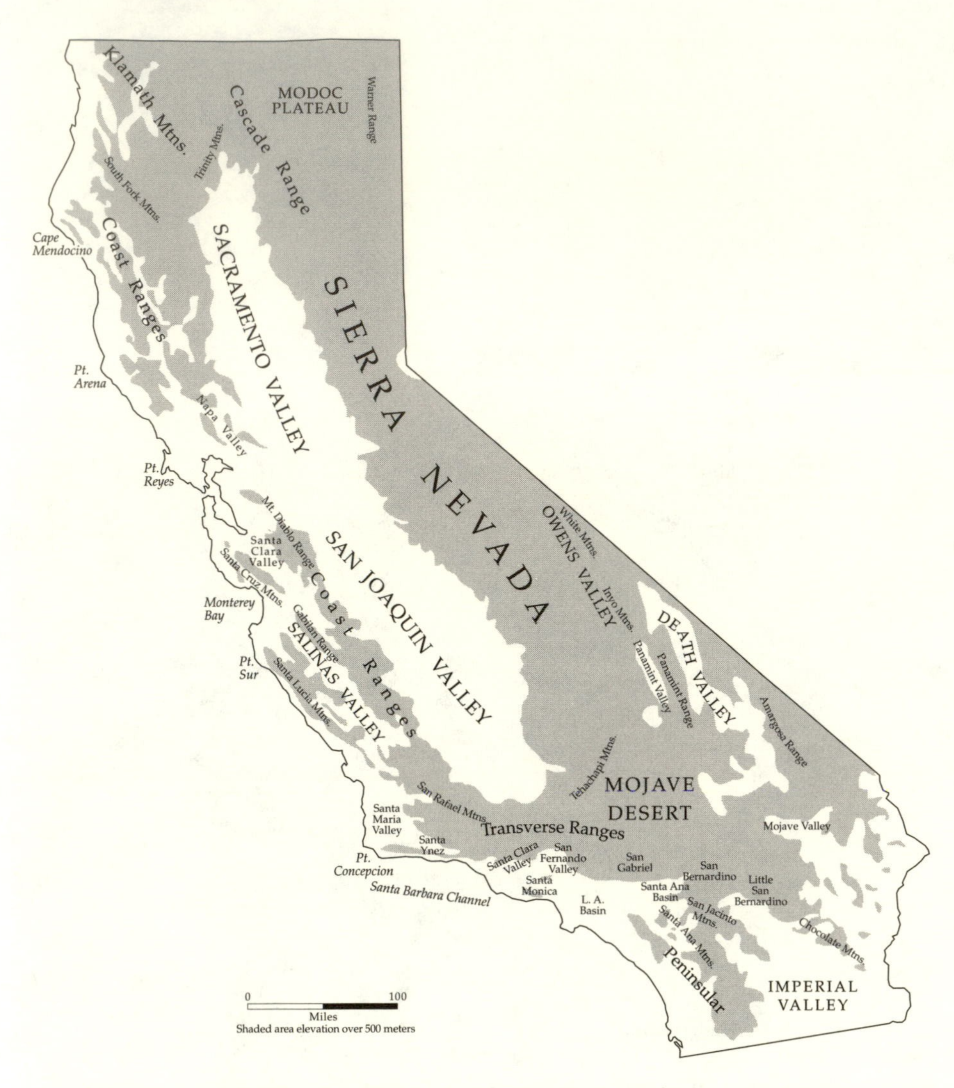


Land Features of California. (Courtesy of Tina Espinoza).

Major Rivers, Lakes, Towns, and Cities of California. (Courtesy of Tina Espinoza).

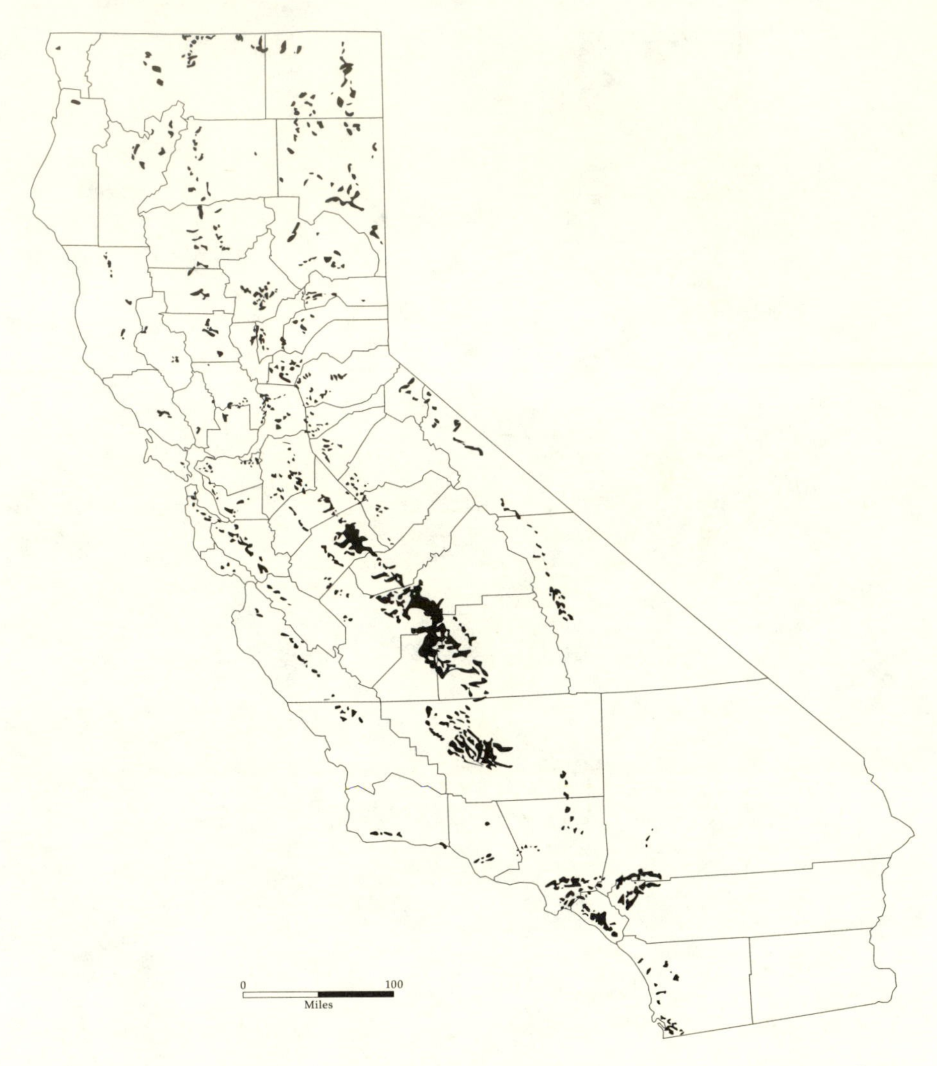


Approximate Location of Irrigated Areas of California, 1900. (Courtesy of Tina Espinoza).

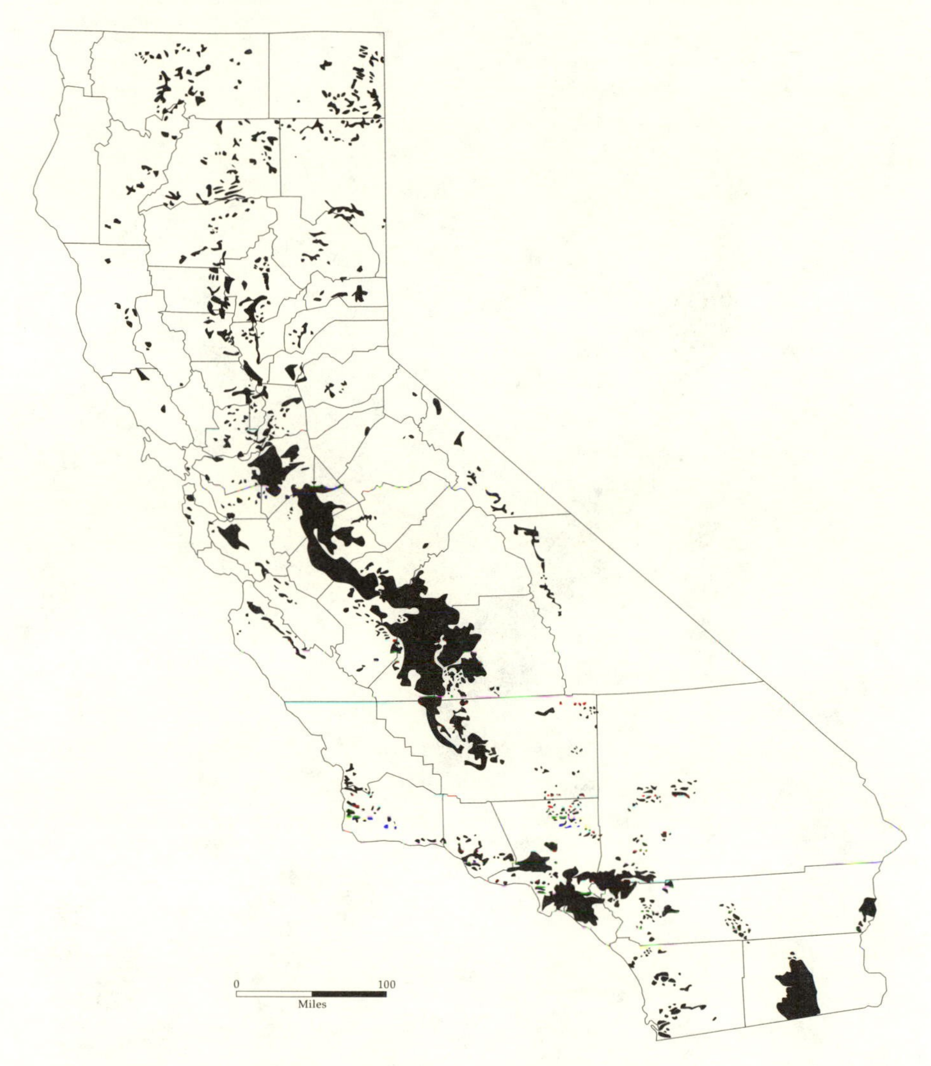


Approximate Location of Irrigated Areas of California, 1920. (Courtesy of Tina Espinoza).

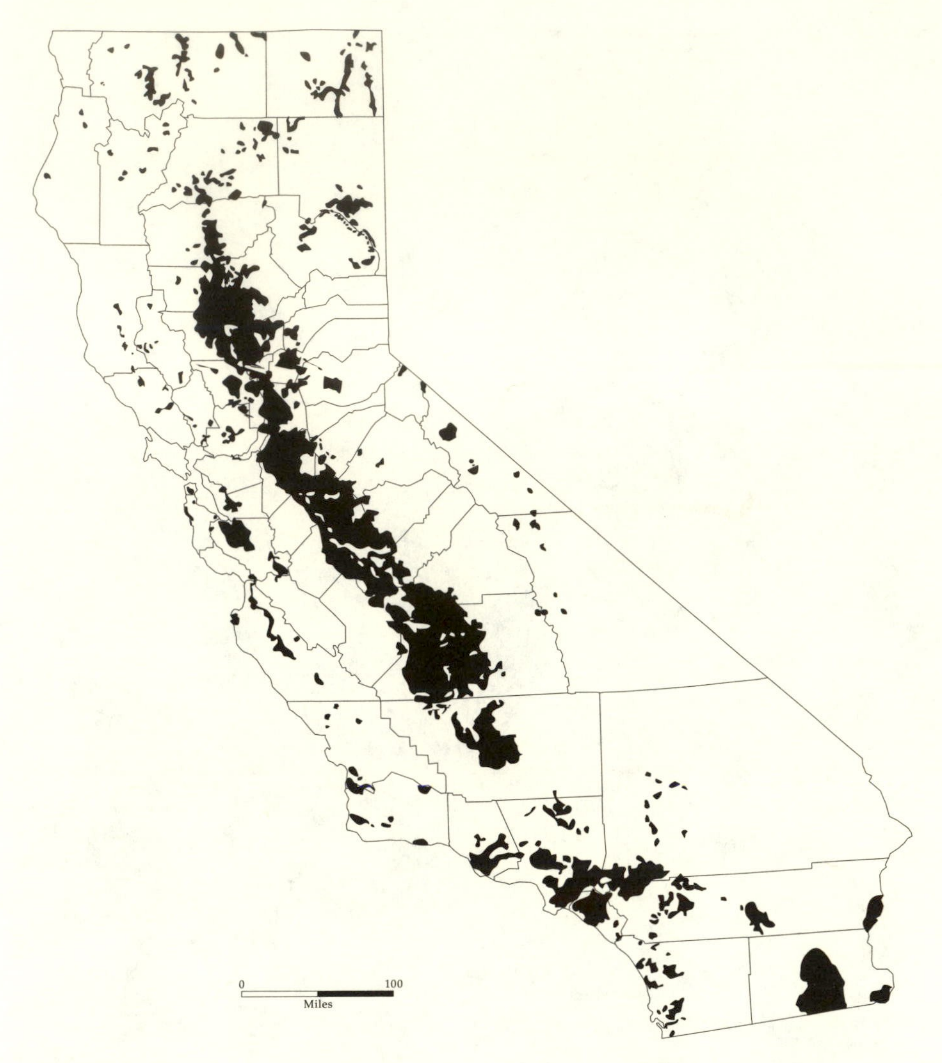


Approximate Location of Irrigated Areas of California, 1930. (Courtesy of Tina Espinoza).

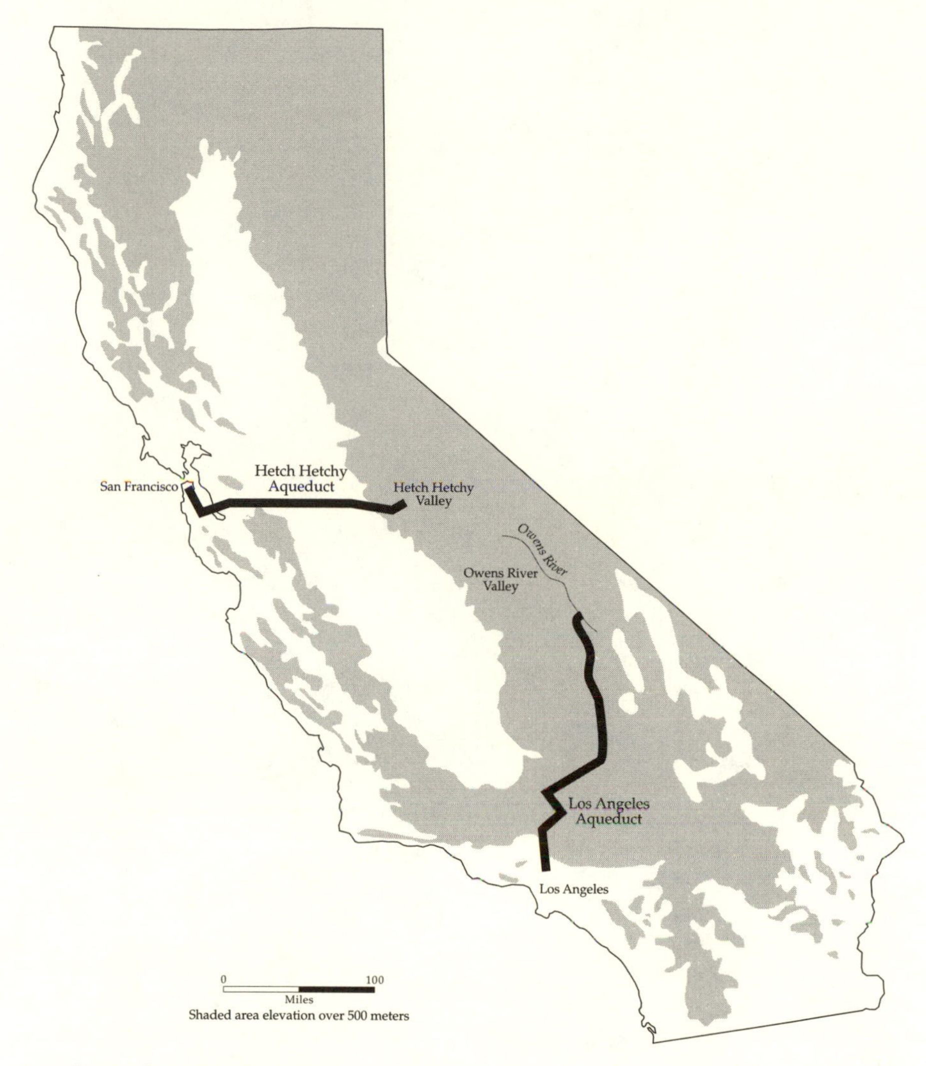


Hetch Hetchy Aqueduct and Los Angeles Aqueduct. (Courtesy of Tina Espinoza).

# PART I

## MAKING GEOGRAPHIES

# 1

# Rural Commodity Regimes

## *A Primer*

It has become something of a truism that after the 1840s, California's development was radically foreshortened—"telescopic," as Carey McWilliams has said (1976). From mining to livestock and grain ranches, to irrigated specialty cropping—in a matter of decades it seems that rural California reinvented itself several times over without ever looking back. In reality, these production regimes, the very stuff of California's rise to national prominence, were monetarily and otherwise connected. The crisis of the mining economy in the Sierra foothills in the 1870s, for example, was in part resolved as a massive shift to wheat in the Central Valley, just as profits from the grain economy were pumped into Southern California's struggling ranch lands and then surfaced as fabulously productive orange orchards. Around each of these transitions, each resolution of crisis, arose a new labor system, a new built environment, a new production apparatus, and widening division of labor (including California's highest-grossing industries in the early twentieth century—sugar refining, flour milling, meatpacking, canning, and packing).[1] California was a virtual laboratory for successive rounds of investment, disinvestment, and reinvestment of capital, far surpassing any place west of Chicago and its hinterland (cf. Cronon 1991).[2] Boosted by the periodic migration of new money, California's surplus values not only circulated in place, allowing single commodity sectors to prosper, but were switched from one sector to another in an intensifying brew of rural commodity production and innovation.

No single essay can do anything near justice to the story of these commodity revolutions. The point of this chapter is to simply tease out for unfamiliar readers a thumbnail sketch of rural California's commodity history through discussion of its major features—the shift to and out of wheat; large-scale and sometimes hyper-commodified appropriations of land and water; the rise of high-value specialty crops and the economy of land subdivision; the problem of markets; the uneven development of the irrigation apparatus; and the wider social division of labor, which connected rural and urban economies to each other. This thumbnail sketch is drawn with the next, much longer, and more detailed chapter in mind. For if, as I've suggested, rounds of investment and movements of surplus value moved commodity production along, we will see in chapter 2 that farm production in California and the United States relied increasingly, from the late nineteenth century onward, upon massive infusions of spatially mobile finance capital, especially in the form of farm credit. This farmward moving capital enmeshed California farms in circuits of finance that tried to exploit (not always successfully) rising agricultural values and underwrote those values at the same time. These circuits saw California farmers through as commodity producers (including their time as employers of wage labor, a subject I will primarily take up in chapter 3), just as it held them fast to the rules of the credit-commodity purchase. The single most important rule of that game, quite obviously, was that although credit fueled production, it always would have to be validated and undergirded by production. For this reason, it is essential, even for already knowledgeable readers, to keep a production history close to mind. We turn now to production and its means.

## The Logics and Illogics of Production: The Shift to and out of Grain

In the latter 1860s, after a stunning collapse of California's cattle economy and looming insecurity in the mines, rural lands were planted to bonanzas of wheat acreage.[3] Though an *un*-sustainable solution to the cattle crash, as it would be to mining, it was nonetheless gold for a while—and in volume. California wheat lands grew to spectacular dimensions in the '70s, when twice they led the United States' annual output of wheat and ran a very close second all the way up to the 1890s. During the best harvests, wagon trains, loaded down with sacks of wheat, stretched for a mile or more, at the dozens of warehouses dotting the San Joaquin Valley. Drivers in back of the lines waited two and three days to reach the front, and sometimes a week (Smith 1939: 247). In the middle of this accelerated production, which helped nudge California out of the 1870s depression, the state's banks, primarily those located in San Francisco, backed this straw gold by moving ten million dollars of their loan capital out of the mines and onto the ranches (California Bank Commissioners 1881). But by the end of the seventies, production declined. Due to international overproduction—the Ukraine, Australia, Argentina, and Canada all being major competitors—prices dropped, thus making the wheat economy more cutthroat than ever. It was then that large producers, more mechanized, more able to command harvest labor, and better connected to sources of financing, beat out many of the small farmers, who in the thousands had been successful wheat growers in the competition for wheat profits (Liebman 1983). Isaac Friedlander was one of those dominant few who, as kingpin of a multinational consortium of warehouses, grain-sack factories, transport companies, and banks, commanded thousands of acres (Bloom 1983). Typical of the wheat years was that California tapped foreign markets, principally Britain, since the eastern United States was glutted with Great Plains wheat. (Later, when California turned to high-value, perishable specialty crops, farmers would learn how to effectively elbow in on those eastern markets.) The glutted East was only one factor that kept growers tied to the international trade. In fact, there was substantial precedent already laid down. The distant markets and the routes to them had been defined during the Civil War, when California was forced to buy manufactures from Europe (Hardy 1927). With doses of British capital and California's own growing indigenous sources, wheat thrived (Paul 1973 and 1958).

Wheat production made sense, given the context of the development of and access to means of production. Because irrigation was poorly developed at best, wheat could be raised in the Central Valley without it. Before railroad car refrigeration, wheat was the only major crop that could be exported. (Defying the logic of the *transcontinental* railroad system, the local branch lines and a network of ocean-going vessels connected the new growers of wheat to local merchants and distant markets.) Wheat cultivation required little in the way of skilled labor and was popular with growers precisely because there was so little labor to be had. In this context, wheat production was mechanized in the state almost from the onset of the American takeover. And wheat did not demand much from its largest growers. The fact that labor requirements on the mechanized farm were low was socially and spatially liberating for the landowning class; it reinforced the tendency of land barons to set up residences among the bon ton of Stockton, San Francisco, and Oakland. From these heights, they redoubled their earnings as merchants and shippers and as investors in industries other than grain (Pisani 1984).

Compared to the specialty agriculture of later decades, profits per acre were small. This reinforced a land-extensive agriculture. Because few improvements were necessary, grain production made double sense in a period when land titles were still embroiled in disputes over land grant verification. Finally, Frank Norris's observation in *The Octopus* that large-scale wheat ranching amounted to soil mining created an apt analogy with placer and hydraulic mining: when the harvest was bountiful, the realization of value was quick (Pisani 1984; Hardy 1929; Norris 1901).

The logic of wheat production was not, however, uncontested. Rapidly solidifying, lopsided social relations in agriculture forced large wheat growers to fight for their economic and class interests. Contemporary critics recognized that wheat production retarded the spread of the small family farm and forestalled the growth of viable rural communities, that it degraded rural labor and created a permanent class of dispossessed harvest workers (Pisani 1984). How to eliminate the class conflict that emanated from opposing social poles, land rich and land poor, preoccupied the social conscience of the Far and Middle West (see Smith 1978). But it was not a preoccupation for everyone in these regions, or at least not in the same way. Large wheat farmers (with some exceptions, such as William S. Chapman) opposed small farming well into the 1890s, in fear of the increase in property values and taxes that ostensibly would follow population growth. In the end, despite year after year of political skirmishes and a muckraking media, the decline of wheat production had less to do with class conflict than with shortsightedness and structural change: overproduction in a limited market; declining per-acre yields; the increasing land values that did indeed follow the beginnings of diversification into higher value crops; and cheaper credit money, which eventually made the high costs of specialty agricultural cropping more viable (Pisani 1984; Hardy 1929; Rhode 1995).

## Appropriation of the Space Economy: Land, Water, Transportation

Wheat production had been predicated upon a wholesale transformation in land tenure and ownership. Most important—because it would later be at the center of debates over subdivision—was the private acquisition of large landholdings; that is, the commodification of land that had been in the public domain or held by Spanish and Mexican land grantees. The resulting skewed pattern of land ownership was precisely what the proponents of small farms in California had in mind as retrogressive and reprehensible. During the first few years of the 1860s, San Francisco bankers and financiers, looking to diversify their investments, starting buying up the Spanish and Mexican ranchos. Other capitalists amassed their latifundia by focusing on the public lands (see Bloom 1983). Even as the number of farms, the vast majority of them fewer than 500 acres in size, rose to over 23,000 by 1870 (from less than a thousand in 1850), the large ones, of 70,000 acres and more, controlled the most land. As Gerald Nash writes, "The attempt to reproduce in California the Middle Western pattern of family homesteads had failed" (Nash 1964: 135; see also Bloom 1983). So polarized was the California farm structure that, still, in 1900, 45% of all land cultivated was done so on only 2% of the farms; 40% of farmers were tenants (Nash 1964).

Control over water similarly fell under the sway of baronage. Big landowners dominated the private irrigation companies and set water rates in their favor. Acting alone or through partnerships (as was most often the case), several of California's legendary and infamous land barons capitalized on these transitional years: Henry Miller, Charles Lux, Lloyd Tevis, James Ben Ali Haggin, William S. Chapman, Isaac Friedlander, William Ralston. The doings of most of these men well represent the circulation of capital from one commodity sector to another and thus the laying of the groundwork for new pulses of regional development. Taking the earnings from his meatpacking business in South San Francisco, Henry Miller turned to raising cattle and, through masterful abuse and manipulation of public land law, acquired pasture lands, which he irrigated with his privately developed canals. His most famed province was in the northern reaches of the San Joaquin Valley, where he came to own a 100-mile swath of land on both sides of the San Joaquin River. By the time of Miller's death in 1916, his California holdings numbered 1.25 million acres, most of them in the San Joaquin Valley (Bean 1968).

Lloyd Tevis and James Ben Ali Haggin were two other exemplars of the go-go years. Tevis (president of Wells Fargo) and Haggin made their fortunes as private bankers and lenders in San Francisco during the gold rush and as venture capitalists in the Comstock. They bought San Joaquin Valley lands around Bakersfield, using the acreage and whatever water they could get to raise feed for cattle operations in New Mexico and Arizona. The cattle were driven, in turn, to the growing market in Los Angeles. In 1890, a new company was formed, the Kern County Land Company, to operate Tevis and Haggin lands.

There were situations when these and other men acted in concert. One of these was the San Joaquin and Kings River Canal Company (organized in 1866). This concern was the joint creation of the reigning captains of agro-industry: William Ralston of the Bank of California, Lloyd Tevis, land magnates William S. Chapman and Isaac Friedlander, and land and cattle kings Henry Miller and Charles Lux (Nash 1964). Ill-fated, the company folded in the depression of the 1870s after only 40 miles of the planned 230-mile aqueduct had been built. While the failure of the canal tied Chapman's, Friedlander's, and Ralston's hands, Miller and Lux added Chapman's and Friedlander's best acreage to their own and continued work on the aqueduct for another 60 miles. Absorption of this kind was not unique; it was a repeat in kind of James Ben Ali Haggin's acquisition of land from another failed irrigation company (see Pisani 1984 for full discussion of the San Joaquin and Kings River Canal Company).

The San Joaquin and Kings River Canal Company demonstrates an important point about the flow of capital in nineteenth-century California: through purchases of land and water, a new round of investment and accumulation was inaugurated based on profits being funneled from the mining economy and its spin-offs. To bring this new regime into existence, it was not unusual that some of California's biggest capitalists would combine their efforts in order to back new projects with the largest sources of financing then available. That individual companies might be short-lived, and that capital would be typically withdrawn at the first signs of trouble, was inconsequential to the basic structure and long-term process of capital's shaping of the countryside.

But of all landowners, none exceeded the Southern Pacific Railroad in size and influence. As such, the railroad ranked high among those institutions (banks are another example) that would push agriculture toward high-value specialty crops. Southern Pacific's land mass, as it were, eventually totaled 11,588,000 acres, carved from the federal land grant system. (For actual construction it wrought subsidies from government at every level: city, county, state, but especially federal.) Yet landownership was only one of its activities and perhaps among the less important. (One might even say that the railroad was saddled by this land. See chapter 4.) By 1880, the Southern Pacific, directed by the Pacific Associates (Charles Crocker, Mark Hopkins, Collis P. Huntington, and Leland Stanford), held a virtual monopoly on the shipment of goods. Beginning in 1869, the "Big Four" controlled all routes by rail to San Francisco. This was only the coup de grâce, however. Before the transcontinental line was finished, the railroad had begun a massive campaign of buying up shipyards, ferry and steamship lines, and waterfront facilities around San Francisco Bay. It out-competed rival companies by controlling important mountain passes, harbors, and river crossings. After passenger ridership and land sales dipped in the 1870s, it moved large amounts of capital into longer-term investments in agricultural research, settlement promotion, and irrigation. (These functions will be treated later in this chapter.) The Southern Pacific thus clinched its position as the premier shipper of agricultural produce, even after the Santa Fe railroad completed its transcontinental line to Southern California in 1887 (Nash 1964).

## The Regime of Specialty Crops

Between 1870 and 1900, in the twilight of the wheat boom, California agriculture altered its form again. Thousands of farmers, newly and heavily capitalized and mortgaged, turned specialty crops into the next dominant industry. A few numbers reveal the impact of the new crop regime on farms' worth alone. In 1870, California's farms were worth $141 million (farmland, buildings, and implements included). By 1900, the number of farms had tripled; their worth, $708 million (Rice et al. 1988). There were antecedents, it is true: limited diversified agriculture had been given impetus by the gold rush, but most of these farms concentrated near the cities and mining districts of northern and central California, especially around the Bay Area, where streams or artesian wells were easily tapped.[4] After agricultural production was opened up by the Southern Pacific Railroad in the San Joaquin Valley and after the railroad built into Southern California where a few agricultural colonies were already in place, it became possible to think more practically than before about other sorts of products which rural areas could produce to take up the slack left by thinning wheat exports. Table 1.1 shows that by the 1890s, a solution had been set upon and seemed to be working. This is the decade during which intensive, specialty crop agriculture rapidly came into its own, seriously challenging the place of grain production in the agricultural hierarchy.[5] Yet, as Liebman points out, if orchards and vineyards paid relatively larger returns during the 1890s, and if in any event it takes years to get bearing plants, then the transition had really come in the previous decade. Intensive agriculture, and the financial backing and land subdivision that went with intensive uses, was thus being developed in earnest during the 1880s, when grain prices were in decline (Liebman 1983).

Indeed, the pattern that was to unfold recurringly was not simply the successive addition of crops to California's repertoire, but the strategic emplacement of the "new" to absorb the losses of the "old." California agriculture in a sense generated its own economic rhythms to which it consequently had to adjust, the downside of these typically being unintended outcomes. Such was the case with fruit production in the 1880s: It had been pursued with abandon so that in the next decade overproduction, worsened by the 1890s depression, haunted California farmers once again. Until fruit producers got more firmly on their feet (after the turn of the century), many of them having been dislodged from agriculture anyway, sugar beet production and sugar refining—led by the Spreckels family—helped buoy the transition away from grain and pasturage. This was especially so for the years 1892 to 1900 (McWilliams 1939). In 1899, in fact, sugar and molasses refining was California's number one industry, the value of the product bringing in very close to $16 million. That was about a half million dollars more than gold production for that year (Cleland and Hardy 1929).[6]

Characteristic of the industry, and something that gave the lie to specialty crops as the answer to the call for an end to the large farm, was its degree of economic concentration. With Claus Spreckels and the Sugar Trust at the fore, sugar refining was undertaken by only a half dozen refiners, most of whom were directly or indirectly linked to the half dozen largest sugar beet growers.[7]

> Like wheat, sugar beets were cause and consequence of the urban-rural nexus: To function effectively, sugar-beet factories had to be located near beet fields, so the factories moved in to the countryside. The factories, in turn, demanded excellent communications and brought into existence a well developed network of highways. In this manner, 'sugar beets helped to bring into existence the whole system of agricultural, orchard, and gardening industries in California' [quoted from *Pacific Rural Press,* Decem-

Table 1.1. Transition from Extensive (Grain) Agriculture to Intensive (Specialty Crop) Agriculture, 1869–1929

| | Value of Crop ($000) | | Percent of Total | |
|---|---|---|---|---|
| Year | Extensive | Intensive | Extensive | Intensive |
| 1869 | 35,007 | 2,444 | 93.4 | 6.6 |
| 1879 | 69,304 | 2,814 | 96.1 | 3.9 |
| 1889 | 62,602 | 6,852 | 90.0 | 10.0 |
| 1899 | 53,111 | 40,442 | 56.7 | 43.3 |
| 1909 | 70,246 | 68,887 | 50.5 | 49.5 |
| 1919 | 204,492 | 346,249 | 36.6 | 63.4 |
| 1929 | 109,902 | 397,030 | 21.6 | 78.4 |

*Source*: Liebman 1983: 52, Fuller 1934: 330, and Taylor and Vasey 1936: 286.

ber, 1897]. In those communities where a sugar-beet factory was established, a cluster of small farm industries soon sprang into existence. (McWilliams 1939: 90–91)

The multiplier effects to which McWilliams alludes were no mere serendipitous events, but structural features at the heart of the agricultural economy. The interweaving of strawberry production is a case in point. When laid off from the beet fields, laborers (especially Japanese and Japanese Americans) found work in the strawberry fields. From a labor market standpoint, the two industries depended upon each other. In contrast to this sort of spatial integration of crop production and highway expansion was the spatial division of labor among the migratory class. As expressed in 1910 by the Labor Commissioner, John D. MacKenzie,

> The lower rates of pay of agricultural laborers had not a little to do with the agricultural expansion which has been witnessed. The presence of a nomadic labor force, so fluid that some migrated from northern California to the opposite extreme of the state in the course of twelve months, and the ease with which its daily needs could be provided for made it possible to expand by developing beet and other industries in new territory, in advance of a settled population at all commensurate with the enterprises undertaken. (Quoted in McWilliams 1939: 92)

Agriculture in advance of settled population was also perfected in the Imperial Valley. In 1921, a Commonwealth Club report noted that the Imperial Valley, at one time the proposed mecca for the landless, had absentee ownership rates of 85% (Commonwealth Club 1921). This sort of pattern was not always the case, however. Southern California citrus (the next crop to bound out of California) was a central feature of that region's urban-rural development, in which orchards, ranch houses, and electric rail lines more or less carpeted the land together. Moreover, at the very same time, Southern California was studded with communities of harvest workers—Chinese and Japanese at first, but then Mexicans between 1910 and 1930 (see González 1994 for a superb study of Mexican citrus worker villages). But whether or not agriculture expanded into areas where absenteeism would rule the fact remains that agriculture was not merely a matter of crops growing in the ground. It was a produced space, a geography of numerous dimensions—social, biological, economic.

California's diversified agriculture was eventually expressed as a highly nuanced geographic pattern of crop production and a mutually developed labor market (more about this in chapter 3). Each was essential in the creation of the other—that is, in the production of a spatial division of labor.[8] Because specialty crops demanded specialized skills and large capital investments in harvest labor, machinery, and land and water, farmers tended to specialize in one or two crops (Crawford and Hurd 1941), the result being, in just a few decades, crop regions, with spatial concentrations of support services and inputs. It was typical, though, that more than one region produced a given crop. Looking at just a few examples, before 1900, orange orchards came to dominate the uplands of Southern California. Lemon growers, whose crops demanded a different sort of microclimate, stuck to the southern coast. Viticulture and wine production expanded in the Bay Area counties and the southern San Joaquin Valley. Deciduous fruits and nuts claimed the northern San Joaquin Valley, the Sacramento Valley, and the Bay Area, with prune-plum orchards especially spreading through the Santa Clara Valley south of San Jose. Raisin grapes concentrated around Fresno (because of the concentration of Armenians there). After the turn of the century, because of developments in irrigation, refrigeration, and marketing, crops such as lettuce, melons, tomatoes, and dates moved into the Imperial and Coachella Valleys in the south and the Salinas Valley in the north. Huge acreages in the Imperial Valley opened up after the depression of the mid-1890s as investors sought new outlets for their capital, which had previously been tied up elsewhere. Imperial became a producer of winter-harvested produce timed in accordance with the summer and fall harvests of the north (Taylor and Rowell 1938). The basic facts of the overall pattern were that different crops ripened at different times and the same crop ripened at different times in different places. Peak labor (and credit) requirements followed accordingly.

Such was the general pattern, or at least one slice of it in time. In actual locales, the experience was typically that of transitions from one regime to another, made more complex by considerable overlaps and variations in social relations. Looking at just one case, in the Salinas Valley, a Spanish land grant (Posa de los Ositos Rancho) was eventually subdivided, a portion going to the 13,000-acre Dumphrey Ranch. Until the 1910s, the Dumphrey was a grain (wheat and barley) and cattle producer. In 1917—the soil having gradually lost much of its nutrient content, but financial relations in California agriculture having become much more complex—three investors bought the property: A. L. Hobson, a cattleman and president of his family's packing company; John Lagomarsino, a farmer and director of one of the Bank of Italy's branches (see next chapter); and Charles Teague, a farmer and manager of the large citrus-producing firm Limoneira Ranch Company. With their purchase, the three formed the Salinas Land Company and began sinking wells along the Salinas River which bordered the property. As Teague later recalled, "We were just getting well under way with this development when Mr. Carlyle Thorpe [general manager of the California Walnut Growers Association] . . . became interested in the opportunity to raise fruit in that area" (Teague 1944: 136; also, California Orchard Company 1921). Thorpe got together with several of his friends and bought 1,900 acres from the Salinas Land Company, constituting them as the California Orchard Company. Teague and his associates, instead of taking cash, took stock in the orchard company as payment, thereby keeping their original capital in circulation in the new enterprise. The Salinas Land Company went ahead with its water development and sold off another 4,000-plus acres before deciding to take the rest of the land off the market. The Company had been so successful in its experiments with growing beans that it reserved land it might otherwise have sold and leased 3,000 acres to sharecropping tenants—proof that specialized, irrigated agriculture would not always mean small-scale farm ownership. Meanwhile, on California Orchard Company land, hundreds of acres each were being planted to tree crops—walnuts, apricots, and almonds—and to peas, grain, sugar beets, tomatoes, paprika, spinach, broccoli, and, of course, more beans. "These pioneer agricultural enterprises," Teague concluded, "are splendid examples of what the business enterprise system, actuated by individual initiative and the profit motive, has meant to America" (139).

## Land Subdivision

When grain prices dipped, the most profitable course for many large landholders to follow was not to automatically convert to fruit or vine, but to sell the land or some subdivided portion of it—thus the ascendance of specialty agriculture in the San Joaquin Valley, Southern California, and the Imperial Valley. Babbitry was reproduced on a grand scale as landowners (speculators during the previous epoch of large-scale privatization) turned over this process to land speculators, who would undertake to buy the land, plan for a water supply, install a few model plantings, then subdivide and resell for a profit. Whether it was in anticipation of irrigation and reclamation or an advancing railroad line, large amounts of land were bought up only to be resold (Liebman 1983). The ultimate landowner—unless the intention was to fully develop farmland and lease it out, as in the case of the Salinas Land Company—was thus usually relieved of having to front the costs of leveling and grading, of installing an irrigation system, of buying the necessary specialized implements, and of paying the interests on loans that would facilitate these things.

Most often, "when conversion [to specialty crops] occurred," Ellen Liebman notes, "the holding was subdivided. The basic reason why this occurred is that fruit prices did not warrant the high costs conversions [without subdivision] entailed" (Liebman 1983: 55). Conversion to specialty cropping, therefore, was not just a structural readjustment within agriculture, but a powerful spur to that sector of the economy which could help bring specialized agriculture to the forefront: the real estate industry and the motions of finance capital that underwrote it. The development of real estate interests paralleled and enabled agricultural transformation, as hundreds of advertisements over decades worth of the *Pacific Rural Press* and every major urban newspaper (*San Francisco Chronicle, Los Angeles Times,* or *Sacramento Bee*) attest. As one writer for the *Labor Clarion* (published by the San Francisco Labor Council and the California State Federation of Labor) put it: the transition to irrigated agriculture

> had created a new industry—land selling. The almost worthless stock ranges and worn out grain farms had found new value in the land hunger of the

> wage earners of the cities, who generally were the purchasers of the small holdings by which only is it possible to carry on diversified farming. The land-poor [poor-land?] range owner, the real estate boomer and the corporation promoter formed a triumvirate of interests solely bent upon the exploitation of this wage earning class. And now it is a wild mid-summer scramble for water. (Williams 1913: 3)

### Markets

New and indebted small farmers still faced numerous difficulties in converting land for specialty crop use. For starters, newly planted trees and vines did not reach bearing age for several years (intercropping with sugar beets and other vegetables was one of the recommended solutions). Then came the juggling act. Fruit prices were initially often low, land payments were high, and getting the product to market required more than a little ingenuity. The last of these—meticulously worked upon by growers' cooperatives and the brilliant campaigning of their brand names, such as Sunkist (citrus), Sun-Maid (raisins), and Blue Diamond (walnuts)—was the clincher. (Ironically, the cooperatives paved the way for large-scale, corporate production of specialty crops during the 1910s and continuing after World War One. Once again the rural economy would come to resemble the bipolar structure of the wheat years: many small producers in the industry, but a relatively few number of very large producers dominating. The main difference was that large-scale specialty crop production, on large landholdings, such as those of the Earl Fruit Company and Calpak, was realized through the purchase and consolidation of smaller holdings [Liebman 1983].) Producers of specialty crops got their goods to *local* markets comparatively easily, despite perennial complaints about freight rates.

But building distant eastern markets was a different story. There the field was crowded with the fruits and vegetables of local producers. After the Civil War, the East had had its own boom in truck farms. New York, Pennsylvania, Delaware, Maryland, and New Jersey were heaping the supper tables of the east coast with peaches, strawberries, fresh beans, corn, melons, and tomatoes.[9] What cracked open these markets, apart from the extremely shrewd marketing organizations, were speedier, lower cost shipments by transcontinental rail and canning and drying technologies.

Southern California became an early and major player in the fresh fruit market, motivated by an overflow of citrus. Newcomers planted orchards like gangbusters when the southern route of the Southern Pacific joined the region to New Orleans in 1881 and especially when the Santa Fe railroad's transcontinental line entered Southern California a few years later. In 1889, the Southern Pacific unveiled its latest innovation, the refrigerated railroad car, which revolutionized fresh fruit marketing in the next decade.

Food preservation was no less important in marketing and shipping a product prone to overproduction. Whereas the associations set out to resolve the problems of overproduction by evolving a sophisticated approach to marketing *fresh* produce, canning and drying physically altered certain products, allowing them to be stored for a much longer period, so that supply and demand could be more easily manipulated. Food preservation caught on like wildfire. (All sorts of produce could be canned, but drying was restricted to grapes, apples, plums, pears, peaches, and apricots [Cleland and Hardy 1929].) The value of canned and preserved fruits and vegetables grew from $6 million in 1889 to $60 million in 1914 and $220 million in 1920. Cleland and Hardy (1929) report that in 1919, it was the *second-ranked manufacturing industry in the state*, after petroleum refining, and the *second-largest employer* (19,575), after wartime shipbuilding (which would soon plummet).

## Irrigation

Of his self-proclaimed "shaggy excursion" through the San Gabriel Valley of Southern California during the parched year 1877, John Muir quipped, "People mine here for water as for gold" (Muir 1894). His statement combines two salient perceptions. On the one hand, water has been the single greatest natural limiting factor to growth. Its distribution is uneven, both spatially and temporally. Northern and mountainous California have most of the state's water supply, while the south and the interior valleys suffer. Yet water can be as prone to descending in torrents as it is to being withheld for years at a time. On the other hand, water has been developed as a means of production as powerful and important as the development of the railroad and as much a center of political debate and struggle. By 1900, the distance traversed by main irrigation ditches was equal to those traversed by the railroad—about 5,000 miles. The imperialistic growth of the San Francisco Bay Area and the Los Angeles basin would not have been possible without these cities reaching out—ultimately at a great distance, or down into underlying aquifers—to import water. Early water projects were undertaken by private water companies, which drilled wells for ground water, drew off local rivers, and constructed reservoirs to trap runoff. After the turn of the century, long distance aqueducts, constructed by publicly owned utilities, brought water from the Sierra to the San Francisco Bay Area and to Los Angeles. The urban search for water brought about conflicts between city and countryside in California, the most notorious being a series of pitched battles and acts of resistance during the 1920s in the Los Angeles "colony" of Owens Valley (see Kahrl 1982; Walton 1992). The lion's share of developed water resources, however, went to agriculture in the form of irrigation. Here, California would excel once again and extend its influence throughout the West.

In *From the Family Farm to Agribusiness,* Donald Pisani emphasizes that irrigation involved practical, as well as ideological, issues, including the debate over whether to irrigate at all.[10] Early boosters often claimed that it was simply unnecessary. Farmers frequently thought so, too, arguing that deep plowing would suffice or that rain would follow the plow. Many investigators asserted that irrigation was a danger to crops, land, and human health; or they argued that it was just too costly. Some of these fears were based on the results of poor irrigation practices. According to other critics, irrigation was just another form of land speculation that would threaten the prospects of family farming rather than foster them. They warned of monopolies over land *and* water as private companies and speculators grabbed the most promising tracts. Eventually, these initial arguments paled next to the tally of successful irrigation projects.

In 1870, only 60,000 acres, a small proportion of California's cultivated acreage, were "under ditch." Small, private water companies were primarily responsible for raising the irrigated acreage to 1,000,000 by 1889, although cooperative agricultural colonies and wells on individual farms contributed a share. Through distinct phases of development—corresponding to the availability of investment capital and the general profitability of California agriculture—the production of irrigated space would expand many times over, especially in the San Joaquin Valley, Southern California, and the Imperial Valley (table 1.2). But while farmers as a group soon found that irrigation paid, now they would have to ardently pursue new investors, for the new problem was how to keep irrigation expanding. The old promotional rhetoric would find its life renewed over and over. Proponents would argue that irrigation would quicken the process of crop diversification and stimulate immigration because land would be subdivided. These processes, they would assert, would inevitably lead to more evenly distributed wealth and settlement: irrigation would strengthen family institutions, build up a middle class, and eliminate migrant labor because crop production would be a year-round activity. Promoters of irrigation in California, such as William Ellsworth Smythe, contributed to the larger movement for irrigation, which eventually touched every western state.[11] This larger crusade began during the late 1880s, strongly influenced by Southern California interests, and was renewed with particular fervor after 1893 when investment capital was vanishing from the region and bourgeois fears of unbridled worker uprisings were widespread (Pisani 1984).

Backed by fortunes that had been made from mining, banking, wheat, and stock raising, the San Joaquin and Kings River Canal Company was the first really ambitious project to emerge. As I have noted already, the company failed, but largely because it was never able to prove itself. Its foray into irrigated agriculture came, in effect, too early and collided with general financial depression. The project's engineering was also accused by local papers of being faulty. Attempts to raise some kind of federal subsidy failed, stymied in part by anti-monopoly sentiments. As Carey McWilliams points out, the downfall of the company was the gain of Henry Miller, who acquired a controlling interest for one-third the original cost. This move left Miller enough water to irrigate over 150,000 acres. He completed the canal works in the 1890s, a decade of particularly depressed farm-labor wages (McWilliams 1939).

The 1870s nonetheless inaugurated a spate of ditch and dam building. In 1871, the Gould Canal was dug at Fresno, and north of town, three years later, the Chowchilla Canal diverted a portion of the San Joaquin River. In 1872, at Bakersfield, the Kern Island Canal was completed, and in 1874, the Goose Lake Canal traversed part of the Tulare Valley. Fresno became the site of a number of speculative irrigation colonies that competed with each other for settlers. Among these colonies was the Central Colony, brainchild of land and wheat baron William Chapman and Bernard Marks, a San Francisco speculator in agricultural lands. This colony and another, the Washington Colony, instigated a minor boom in the Fresno area. By 1886, there were 21 colonies covering approximately 45,000 acres and housing 7,500 residents. As investors had hoped, land values rose sharply. Land selling at $2 per acre in 1870 was available by 1890 for $50 to $100 per acre, or potentially triple that if under ditch. Although there was an outlying concentration of irrigated acreage north of the San Joaquin-Sacramento delta, most irrigation developments by the late 1870s were in Southern California and the San Joaquin Valley.[12]

Table 1.2 Top Ten Counties Ranked by Irrigated Acreage, 1899–1929

| County | Acres Irrigated | County | Acres Irrigated |
|---|---|---|---|
| | 1899 | | 1909 |
| Fresno | 283,737 | Fresno | 402,318 |
| Kern | 112,533 | Tulare | 265,404 |
| Merced | 111,330 | Kings | 190,949 |
| Kings | 92,794 | Imperial | 190,711 |
| Tulare | 86,854 | Kern | 190,034 |
| Los Angeles | 85,644 | Merced | 151,988 |
| Modoc | 78,016 | Los Angeles | 145,586 |
| Mono | 59,202 | Modoc | 82,075 |
| Lassen | 49,634 | Lassen | 77,079 |
| Siskiyou | 49,108 | Riverside | 71,436 |
| *State* | *1,446,114* | *State* | *2,664,104* |
| **County** | **Acres Irrigated** | **County** | **Acres Irrigated** |
| | 1919 | | 1929 |
| Fresno | 547,587 | Fresno | 533,992 |
| Imperial | 415,304 | Imperial | 432,240 |
| Tulare | 398,662 | Tulare | 410,683 |
| Los Angeles | 248,412 | Merced | 318,244 |
| Kern | 223,593 | San Joaquin | 281,629 |
| Merced | 212,851 | Kings | 269,994 |
| Stanislaus | 197,249 | Stanislaus | 241,712 |
| Kings | 187,868 | Los Angeles | 205,837 |
| San Joaquin | 183,923 | Kern | 180,106 |
| Riverside | 106,212 | Madera | 140,637 |
| *State* | *4,219,040* | *State* | *4,746,632* |

*Sources*: U.S. Department of Commerce, Bureau of the Census 1899, 1909, 1919, 1929.

At this time, irrigation was a checkerboard of financial and social arrangements, wholly uncoordinated and without oversight. This was a disturbing development to sectors of the population who worried about the potential for monopolistic control of water and the as yet insecure future for California as a society of small, diversified farmers. A new idea began to take hold: might there not be a way to set the financial basis of irrigation expansion on a firmer, more reliable footing and at the same time retain local control over water? Out of this notion was born the argument for state-regulated irrigation districts.

Among the first organizations to promote the irrigation district idea was the California Grange, whose interest in the irrigation district was but an extension of its politics of local control. The constituency of the Grange embodied the changing geography of rural settlement. Its members were largely latecomers in wheat production, savvy smallholders resident on their farms rather than absentee landowners. The Granger attempt to establish trade and marketing cooperatives, irrigation, farmer-owned banks and insurance companies, and stores put it in opposition to the California State Agricultural Society, a group representing entrenched agricultural interests with ties to the business elite of San Francisco. Grangers organized a "wheat revolt" to oppose unfair shipping rates and to protest the attempt of the San Joaquin and Kings River Canal and Irrigation Company to make landowners adjacent to the canal help pay construction costs (Pisani 1984; Jelinek 1982).

Well into the 1880s, legislators experimented with irrigation district legislation, but popular suspicions abounded. The proposed districts might be merely land and water company grabs (sometimes they were); the state might be forced to pay otherwise unpayable irrigation construction costs (this would happen later at the federal level); one section of the state might prosper at another's expense (uneven development was intrinsic to every phase of capitalist expansion). With the erosion of the Grange's constituency, the beginning of wet years again in 1878, and the discovery that Tulare Lake—the water source proposed by the potentially most promising irrigation district—was insufficient, the district idea languished.[13]

As if these hindrances were not enough, an even more fundamental barrier to irrigated agriculture lay in the waves of litigation that inevitably resulted from the tangle of California water law. Through the 1870s, litigation intensified, especially in the drier counties of the San Joaquin Valley—Tulare, Kings, and Kern. Spurred by the "canal boom" that followed the progression of the Southern Pacific through the valley, warring farmers and stockmen and the representatives of competing ditch companies jammed the courts. (Moreover, contests for water were heightened by the dry years 1877–79.) Then in 1886, *Lux v. Haggin*, a closely watched case that had been making its way for a decade through the judicial tangle and which California water users thought might decide water-use doctrine and its impact on small farm settlement once and for all, was finally settled.

The infamous ruling in *Lux v. Haggin* turned out to be a bitter disappointment to promoters of intensive rural settlement. Ominously, the litigation had not been brought between large and small farmers at all, but between the Goliaths of the San Joaquin Valley: Charles Lux and Henry Miller paired against James Ben Ali Haggin and Lloyd Tevis. Haggin and Tevis, whose pasturelands were isolated from the Kern River, had acquired rights of appropriation to irrigate them. Miller and Lux, claimants to extensive riparian rights on the Kern, filed suit to have the diversion halted. In a stunning decision, the State Supreme Court ruled for Miller and Lux, but because Miller knew that Haggin would file appeal after appeal, he allowed that each party would appropriate water at different times of the year.[14] Still, the court's decision, with its implied sanction of land speculation and ranching, instead of diversified agriculture, propelled debate in the legislature and paved the way for irrigation district legislation the next year.

In practically the same breath as the court's decision was announced, the agrarian idealists fought back. Within a year, C. C. Wright, a senator from the San Joaquin Valley town of Modesto, pushed his Wright Irrigation Act through the California legislature. Meant in part as a corrective to *Lux v. Haggin*, its aim was to allow landowners in a given area to form public irrigation districts. These districts were to be political entities with certain powers vested in them.

> A board of directors, elected by the landowners, had the authority to overcome riparian water rights by invoking the right of eminent domain. With the

> concurrence of the landowners, the board could issue bonds, tax the participants for interest payments, and build irrigation works. (Jelinek 1982: 56)

The irrigation district, then, was a political division functioning on a one-man, one-vote basis. All property within a district was taxable according to its value; but the owner of the water was the district itself, not the consumer or the landowner. Irrigation district promoters hoped that the district would transcend the financial limitations and chaos of competitive private water development. It was the new panacea, Pisani observes, which would supposedly accomplish for California what purely capitalistic control of water could not. After numerous false starts in the late '80s and '90s, irrigation districts eventually became an essential instrument in the development of an irrigated agriculture, even if they remained mired in the world of finance and competition.

Private groundwater pumping and an alternative form of community controlled water, the mutual water company, took up the slack that the irrigation district left—although it may be more accurate to word it the other way around. The U.S. census for 1900 reported that wells (as opposed to streams) were responsible for up to 50% of Southern California's irrigated acreage. The percentage was even higher for farms around the San Francisco Bay. In the Sacramento and San Joaquin Valleys, by way of contrast, irrigation from streams supplied well over 90% of the irrigated acreage (see U.S. Department of Commerce, Agriculture 1900: 829). The mutual water company proved most successful during the 1880s and 1890s in sections of the San Joaquin Valley and the Los Angeles basin. It differed from the irrigation district in that the number of stock shares depended on the size of one's landholding. Obviously, it appealed to the well-endowed landowner in a way that the irrigation district did not.

By the end of the nineteenth century, rural California had still not been able to use irrigation to reinvent itself in the image of the small independent farmer. Rather, as Pisani, and many other historians, have emphasized, the countryside was bipolar. The state contained more small irrigated farms (of approximately 10–30 acres) and more large irrigated farms (of approximately 550 acres) than most of the rest of the arid West. Moreover, the San Joaquin Valley and Southern California, together comprising 75% of irrigated land in the state, had each pursued divergent paths. Tulare and Kern counties used much of their water for forage crops on large landholdings still devoted to stock raising. Conversely, the three leading Southern California irrigators—Los Angeles, Riverside, and San Bernardino counties—comprised an empire of smaller citrus producers.

In the early twentieth century, Progressive politics began to reshape water development. Under Governor Hiram Johnson, laws were enacted in 1911 and 1913 which helped to crack open new circuits of capital for investment in irrigation district bonds. These laws further regulated district formation and put a ceiling on how much debt the districts could incur by issuing bonds. In return, cities, school districts, and counties were free to buy the bonds and, very importantly, irrigation districts could sell hydroelectric power to defer the cost of irrigation works. Progressive-era legislation helped produce a public sector market for investment in irrigation.[15] Private water company rates were now to be regulated as well.

These factors, in concert with high crop prices during World War One, made for a dramatic rise in the number and success of irrigation districts. I have noted that irrigation districts were responsible for only 5% of irrigated acreage statewide in 1910. By 1928, California's 73 irrigation districts were irrigating over a quarter of the total acreage under ditch: 1,467,500 acres out of a total of 4,000,000. What these numbers really show, however, is that the irrigation economy was being restructured: irrigation districts were now responsible for nearly two-thirds of the expansion in irrigated acreage since 1910.

During the 1920s, irrigation in California reached a crossroads. San Joaquin Valley irrigators, who had increased groundwater pumping so that it supplied a third to a half of their acreages, were seriously overdrawing the supply. By the end of the decade, 20,000 acres would be abandoned as a result. As for surface water projects, all the small projects that could be constructed by the irrigation districts, mutual water companies, and private enterprise had already been built. The next phase was for the irrigation districts to plan a series of larger, more expensive reservoirs on rivers such as the Kings, Tuolumne, San Joaquin, and Kern. The net effect would be that irrigation, already expensive, would become more so.

Ellen Liebman's point bears repeating: irrigation was not the undoing of the large California farm. Yes, it stimulated subdivision, but it also supported the continuation of large farms. It abetted California's polarized rural social structure. While it nearly always accompanied intensive specialty cropping, most of the irrigated acreage in fact went to extensive uses: cereal crops, forage, and pasture. And even though small farms grew these crops, they were mostly grown on large holdings (Liebman 1983).

## A Wider Division of Labor: The Country in the City

All along, agricultural production was fed by urbanizing processes (urban banks, urban railroads, and urban markets), but urban spaces themselves were altered by the "ruralizing" project. During the wheat boom, for example, San Francisco (and other transhipment cities around the bay) extended long wharves out into the shallows for efficient handling of grain, imparting a distinctive shape to the urban waterfront (Vance 1964). A few miles away, in what would become South San Francisco, an entire industrial suburb was built to house large-scale cattle slaughtering and meatpacking plants (Blum 1984). In Oakland and San Jose, agribusinesses built their canneries to process Central California produce. In the largest such operation, owned by Mark Fontana, "The Santa Clara Valley provided the produce while the North Beach Italian neighborhoods in San Francisco and similar Italian communities in San Jose and Oakland supplied the labor," mostly immigrant women (Reis 1985). Perhaps it is too self-evident to say, but wheat, cattle, and produce—being material commodities—needed material landscapes for their survival at every stage of their production.

This was not lost on those Californians awestruck by what they'd wrought. Agricultural industry promoters delighted in the details, the hardware, the sheer amount of space that the agricultural economy took up. (Less delighted were workers exploited by low wages and dangerous working conditions. See Reis [1985] on the 1917 cannery workers strike.) On New Year's eve, 1921, with the world war over and California ironically poised for agricultural depression, the cover story in the *Pacific Rural Press*—California's major mouthpiece for "progressive," "scientific," technologically sophisticated agriculture—was about Los Angeles's sprawling produce district. The caption for the cover photo, an aerial view of warehousing facilities at the railroad terminal, reminded readers that it was now *only* through a bird's-eye view that this economy could be taken in. Only the aerial view could show the full impact of the "mass of machines, trucks, produce and bargainers" squeezed into the enormous open square that was bordered by the blocks-long buildings housing the produce commission houses and the warehouses of the growers cooperatives. But even as it transcended the dimensions of simple landscape—that is, "country that ordinary mortals know only from the ground"—the view missed all the important details. For the district was a very finely tuned space produced by and for the circulation and final production processes of agrarian capital. Moreover, this micro-geography had precise time coordinates and, as the following passage also describes, embodied California's racial and ethnic relations, comment upon which was nearly always ready to surface:

> All the wholesaling of fruit and garden truck for the city gathers at the buildings of the Los Angeles Union Terminal Company. Cars can come up and unload on tracks on one side of the 20-acre area used, and can be handled after that any way desired. Most of the bigger dealers have their quarters so that they can unload produce from one side and sell it out at another . . . [At the Wholesale Terminal Company] carlots are assembled and shipped east in large quantities by several large firms who have specially favored locations for that purpose. The selling to retailers and peddlers is practically all done in a large paved space surrounded by buildings. Around the edges are the stores of the regular wholesale companies. In the center is space for truckloads of fruit and vegetables brought in by farmers or others. A man can rent space here for 50 cents a day or $7.50 a month . . .
>
> Early hours are the rule. By one in the morning, or very little later, the heavy laden trucks come moving forward to their places and from car or truck produce is hurried to [the] floor of the regular dealer[s] around the border of the trading area. Without delay the procession of buyers begins and from two o'clock in the morning, or earlier, until about eight o'clock, the area is a Babel of bargaining . . . Those early buyers are usually men from the big grocery and retail fruit stores . . . For hours after they have gone there is a bustle and stir in the trading area by peddlers, owners of small fruit stands, and buyers hunting for cheap stuff . . . Naturally the fellows engaged in this work are seldom, if ever, "white men" in the sense of being of old-line American stock, or in other senses either. The old-line American stock is not very plentiful out in the bargain area any way. The big, reputable commission houses are largely owned and manned by real Americans. Buyers from the retail stores also are, but the peddlers, the fruit dealers and other small buyers are made up in an extensive degree by Orientals, Greeks, Italians, and others. (Whitney 1921: 679)

*Naturally.*[16]

Urbanization went hand in hand with industrialization and the production of nature in the countryside (Rice et al. 1988; Bean 1968; Cleland and Hardy 1929; see also Niklason 1930). Hinterland economies such as mining, lumbering, and crop production fueled an expanding division of labor which, along with a predominantly urban-oriented immigrant population, gave rise to multiple city and town growth around the San Francisco Bay (see Vance 1964). Western mining became large-scale and more capital intensive in as much as industries in San Francisco produced mining machinery, boilers, iron pipe, cables, pumps, stamp mills, steam engines, machine tools, rails, and locomotives. The expansion of lumbering spurred mining activity (especially flume construction) and, needless to say, fed the overall construction of a built environment. It gave impetus to and was enabled by, the production of heavy lumber-milling equipment and the consumption of wood in activities as diverse as railroad-tie making, furniture making, and architectural millwork. Shipbuilding in the 1860s was a necessary outgrowth of California's productive activities. Investment soon began to flow into the making of marine engines and specialized metalworking. At first, steel was imported for these activities, but by 1910, the Bay Area cities of Pittsburgh and South San Francisco housed their own steel plants (Vance 1964).

During the "wheat era," profits went less to the development of a built landscape of towns and residences in the countryside—though to some extent these were necessary, too (Smith 1939)—than to the speeding up of urbanization around San Francisco Bay, just as wheat drew on that urbanization to begin with. The large-scale wheat ranches of the 1870s laid a foundation for an agricultural-implements industry—steam-powered tractors, combined harvesters, and gang plows. The exchange of wheat for shipments of coal and iron stimulated those industries. Boilermakers produced boilers for use in flour mills and for making the power tools that were used in the manufacture of agricultural implements. These industries made wheat production in California one of the most mechanized in the world.

As we have seen, the industrializing process also involved food processing and mercantile activities that captured the "value added" component of agricultural produce. One might say that it was these industries *for which* agriculture expanded. At first, these activities were rooted in San Francisco, San Jose, and Oakland. With the resurgence of the Southern California economy in the 1880s, they expanded below the Tehachapis (Moses 1994). Irrigated agriculture, especially beginning with the use of groundwater, spread by virtue of the production of urban-made spray pumps and irrigation pumps. The raising of livestock, once this industry recovered, was essential to tanning, boot making, and textiles.

City and countryside developed in tandem, though far from equally. In step with the advance of the Southern Pacific Railroad down the San Joaquin Valley and into Southern California, breweries, wineries, and grain mills sprang up at railroad sidings. Indeed, a railroad subsidiary, the Contract and Finance Company (later, the Pacific Improvement Company), became California's biggest promoter and developer of new towns (Rice et al. 1988). The Southern Pacific's activities included laying out streets; building shops, stations, yards, warehouses, loading docks, stock pens, railroad worker housing, hotels, and restaurants; installing and operating water systems; and dispensing cash and money for schools, churches, and businesses. The Big Four realized full well that this massive outlay exposed them to unpredictable business cycles and risky agricultural ventures. Initially, in fact, they wanted out of railroading once construction of the transcontinental line was complete; but they could find no buyer (Bean 1968)! The next best strategy was to organize their massive campaign to sell California—that is, Southern Pacific's lands—to would-be farmers. The railroad did not merely link one place to another, but produced an extensive geographical framework in which a wide variety of social and economic activities were undertaken. For the railroad—as for the irrigation district, for San Francisco's and Los Angeles's produce warehouse districts, and, as we shall see in chapter 2, for Giannini and his San Francisco–based branch banking empire—space itself was a commodity.

Industrialization was a multistep process, then. It was first made possible by early mining profits. These then fostered a new phase of capital-intensive mining through which deep and fugitive ores were wrested out of the earth. A new round of industrialization came after those mining profits began to decline. Before long, capital was again redirected—into urban manufacturing enterprises such as food and textile plants, agricultural implements, and machine tool shops.

In truth, phases of agricultural growth fed industrial growth, and, in turn, capital formation off-farm made possible the continued elaboration of California agriculture. One of the mechanisms allowing for this dialectical relationship was the mobility of finance capital. Let us close this chapter with an exercise in visualizing California's finances.

Beginning in 1878, the California Board of Bank Commissioners began to track where the money from California banks was going (see figures 1.1–1.4; tables 1.3 and 1.4). First, it is apparent that most of the capital that banks made available for rural circulation was in the form of "loans on real estate," a somewhat catchall category that apparently included loans extended for land purchases, loans extended for other purchases—with land as the collateral—and land-backed loans sold to extend the life of previous loans. No matter what variety of loan, we can take the rise and fall, and the geography, of the loan amounts to indicate the urban bid for rural profits. It should also be noted that until well after the turn of the century, savings banks were the premier investors in California land. Neither national banks, which were prohibited from making real estate loans, nor commercial banks, which loaned on real estate in very small sums, came close to those institutions. Moreover, savings banks—which consistently had more capital than

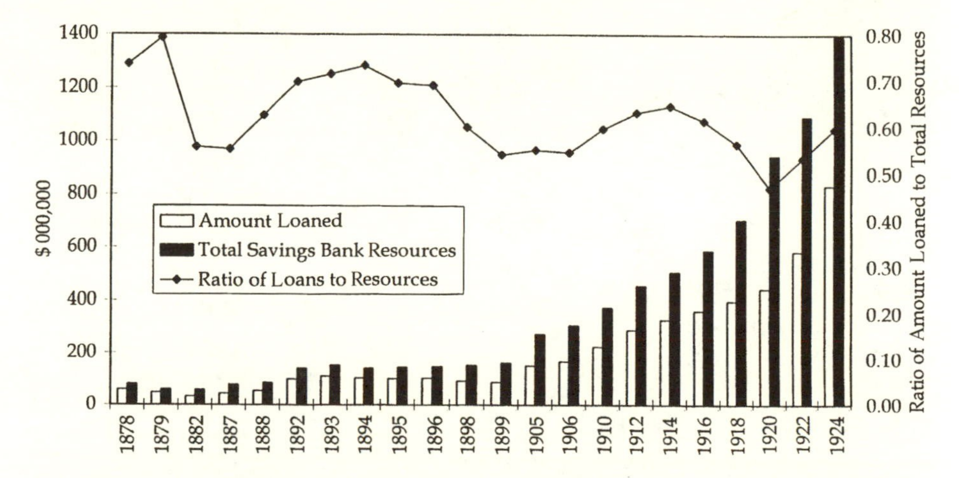


Figure 1.1. California Savings Banks' Loans on Real Estate, 1878–1924. (*Source*: California Board of Bank Commissioners, *Annual Reports,* selected years).

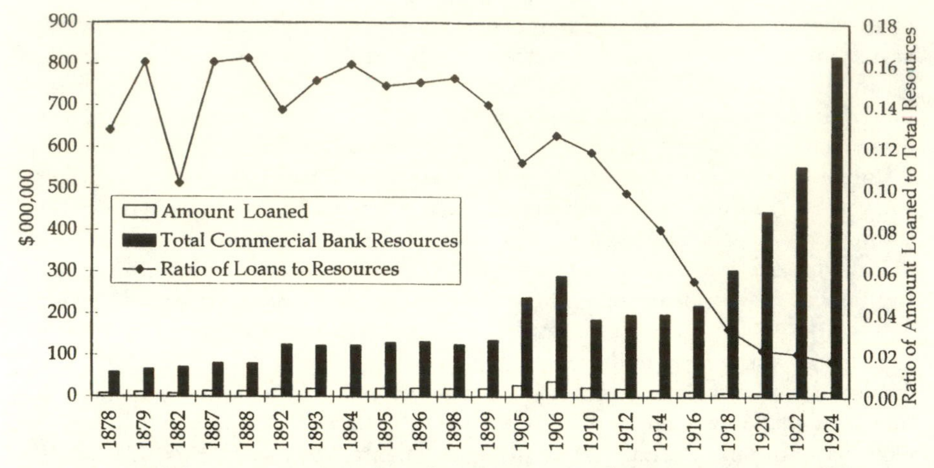


Figure 1.2. California Commercial Banks' Loans on Real Estate, 1878–1924. (*Source*: California Board of Bank Commissioners, *Annual Reports, selected years*).

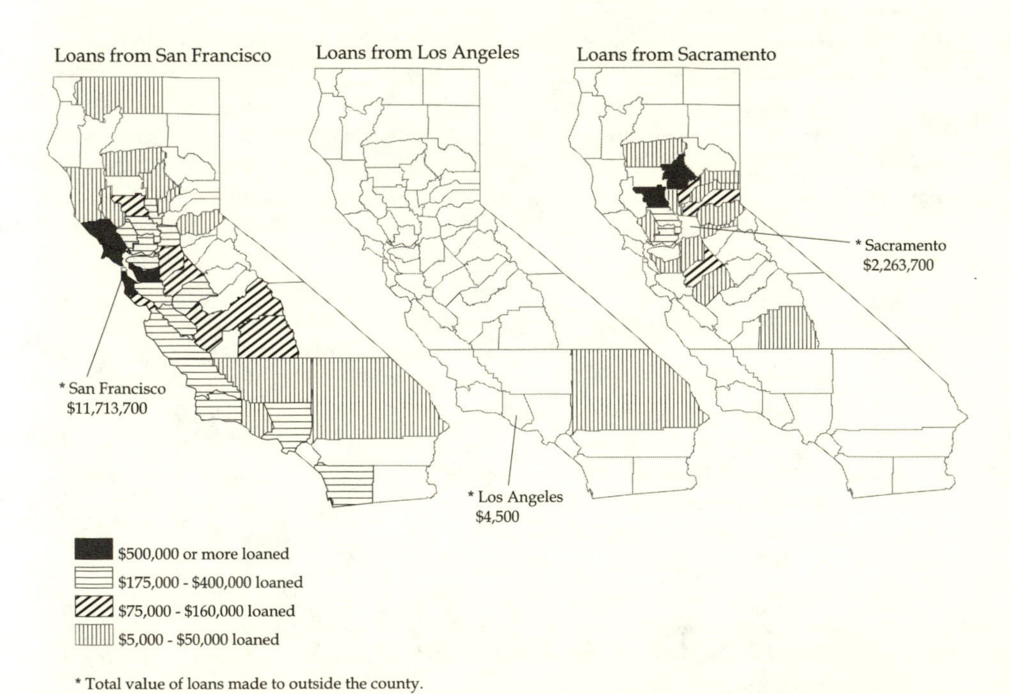


Figure 1.3. Real Estate Loans from Savings Banks in San Francisco, Los Angeles, and Sacramento Counties 1879. (*Source*: California Board of Bank Commissioners, *Annual Reports*).

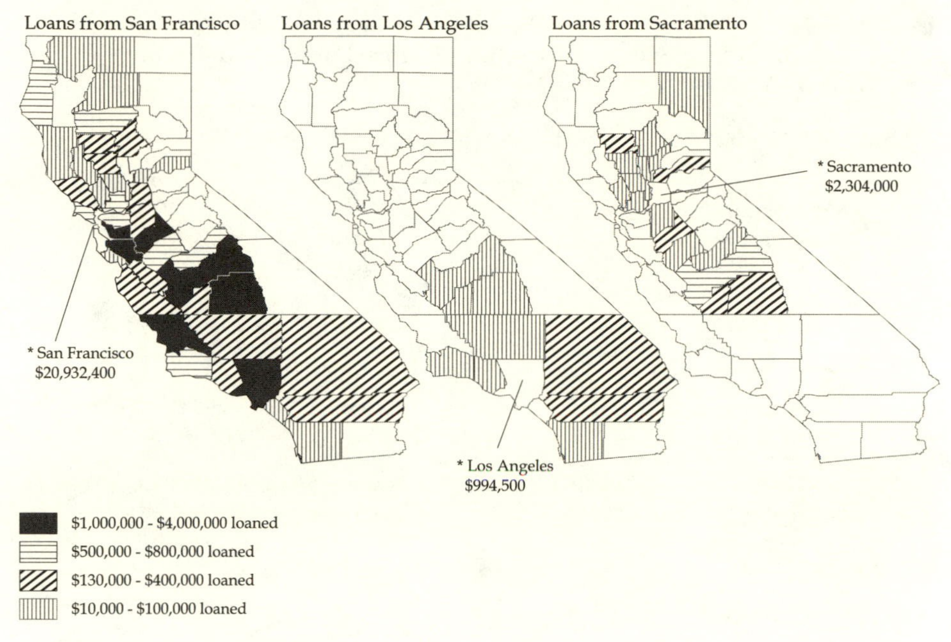


Figure 1.4. Real Estate Loans from Savings Banks in San Francisco, Los Angeles, and Sacramento Counties, 1899 (*Source*: California Board of Bank Commissioners, *Annual Reports*).

the commercial banks, anyway—put up more money for real estate than for any other single kind of economic activity for which they sold credit, which was, as would be expected, subject to temporal rhythms. While savings banks cut back on real estate loans during the downturns of the late 1870s and the middle and late 1890s, only once, after the First World War, did these loans—as a share of the banks' total resources—dip below 50%. By contrast, the commercial banks rarely exceeded 15%; and after the turn of the century, they disinvested from real estate almost entirely (see figures 1.1 and 1.2). From their annual reports, an initial picture emerges of where capital that had been invested in the lands of the largely rural counties of the late nineteenth century came from.[17]

Not surprisingly, money for loans on real estate came primarily from the major urban financial centers: the San Francisco Bay Area, Sacramento, and—once the 1880s boom put "Southern California" on the map—Los Angeles (see figures 1.3 and 1.4). The message we can glean from these maps is that each city developed its own financial hinterland. San Francisco was the major player. From its deep pockets, it sold loans to all the major agricultural areas of the state, from Southern California to the entire Central Valley and the coastal counties. Sacramento and Los Angeles played out fiscal command and control functions, too, the former vying with San Francisco in the San Joaquin and Sacramento Valleys; the latter developing a tributary region in the south San Joaquin Valley and most of the agricultural areas south of the Tehachapi Mountains.[18] If we contrast the geogra-

Table 1.3. Geographical Sources of Loans ($000) on Real Estate in Counties of the San Joaquin Valley (*Source*: California Board of Bank Commissioners, *Annual Reports*).

Location of banks (by county) loaning on real estate in San Joaquin County

| 1879 | | 1899 | |
|---|---|---|---|
| *San Joaquin* | *605.4* | *San Francisco* | *182.4* |
| *San Francisco* | *78.4* | *Sacramento* | *57.7* |
| *Sacramento* | *42.5* | *Alameda* | *15.8* |
| *Alameda* | *4.0* | | |
| Total | 730.3 | Total | 255.9 |

Location of banks (by county) loaning on real estate in Stanislaus County

| 1879 | | 1899 | |
|---|---|---|---|
| *San Francisco* | *157.9* | *San Francisco* | *1,158.4* |
| *San Joaquin* | *155.1* | *Sacramento* | *553.8* |
| *Sacramento* | *87.5* | *Stanislaus* | *160.4* |
| *Stanislaus* | *59.6* | *Alameda* | *20.2* |
| | | *Merced* | *1.4* |
| Total | 460.1 | Total | 1,894.2 |

Location of banks (by county) loaning on real estate in Merced County

| 1879 | | 1899 | |
|---|---|---|---|
| *San Francisco* | *203.9* | *San Francisco* | *627.2* |
| *San Joaquin* | *128.3* | *Merced* | *292.8* |
| *Santa Clara* | *102.9* | *Sacramento* | *27.7* |
| *Merced* | *97.7* | *Stanislaus* | *10.2* |
| *Sacramento* | *22.5* | | |
| *Alameda* | *13.0* | | |
| *Stanislaus* | *3.0* | | |
| Total | 571.3 | Total | 957.9 |

Location of banks (by county) loaning on real estate in Madera County

| 1879 | | 1899 | |
|---|---|---|---|
| | | *San Francisco* | *568.7* |
| | | *Sacramento* | *98.3* |
| | | *Stanislaus* | *2.8* |
| | | *Fresno* | *1.5* |
| | | Total | 671.3 |

Table 1.3. (*continued*)

Location of banks (by county) loaning on real estate in Fresno County

| 1879 | | 1899 | |
|---|---|---|---|
| *San Francisco* | *140.5* | *San Francisco* | *1,753.5* |
| *San Joaquin* | *30.3* | *Sacramento* | *496.2* |
| *Santa Clara* | *4.9* | *Fresno* | *216.0* |
| | | *Alameda* | *21.7* |
| | | *Los Angeles* | *15.4* |
| | | *Merced* | *6.1* |
| | | *Santa Barbara* | *1.0* |
| Total | 175.7 | Total | 2,509.9 |

Location of banks (by county) loaning on real estate in Kings County

| 1879 | | 1899 | |
|---|---|---|---|
| | | *San Francisco* | *375.1* |
| | | *Sacramento* | *136.5* |
| | | *Kings* | *39.0* |
| | | *Los Angeles* | *10.0* |
| | | *Tulare* | *7.6* |
| | | *Santa Cruz* | *3.0* |
| | | Total | 571.2 |

Location of banks (by county) loaning on real estate in Tulare County

| 1879 | | 1899 | |
|---|---|---|---|
| *San Francisco* | *76.5* | *San Francisco* | *1,345.4* |
| *Sacramento* | *6.0* | *Sacramento* | *169.8* |
| *Alameda* | *2.0* | *Tulare* | *92.3* |
| *Merced* | *1.3* | *Los Angeles* | *57.3* |
| *Stanislaus* | *1.1* | *Santa Clara* | *12.0* |
| | | *Fresno* | *1.8* |
| | | *Alameda* | *1.6* |
| Total | 86.9 | Total | 1,680.2 |

Location of banks (by county) loaning on real estate in Kern County

| 1879 | | 1899 | |
|---|---|---|---|
| *San Francisco* | *34.5* | *San Francisco* | *197.0* |
| *San Joaquin* | *15.6* | *Kern* | *142.2* |
| | | *Los Angeles* | *37.5* |
| | | *Santa Clara* | *11.4* |
| | | *Sacramento* | *3.3* |
| | | *Orange* | *1.5* |
| Total | 50.1 | Total | 392.9 |

Table 1.4. Geographical Sources of Loans ($000) on Real Estate in Counties of Southern California (*Source*: California Board of Bank Commissioners, *Annual Reports*).

Location of banks (by county) loaning on real estate in Los Angeles County

| 1879 | | 1899 | |
|---|---|---|---|
| *San Francisco* | *326.4* | *Los Angeles* | *4,575.1* |
| *Los Angeles* | *325.1* | *San Francisco* | *2,074.0* |
| | | *Orange* | *24.3* |
| Total | 651.5 | Total | 6,673.4 |

Location of banks (by county) loaning on real estate in San Bernardino County

| 1879 | | 1899 | |
|---|---|---|---|
| *San Francisco* | *16.7* | *San Francisco* | *419.4* |
| *Los Angeles* | *4.5* | *Los Angeles* | *358.6* |
| | | *San Bernardino* | *79.4* |
| | | *Santa Clara* | *50.0* |
| | | *Riverside* | *39.3* |
| | | *Orange* | *1.3* |
| Total | 21.1 | Total | 948.0 |

Location of banks (by county) loaning on real estate in Santa Barbara County

| 1879 | | 1899 | |
|---|---|---|---|
| *San Francisco* | *224.4* | *San Francisco* | *542.6* |
| | | *Santa Barbara* | *257.0* |
| | | *Alameda* | *32.8* |
| | | *Los Angeles* | *25.0* |
| | | *Santa Cruz* | *3.5* |
| Total | 224.4 | Total | 860.9 |

Location of banks (by county) loaning on real estate in Ventura County

| 1879 | | 1899 | |
|---|---|---|---|
| *San Francisco* | *26.4* | *San Francisco* | *152.9* |
| *Alameda* | *20.5* | *Los Angeles* | *112.8* |
| | | *Santa Barbara* | *5.7* |
| Total | 46.9 | Total | 271.4 |

Location of banks (by county) loaning on real estate in Orange County

| 1879 | | 1899 | |
|---|---|---|---|
| | | *Orange* | *157.9* |
| | | *Los Angeles* | *128.8* |
| | | *San Francisco* | *64.3* |
| | | Total | 351.0 |

Table 1.4. (*continued*)

| Location of banks (by county) loaning on real estate in Riverside County | | | |
|---|---|---|---|
| 1879 | | 1899 | |
| | | *Riverside* | *239.5* |
| | | *San Francisco* | *230.4* |
| | | *Los Angeles* | *224.6* |
| | | *Orange* | *23.2* |
| | | *San Bernardino* | *1.8* |
| | | Total | 480.0 |

| Location of banks (by county) loaning on real estate in San Diego County | | | |
|---|---|---|---|
| 1879 | | 1899 | |
| *San Francisco* | *185.5* | *San Diego* | *207.0* |
| | | *San Francisco* | *43.7* |
| | | *Los Angeles* | *21.5* |
| | | *Orange* | *2.4* |
| Total | 185.5 | Total | 274.6 |

phy of real estate loans for 1879 and 1899 (see especially tables 1.3 and 1.4), a secondary pattern emerges, especially by the latter year. Quite clearly, an undercurrent of localism also drove rural economy. Southern California and the San Joaquin Valley each was home to regional circuits of finance, apart from the imperial finances of the San Francisco Bay Area. (Unfortunately, a change in the Commission's annual reports prohibits tracking bank capital at this level of detail into the twentieth century.)

The bid for real estate profits in the hinterlands where economies were largely underwritten by agriculture thus involved a cast of distant players from the major cities and of local players, too. This was precisely the geographic fabric that would be profited upon in the next major development of California's financial institutions, branch banking. Those details, along with an extended discussion of the role of the financial circuits of capital on California farms, are the subject of the next chapter.

# 2

# Nature and Fictitious Capital

## *The Circulation of Money Capital*

### Capitalism and Nature: The Agrarian Nexus

There is seemingly no lack of evidence for the agrarian turn of post–Gold Rush capitalism. It is writ in the state's changing occupational structure—hence, the precipitous decline in the number of miners and preponderant increase in the number of farmers in the 1870s. It is woven in the fabric of industrial growth—thus, four of the top five industries by the turn of the twentieth century were processors of farm products like sugar beets, beef, grains, fruits, and vegetables (Cleland and Hardy 1929). And it is embedded in the social and spatial division of labor—as discussed in the previous chapter, a widening production matrix joined together an assortment of commodities validated through complex chains of inputs and outputs: the production of boilers that fueled machine shops and metal works, which in turn furnished product for plows and threshers, which in turn allowed more labor-efficient grain production, which stoked the growth of mills that filled the hulls of ships, and so on.

But as suggestive as these observations are, they actually do not tell us much about how capital enters the farm, about what might make farming capitalistic, nor about how farm production, as an economy centered on natural processes, recursively shapes the ways in which it is shaped by capital. It is the purpose of this chapter to broach this problem theoretically and historically.

As simple as the question may seem—"How ought capitalism in agriculture to be recognized?"—the answer is rife with complexity. There are two axes of concern. Along the first, what counts is whether farm *production* is organized in a capitalistic manner. Here, the issue is the employment of wage labor in on-farm production versus the persistence of forms of non-wage labor, or some combination of waged and non-waged labor. The sticking points are whether farming is capitalistic as soon as farm products are grown for exchange in the market, by farmers who own or control their means of production, or if it is capitalistic only when surplus value is extracted from wage laborers employed in farm production (the commodification of labor power).

The other axis concerns the circulation of money capital, especially in the form of farm credit and mortgages. Within this framework, farm production does not have to be capitalistic in itself nor non-capitalistic; what matters is whether money can be plowed into the farm from elsewhere, making the farm an instrument for capitalist exploitation and a site among others for circulation.

Along both of these axes, and for the various theorists concerned to explore the reaches of agrarian capitalism, *the fact that farm production is centered in nature is a crucial point.* Nature, it is said, is an active agent which can actually keep capitalist relations of production from completely taking over the farm economy. Nature thus helps account for the survival of family farming (even while non-wage family labor may be supplemented by wage labor). Amidst an otherwise enveloping industrial world of capital/wage-labor relations, industrial capitals, this argument goes, wish to avoid directly undertaking farm production when the hard-to-predict risks presented by nature can be left to another class, the farmers. This argument should not be taken to mean that the farm economy is devoid of wage labor; quite the opposite. Rather, the transformation to the wage relation is incomplete and resisted. As I shall spend most of this essay arguing, however, nature shapes opportunities for the investment of money capital for precisely the reasons that industrial capital may shy away from the farm. Bankers, insurance companies, shippers, or other entities interested in putting interest-bearing capital into circulation are enabled to do so, for example, because the long period of time in which nature "takes over" production (e.g., the period of waiting for crops to mature) means that farmers must often buy credit in order to, quite literally, buy time. The demand for credit, it must be cautioned, is not a product of nature; it is imbricated in the more general throes of the agricultural economy, which—over the course of the late nineteenth and early twentieth centuries—made increasing and multiple demands on farmers' own capital.

In what follows, I place an emphasis on the second axis, the one concerning the sale of credit, the circulation of money, and why nature matters in that process. There are three reasons for this. One is that, whereas there is a substantial and sophisticated theoretical discussion of the social relations of on-farm production, developed especially by rural sociologists, the role of money capital has been relatively underdeveloped in recent debates. Another reason for this slant follows from the fact that, alongside its farm labor regimes, California excelled at the circulation of money capital through the farm. In other words, we miss something in California's historical geography by not paying attention to the financial circuit. In order to shore up the argument that California should not be overlooked in this capacity, I offer a comparative discussion of the United States.

Still a third reason to emphasize the circulation of money is that a picture of the political economic situation of California agriculture emerges—a picture more interconnected than would otherwise be possible. Though *interconnected* is perhaps not quite the right word. I mean something closer to decentered and destabilized. That is, the view of the farm from the position of off-farm money capital is a picture of the farm not as its own center of capitalist production but as an instrument of capital. Obviously, that is not all that the farm is, but we will need to cultivate that side of things nonetheless, because there is no other way to understand the representation of California economy and its social transformation of nature, explored in part two, except through such a lens.

The reader will notice in due course that this chapter relies upon a theoretical discussion of Karl Marx's thoughts on capital circulation and agriculture, especially as developed in his second volume of *Capital.* I deem this discussion necessary because Marx is a key figure for the rural sociologists that I turn to in my discussion of the capitalism question in farm production. But a better reason is that Marx offers ways of thinking through the relations between capitalist production and circulation as relations that are at once full of profound contradiction and of stunning innovations geared to displacing contradiction. Marx once wrote that the true barrier to capital is capital. Teasing out the meaning of such a riddle demands that the circulation of capital, and not just the narrower sphere of production, be kept in view.

As much as I think Marx provides an invaluable analytic touchstone (if not more), my acceptance is not uncritical. In some of his analysis, I argue, there is a loss of clarity about the development of capitalism through agriculture and what that development means. But even these instances, I would argue, have a great deal to do with the fact that Marx was an exceptionally supple thinker, with a provocative ability to turn objects of study around this way and that, so as to put them in contrasting lights and extend their interpretive possibilities.

## Axis One: The Mann-Dickinson Thesis, Nature as Obstacle

It has been twenty years since two rural sociologists, Susan Mann and James Dickinson, wrote an article which has proven an indispensable tool for thinking about the turbulent intersection of capital and nature, particularly as expressed in a significant rural holdout, the non-wage rural labor regime most symbolically embodied in the "family farm" (Mann and Dickinson 1978). Appealing to a tradition stretching back to Marx, Lenin, Kautsky, and a host of others, Mann and Dickinson were concerned with what role nature might play in keeping the development of capitalism at bay. By *capitalist development* they meant the extent to which labor in a given sphere of production was wage labor. Agriculture, it appeared, stood as a rather strange obstacle to this sort of development when it came to the on-farm production of certain commodities. In spite of the social relations prevailing in "industry" (not just, say, steel or automobiles, but agro-industrial capitals such as fertilizer and implement producers who over time appropriated operations once performed on-farm), forms of non-wage labor were persisting or being revived in the production of particular crops even as the authors wrote. These forms included independent family labor most especially, but also share-cropping and leasing arrangements. Even if non-wage labor wasn't always the rule in agriculture, it seemed that it was only in agriculture that that sort of social relation persisted in any really meaningful way.[1] The question was, why?

The strength of Mann and Dickinson's political economic approach was its characterization of the relations between capital and nature not as in any way direct but as mediated by and made out of social relations. Susan Mann developed her ideas further and responded to her critics in a thoroughgoing, exceptionally clear book, *Agrarian Capitalism in Theory and Practice* (Mann 1990, especially chapter 2; for critics of Mann-Dickinson, see, for example, Davis [1980], Singer et al. [1983], Mooney [1982, 1986, 1987], and Kulikoff [1992]). I will refer to the book rather than to the "Peasant Studies" article for a brief review of the Mann-Dickinson (M-D) thesis. The M-D thesis begins with a relatively simple question: of what importance to a theory of agricultural production in a capitalist society is it that this production is centered in nature? Mann notes that earlier theorists such as Marx and Kautsky put emphasis on land as a potential obstacle to capitalist penetration of agriculture. Land is generally neither mobile nor subject to reproduction. For Marx, this problem is deepened by what he called "differential rent," a concept employed in part to explain why capital avoids lands unfavored by nature (rocky, steep, nutrient-poor, etc.). For Kautsky, who drew directly on Marxist theory, it was important that capitalists seeking to develop agriculture on a large scale would need to lay out a large capital at the very first before even beginning production. In Marx's terms, this type of high "organic composition of capital" (i.e., the proportion of capital invested in land, machinery, and technology to that invested in labor) would stall the appropriation of labor-produced surplus values in agriculture, because land is not an investment that usually increases labor productivity. Also, as Marx discusses at length in the third volume of *Capital,* to the extent that land is held by a class of landowners who can sell and/or rent to capitalists and non-capitalists alike, capitalists may be presented with a barrier to the free flow of their capital. Every way that land poses a problem for the capitalist—by virtue of its "natural" properties and/or its control by a landholding class (or at least a class that facilitates access to land, such as mortgage sellers)—potentially protects the independent, non-wage rural producer.

For the M-D thesis, the crucial issue is how to explain "why some branches of agriculture become capitalist more rapidly than others" (Mann 1990: 32). Drawing on other writings of Marx, especially in the second volume of *Capital,* the M-D thesis looks to how the capital-nature nexus is shaped by the more fundamental laws of circulating capital, not just by land or rent per se. Of special importance is the turnover time of capital and the problem presented when the time that capital spends in production (production time) is not matched by the time that capital spends embodied in labor (working time). In principle, whereas time spent on labor is always production time, production time is not always labor time. Moreover, every period that capital spends in production without labor applied is a period where value is not being created. This disunity between production and working time is evident in agriculture, for example, when the time during which crops mature in the ground involves little or no application of labor.

The M-D thesis argues, therefore, that "capitalist development progresses most rapidly in those spheres where production time can be successfully reduced and where the gap between production time and labor time can be minimized. Conversely, . . . spheres of production characterized by a more rigid nonidentity of production time and labor time . . . [are] likely to prove unattractive to capitalist investment and thus were more likely to be left in the hands of petty producers" (Mann 1990: 34). (Subsidiary problems devolve from the disunity of production and working times. For example, production schedules that may be flexible in industrial, factory production in response to price fluctuations can be impossible to adjust rapidly in agriculture. Or, farm machinery may be idled during the portion of production time when crops are maturing. Or, continuous production which may be achieved in food processing may not be matched by continuous production in the field.) The more production time is fixed, the more capital's turnover time is, too. Capitalists are faced with deciding where to put their capital within those constraints. Also, given that capitalists compete with each other, the fixed turnover time in some agricultural spheres impedes a capitalist's attempt to meaningfully reduce the social necessary labor time involved in the production of those particular commodities. Finally, it is not only the disunity of production and working times that can stall the capitalist development of agriculture. Capital's time in circulation—that is, the time capital spends in the commodity form, from the moment it is put in storage (whether a box or a grain elevator), on through its journey to market, to the moment the capitalist receives payment from sale—can present an obstacle. The fact that an agricultural commodity may spend a long time in storage and be sold over the course of a year may be restrictive. Or the fact that a commodity may travel a long distance or may sit in a merchant's warehouse will shape the direction of capitalist development. In spite of the fact that capitalists have designed ways to overcome these obstacles in the production of a variety of agricultural commodities or for portions of the production process within certain commodity chains (see, especially, Goodman, Sorj, and Wilkinson 1987), other commodities and/or portions of the production process have proved resistant to production based solely on wage labor.

### Axis Two: Exploiting the Natural Obstacle

A primary aim of the M-D thesis is to understand the variable class structure of agriculture as it is shaped by the potential obstacles to capitalist development presented by nature. The circulation of capital is indeed a pivotal analytic. But I want to use the model of circulating capital to open up a rather different horizon. My argument will be that whereas the centering of agricultural production in nature may impose constraints on capitalist development, this same nature-centered production poses opportunities for capital precisely because it must circulate and precisely because the disunities of production and working time (necessitated by natural processes) and capital's time in circulation (in part, nature as distance or as space) exist. That is, if these things exist for potential capitalists as a cost to be averted, then they exist as areas of investment for capitalists looking to fund anyone who does get involved in having to cover the cost. Much of this argument hinges on an analysis of credit in late nineteenth- and earlier twentieth-century U.S. and California agriculture. Where Mann downplays credit, because she argues it does not alter the class location of debtors (i.e., does not really proletarianize them), her critics sometimes get caught in the same typologizing trap (e.g., Davis 1980). (In fact, I would argue that the attempts to essentialize and fix class locations would be better spent on understanding the ways in which class locations may change as capital circulates through the actors who come into contact with it.) Consequently, the opportunity is missed to develop the links between nature as constraint on capital, on the one hand, and opportunity for capital, on the other. Where credit and debt relations are argued to be "detours" that capitalists devise to get past their inability to directly shape the labor process and to subsume all farms into the wage relation, they are not well articulated in terms of the space-times of circulating capital that are so compelling a feature of the M-D thesis (e.g., Mooney 1982)—or, surprisingly, they are only barely theorized as "supply-side" *investments* (Mooney 1986).

The issue here is not so much the class structure in agriculture that devolves from nature-centered production (though I will have one or two comments to offer), as it is that nature repels and attracts capital in different ways according to the historically contingent tendencies of circulating capital.[2] Some may object, in what follows, that the distinction between the roles of industrial and merchant (financial) capital in the historical and continuing development of capitalism is not given enough due, the former being more the "Right Stuff." I would respond that the distinction has been made too much of, if the implication of a hard and fast distinction is the trivialization of mercantile capital (cf., McMichael 1987). Some may also object that I use a broader concept of capitalist development than the predominance of wage labor. I would respond that wage labor is no easy answer to the question of capitalist development, that human wage labor may be conceived of as itself an obstacle to capitalist development—which, as we will see, Marx theorized at one point as having been overcome more in agriculture than in industry (even while the *pace* of accumulation was faster in industry). It may also be objected to that I pay insufficient attention to the production of value by labor. In addition to the facts that there are many excellent histories of labor in California agriculture and that precious little exists on circuits of capital and rounds of investment, I would respond that the ideas here are compatible with a labor theory of value and, indeed, depend on such a theory. I would also argue that the circulation of capital, even as it circulates through the hands of people who produce value in the first place, constitutes a semiautonomous process. (Indeed, this semiautonomous process can be the target of labor actions.) Lest bells go off as I repeatedly invoke "the sale of credit" later in the essay, I am not arguing that sellers make profits merely from exchange in the money market. I am arguing that debt paid with interest is a form of appropriated value. Here and there, especially in the discussion on California, we will see that this constituted a social relation of its own on the farm when it led to creditors trying to discipline the production process.[3]

Natural processes are both invitation and barrier to capital. This can best be intellectually grasped through attention to the circulation of capital and to capital not as a thing, but as a relation, a function of the purposes that values embodied in capital are directed to serve. Confining the issue of capitalism's relation to agriculture to the question of the perpetuation of non-wage forms of rural labor (i.e., family farming) leaves out some of the very crucial ways in which capital is actually present, and present precisely because of "nature." The value of the M-D thesis, for the argument here, is that it forcefully brings to the surface the dynamics of circulation as a way of getting at how capital and nature confront each other. I want to look through that optic as well, but extend the range of the inquiry.

## Keeping Capitalism Out or Letting Capital In? Marx on Circulation

We can begin with Marx's discussion of how it is that non-capitalist modes of production intersect with the capitalist mode. A key set of passages are found in the second volume of *Capital*, where Marx begins to think through the circumstances whereby the circulation of capital set in motion by one set of capitalist producers is completed by the sale of their finished commodities to other producers, who use them as means of production in their own as yet incomplete circuit: "A large portion of the commodities composing MP, the means of production, is itself functioning as the commodity-capital of someone else. From the standpoint of the seller, therefore, C'–M', the transformation of commodity-capital into money-capital, takes place." Marx notes, however, that "this is not an absolute rule" and that quite the contrary can take place.

> Within its process of circulation . . . the circuit of industrial capital, whether as money-capital or as commodity-capital, crosses the commodity circulation of the most diverse modes of social production, so far as they produce commodities. No matter whether commodities are the output of production based on slavery, of peasants . . . of communes . . . as commodities and money they come face to face with the money and commodities in which the industrial capital presents itself and enter as much into its circuit as into that of the surplus-value borne in the commodity-capital . . . The character of the process of production from which they originate is immaterial. They function as commodities in the market, and as commodities they enter into the circuit of industrial capital as well as into the circulation of the surplus-value incorporated in it. (Vol. 2: 109–10)

Once those commodities are purchased for means of production, they may be put to use as productive capital. The point being made is that what becomes capital can in fact originate from outside the social relations of production of capitalism per se, outside the relations whereby capitalists otherwise extract surplus value in labor processes they control. To the extent that these commodities, these means of production, must be sought after again and again, "the capitalist mode of production is conditional on modes of production lying outside of its own stage of development." This is not a steady state of affairs, however, for "it is the tendency of the capitalist mode of production to transform all production as much as possible into commodity production. The mainspring by which this is accomplished is precisely the involvement of all production into the capitalist circulation process . . . The intervention of industrial capital promotes this transformation everywhere, but with it also the transformation of all direct producers into wage-labourers" (Vol. 2: 110.) Marx's language embodies the tensions over the M-D thesis. Critics like Patrick Mooney suggest that although forms of production, such as the family farm, may not be capitalist in the strict sense of the word, they are subjugated to forms of capitalist exploitation. That is, if industrial capital promotes "transformation everywhere," that transformation does not have to be complete in order to be exploitative. And yet Mann has come back again and again to the question of why it is that these processes of transformation remain incomplete where they do.

What *is* stopping them? What forces decide whether capital's tendency will come to pass that all production will become commodity production and all direct producers will become wage laborers? And will these tendencies emerge differently in different branches of production? The answer to these questions cannot be found once and for all; it is full of contingencies of time and place over which actual social relations vary. I would want to argue anyway, though, that the questions are very thorny in the first place. What makes capitalist production *capitalist* (i.e., appropriation of surplus value through wage labor as opposed to only rents, piece-rates, interest payments, liens, etc.) is the subject of continual debate within the Marxist tradition. Thus, Mann-Dickinson's critics want to argue that those non-wage family farmers are in fact piece-rate workers, for example, with the supporting view from Marx that a piece-rate is a form of wages. The complexity works the other way around, too, as I will discuss below: no sooner are the "capitalist farmer" and "capitalistic agriculture" identified in *Capital* then arises the unanswered question of what those terms really mean. In the meantime, let us follow Marx's initial insight that the capitalist mode of production is at once conditional on other modes and promotes the transformation of those modes, precisely because the circulation of capital itself is to be reproduced. Marx's observation can be appropriated and altered into one that understands that actual social relations of production at any point in time will lie along a continuum and that the circulation of capital is *a* primary axis along which intersecting social relations form. The answer to the question of why the capitalist transformation is complete or incomplete is that it is neither complete nor incomplete. Certainly a generation of post-Fordist history tells us acutely that the question smacks of teleology. The mandate that capital circulate has taken numerous societies along the "path" of transformation "toward" industrial capitalism proper (the capital/wage-labor relation as the exclusive class relation, subject to debate of course) and has allowed the persistence or resurgence of non-capitalist modes, or quasi-capitalist ones (also subject to debate), and has allowed these in combination. Inquiry into the nature of circulating capital is, therefore, a key to examining both the nature of transformation and the persistence. What this means, though, is that if we ask, as Mann and Dickinson do, about how a social formation confronts circulating capital and vice-versa, we will want to recognize that *Marx's theory of circulating capital is always already a theory of barriers and interruptions to capital.* For example, capital needs blockages; it invests in them so that it has access to something corporeal through which to circulate. This is partly what lies behind Marx's quip that "The *true barrier* to capitalist production is *capital itself*" (Vol. 3: 358).

Virtually the entirety of Marx's second volume of *Capital* is devoted to the subject of circulation. Of special interest, though, is his examination of the interruptions to the circulation and turnover time of capital. Marx speaks of these points of friction within the turnover time of circulating capital as differences in the *working time* or *working period* (the time that labor is actually applied in a given round of production), *time of production* (the time during which capital is actually tied up in the production of a commodity), and *time of circulation* (by which Marx means not the general circulation of capital but the time involved in getting commodities to market, time involved in selling all the articles from a particular production run, time involved in receipt of payment, etc.). These interruptions,

Marx theorizes, pose serious limits on what capital can do and where it can go at any given time. In this part of Marx's analysis, the claim is that capital investments come at a cost to capitalists not so much because means of production cost something but because capital is tied up for varying periods of time in the very process of production and cannot immediately be returned back to the capitalist in its enhanced form, M'. In one branch of production, the problem may be disequilibrium between production and working times. Means of production are bought and then must be left idle for a large portion of the production time, which far exceeds actual working time. This inordinately lengthens the period of time during which the capital invested in those means of production can be turned over. In another branch, it might be that the time taken in selling the goods from a production run is excessively long, thus requiring large portions of capital reserved as money capital to be invested in a new production run before the total sale money of the first production run is obtained—or else requiring that machinery, buildings, and labor lay idle. Relations among working, production, and circulation times vary according to the different (and changing) requirements of different kinds of commodity production and, consequently, are partly the reason why capital, in the broader sense, may be invested now in one industry and now in another. And they are partly the reason why social relations of production emerge differently in different commodity sectors. As we have seen already, Mann uses these concepts, which are crucial to Marx's analysis of circulating capital, in order to make the case that nature presents an obstacle to capitalist development. But perhaps Marx's argument concerning circulation poses a more basic point about the relations between nature and capital. Let us continue and see where Marx goes.

Agriculture is the classic example of the first of the cases named above, the non-identity of working time and production time. "The difference between production time and working time," Marx writes, "becomes especially apparent in agriculture" (Vol. 2: 240). Labor is expended for a period of time, after which (typically) production time is determined by the biological processes of plant and animal growth, with minimal application of labor and minimal use of tools and implements (although a lot of variability from crop to crop and animal to animal). Furthermore, in "moderate" climates, crops mature once a year. So, whereas in many branches of industry, commodities may be produced in a matter of weeks, days, or hours, a production run in agriculture is very long indeed. (Although Marx points out that production and working times in various branches of "industry" are highly variable. "In one of these branches a definite quantity of finished product, cotton yarn, is turned out daily or weekly; in the other, the labour-process has to be repeated for perhaps three months in order to manufacture a finished product, a locomotive . . . [A]n armoured man-of-war requires one year or more" [Vol. 2: 228]). And Marx concludes that "in agriculture we have a combination of both the longer working period and the great difference between working time and production time" (Vol. 2: 242). Add to this the facts that production in agriculture in any given season can be speeded up by only a very limited amount and that varying conditions of weather that impinge on yields can be predicted only in a limited fashion. *In terms of circulating capital*, these particularities do not signify a fundamental difference from industry, and I think they form a major, perhaps the major, departure from how Marx elsewhere tends to essentialize distinct forms of production in the social division of labor. The limitations presented to capital in agriculture versus industry are qualitatively similar (each must deal with a degree of interruption due to working, production, and circulation times), though quantitatively different (working, production, and circulation times will affect the pace of the development of the capitalist mode in different branches of production).

There is still the question, however, of the extent to which farmers themselves become capitalists—in the context of English history, a question related to the processes of peasant uprooting—and the extent to which autonomous, simple commodity producers are "left alone" to produce commodities as means of production to be bought by industrial capitals. (That is, there is the question of how much "diverse modes of social production" will be maintained.) It's pretty clear that Marx sees farmers disappearing as mere farmers and being reborn as either wage workers (the many) or industrial capitalist farmers (the few) (Vol. 1: 742–44). Once industrial capital achieves high levels of concentration, the majority of farmers left *will be* capitalist farmers producing at highly efficient rates as a cause and consequence of the many no longer producing food for themselves. In the long, historical transformation "toward" capitalism in England, which saw both the political usurpation of peasant lands and technical improvements in agricultural production, masses of rural people became masses of "free" labor—mostly "free" to migrate to town centers to work for wages, where they fueled the rise of industrial capital, and also "free" to work for wages on the lands of now a few capitalist farmers, who assumed control of those usurped lands. Either way, in town or in the field, the wage workers came to comprise the home market for industrial goods. And what else are these goods but the very usurped use values they once produced domestically?

> The events that transformed the small peasants into wage-labourers, and their means of subsistence and of labour into material elements of capital, created, at the same time, a home-market for the latter. Formerly, the peasant family produced the means of subsistence and the raw materials, which they themselves, for the most part, consumed. These raw materials and means of subsistence have now become commodities; the large farmer sells them, he finds his market in manufactures. Yarn, linen, coarse woolen stuffs—things whose raw materials had been within the reach of every peasant family had been spun and woven by it for its own use—were now transformed into articles of manufacture, to which the country districts at once served for markets. (Vol. 1: 747)

Nodding in the direction of the continuum of social relations, Marx notes that this historical transformation was not only *not* unilinear, but produced what seemed to be countertendencies along the way. Before the period of so-called modern industry, dominated by machinofacture,

> manufacture . . . always rests on the handicrafts of the town and the domestic industry of the rural districts as its ultimate basis. If it destroys these in one form, in particular branches, at certain points, it calls them up again elsewhere, because it needs them for the preparation of raw material up to a certain point. It produces, therefore, a *new* class of small villagers who, while following the cultivation of the soil as an accessory calling, find their

> chief occupation in industrial labour, the products of which they sell to the manufacturers, directly, or through the medium of merchants. (emphasis added)

Moreover, over the course of English history, one finds the penetration of capitalist farming in rural districts, *as well as* the peasantry, "turning up again, although in diminished number, and always under worse conditions. The chief reason is: England is at one time chiefly a cultivator of corn, at another chiefly a breeder of cattle, in alternate periods, and with these the extent of peasant cultivation fluctuates" (Vol. 1: 748). Then, however, comes the modern era, which seemingly has no truck with indeterminacy. "Modern Industry, alone, and finally," he writes in the eternal present tense, "supplies, in machinery, the lasting basis of capitalistic agriculture, expropriates radically the enormous majority of the agricultural population, and completes the separation between agriculture and rural domestic industry, whose roots—spinning and weaving—it tears up. It therefore also, for the first time, conquers for industrial capital the entire home-market" (Vol. 1: 748–49).

## Blurred Boundaries and Fugitive Bodies

Even if we were to presume that in Marx's time the conquests of "modern industry" and the capitalist transformation of the countryside were *complete* (a word we should use with particular caution, even applied to the present), let us take note of a couple of unsettled theoretical points. Marx does not say if he means that capitalist farmers, as producers of (mere?) raw material, are themselves subordinated to industrial capitalists—though later, in the third volume of *Capital*, Marx more consistently invokes capitalist farmers as industrial capitalists—or if these two classes are one and the same wage-labor–employing capitalist class, albeit two separate capitalists competing against each other. He does not say, in other words, whether the fact that one capitalist's commodity capital being another's means of production subordinates the former to the latter. Nor, when he mentions "capitalistic agriculture," does he say if he means something like "agriculture as it will be under capitalism" as distinct from "agriculture will become capitalist" (the distinction resting on the place of capitalist farmers within the circulation of capital). It is not clear whether the process whereby the mass of rural peasants were made "free," leaving a class of capitalist farmers to rule the country districts, would eventually extend to the capitalist farmers, too, "freeing" them to be proletarians and leaving the farms to be appropriated by specifically industrial capitalists. Having appropriated the labor power of "freed" peasants, wouldn't industrialists want to also find a way to usurp and "free" the capitalist farmer, given certain forces of production that have the potential to reorganize the social division of labor? And if not, why not? In fact, Marx has a way of writing about these processes as if the capitalist farmer (occasionally referred to as the "large" farmer) were still outside the domain of capitalist production proper, a mere producer of commodity capital which becomes means of production for industrial capital when the two encounter each other in the market. Marx does not confront, once and for all, what keeps agriculture and industry separate in capital's anatomy and seems to finesse the point by applying the term "industrial capitalist" occasionally to both.

The theorized particularities of agriculture are trickier still, for the issue concerning the rise of the capitalist farmer and capitalistic agriculture is intimately connected to what Marx means when he calls farmers and agriculture capitalist at all. Capitalist agriculture, I've said, seems to stand theoretically apart as something capitalist and something left over by capitalism at the same time. The textual outcome in *Capital* is that whereas the capitalist farmer is more than once held up as an example of what a capitalist is, urban industrial capitalism is usually attributed with being at history's progressive edge. Yet, even this is not quite right. For Marx's divergent thinking is redoubled.

On the one hand, he is adamant that the advance of capitalism was indeed *most evident* in agriculture. In volume one of *Capital*, Marx writes, in his discussion of the "revolution called forth by modern industry in agriculture," that "if the use of machinery in agriculture is for the most part free from the injurious physical effect it has on the factory operative, its action in superseding the labourers is *more intense*" (Vol. 1: 504–5, emphasis added). The reason is, of course, that a process was set in motion that made many laborers superfluous—as opposed to industry, which was, by contrast, amassing the majority of that surplus of laborers. And he's not suggesting here that as industrial capital absorbs rural labor, it leaves agriculture as a sort of residue. Modern industry in agriculture, capitalism in agriculture, is subject to internal transformative processes. "In the sphere of agriculture, modern industry has a more revolutionary effect than elsewhere, for this reason, that it annihilates the peasant . . . and replaces him by the wage-labourer"—and a decreasing number of rural wage laborers at that (Vol. 1: 505). If one insists on seeing the motor of change firmly emanating from industrial capital, at the very least we apparently find in capitalist agriculture a branch of production that seemingly outpaces the parent. No process being without contradiction, however, the capitalist countryside, without its masses of small, thriving producers, finds itself in the throes of labor shortage at harvest and, at other times, in the throes of labor surplus as the impoverishment of the remaining rural population reveals itself. "There are always too many agricultural labourers for the ordinary, and always too few for the exceptional or temporary needs of the cultivation of the soil" (Vol. 1: 693). Nonetheless, in removing human bodies from production, Marx seems to view agriculture as potentially moving faster than industry.

On the other hand, in his discussions of how varying arrangements of production and working times relate to the constraints on circulating capital, agriculture does not come off nearly so advanced as, say, yarn-spinning. And if agriculture, as discussed in volume two of *Capital,* turns out to be not quite residual, it *is* a troublesome site for the circulation of capital—an observation that has to be tempered by the realization that Marx's whole point is to set forth reasons why the circulation of capital is almost always troublesome, whether for agriculture or industry! The aim of the discussion, that is, is not to rank branches of production as most or least suitable for capital, but to map out the difficulties encountered by all capitalists, given that their capital must circulate. Nonetheless, Marx's readers here and there still gain a picture, however spotty, that agricultural production is rather something to be reckoned with. We may be reminded, for example, that Marx agreed with the English political economist Thomas Hodgskin that the "monopolisers of all the land" (the agriculturists) are doomed to dependence on creditors: dependence and debt are the *specific* costs exacted by the disunity of production and working time as this disunity stalls the turnover of the "monopolisers'" circulating capital. And one of the branches of production mentioned as specifically an obstacle to the capitalist mode is forestry, where nature demands absurdly long production times of 20, 40, or 150 years, making it "an industry of little attraction to private and therefore capitalist enterprise" (Vol. 2: 244)—but just such enterprises with very long working periods, like road building, are taken on at state expense rather than at private capital's, at least until huge capitals become concentrated and centralized and the credit system has developed (Vol. 2: 233).

By far, the weight of Marx's discussion about agriculture in volume two simply concerns the problems encountered by the circulation of capital. It is not really a discussion of why agriculture fails to be or become capitalist. In fact, the dividing line between how Marx assesses agriculture and industry and their respective capitalists is simply the line that divides and joins two of capital's tendencies. What of Marx's divergent thinking then? It is two sides of the same process, wherein capital just looks different and is evaluated differently as glimpsed through the different processes where it circulates. Take the capitalist farmer, then. Having excelled in reducing labor time (the amount of labor actually applied in production, as distinct from working period, which is an indication of the length of the period during which any labor is applied in production), the capitalist farmer at the vanguard of modern industry in agriculture dramatically evinces a tendency of capital to do with as little labor as possible, thus perverting the assumption of more "advanced" industrial capitals. It is as if he is suggesting that the mark of a highly developed industrial capitalism, with respect to the massing of workers into great centers of population, is simultaneously the mark of a capitalism not as developed as the capitalist agriculture that makes such a massing possible. That agriculture was doing away with so many workers altogether constituted a real victory for capitalist social relations. But *to the extent that industry could not do away with them in the same proportion* signaled a, or *the*, opportunity for workers. Viewed from the capitalist countryside, the capitalist city then takes on new meaning. It is less the site of capital's complete conquest than the site of something not yet accomplished, that something making all the difference for the progressive edge of history: "Capitalist production, by collecting the population in great centres and causing an ever-increasing preponderance of town population, on the one hand concentrates the historical motive power of society," whereas it "destroys . . . the intellectual life of the rural labourer" (Vol. 1: 505). Then take the industrial capitalist. Having excelled at extracting surplus value from labor power only partly repaid in wages, industrial capitalists dramatically evince the tendency of capital to amass biopower, *and* keep a portion in reserve. This, too, is what capitalism does, and can do, exceedingly well.

But to the extent that the long, historical transformation of independent producers into wage workers and the reproduction of wage-work social formations are the signal events of capitalist penetration, and the theory thereof, there is an express contradiction: the perpetuation of waged bodies is simply another skin of "nature" that capital fails to penetrate; it does not represent the antipode to non-wage rural labor. The "nature" that prevents capital from subsuming non-wage rural labor is represented in miniature in the (waged) body itself. (The body's own production time exceeds its time as variable capital embodied in labor.) Unless capital does away with the human body, it will always face the "natural limitations of the labour-power itself" (Vol. 2: 238) as a barrier to increased rates of production. Workers are sites of biological processes and energy flows for which capital has only partial substitutions (e.g., robotics). They are themselves obstacles to capitalism. Bodies persist. That they are *waged* bodies is a capitalist solution. That they are waged *bodies* is a capitalist problem. (In chapter 3 I will examine the implications of this dynamic for the racializing process.) Of course, within this constraint there is also opportunity, for the inability to fully substitute for the bodily reproduction of the worker and labor power has come to occasion a whole realm of capitalist production for consumption and reproduction, the realm of capitalist-produced commodities that are sold and bought *for* reproduction (food, housing, etc.). That the very hallmark of capitalist penetration would also signal that which capital cannot itself make and that thereby capitalism must ultimately remain incomplete if it is to be overturned are delectable ironies.

I have wanted to raise certain questions regarding what's capitalist about capitalist agriculture and about the different inflections in Marx's thinking about agriculture and industry, countryside and city, because I don't think they should be answered hastily and without reference to how certain answers (perhaps contradictory) can arise from within different aspects of one and the same analysis of circulating capital. An important contention of the Mann-Dickinson thesis is that the disunity of production and working times presented by the agency of nature is an obstacle to capitalist development (even though the society-nature encounter is admittedly shaped by the quest for commodity production); that the result is the persistence of non-wage rural enterprises, the family farm; and that on each of these counts, industry may contrast sharply with agriculture in advanced capitalist societies. But in Marx's thought, the extent of capitalist development—even when the capital-wage labor relation is considered definitive of that development—can be appraised otherwise: more developed in agriculture, to the extent that labor has been radically dispensed with (and certainly with the express aid of nature), and less developed in industry, to the extent that the massing of labor is a crude accomplishment of industrial capital. While I do not want to argue at all the question of whether U.S. family farms persist in certain commodity sectors as a form of non-wage rural labor—that is, as non-capitalist—I am saying that the presence and concentration of wage labor is not the be-all and end-all of capitalism. (There is also a certain irony in the fact that the disunity of production and working time, which ostensibly blocks the development of agrarian capitalism in, say, California strawberry share-crop production, is also one of the very things that makes hiring masses of migrant laborers necessary for the harvest [Wells 1996]. This leaves us with the very undesirable contradiction that capitalist social relations would exist for the workers but not for the non-capitalists who appropriate the surplus value!) It can be as capitalist a tendency to replace human labor as it is to amass it and exploit labor power. Capitalist development can mean both the obsolescence of labor and the concentration of labor. Whether nature is an obstacle to capitalist development must also be opened to question. Let us now turn to it.

### Nature and Circulation

Here, recognition of the social division of labor and the circulation of capital through it, and by virtue of it, is crucial. For Marx, again in the second volume of *Capital,* the effect of the disunity between production time and working time in agriculture, a disunity produced by time absorbed in the stages of biological production, is at least twofold. First, "the divergence of the production from the working period, the latter being but a part of the former, constitutes the natural basis for the combination of agriculture with subsidiary rural industries," there being regular surpluses of labor (Vol. 2: 241). Marx's choice of the words "natural basis" is fortuitous indeed. Where nature presents grave problems for the circulation of the farmer's capital, it is the very basis upon which the social division of labor in the countryside can be erected and upon which the circulation of other capitals (rural and non-rural) can proceed—thus David Harvey's point, as we'll see below, that the restrictions on capitalist development appear much more severe for the individual holder of capital than for capital in general. Second, "these subsidiary industries in turn offer points of vantage to the capitalist, who intrudes first in the person of the merchant" (Vol. 2: 241). Marx allows Thomas Hodgskin, the English political economist mentioned above, to speak for him on the logic of this point:

> [Agriculturists] cannot bring their commodities to market in less time than a year. For the whole period they are obliged to borrow of the shoemaker, the tailor, the smith, the wheelwright, and the various other labourers, whose products they cannot dispense with, but which are completed in a few days or weeks. Owing to the natural circumstance, and owing to the more rapid increase of the wealth produced by other labor than that of agriculture, the monopolisers of all the land, though they have also monopolised legislation, have not been able to save themselves and their servants, the farmers, from becoming the most dependent class of men in the community. (Quoted in *Capital,* Vol. 2: 242)

Marx adds that to the extent that agriculturists are able to stretch working time over a greater part of the year by planting a variety of crops whose planting, cultivation, and harvest occur at different times of the year, even greater amounts of circulating capital will have to be advanced in production in the form of fertilizers, seeds, wages, and the rest. Farmers, like industrialists in general, will need *more capital* up front in order to employ capital more smoothly over time and reap the rewards more smoothly as well. To avoid one interruption in the circulation of their capital, they thereby court another whose avoidance often means more credit and debt. So it is that what works to agriculture's disadvantage vis-à-vis the gaps between working and production times works to someone else's advantage. And that is the general run of things. *The very processes that interrupt the circulation of one capital are processes which may be the condition for the circulation of another.* This is so not only in agriculture. For example, long circulation time (in that more specific sense) determined by the necessity of delivering commodity capital to a distant market for final consumption (even as only some capitalist's means of production) is time presented for some other capitalist—a shipping company, a packing company, and so forth—to circulate their own capital. The intersection of capitalist development with nature has to be observed across the whole social division of labor if it is to make any sense.

Certainly, credit developed as an integral mechanism with capitalist production, although this development represents a kind of duality. It signifies that capital is at once incapacitated and often brilliantly mobilized. Again, Marx:

> [F]rom not having sufficient capital of his own at the very outset . . . A borrows from banker C a portion of the productive capital with which he starts in business or continues it during the year. Banker C lends him a sum of money which consists only of surplus-value deposited with the banker by capitalists D, E, F, etc. As far as A is concerned there is as yet no question of accumulated capital. But with regard to D, E, F, etc., A is, in fact, nothing but an agent capitalising surplus-value appropriated by them . . . The money-capital which the capitalist cannot as yet employ in his own business is employed by others, who pay him interest for its use. It serves him as money-capital in its specific meaning, as a kind of capital distinguished from productive capital. But it serves as capital in another's hands. (Vol. 2: 320–21)

These relations can be specified further such that the social division of labor, social and geographical space, and fictitious value (e.g., credit) must be coordinated in order for capital to circulate in as uninterrupted a way as possible. In *Limits to Capital,* David Harvey has suggested what sort of opportunities and constraints may be present in these relations. Given that spatial movement is required for capital to circulate, it must take a fixed form such as money or commodities while it does so. As would be expected from the foregoing discussions, capital's turnover time is thereby increased, which thereby sets limits on capital's geographical mobility in the first place. But enter the social division of labor—for the restriction placed on capital's mobility "applies in the strict sense to an individual capital undergoing its standard process of self-expansion." This is opposed to circulation in the aggregate, where countless numbers of individual capitals circulate, "each beginning and ending at different time points. The opportunity arises, therefore, for myriad spatial substitutions between different temporal processes." In other words, it's not simply that capitalists can buy credit to keep production running. As surpluses of capital are produced, these moneys are free to jump, quite geographically, into other circuits elsewhere, which have yet to reach completion and may not reach completion at all lest credit be available for sale in the first place. "Capitalists in an industrial region can lend the money they earn in the first part of the year to farmers in another region who pay them back after harvest time," whether or not capitalist farmers are the ones buying the credit. "What appears as very tight constraints to spatial movement at the individual level are much reduced when the circulation process is viewed as a whole. The credit system, in particular, facilitates long distance transfers and substitutions between highly divergent temporal processes" (Harvey 1982: 406). So it is not only nature that, in freeing up rural labor, allows for the subsidiary industries to be established. Spatial substitutions that arise out of the circulation process in the whole of the social division of labor enable crucial urban-rural ties. Where nature as the process of biological production "takes over," rural labor may be available for other enterprises. Where other enterprises have credit for sale, they may wish to avail themselves of the opportunity to cash in on biological production time. These are conditions that may or may not be acted upon; there is nothing strictly deterministic about them.

As both Marx and Harvey insist, the circulation of capital through the mechanisms of credit is by no means a stranger to the sphere of capitalist production. Nor is credit a curious, antiquated relic from the days of merchant capital. While credit must ultimately be valorized in production (somewhere, sometime), production, over the history of capitalist development, has increasingly come to rely on credit. This describes a particular history. For "as conditions change," notes Harvey, "so different kinds of capital tend to take on a leading role. The movement of commodities and gold, once the cutting edge of the internationalization of capital, was steadily supplanted during the late nineteenth century by the movement of money capital as credit" (Harvey 1982: 407; see also Leyshon and Thrift 1997, especially Part I). And so we have the seeming irony that it is, as Marx observed, "impossible for capital to be produced by circulation, and it is equally impossible for it to originate apart from circulation. It must have its origin both in circulation and yet not in circulation" (Vol. 1: 165–66). The circulation of capital and the credit system develop together (Vol. 2: 321).

## Capital, Nature, and the Space-Time of Agro-Credits in the United States

Harvey's observation stands true of agriculture. Long-term changing conditions in agriculture indeed were accompanied by and expressed the rise of sophisticated credit mechanisms. Through these, nature presented itself as a pivotal opportunity, not as an obstacle to the circulation of capital—I take circulation to be a sine qua non of capitalist development. In the following discussion of the late-nineteenth- and early-twentieth-century United States, I want to illustrate how the nexus of nature and capital, as mediated by the sale of credit, was comprised of specific space-times. What this means is that credit was mobilized at different scales (primarily national, regional, and local, but also international), through different capitalist actors, and across the cyclic motions of capital accumulation.

A key period during which to track the movements of loan capital in U.S. agriculture is 1910–20, the reason being that it includes the boom years of World War One, when finance capital's confidence in American agriculture was at a peak. While I will discuss the expansion of agricultural credit in the latter decades of the nineteenth century, which provided a critical opening to the growth of finance capitals in agriculture, the dramatic output of the 1910s makes the earlier period pale in comparison. Tables 2.1 and 2.2 offer a quick snapshot through which the story can begin to be told.

Immediately apparent in table 2.1 is that the amount of interest-bearing capital tied up in farm mortgages secured by real estate—and representing a combination of credit used for land and equipment purchases and for purchase of seasonal inputs (labor, fertilizer, seeds, etc.)—skyrocketed in the 1910s, going from $3.3 billion to $7.8 billion. (This bulk sale of credit would resurface in the 1930s as a devastating catastrophe for agriculture—another reason why the 1910s is an absolutely critical decade to be mindful of.) The lion's share of capital tied up in these farm loans was in the Midwest and Great Plains regions—especially the latter,

Table 2.1. The Westward Tilt of Financial Capital in Agriculture, as Indicated by Farm-Mortgage Debt, 1910 and 1920.*

| Geographic Division** | Farm-Mortgage Debt ($000) on Jan. 1 | | Share (%) of U.S. Farm-Mort. Debt | | |
|---|---|---|---|---|---|
| | 1910 | 1920 | 1910 | 1920 | Δ% (+/–) |
| U.S. | 3,320,470 | 7,857,700 | | | |
| New England | 76,110 | 120,860 | 2.29 | 1.53 | – |
| Middle Atlantic | 281,530 | 396,640 | 8.47 | 5.04 | – |
| South Atlantic | 141,250 | 347,470 | 4.25 | 4.42 | + |
| East South Central | 123,560 | 320,100 | 3.72 | 4.07 | + |
| East North Central | 794,950 | 1,591,420 | 23.94 | 20.25 | – |
| West South Central | 291,210 | 703,680 | 8.77 | 8.95 | + |
| West North Central | 1,296,080 | 3,199,690 | 39.03 | 40.72 | + |
| Mountain | 113,710 | 544,550 | 3.42 | 6.93 | + |
| Pacific | 202,070 | 633,290 | 6.08 | 8.06 | + |

*Source*: Wickens, David L. 1932. "Farm-Mortgage Credit." *Technical Bulletin No.288* (Washington, D.C.: USDA), pp. 3–4.

*The amounts listed in this table, and table 2.2, may not be comparable with other studies of the period. Economists employed different methods to estimate farm indebtedness on other than owner-operated farms (e.g., tenant farms and manager-operated farms) because of the difficulty of obtaining data. In this 1932 study, the authors used ratios of farm mortgages to total farm value on owner-operated farms and applied them toward calculating the indebtedness of farms of different tenure.

** States within each division: New England (ME, NH, VT, MA, RI, CT); Middle Atlantic (NY, NJ, PA); East North Central (OH, IN, IL, MI, WI); West North Central (MN, IA, MO, ND, SD, NE, KS); South Atlantic (DE, MD, D.C., VA, WV, NC, SC, GA, FL); East South Central (KY, TN, AL, MS); West South Central (AR, LA, OK, TX); Mountain (MT, ID, WY, CO, NM, AZ, UT, NV); Pacific (WA, OR, CA).

whose share of the value of all real-estate–based farm-mortgage debt nationwide hovered around 40%. The flip side of the Midwest's and Great Plains' heavy share, itself a measure of how credit was tied to those regions' production regimes, is that the concentration of finance capital in the West was highly uneven. Before the world war, credit was notably absent in the Mountain states and many of the states in the lower Mississippi Valley. Investors were relatively more tied to the Pacific Slope, by comparison. (In due course, we shall look at where investors themselves were geographically based.) After the war, the westward tilt was even more apparent. Most of the regions where the share of finance capital increased were western, especially the Mountain and Pacific states, whose production bolted upward during the 1910s. From table 2.2 a few more details are discernible.

Table 2.2 is a ranking of the ten states where the most amount of credit (of the same type as indicated in table 2.1) was sold. The top ten states are a good measure of just how geographically concentrated finance capital was. In both 1910 and 1920, the top ten accounted for about 60% of the value of farm-mortgage loans. (If the next five ranked states are thrown in for good measure, all fifteen would account for about 75%). As might be expected, there is some overlap of the patterns indicated in table 2.1. States in the Great Plains and Midwest are well represented, especially the corn belt, which stretched across the latter. Also revealed are large pockets of loan capital in states—particularly Texas and New York—that are within regions whose farms attracted a relative dearth of such capital.

Table 2.2. Farm-Mortgage Debt, Top Ten States, Jan. 1, 1910 and 1920, and Share of National Farm-Mortgage Debt.

| 1910 | | | 1920 | | | Δ% |
|---|---|---|---|---|---|---|
| State | Debt ($000) | Share (%) | State | Debt ($000) | Share (%) | 1910–20 (+/–)* |
| Iowa | 431,500 | 13.00 | Iowa | 1,098,970 | 13.99 | + |
| Illinois | 266,780 | 8.03 | Illinois | 502,850 | 6.40 | – |
| Missouri | 202,650 | 6.10 | Minnesota | 455,540 | 5.80 | + |
| Wisconsin | 193,600 | 5.83 | Wisconsin | 455,470 | 5.80 | – |
| Texas | 172,240 | 5.19 | California | 425,460 | 5.41 | + |
| Kansas | 163,770 | 4.93 | Nebraska | 416,860 | 5.30 | + |
| Nebraska | 161,850 | 4.87 | Texas | 396,670 | 5.05 | + |
| New York | 154,190 | 4.64 | Missouri | 385,790 | 4.91 | – |
| Minnesota | 146,160 | 4.40 | Kansas | 295,870 | 3.77 | – |
| California | 122,080 | 3.68 | South Dakota | 278,880 | 3.55 | na |

*Source*: Wickens, David L. 1932. "Farm-Mortgage Credit." *Technical Bulletin No. 288* (Washington, D.C.: USDA), pp. 3–4.

*Provided only for states which ranked in the top ten in 1910.

Table 2.2 makes clearer that a large amount of credit was poured into the Pacific Slope, especially California. This reflects a national shift in the agricultural economy; toward the West in geographical terms and toward a capital-intensive, industrialized agriculture in social terms. In 1910, California was the tenth-ranked state with regard to the amount of loan capital invested; after the war, it ranked fifth. In terms of the *growth* in percentage share of loan capital nationwide, no other state attracted as much of that kind of investment as quickly as California, although many states increased their share of total credit sold in the United States.

But if the case of California is exceptional, it also indicates the tendency for particular states to dominate within their regions, giving us a better idea of the shape of things. Thus, while much of the growth along the Pacific Slope was really California's, Iowa clearly dominated the West North Central states, where it sits at the eastern edge, considerably removed from its more arid neighbors and more tied to the midwestern farm economy proper. Texas dominated in the West South Central, where its combination of livestock, forage, and cotton crops dwarfed its neighbors. New York, whose dairies and orchards had access to credit emanating out of Manhattan, was a relatively important magnet before the war. With the general picture of an uneven landscape in mind, we can develop some of the details. I will proceed in three "takes"—first, a look at the growing recourse to credit over time; next, an examination of the changing actors who sold credit; and last, an analysis of the geography of credit through the meshing of local and nonlocal actors.

## Historical Growth of Credit Investments/Purchases

The expansion of the credit system into agriculture from the late nineteeth to the early twentieth century was a complex affair. On the one hand, the maturing of the credit system meant both an absolute rise in the dollar sales of credit and an increasing proportion of farmers who bought credit. On the other hand, with its deepening grip, the credit system was capable of extracting values out of farm production in good times and bad. Creditors could make money by fueling farm expansion *and* by floating farmers during periods of contraction.

In the late nineteenth century, but before the crash of the mid-1890s, the percentage of U.S. owner-occupied farms that bought credit was under 30%—27.8% in 1890. This low percentage was a reflection both of state-subsidized forms of land purchase under various homestead and reclamation laws and of land prices that were still low enough on average to permit ready purchase with savings. Wickens (1932) speculates that the 1890 figure is greater than for the preceding years as it represents the flow of capital toward midwestern farms established in the previous generation.[4] After the 1890s depression, when prices began rising, the sale of credit continued to multiply. Some 30% of owner-occupied farms were mortgaged in 1900, 33.2% by 1910. During the 1910s, the percentage of farms mortgaged reached 37.2%, a rate that conceals the fact that actual dollar sales of credit more than doubled. The sheer number of land sales during these years, coupled with the rising price of land and other means of production, virtually guaranteed a growing market for farm loans (Wickens 1932: 41). It must be mentioned that loans were sold based on forms of security other than real estate. Most of these were short-term seasonal loans that explicitly extracted surplus values based directly on the disunity of production and working time. Such loans were backed up by everything from a farmer's own word to crops, livestock, warehouse receipts, and stocks and bonds. For banks alone, these personal and collateral loans amounted to an estimated $3.8 billion in 1920 (Valgren and Engelbert 1922: 2–3). Farmers would be forced to refinance loans such as these after the war, on the basis of their farmland—see below (Horton et al. 1942: 2). In the postwar downturn, the sale of credit money kept increasing, by almost a fifth from 1920 to 1925, although the percentage of farms mortgaged declined from 37.2% to 36.1%, a reflection of foreclosures in hard-hit areas of the American West (Wickens 1932: 41). As this history implies, increasing mortgage indebtedness can, in fact, indicate contradictory trends. It can point to rising trends in the rural economy, as with mortgaged-financed sales of farmland during the high-price, expansionary 1910s. Conversely, it can reflect a downturn, as when the 1920s' drop in farm prices spurred farmers to buy credit from banks to meet their operating expenses, to pay off old debts, and/or to purchase machinery to increase on-farm productivity (Wickens 1932: 5). Of course, considerable geographic variation existed in these trends. In the 1920s, farmers in the upper and lower portions of the Mississippi Valley and the Great Plains states suffered under the weight of farms mortgaged at a high share of their value. For many California farmers, it was easier to take on more debt given that land values remained more constant (Wickens 1932: 58–59). Because sales of credit may increase in good times *and* bad, creditors are positioned to "win" either way; a mechanism for the appropriation of surplus values survives either way and is tied directly to what "either way" means in the first place. This is the reality lying behind the contradiction that whereas most loans sold were for a term of five years or less, most farms, once mortgaged, remained so for thirty years or more, as farmers tended to renew their debts rather than pay them off once and for all (Wickens 1932: 76). With "nature" as a perpetual draw for sellers of credit—though sellers differ over time and space, as we'll see next—farmers themselves had to arrange and negotiate renewals of their debt over the years.

### Changing Sellers of Credit through Credit-Debt Cycles

Yet another look at the secular growth of the credit "system" reveals that the actors change at certain critical junctures and that the credit itself circulates differently. Here the story is not just of the greater mass of credit but also of changes in its institutional form. For one thing, more mainstream, larger capitals get involved with financing agriculture (as we will see, especially in the case of the Bank of Italy in California). Credit also more clearly becomes a commodity that can be traded; it becomes a more advanced form of capital (though not in so nearly sophisticated terms as we observe today [see Leyshon and Thrift 1997]). In theory, credit begins as what Marx calls "fictitious value." Fictitious value is simply credit sold for a price that is predicated upon as yet unproduced surplus values. If credit in this form were to itself circulate as a medium of exchange, it would become "fictitious capital." So it is along the lifeline of the farm mortgage through the business cycle.

We can begin with what happens during a crisis. In the economic downturn of the farm economy, mortgages held by parties concerned about keeping a maximum of capital in circulation (e.g., individual investors or former farm owners who accepted a mortgage as part of the purchase price for a farm they sold during a previous period of rising prices) may be sold to entities who can greater afford to circulate their capital over a longer period (e.g., banks or companies who specialize in long-term loans). At the same time, banks—which already hold mortgages (also procured during the previous period of rising prices)—may prod farmers into securing their short-term loans with land rather than with crops, whose values are more volatile. By these means, banks not only reduce the risk of selling credit but also compete with other firms (e.g., warehouses, fertilizer companies, shippers, etc.) that sell short-term credit—the purchase of which is absolutely essential if the farm economy is to function at all. No sooner do these banks fix on land securities, however, then they potentially run into the problem of being legally limited by how much capital they can fix in land—a legality that came into play especially in the post–Civil War period as a safeguard for both bank depositors and holders of a bank's capital stock. It is more than a legal question, however, for banks also wish to reserve a portion of their circulating capital for other kinds of loans besides those based on rural lands. In consequence, banks may then sell a portion of these land-based short-term loans to yet other entities whose business is farm loans. These entities include the government-backed land banks begun in the 1910s and the generally cash-rich life insurance companies. From the farmer's point of view—the farmer being the one who must cover the cost of the disunity between production and working times—the circulation of these fictitious capitals is experienced, on the one hand, as definite debt that demands surplus values in payment and, on the other hand, as an opportunity to repeatedly refinance short-term debt (sometimes before it comes due), thereby making a long-term loan out of a short-term one. As prices continue to fall in the course of the downturn, this is experienced (by those who have money and are positioned to use it) as greater purchasing power for a given quantity of money. In this context, new loans are made, albeit in small amounts—small because the crisis has not yet run its course and because purchasing power is relatively high. With this begins a gradual upturn in the credit cycle (Wickens 1932: 19–20; see also Horton et al. 1942). The sum total of these transactions makes the circuit of fictitious capital a wheel within a wheel. The circuit disaggregates into the hands of its separate actors as prices *begin* to decline and starts to reaggregate *before* prices fully recover. All the while, "nature" is relied upon and capitalized on throughout. Over the course of the cycle and stretching across cycles, fictitious capitals exist by virtue of expected rents to be extracted over the constant life of the farm (i.e., the farm's use value as land always being potentially convertible to exchange value as real estate) and by virtue of credit's ability to mend and profit from repeated seasons of production/working time disunities.

## The Mesh of Local and Non-Local Circulation of Credit

Still another cut at the credit system reveals a distinctive geography, whereby local sellers of credit tend to be more involved than geographically distant creditors during a period of rising prices, and vice versa during downswings. Let us look at the process at the beginning of a period of rising prices—that is, from the point of view of farmers looking to expand. "Out of a period of generally rising commodity prices," Wickens writes, "increased activity in land transfers develops." With this, land prices themselves increase and, with them, the demand for mortgages (potentially blinding producers and creditors alike to the fragility of farm incomes and their purchasing power). In this same climate, farmers seek to expand their access to money for use as fixed, productive capital, in the form of new purchases of equipment and livestock, for example. For these they need loans. "Lenders grant these loans on the assumption of continued higher prices" (Wickens 1932: 19).

Geography matters here. At first, the bulk of the lenders (although it is crucial to see them as sellers-of-credit/extractors-of-value, so as not to confuse what sort of transaction takes place) are near at hand. Lenders may at first be the very farm owners (or real estate developers) who take a part of the selling price as a mortgage on the land they're selling. But when exchange values are being directly sought, "the local banks that stand closest to the farmer are the first of the institutions to encounter the demand" (Wickens, 1932: 19). The funds they have at the ready are generally made up of local surplus values. At the point where prices begin to fall, other sellers of credit intervene, as we saw above. The point about these other actors now is that they are often non-local, meaning that they may be based in the nearest large city or outside the region altogether. At any rate, there is a palpable "shift of farm mortgages from local agencies dependent upon local funds to large centralized institutions drawing their resources from a wide area" (Wickens 1932: 25). Thinking back to the previous section, this is generally the difference between commercial and savings banks, on the one hand, and life insurance companies and federal and joint stock land banks, on the other. The movement of farm-mortgage debt from local to non-local sellers during the post-World War I price downturn is suggested by table 2.3. Aside from the rising importance of non-local sellers of credit during a price downturn, they may also be

Table 2.3. Percent of Farm-Mortgage Debt in the United States Held by Principal Selling Agencies, Jan. 1, 1920, 1925, and 1928.

| Selling Agency | 1920 | 1925 | 1928 |
|---|---|---|---|
| Commercial Banks | 18.4 | na | 10.8 |
| National Banks | 21.0 | 2.7 | 3.4 |
| Life Insurance Companies | 12.4 | 20.7 | 22.9 |
| Federal Land Banks | 3.6 | 9.9 | 12.1 |
| Joint-Stock Land Banks | 0.7 | 4.8 | 7.0 |

*Source*: Wickens, David L. 1932. "Farm-Mortgage Credit." *Technical Bulletin No. 288* (Washington, D.C.: USDA), p. 23.

of importance during a period of rising interest rates. During such a period, local banks will withdraw a portion of capital for investment in central money markets, thereby reducing what is locally available to farmers. To the extent that this is the case, local banks will direct farmers to the local agents of non-local lenders who, in this newly created environment of credit shortage, see a new market into which their exchange values can be ploughed (Wickens 1932: 71; Horton et al. 1942). We must remember that these non-local sellers of credit may themselves be attracted to strong money markets and that this may interrupt the flow of fictitious capital into farm mortgages. For example, in 1919, 1922, and 1924, insurance companies pulled a large portion of their farm-mortgage capital out of those mortgage markets because those were years when U.S. Government bond yields were high.

## Local and Non-Local Credit Tied to the Farm as an Economic Institution

From where most farmers who "owned" their land stood, the disunity of production and working times, the swings in the economy, and the varying geography of credit came together in a way that emphasized just how mortgages could be both a cause and consequence of family farming (despite the fact that family farms were very often seasonally waged, to the extent that wage labor was used during periods of peak working time). At the risk of some repetition of the previous section—though now viewing the situation from an alternate perspective—let us look at a period when high money rates coincide with a farmer's mortgages falling due. The farmer starts the agricultural year with a need for some quantity of advance capital to begin production and carry him through the period when his commodity is maturing in the ground in its own time. The farmer has also begun the year with back debt to pay off. Were this farmer a corporation, he might have the option of issuing notes for sale on the market or of raising capital by selling stock—either way, acquiring capital without having to buy credit at high rates. Instead, the farmer must look to buy that credit. Given that money rates are high and that a sizable portion of surplus values has consequently fled the countryside for the central money markets, local banks may not have the money on hand that the farmer needs. "He must borrow on his own security"—from outside lenders or from a local bank willing to trade in its opportunities on the money market for values produced by the high-interest paying farmer—"and contract to pay the rate of interest current at the time. The great part of the farmer's financing thus tends to take the form of mortgage on real estate" (Wickens 1932: 72). Farmers take on mortgages, rather than other types of debt, then, because their business prevents them from doing otherwise, while mortgages are sold *to* them, because it can be good business for sellers to capitalize on the gap between production and working times. In other words, in theory, *the way that capital exploits "natural" time in production is partly responsible for the persistence of non-wage rural enterprises.* Also key to the persistence is that the debts incurred are private debts based on private property alienable to individuals. Farmers, thus in possession of land, are more likely to remain locked into the mortgage option than to collectively incorporate at the point of production. (Through marketing cooperatives, however, California farmers excelled at collectively incorporating in order to see their capital more efficiently through its time of circulation; and through irrigation districts, they essentially did the same in order to finance the costs of capital fixed for very long periods in the irrigation apparatus—what Marx calls "earth-capital").

## The Uneven Landscape of Capital and Nature

There were innumerable variations on the model of credit circulation that I have been laying out here. These resulted from all sorts of determinations that operated at multiple scales and through the hands of various actors. Recall first, from tables 2.1 and 2.2, that investments in mortgages were highly regionally differentiated when it came to the share of the total amount that particular places had. In the western states, and to an extent in the South, the growing share was due at once to the expansion of production onto new agricultural lands and to higher ratios of debt to real estate value (Horton et al. 1942: 6). Second, geographical variations on the model were also expressed in the changing kinds of investors who were active in one place as opposed to another.

A few examples from the 1920s will serve to make the point. Among all agricultural regions, life insurance companies were most attracted to mortgage investments in areas where agriculture tended to be more standardized—that is, areas dominated by a crop regime that did not vary too markedly over space and where, consequently, a large number of mortgages could be sold based on that regime. Life insurance companies looked for clusters of counties that had these sorts of qualities (Horton et al. 1942: 16), the basic idea being to become "educated" about a relatively small knowledge set of risks and earnings, which could be applied over a wide swath of landscape. By the mid-1910s, insurance companies had made a strong bid for the loan markets of the Midwest and Great Plains regions. Mortgages sold by insurance firms showed up most strongly in the Iowa corn belt, but also in Missouri, Kansas, and Nebraska. Almost half of all insurance companies' farm-mortgage sales were in these four states by 1915 (Thompson 1916: 7–8). In the Middle Atlantic and New England regions, credit sold by those whom farm economists called "individuals other than retired or active farmers," remained relatively strong during the 1920s downturn. In these regions, where the density of towns and cities was high, loans were sold by "professional men living in towns adjacent to farming territory," and by "merchants or other dealers who [took] mortgages often as a means of funding short-time credit extended at an earlier date." Loans sold by the federal land bank system showed up most strongly in the southern states, where there was a historical shortage of other forms of fictitious value. In the Pacific states, the rural credit market was dominated by commercial banks (including savings banks) and by individuals (Wickens 1932: 25–27). Historically important in this region were the nineteenth-century gold and silver rushes—accruing especially to California—which fueled a fast-growing and exceptionally strong local banking system well prepared to circulate surplus values into agriculture. Finally, in actual practice, it was not the case, as the foregoing might suggest, that these various actors unproblematically divided up their territory. For example, consider that because local lenders could oversee their investments more closely and quickly impose sanctions when they perceived a threat to their investments, they took on risks that distant lenders shied away from. Loans made on these higher risks were sold at a premium precisely because there was little outside competition. At the point where outside lenders became interested in a local area (presumably on the downside of the business cycle), the local lenders lowered the interest rates to a more competitive level (or even below cost) for farmers who qualified for the loans from outside and raised interest rates on farmers who did not qualify, in order to make up the difference. Farmers who had no choice but to buy credit locally subsidized both farmers who were better off and the flow of capital from outside (Horton et al. 1942: 164). There were specific dynamics internal to the accumulation of finance capital, therefore, that drove how fictitious values circulated and determined the shape of profits derived from "nature."

## Capital, Nature, and the Space-Time of Agro-Credits in California

At several points, I have alluded to the exceptional circumstances of the circulation of values through the California countryside. Not least was California's leap in the ranking of credit sales to farmers during the 1910s. California agriculture, aided by the circulation of agro-credits, challenged the nation. Just as the Northeast had had to compete with a rising Midwest, so did the Midwest watch California emerge seemingly from nowhere. As in the above discussion, I will examine the circulation of values in three different takes: a general comparative overview and historical discussion, an examination of the different actors who sold credit, and a look at the space-times of capital and nature.

### Historical Rise of Credit Investments and Purchases in California

Whereas farm-mortgage debt in the United States more than quadrupled between 1890 and 1925, it increased in California by more than five times. Over that period, more California farmers borrowed more money and borrowed it in larger amounts than farmers in the United States as a whole (table 2.4). These conditions accord well with what is widely known among students of American history, that California was a magnet for migrating farmers in an atmosphere of extremely rapid land commodification and that its crop regimes were capital intensive. (The basic answer to the question of why California agriculture was

Table 2.4. Farm-Mortgage Debt of Owner-Operated Farms in California and the United States, 1890–1925.

California

| Year | Total Farm-Mortgage Debt ($$) | % of Farms Mortgaged | Indebtedness As % of Farm Value | Average Mortgage ($$) |
|---|---|---|---|---|
| 1890 | 46,767,837 | 31.6 | 30.3 | |
| 1900 | ——— | 31.3 | — | |
| 1910 | 60,036,660 | 40.1 | 24.0 | 2,802 |
| 1920 | 224,063,903 | 50.4 | 29.3 | |
| 1925 | 295,688,806 | 46.3 | 33.8 | 6,379 (4,224 in 1913 dollars) |

United States

| Year | Total Farm-Mortgage Debt ($$) | % of Farms Mortgaged | Indebtedness As % of Farm value | Average Mortgage ($$) |
|---|---|---|---|---|
| 1890 | 1,085,995,960 | 27.8 | 35.5 | |
| 1900 | ——— | 30.0 | — | |
| 1910 | 1,726,172,851 | 33.2 | 27.3 | 1,715 |
| 1920 | 4,003,767,192 | 37.2 | 29.1 | |
| 1925 | 4,517,258,689 | 36.1 | 41.9 | 4,004 (2,651 in 1913 dollars) |

*Source*: West, Charles. 1929. "The Use, Value, and Cost of Credit in Agriculture." *California Agricultural Experiment Station, Bulletin 480* (Berkeley: California Agricultural Experiment Station, University of California [Contributed by Giannini Foundation of Agricultural Economics]), p.12.

capital intensive is because it could be, given the early concentration of finance capital in San Francisco and the regular migration of new capital and labor into the state.) That this would be so was not a given, for in the 1850s and sporadically through the '60s, a large proportion of capital was tied up in western mining and associated enterprises. Though economic change did come quickly to California, it was not automatic (for general histories, see Bean 1968; Blackford 1977; Jelinek 1982; McWilliams 1969, 1979, 1983; Odell 1992; Orsi 1974, 1975; Pomeroy 1965; Paul 1947; Pisani 1984; Almaguer 1994; Wright, 1980). Portions of capital accumulated in the mining-fueled economy were funneled into massive land purchases in the large interior basin, the Central Valley, and in the coastal and interior valleys of Southern California (see, for example, Glasscock 1933; Lavender 1981; Zonlight 1979; Odell 1992). These, then, became the basis of an extensive grain and stock empire—another regime in which a vast quantity of capital was fixed. Only later was a foundation laid for more intensive, irrigated crops. This last transition, to intensive agriculture, was finally well under way by the turn of the century, fueled, on the one hand, by capital that had been accumulating and by the declining cost of money, on the other (Rhode 1995).[5] Between 1900 and 1910 alone, irrigation expanded by over a million acres, in a near-even exchange with decreasing grain acreage. Investments in irrigation works practically tripled (Agricultural Economics Staff 1930: 11; also Pisani 1984). Capital was maneuvered into a far-flung, new production apparatus including newly leveled land, lateral ditches linking canals and aqueducts to fields, orchard and vineyard plantings, livestock, barns, and houses—much of this accompanied by highly exploitative labor conditions. Integral to the rise of irrigated, agriculture was the subdivision of large landholdings acquired both before the period of U.S. hegemony and after the Gold Rush. (Though many large landholdings were in fact irrigated, too, land subdivision hardly ever went unaccompanied by irrigation [Liebman 1983]. In fact, despite subdivision, large landholdings in California persisted [California Commission of Immigration and Housing 1919].)

A number of reasons combined, then, to make rural California a heavy buyer of credit. More agricultural specialization under competitive conditions meant the purchase of more specialized machinery and equipment. It also meant more purchases of household goods rather than their domestic production. Specialization often went hand in hand with the fact that subdivision translated into large numbers of real estate turnovers, increasingly facilitated by mortgages. These things took on special significance for Elwood Mead, who, as California's tireless champion of irrigation, land subdivision, and colonization, insisted at a luncheon of the California Development Association that

> The settler of moderate means cannot pay for a farm if we leave him to struggle alone. In the last ten years the cost of land has more than doubled. The cost of water for irrigation has made a like increase. Everything needed to change raw land into improved farms costs more. These things give a new importance to credit because the capital of settlers has not increased. But if the money invested and the money borrowed is increased, the earning power of the farmer also must increase, and that means he must work with better tools, own better stock, use more science and skill in cultivation. Along with the greater credit must come a better organization of the rural community and expert advice and direction in development. (Quoted in Hodges 1921: 659)

Whether this really meant "an urgent call to service," as one real estate dealer put it, realtors with their ears to the ground knew that, at least potentially, such service brought a "high money reward in the great, scarcely developed West," as put by the same dealer (Mendenhall 1924: 287).

But in other ways, too, farmers could not be left to "struggle alone." Specialization in labor-intensive crops also demanded a mobile pool of labor that had to be paid (e.g., Daniel 1981; Mitchell 1996)—often leading to farmers' complaints, presaged by Marx many years earlier, that the labor market was never big enough when needed and always too big when little called for. Finally, specialization typically corresponded with the fact that many California crops were grown in order to compete for a place in large, distant markets. Careful harvesting, processing, refrigeration, and transport, therefore, all added costs and provided opportunities to extract profits through the sale of the fictitious values that were pumped into agriculture. High competition and capital intensity put a premium on getting high prices. As one agricultural economist observed,

> A crop may be held for some time to await more favorable prices, and if of a semiperishable nature may be marketed through a period of more than a year. If the farmer deals through cooperative marketing organizations it

> usually requires nearly a year after delivery to obtain a complete return on his crop. The use of more capital in production and the sale of larger quantities of products over a longer period of time have made necessary the use of more commercial credit for efficient operation of the farm. (West 1929: 14)

But not *just* commercial credit, for what was being coordinated were credits sold at one point to mend the gap between production and working times and at another point to fill the void created by commodity capital's time in circulation, an observation that will be explored later.

The long period of growth in intensive, irrigated agriculture began to turn around after the world war, when overproduction problems finally reared up (as indeed they had in the mid-1890s, when the production of fruit growers proceeded far apace of their capacity to open up new markets). Growers continued to plant fruit crops, especially trees and vines, through the early 1920s—a 42% increase in fruit acreage between 1920 and 1925 (Agricultural Economics Staff 1930: 17). Because it takes several years for these crops to come into bearing, it became apparent late that they'd been overplanted. Moreover, the long time spent by capital in the production of irrigation facilities had the effect of extending the period of overdevelopment. The case of the rise of and crisis in California irrigated agriculture illustrates the fact that different kinds of agricultural regimes yield different problems for the circulation of capital through agricultural landscapes. As a group of economists at the California Agricultural Experiment Station put it: "While production cycles occur in other states and for other products entirely independent of irrigation, in California the time required to bring fruit trees into bearing is a greater disturbing element when superimposed upon the other difficulties of irrigation development." The sum of which can be confusing for creditor and debtor alike since the fall in prices leads to cutbacks in planting and credit, which in turn means that with a turnaround in the business cycle, farmers cannot respond so quickly (Agricultural Economics Staff 1930: 37).

## Changing Sellers of Credit in California

A second look at the circulation of value in California makes clear that finance capital was put into circulation by a changing set of actors. In the grain and livestock economy, production was more self-financed than in intensive agriculture, "which, for a period of years, [had] to be supported by capital originating mainly from sources other than agriculture," including buyers of irrigation bonds, land developers, and irrigation companies (Agricultural Economics Staff 1930: 10). This is a relative evaluation, however, for there is no question that California banks were important backers of the wheat economy and that in local places all over the wheat landscape, merchants, warehouses, and shippers sold credit to farmers. In the case of one "shipper," the Southern Pacific Railroad, millions of dollars worth of credit for land purchases were sold to farmers throughout the later wheat years and well into the transition to irrigated agriculture (Orsi 1975). With table 2.5 we have a general picture of the different real estate mortgage lenders who sold their wares in the era dominated by specialty, irrigated agriculture. This table, though constructed for the Pacific region and though omitting companies like the Southern Pacific Railroad, makes plain that banks remained a strong player

Table 2.5. Farm-Mortgage Loans ($000) Sold by Insurance Companies and Banks, Pacific Region, 1914–1927.

| Selling Agency | 1914 | 1918 | 1920 | 1923 | 1927 |
|---|---|---|---|---|---|
| Insurance Companies | 12,621 | 20,888 | 19,940 | 34,771 | 53,102 |
| Federal Land Banks | — | — | — | — | 78,959 |
| Joint-Stock Land Banks | — | — | — | — | 42,974 |
| State and National Banks | 65,200 | 138,951 | 114,321 | 227,872 | 194,840 |

*Source*: Wickens, David L. 1932. "Farm-Mortgage Credit." *Technical Bulletin No. 288* (Washington, D.C.: USDA), pp. 30–32.

in the California farm-mortgage market well into the postwar downturn. This was especially true of savings banks, whose investments in real estate loans far exceeded other banks (see chapter 1) and which were required to hold at least half of these mortgages on in-state properties (Odell 1992: 105). In 1914, they held some 45% of California farm mortgages, and as the decade wore on, they yielded little to the non-local agencies that became important creditors elsewhere in the country (Thompson 1916: 10).[6]

In fact, where life insurance companies have often signaled the presence of non-local finance capital (Bogue 1963), in California they signaled primarily the accumulation of more local capital, which was circulated into California agriculture. At the end of 1922, for example, only 20% of the loans that insurance companies made to farmers in California were sold by companies headquartered outside the state; these came mostly from Ohio, Illinois, and Indiana firms. Of the fourteen life insurance companies based in New York that conducted business in California, none invested any money in farm loans. Farm-mortgage loans sold to farmers were primarily sold by California firms. Among these, one loomed far above the rest—the Pacific Mutual Life Insurance Company, a phalanx of the Southern Pacific Railroad, headquartered in Los Angeles. Pacific Mutual held $8 million in farm loans in the state, about 40% of the total farm loans sold by insurance companies to California farmers (Chenowith 1923; also Odell 1992).

Pacific Mutual's investments were still dwarfed by the activities of California banks (though not the land banks, with which California farmers were frustrated because credit could only be bought in insufficient amounts for their intensive operations [Agricultural Economics Staff 1930: 52–53]). So heavily had the savings banks, in particular, sold land-secured credit—probably in the form of both long-term loans for land and equipment and short-term loans for advance capital to be consumed immediately in production—that by the end of the world war, they had saturated their own market. In 1920, the California Superintendent of Banks was compelled to write:

> A very conspicuous development . . . has characterized the past few years in the savings banks of California. Due to the tremendous prosperity of our state, mortgage loans of every sort have been retired in very large number. During the past year or two there has been a dearth of acceptable mortgage loans. During this interval savings bank deposits available for loans have tremendously increased. As a natural result of this decrease in the quantity of acceptable mortgage loans and increase in savings bank resources, we find

> that while in 1914, 64% of the resources of savings banks were invested real estate loans, in 1920 only 47% were so invested. This points unerringly to the necessity for a wider field for savings bank investment and activity. (Quoted in Chenowith 1923: 9)

Many successful farmers had apparently outcompeted these banks for a share in agricultural values. Savings banks, whose primary business was land development, were consequently prompted to switch capital into other circuits. They found at least a partial outlet in the agricultural bond market, a new brand of fictitious values that appeared with a trend that had been growing in the prewar period alongside land subdivision: the reconsolidation of land by large agro-capitals (Jelinek 1982; also California Commission of Immigration and Housing 1919).

The 2,000-acre Salinas Valley ranch, owned and developed by the California Orchard Company, is one such example. "You can make BIG money on CHEAP land," the company officers proclaimed to potential bond buyers (California Orchard Co. 1921: 26–27). Formed in 1920, the company was presided over by C. C. Teague, manager of the much larger agribusiness the Limoneira Company; J. Lagomarsino, president of the California Lima Bean Growers Association and a director of the Bank of Italy (see below); and C. Thorpe, the manager of the California Walnut Growers Association. Placing their bets upon diversification of crops, harvest times, and markets, they had the orchard planted to apricots, almonds, walnuts, apples, peaches, prunes, pears, and plums by workers who lived in the boarding house and bungalows on the property. Some of the produce was sold fresh, some dried, and some canned. In the interim before the trees went into bearing, they intercropped with lima beans, peas, and other vegetables, thus enabling bond buyers' capital to circulate more quickly. It was the job of the bank superintendent's office to certify bond issues such as these. In the six years up to 1919, his office certified $32 million worth of bond issues. During the next year, he certified $47 million more. "This function has become one of the most important within the department," he wrote in his annual report for 1920. "Through the medium of land bonds the larger agricultural enterprises in California are being carried forward," though the banks, he insisted, were especially interested in the bonds "predicated upon properties . . . that are marching forward progressively toward subdivision" (quoted in Chenowith 1923: 10). While the superintendent certified the bonds of the farm companies and encouraged California's banks to buy them, most were bought by individuals through investment companies in Los Angeles and San Francisco (one such firm, E. H. Rollins and Sons, begun in 1894, had bought $8 million in bonds as of 1923 and another $9 million of irrigation and reclamation district bonds) (Chenowith 1923: 11).

When it came to the sale of short-term credit to farmers, the kind of credit most used to bridge the gap between production and working times, banks were again in the vanguard. The dollar value of outstanding short-term loans that were backed up with securities other than land was estimated to be over $119 million in 1920. (Recall that loans made on the basis of real estate were also partly used as short-term credit.) These so-called personal and collateral loans were most often backed up with nothing more than a written promise. Survey data collected in 1920 and presented in table 2.6 reveal this quite dramatically. The large proportion of loans backed up with unendorsed written promises was 50% for California and 36%

Table 2.6. Percent of Farmers' Personal and Collateral Short-Term Loans Backed Up with Various Types of Security, United States and California Compared, 1920.

| Security (% of Number of Loans) | United States | California |
|---|---|---|
| % loans backed up with written promise only | 36.0 | 50.0 |
| % with written promise, one or more endorsements | 32.0 | 13.1 |
| % with mortgage on livestock | 18.3 | 11.8 |
| % with crop lien | 6.2 | 7.5 |
| % with warehouse receipt | 1.4 | 4.5 |
| % with stocks and bonds (mostly government) | 4.2 | 11.6 |
| % other | 1.9 | 1.5 |
| Total # banks reporting | 7,590 | 189 |

*Source*: Valgren and Engelbert. 1922. "Bank Loans to Farmers on Personal and Collateral Security," *Bulletin No. 1048* (Washington, D.C.: USDA), p. 21.

for the United States as a whole, a testament to the good security that banks considered California farms to be (Valgren and Engelbert 1922: 21).

Banks were not the only sellers of short-term credit. To varying degrees all over the country, marketing agencies, manufacturers, shippers, individuals, and stores (especially in the southern states) all sold such credit. The problem is that it is laborious, to say the least, to reconstruct the picture. What can be said is that most of this credit was sold by parties who had a direct interest in the products the farmers grew. What can also be said is that this credit tended to be sold at a higher interest rate than what banks charged. For the farmer, this meant a particular kind of bind:

> If credit is obtained from a company to which one must sell, bargaining ability is reduced. The grower must accept what is offered him, if by the terms of the loan he is compelled under contract to deliver his products to this particular concern; he is usually handicapped as compared with the grower who is free to sell where and when he chooses. (West 1929: 31–32)

Just how much these short-term lenders sold credit most likely varied by commodity sector—although they dominated in the early development of some areas in the absence of banks (see Wangenheim 1956, on the San Joaquin Valley grain hinterland). Grape growers, for example, bought the majority of their short-term credit from banks (58.0%), but most of the remainder from shippers and commission houses (15.8%) and "individuals, stores, and other sources" (16.2%). Some of the shippers' credit itself came from eastern wholesalers and jobbers who funneled funds through California shippers to the farmers, but this amount would have been relatively small and would not alter the argument here that California was the primary financier of its own agricultural development (West 1929: 15, 32). There were also variations marked by race. For example, historian Sucheng Chan found that Chinese tenant farmers in the California Delta region were almost exclusively financed by Anglo merchants and shippers, who both sold the tenants credit and contracted for their produce (Chan 1986). For the most part, these workers were denied access to credit by the usual financial intermediaries.

In theoretical terms, fictitious values sold to farmers by shippers, commission houses, and marketing agencies to cover in advance the cost of capital's time in circulation were values already extracted by these concerns during previous rounds of time in circulation, a portion of which was held in reserve for the new season. Nature was in no sense absent here. For in part, these loans represented capitalizations on "nature" as space and distance, and on "nature" as perishable goods whose value had to be preserved in transit. If these loans were also used by farmers as advance capital for production, then this represents values that, once, were put into the circuit defined by time in circulation and then, twice, were put into the previous circuit opened by "nature"—in essence, the familiar gap between production and working times.

How much did creditors actually make from selling farm loans, both long- and short-term? Table 2.7 provides a 1920 estimate for California and the United States of the total amount of all outstanding loans, short-term and long-term, sold to farms—owner-, manager-, and tenant-operated—by banks, shippers, individuals, and the rest. For California, the total came to more than half a billion dollars. But these figures do not reflect the annual cost of the credit, since they do not include the interest that would have been paid. With prevailing interest rates in California at 6.6%, 7.63%, and 12%, for long-term credit, bank short-term credit, and other short-term credit, respectively, the annual costs would be $28.1 million, $9.1 million, and $4.2 million. This is a total of over $40 million dollars of value extracted annually from California farmers. For the United States as a whole, which enjoyed a lower prevailing rate of interest and whose outstanding debt in 1920 was $12.5 billion, the total annual cost was $877.3 million. These are values not created through the selling of credit but, as Marx reminds us, values extracted by it.

Aside from the aforementioned venues through which credit was sold to farmers, one more became of particular importance. In 1887, the California legislature passed a bill permitting the formation of irrigation districts. These districts, whose rules changed through various other pieces of legislation into the twentieth cen-

Table 2.7. 1920 Estimate of Total Agricultural Credit (Bank and Non-Bank Sources, including Stores, Shippers, and Marketers, etc.) on Owner-Operated and Non-Owner–Operated Farms, United States and California.

| | United States ($) | California ($) |
|---|---|---|
| Long-Term Mortgage Credit* | 7,857,700,000 | 425,500,000 |
| Bank Short-Term Credit** | 3,869,891,000 | 119,181,000 |
| Other Short-Term Credit*** | 750,000,000 | 35,000,000 |
| Total | 12,477,591,000 | 579,681,000 |

*Source*: West, Charles H. 1929. "The Use, Value, and Cost of Credit in Agriculture." *California Agricultural Experiment Station, Bulletin 480.* (Berkeley: Giannini Foundation of Agricultural Economics), p. 16.

*USDA Agricultural Yearbook, 1924, pp. 190, 191 (1925).

**Valgren, V.N. 1922. "Bank Loans to Farmers on Personal and Collateral Security." *Bulletin No. 1048* (Washington, D.C.: USDA), pp. 2, 3, table 1.

***Values estimated by Charles H. West.

tury, essentially permitted the collection of taxes from all property holders within a district for the purpose of issuing bonds to fund the construction of irrigation facilities. Though the districts were filled with tension—holders of town vs. country property, stockmen vs. intensive specialty croppers, large farmers of grain vs. small farmers who could no longer grow grain very profitably—they became an essential instrument through which rural areas bought credit, eventually replacing most commercial irrigation companies (see Hutchins 1930, on such companies). In 1913, $7.5 million worth of these bonds were outstanding, covering over half a million acres. By 1930, $98.1 million worth of bonds were in the process of being paid off (and tens of millions of dollars more authorized but not yet issued), covering nearly three million acres (Agricultural Economics Staff 1930: 45). Their tremendous expansion was due partly to large increases in agricultural production, but also partly to the allowance of irrigation districts to establish hydropower plants at their dam sites and sell electricity. These bonds had a turbulent history, however. The first center of district formation was in Southern California, where districts were formed as part and parcel of the late 1880s real estate boom (Pisani 1984). Following the crash, and for a host of other reasons that need not detain us here, the irrigation district movement slipped into a funk that had district leaders a few years later pleading desperately with San Francisco bankers to endorse their bonds (see "The Irrigator," *Pacific Rural Press*, July 4, 1891: 3). Depression in the middle '90s only made things worse.

In these early years, many of the bond purchases were idiosyncratic, ranging from construction companies who built the irrigation works being paid with the bonds of the districts for whom they were doing the work, to large farmers within the districts bailing them out by purchasing large numbers of bonds, to the occasional San Francisco capitalist doing the same, and to the Southern Pacific Railroad buying up just about the entire bond issue of one district (Imperial Valley) in the 1910s after it was flooded into near oblivion (Rhodes 1943; Henderson 1994). Yet, these idiosyncrasies themselves revealed important features of the capitalist economy—namely, the dominating presence of California's heavy hitters: San Francisco, the Southern Pacific, and large landowners. In fact, "localization" of the irrigation district bond market describes the entire West during the 1910s and 1920s. (California was not alone in forming irrigation districts and selling bonds, though it was the most active.) That is, with the exception of the very beginnings of the district movement, when there was some reason to hope that a reliable market might be built up in the Midwest and East, the largest market for district bonds sold by westerners turned out to be the West itself. After the world war, bond purchases only came trickling in from the financial centers of Chicago, St. Louis, and New York (Hutchins 1923, 1931).[7]

Examined through the lens of the pool of potential investors, the bonds were of course nothing other than, on the one hand, a mechanism by which values could be extracted from agriculture and, on the other hand, a mechanism among other competing mechanisms. During the 1920s, California banks in particular regarded their competition with irrigation district bondholders for a share of agricultural values very circumspectly. Given the stagnation that followed the war and the heavy indebtedness that entrapped some districts, banks began to hold back on their own credit sales to those areas. As put by a group of farm economists at the time, "Most of the areas in California experiencing difficulty in obtaining credit are in reality suffering from too free use of credit, of one form or another, in the past. Landowners in many bonded irrigation, reclamation, drainage, and flood control districts find it impossible to get credit to develop their land, without which they must pay for a service that can not be used." This was a classic accumulation crisis. Capital had been invested in building the irrigated landscape and yet could not be adequately turned over for lack of advance capital to jump-start production. Because, as the banks saw it, the debt to bondholders (the banks themselves, as we'll see in a moment) came first, it was perilous to sell mortgages in more newly developed irrigated areas, since it takes some time for many crops to come into bearing. In areas where agriculture was already established, there were cases where irrigation construction had gone too quickly and too heedless of expense. During the 1920s, Federal Land Banks began withholding credit to farmers in irrigation districts, and the policy spread to other banks. (Not surprising, given that California banks were probably the single most important purchaser of the bonds in the first place! As *The Real Estate Handbook of Califonia* noted in 1929, "The authorized indebtedness of [the irigation districts] aggregates $139,580,000 of which $98,800,000 is represented by certified bond issues variously held throughout the state and mainly by the banks" [Wood 1929: 369].) That these events unfolded during the postwar period made all the difference. That is, let's say that the banks had gone ahead and sold mortgage credit, expecting that their capital would turn over in an acceptable period of time. Once those farmlands had been developed and begun producing, "this would have contributed to the general increase in production and an even faster decline in prices of agricultural products" (Agricultural Economics Staff 1930: 48–49). That sort of conundrum—that is, the kind which results from the relative inability of agricultural production to be regulated over time—is just the sort of problem that might keep capital away. But it is nothing compared to the problem faced by those capitals that did not heed the problem to begin with and dove right in.

## Circulation of Credit in Three California Space-Times

A third look at the circulation of values in California agriculture adds more dimension by narrating events explicitly as a space-time relation. I want to proceed in this section with three examples that I think aptly illustrate the space-times of the nexus between capital and nature. A problem that any student of California faces is the complexity of its agricultural space. A bewildering variety of crops has been grown in California and in many different physical and social environments. This is one of the clichés about the state, and it is, alas, true. But while this poses a difficulty for research, it was just the sort of thing that eventually made certain capitalists eager. The last of the examples that I will present, then, is one of the most important innovations to come out of California in the early twentieth century—the branch banking system led by A. P. Giannini's Bank of Italy, headquartered in San Francisco. Like no other entity, the Bank of Italy knew how to extract values from the California countryside in all its variety. The other two examples represent specific, local conditions. The first that I will present follows a rural county, Fresno, in the San Joaquin Valley—from its stock-raising and wheat-growing days until its turn to intensive, irrigated agriculture—in order to see changes in how credit circulated during an agricultural transition in one place.

The second examines a commodity sector, citrus, in order to see how credit circulated in one of California's crop regions. In varying ways, each of these examples demonstrates the local financing of California agriculture.

## (1) Fresno County: Circulation in Place

California did not start with the Gold Rush, but as we have seen, mining set in motion a widening spatial division of labor. Giving this history a unified "face" is too easy, since it truly was an outcome of thousands of points of struggle, violence, and resistance, including class, race, and ethnic war. Just the same, feats of coordination were often swift and very much to the point: mines in the Sierra foothills; financial command and control functions in San Francisco (though these took some time to coalesce [Paul 1947]); stock raising in the San Joaquin Valley to supply meat to the mines; express and stage coach companies to ferry commodities and bullion; mining machinery production in San Francisco; lumber mills in the forested Sierra and Coast ranges; truck crop production near the mines. As the pace of accumulation slowed in the mining regime and capital began to shift toward grain, a new spatial division of labor undergirded that transition: San Francisco persisting as the crux; grain collection points in harbors around the San Francisco, San Pablo, and Suisun Bays; long tendrils of railroad track ferrying grain up and down the San Joaquin and Sacramento Valleys; grain warehouse towns dotting the tracks. The area that became Fresno County was produced within this matrix as one of many centers of rural production and as the nexus of local and non-local finance.

By the end of the Civil War, Fresno in fact had a mixed economy of grain and livestock, the first oriented toward the Great Britain trade and the second toward California and the West. By the 1890s, yet another switch—toward intensive fruit cropping—was in view. Credit, it will not be surprising, circulated through those changes as partial cause and partial consequence. Historian John Shaw's study of credit relations is the best-known and most thorough chronicle of what happened. Using mortgage records in the county recorder's office, he pieced together the following picture.

Local, California credit was definitive. In no year between the Gold Rush and the end of the century did investment from outside the state, foreign or domestic, eclipse the importance of California itself. The geography of credit in Fresno was highly differentiated, though. San Francisco was the prominent lender, at first, but was then outstripped by Fresno County investors. And, at first, San Joaquin Valley counties, including Fresno, ranked after San Francisco but then were outbid by cities around the San Francisco Bay. The divide seems to have fallen on either side of the 1870s depression, before which San Francisco reigned nearly supreme in financing Fresno, and after which it was outbid by Fresno itself. Certainly the railroad figured importantly. Its freight rates were substantially lower than what stage companies had charged, and, therefore, it allowed more capital to circulate and accumulate within agricultural production proper. Also after the depression, other San Joaquin Valley lenders became increasingly less important as the lending circuit became more bipolar: very local sales of credit at one end (within Fresno) and sales from San Francisco and other bay cities at the other. (Similar patterns were reproduced in many San Joaquin Valley and Southern

California counties [see chapter 1; also Doti 1995].) Fresno outbid both its neighbors and the "City" but retained strong ties to the "City" which it could not afford to do without (Shaw 1969: 152). During the period up to 1890, the actors who sold mortgage credit also changed, following a process similar to the model outlined earlier. Until the late '60s, individuals engaged in agricultural enterprises were the sole lenders. During and after the '70s, local banks made heavy inroads, although they withdrew for a time during the 1893 Panic. Competing with these banks was a vibrant land colony movement around Fresno in the '60s and '70s, which kept alive a circuit of credit initiated by large subdividers (Thickens 1946). Lenders from San Francisco tended not to be bankers so much as real estate dealers and private investors specializing in property markets (Shaw 1969: 154–65).

When farmers needed to buy money on the short-term, seasonal basis, either to expand their operations or to bridge the disunity of production and working times, they turned very often to grain-based merchants and proprietors of one kind or another in the San Joaquin Valley or in San Francisco (precisely because San Francisco was both a financial center and a transportation center for the grain trade). As the pathways of accumulation in Fresno County strengthened, it supplied more and more of its own short-term loan capital, much like the pattern that developed in the long-term mortgage market. In the 1890s, bankers—who before had mostly restricted themselves to the long-term market—finally invested more in the seasonal capital market, having figured out that fruit potentially brought in high returns (Shaw 1969: 166–71).

For the whole decade leading up to 1866, investments of finance capital, in the form of mortgages sold on Fresno County land, came exclusively from within California. For the rest of the century, California remained the major source. Capital from outside California, though rarely in large amounts, began to flow into the county only after the Civil War and especially after the extension of the Central Pacific Railroad to Fresno in the early 1870s. In fact, the last year that California was the sole source was the year the railroad arrived. What made Fresno an attraction to mortgage capital from outside the state was the same thing that made most distant places attractive: higher interest rates. Between 1880 and 1900, the major regions lending to Fresno (New England, Mid-Atlantic, Old Northwest) were also the regions where investments in mortgages yielded a lower return (usually under 6%) than in the Pacific and Mountain states (often topping 10%) (Shaw 1969: 149). Interest rates in Fresno County, in fact, were even higher on average than the already high rates elsewhere in the West. Foreign capitalists, primarily from Great Britain, also sold mortgages in Fresno. In the early 1880s, it was in fact a more important source than non-California, U.S. capital. In 1882, Great Britain sold 18.5% of mortgages on Fresno County land, and in the depression year 1894, it held 8% (Shaw 1969: 145). Looking at the overall picture of Fresno County and comparing it with the Midwest, Shaw drew the tentative conclusion that Fresno stood out as having attracted more capital from outside the county yet less from outside the state. (Quite the reverse was the case in the two Midwest locations upon which the comparison was made.) Why? Because California contained the West's major financial center and "capital mobility to the far west was probably more difficult than between other regions in the United States." In short, capital mobility within California was highly developed from very early on (Shaw 1969:

152). This devolved directly from the peculiar character of San Francisco's emergence as a financial center (center of investment *and* center for rural banks around the state who kept deposits there). It was not only an entrepôt but also a collecting point and the regulation center for gold and silver. The importance of this type of mining, as opposed to, say, iron ore, was that gold and silver were money. Thus, as Marx noted more than once in his third volume of *Capital*, the production of value through labor applications immediately netted money capital, without being stalled in an intermediate commodity form. Money was *already* the commodity form. Returns were swift and direct, at least at first.

### (2) The Space-Time of Citrus

In the 1880s, citrus, especially oranges, was one of the fastest-growing sectors of the California economy. Its wildfire-like expansion was intimately tied to Southern California, a region whose virtual carnival of urban and rural, land and water investments would in a few decades absorb local aquifers of their moisture and drain the mountain slopes above of their waters (Dumke 1944; McWilliams 1983). Orchardists, some in it for the long haul, others just panting for immediate profits, had rushed to plant so many tens of thousands of orange trees that they brought a crisis of overproduction down on their heads in the 1890s. It was not only citrus growers who saw the "problem." Surveying the huge increases in fruit production in general, one fruit grower/writer for the *Pacific Rural Press* asked in 1896, "Have we reached the limit of Profitable Fruit Growing in California?" Not hardly. For "the real question is a commercial one. If we are to sit down and do nothing to extend our market we had better stop planting. The false quantity in the question is in assuming that we may possibly overplant, whereas failure lies alone in our failure to push our wares" (Chipman 1896: 372–73). For citrus growers (as it would be for numerous other commodity producers), the answer was to look to markets, consumption, and production standards, rather than to production cutbacks, as a solution (Cumberland 1917; unless otherwise noted, Cumberland is the source of the following discussion of the orange industry.) Consequently, they went to war with the commission merchant houses to gain control of the citrus economy at exactly those points: the commodity's time in circulation and the portion of production and working time spent on harvesting and packing. Their success in 1905 resulted in the California Fruit Growers Exchange. In a short time, this "cooperative" was harvesting, packing, shipping, marketing, and financing (in part) 70% of the orange crop, eliminating the middleman wherever possible. (Through the decades of the early twentieth century, the citrus economy developed also as an urbanizing, industrializing economy involving a regional landscape of technological innovation; production of processing machinery; packing plants at key nodal points; and a leadership dominated by large growers with strong ties to Southern California banks [Moses 1994 is especially strong on these points; on the dominance of the large producers, see Teague 1944].)

Certain aspects of the early orange economy underscore what was partly at stake in making a go of the Exchange. For one thing, large producers aside, most California orange growers failed to turn a profit on their dozen acres (Beach 1963). Keeping an orange orchard productive was an expensive proposition involving irrigation, frost protection, pest control, pruning, and picking. The turnover of orange lands was high as a result, some estimates putting the average length of ownership at eight years. The high rate was also due to speculative purchases which drove land values beyond what many mortgaged or otherwise indebted orchards could support. Although immensely attractive to prospective farmers who wanted only a small plot to cultivate, the undertaking was risky. Even when orchardists successfully brought their trees to bearing age, their worries had only just begun.

Before the advent of the Exchange, a grower sold the orange crop to a wholesaler at a fixed sum or to commission merchants who would ship and sell the crop and remit a share of the receipts to the farmer. Buying the fruit on the tree was almost pure speculation for a merchant, given that there was no sure way to know how much other merchants were buying from other growers. If prices in eastern cities were low, a buyer had no choice but to pay lower prices to the farmer, given that packing and shipping costs were fixed. Behind the backs of the growers, moreover, commission firms divided up the orange-producing territory and fixed the prices they would offer. Each grower, thus burdened by the monopoly rents extracted during a crop's circulation time (not to mention periodic debts incurred to merchants to cover the production-working time disunity), would get only one bid for the two or three pickings produced by each tree during the growing season. Commission merchants had additional leverage in that they could lie about the condition in which the fruit arrived at its destination or about when the fruit arrived, this latter point being especially important because prices could change quickly. In any event, that merchant shippers had a great deal to lose is evidenced by the fact that when growers began to organize, they fought against them tooth and nail. In spite of these obstacles, orange growers as a group still found themselves in the position of having too much fruit.

The California Fruit Growers Exchange was designed to handle an embarrassment of riches. It was a three-tiered, geographically dispersed organization, composed at the base of dozens of *packing associations* and the individual growers who belonged to them; coordinated by a fewer number of selling agencies, or *district exchanges*, to which groups of packing associations belonged; and topped off by the *central exchange*, simply referred to as the California Fruit Growers Exchange, organized and owned by the district exchanges. The central exchange regulated the mechanisms "through which the district exchanges operate for the local associations in behalf of the growers" (Cumberland 1917: 132). It functioned as a full-fledged corporation, with a claims department, a legal department, sales agents distributed throughout the country, an advertising bureau, and a field department whose strategically dispersed agents insured the quality of the pack and grade at key points within the distributing and shipping process. Essential to the Exchange was its ability to abstract and rationalize the commodity during its circulation time, the time during which the identity of any one grower's harvest was buried, only to be reborn as the cooperative's prominent, national brand name, Sunkist (cf. Cronon 1991). Let us follow this process from the point where the packing association directors, charged with the task of determining harvest dates, announced the time for a harvest, perhaps a March harvest in which growers were to deliver 20% of their crop to their local packing plant. The typical chain of events through to market was as follows:

The local packing association manager phoned growers to inform them when pickers would arrive to pick certain varieties of a defined size. While growers purchased boxes and ladders from the association's packing house, the packing houses (not the orchard owners) organized the pickers, predominantly Japanese and Mexican workers, resident in or migrating to Southern California. When pickers arrived at the orchards, growers assigned each one a number to affix to each box in which they put their picked fruit. Pickers then went from orchard to orchard throughout the district that was being harvested and, usually, were paid a daily rate rather than a piece rate so that they would not exploit and hurry their own labor enough to injure the fruit. (In reality, agricultural wage workers were far from being passive objects of this spatial division of labor. See Mitchell 1996, for an excellent recent account.) The growers last saw their fruit when they took it to the packing houses. There, machines—largely invented and built by Southern Californians in the citrus industry for the citrus industry (Moses 1994)—washed and brushed the fruit and moved it by belt to a grading station, typically operated by women. All this time, the fruit remained separated according to the grower who produced it. A machine weighed the fruit by grade and recorded the figure for each grower. After this, the grower's identity was lost. The fruit went by conveyor to automatic-sizing machines, which dumped it into bins, or "pools," with the same-grade fruit of other growers. (At times, farmers resisted this process of alienation and abstraction. Alienation and abstraction were social relations, and the reality of grading and pooling was that not all fruit within a given grade could be of exactly equal quality. It was therefore not unheard of for groups of growers, disgruntled that their harvest was pooled with lesser-quality fruit, to break away from the cooperative.)

After the fruit was pooled, it was precooled and loaded onto boxcars owned or leased by the Exchange, which were scheduled by the manager of the district exchange. With the fruit on the cars, the district exchange took over responsibility from the packing association. It oversaw transport and played a part in directing the turned-over capital back to the packing associations and growers. Each car traveled in the name of the district exchange to an agent of the central exchange in whatever city was paying a competitive price, perhaps Chicago. At every possible point, inspection agents kept the district exchange managers appraised of the location and condition of the car. Meanwhile, these district managers received daily marketing reports with data on prices and quantities of other citrus shipments from competing companies, including other district exchanges. If it looked to them like Chicago prices were declining or that the city's market was about to be glutted, the manager rerouted to, say, the agent in Detroit. That agent made the sale (or at the last minute sent it somewhere else) and then sent word back to the district manager. All the while that the fruit was en route, the district manager kept in touch with the managers of the packing associations that owned the fruit in the cars. Upon sale, the agents of the central exchange who were posted around the country forwarded the money to the exchange, where it made its way through the organization levels (each keeping a portion for expenses). At the end of the "pool," this term describing not just the activities of the packing house but also all the activities up to the sale, the growers received their shares.

Within the constraints of how well the fruit stood up to the stresses of being handled and shipped (these constraints subject to manipulation through refrigeration technology), the distributing and selling system was designed to balance the need to keep time in circulation to a minimum with the desire to extract high prices from consumers, which sometimes meant lengthening the time in circulation. The system was highly flexible, highly rationalized, and thoroughly penetrated by the telegraph and telephone communications revolution. The system was also an exacting division of labor, like the other phases of the production process. The Exchange divided the United States and Canada into six sales territories, each headed by a division manager in Boston, New York City, Chicago, Minneapolis, Fort Worth, and Seattle. For each of these major divisions, the central exchange assigned sales agencies to smaller market divisions, seventy-seven in all. The salaried agents of the minor divisions reported daily to the division manager on fruit sold, fruit at auction, orders they received for fruit, and new markets they were responsible for developing. These agents, spending thousands of dollars per month on telegrams, also daily sent information on market conditions and, importantly, on non-exchange shipments to the six division heads and to the central exchange office in Los Angeles. The following day, Los Angeles compiled a report of the citrus "situation" nationwide and rushed it to the packing associations and district exchanges via the elaborate regional rail network, which Southern California had built beginning in the 1880s and which helped significantly to launch the citrus boom in the first place. The district exchanges used the marketing information thus sent to decide where the oranges were to be routed next.

The Los Angeles office of the central exchange greased the system's wheels by reassembling the elements of this far-flung landscape into one compressed space. In this process of reassemblage, the oranges were "converted" into data. This is the site where, in Lefebvre-ian terms, the industry's vast "representation of space" was reconceived as the coded "representational space" in opposition to the earlier, decentered commission system (Lefebvre 1991: 38–39). Each boxcar shipped had a so-called history card that bore the date and destination of shipment, the identity and type of car (whether it was iced, ventilated, precooled, etc.), the number of boxes of different varieties of oranges in the car, and the routes over which the oranges traveled. Every day, this information was updated and hoarded on the history cards, which were pigeonholed according to the district exchanges to which the fruit belonged. With a quick look, virtually any detail of the whole system was recoverable from these cards. Apart from the information and distribution apparatus, systematic advertising, spearheaded in Chicago, was a key to the Exchange's success. In 1907, the Exchange invented the Sunkist brand name and selected Iowa as a test market. Fruit went out on specially marked trains with banners announcing the Sunkist label and bearing the slogan "Oranges for Health—California for Wealth." Billboards were splashed with pictures of oranges and scenes of California orchards. Regional sales immediately shot up 50% and nationally went up nearly 18% (Ralmo 1925; Beach 1963). In the hands of the Exchange, citrus was an information economy capitalized by nearly instantaneous data transmission. It was an image economy capitalized by the produced desires extracted out of midwesterners grown used to ham, corn, and winter.

The sophistication of citrus production and circulation was matched by that of the Exchange's finances. In order to keep its momentum, the Exchange relied on two mechanisms: reserves of turned-over capital which were called on to circulate internally within the Exchange, and loans bought from banks (and sometimes from well-to-do Exchange members). As some of the details are reviewed below, it should be remembered what these "mechanisms" represented: the outcome of a class struggle among organized citrus producers, independent mercantile houses and packing plants, and banks, for control of circulating values. A primary concern of the Exchange was where to get the capital that would be fixed in the packing plants run by its own packing associations (see figure 2.1). This included land, buildings, and machinery and other equipment that could cost anywhere from $25,000 to $200,000. The associations first bought credit from local banks in Southern California and used that capital until its internal "revolving capital" plan had accumulated money. With this plan, the packing associations retained a portion of the citrus sales proceeds for seven to eight years. Only then

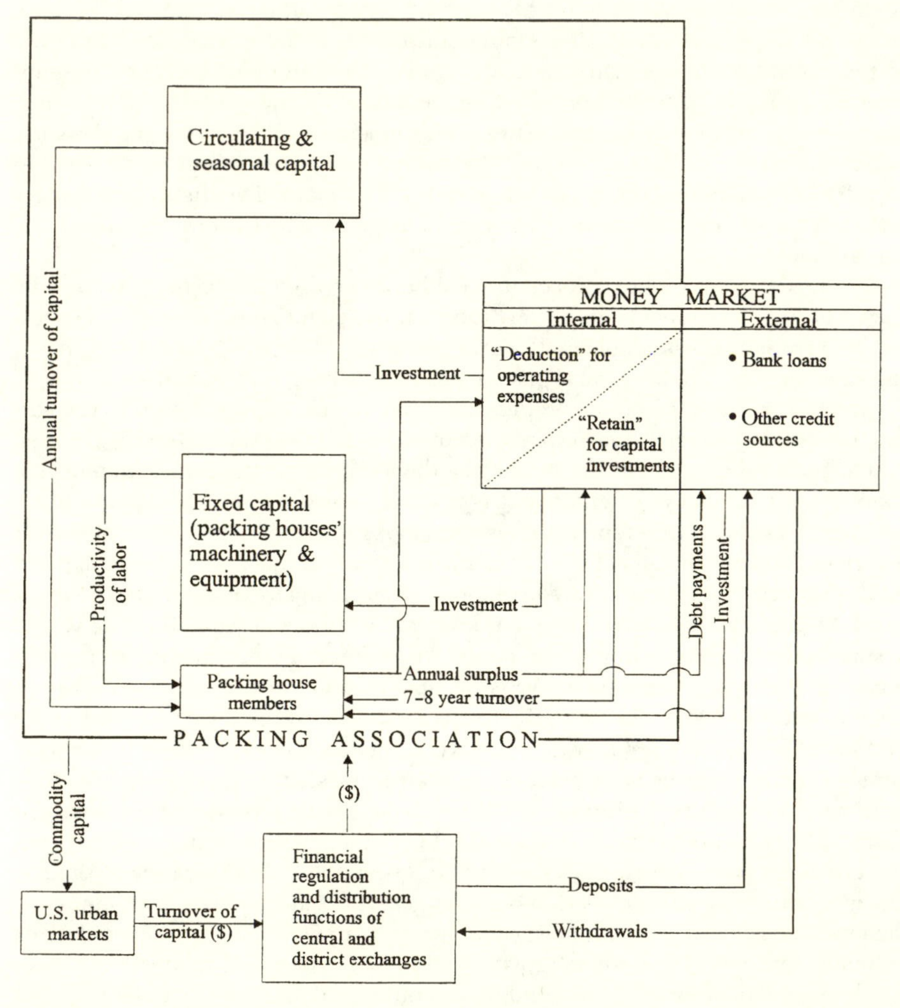


Figure 2.1. Circulation of Capital through California's Organge Industry Packing Association.

would growers be paid back what had been retained, and even then they were paid in the eighth year only what they had put in during the first year. In the ninth year, they were paid what had been retained in the second year, and so forth (Stone 1966: 170–71). The plan was designed to discipline growers into remaining with the associations for a long period of time. It allowed the Exchange to function as a sort of supra-bourgeoisie, regulating the behavior of the member bourgeoisie (so-called, to the extent that they were employers of wage labor). In turn, the banks disciplined the Exchange. They wanted assurances that pools consisted only of like grades and varieties; that fruit was being sold where markets were well developed; that growers were living up to their contracts; that records were kept up to the minute and audits frequently done (Basset and Moomlaw 1915: 209). Forms of discipline extended as well to the growers who bought bank credit. George Stone, who was once a vice president and loan officer at the First National Bank of Pomona, recalled just what that could mean: "Some banks making a large number of citrus loans [long- and short-term], check to see that certain groves are properly irrigated in the summer, heated in winter and treated at the proper time for pests, for only in this way can they be certain of the value of the security" (Stone 1967: 38). Stone's observation is indicative of the fact that while capital was invested in nature, the limitations of nature were forthrightly recognized. Owing to this, however, banks hedged their bets against nature. Crop mortgages often applied not just to a single year's harvest, but to four years. One bad year (due to drought, freeze, or what have you) would not then ruin the security. The bank gave itself an out by stipulating that it could recoup its investment over the long term (Stone 1967: 35–36).

In the next level of the Exchange, the district exchange, the source of capital was also a deduction taken from every carload of fruit sold. But the fact that turned-over capital (the proceeds of sale) went first to the central exchange, which forwarded this realized capital to the district exchange, meant that the district exchange's finances were almost wholly internal to the system. The district exchange (the in-house sales and marketing organization) resorted to banks only to deposit its money there and withdraw it as necessary for citrus's time in circulation. (Given that these bank accounts were often large, they would have offered banks their own opportunity to plough this capital into credit sales elsewhere, as long as the turnover time allowed the district exchange depositor to withdraw needed sums.) The central exchange in Los Angeles, in contrast to the districts, resorted to buying bank credit at the beginning of the harvest season (figure 2.2 charts the flow of capital through the citrus industry in general). It needed this credit—which to the bank represented a cut of citrus values based on time-in-circulation/nature-as-distance—for its regulatory functions, until a few months' worth of remittances had made their trek back from urban markets around the country (Stone 1966: 172–33).

The California Fruit Growers Exchange was a bourgeois revolution in miniature, launched at nearly every level of production, processing, and distribution. Largely because of its success, shipments of California citrus increased 580% between 1894 and 1914, ten times the rate of increase for the United States population. The Exchange kept its members informed of the latest scientific advances in cultivation, from budding techniques to pest control. In 1907, it formed a separate corporation, the Fruit Growers Supply Company, in order to both bust a

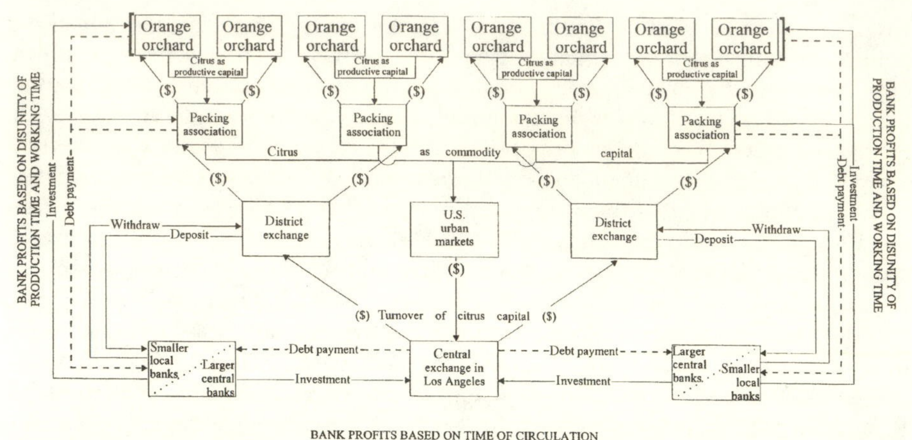


Figure 2.2. Paths of Capital Flow through California's Orange Industry.

monopoly on the manufacture of the pine shooks used for boxes and counter the price increases that followed the 1906 San Francisco earthquake. Later, this company moved into procuring fertilizer, pesticides, and tissue wraps for exchange members. By eliminating growers' early reliance on outside packing houses, the Exchange reduced the cost of packing from 50 cents to 30 cents per box. In nearly eliminating commission agents from the industry, the cost of selling was reduced from the 7%–10% charged by agents to less than 3% charged by the Exchange. As the Exchange solidified its monopoly, it won lower freight rates and highly successful damage claims from the railroads. The Exchange reduced the gap between production and circulation times by coordinating picking, shipping, and selling—and by being willing to sell less than a carload to jobbers whose markets were in small towns and villages. It made huge inroads in the production and working time gap by keeping oranges in the market year-round and defeating the seasonality of the December-to-June harvest period. As such, it very competitively bid against other sellers of credit and internalized much of that demand within its own structure. It was almost as if oranges never grew on trees at all.

### (3) Branch Banking: The Mobility of Capital and the Production of Space

> There is plenty of money, but it is in the wrong place. . . . The best way for the metropolis to get some responsive thrill from the rural object of metropolitan wooing will be to loosen up the purse-strings! All the world hates a stingy lover!
>
> —*Pacific Rural Press* (Vol. 102, July 9, 1921: 29)

> In our judgment that California city, which carries the fairest finance to the country, will be the metropolis of the future.
>
> —*Pacific Rural Press* (Vol. 102, September 3, 1921: 228)

Like theorists elsewhere along the political spectrum, capitalists and capitalist functionaries also dream of planned economies. In 1891, fed up with the uncoordinated activities and policies of the hundreds of banks scattered across the California landscape—and recognizing the barriers to accumulation that this presented—the California Bankers Association began a serious effort to standardize the way banking was done. So as to allow capital to circulate with fewer impediments in space and time, they fought to standardize interest rates among urban and rural banks and to pass legislation for greater state regulation (Blackford 1977). As if to send the point home, the 1893 panic spelled out quite clearly what the Association was up against. As opposed to the north, especially San Francisco—where financial ties among institutions were tighter and access to reserves of money was easier to come by—Southern California banks either closed their doors or fell like dominoes. Out of these two tendencies—the tendency for separate banks to perform differently in reality and the tendency for bankers to try to resolve those differences—branch banking was born. The real nub of branch banking, however, was this: It counteracted the general urbanization of capital during an era when the rural hinterland (i.e., agriculture) had become a leading edge of the economy. It therefore eased a fundamental contradiction of the time.

A. P. Giannini turned to banking in 1904, after a meteoric career as a produce commission merchant. In the 1890s, he was California's leading commission merchant and the first San Francisco agent of the Southern California Citrus Fruit Growers Exchange, the forerunner of the Exchange discussed above (Dana 1947: 35; see also Bonadio 1994 for details of Giannini's life). Giannini's produce fortune would have allowed him to retire and spend his remaining days tinkering with his investments, but instead he took $50,000 and sank it into a new business. The Bank of Italy was practically an overnight success. Giannini not only survived but also capitalized on the 1906 San Francisco earthquake and the 1907 panic. By 1912, he had set up 2 branches, and by 1919, he had added 22 more, by which time his enterprise laid claim to 6% of all California's bank deposits. His banking investments fanned out into agriculture, insurance, real estate, oil, and construction (Dowrie 1930). Along the way, Giannini fought successfully in the post-war period with a state banking superintendent who ostensibly wanted to protect small independent banks but who also favored his cronies in Southern California who were developing a branching system of their own. Though smaller than Giannini's operations, the Los Angeles Trust and Savings Bank, for example, marched up and over the Tehachapi Mountains, in a direct challenge to Giannini, to establish branches in the San Joaquin Valley. Mimicking the Bank of Italy's rhetoric, the Trust and Savings announced to readers of *The Associated Grower* in 1922 that it could now take debts paid off by Southern California orange growers south of the Tehachapis and fund San Joaquin Valley raisin producers on the other side of the mountains. Once those debts were paid off, the money could be brought back over the slopes and re-loaned to vegetable producers in the Imperial Valley. "The San Joaquin Valley Banks have not sold out," it said. "They have become partners in the merged institution" (*Associated Grower*, July 1, 1922: 19). Where the Trust and Savings moved credit amongst some two dozen branches, the Bank of Italy empire grew to 289 branches after the war. Nearly 200 of these were added (i.e., bought) in 1927 alone, the first year in office of Giannini-backed Governor C. C. Young. This same year, the Bank of Italy merged with the Bank of

America of New York and so became a national banking system. By 1930, this empire controlled almost half of California's banks and nearly a third of all deposits (Nash 1964; Bean 1968).

Branch banking remapped the geography of money and restructured city-countryside relations in California. As western historian Gerald Nash rather soberly puts it:

> Mobility of capital was one of [branch banking's] great advantages. Previously funds had been concentrated in San Francisco and Los Angeles. Now branches could spread the resources of urban banks into rural regions. Branch banking also allowed for greater stability and diversity. Agricultural loans would not exhaust the resources of local banks. Moreover, branch banking was less subject to local pressures. (Nash 1964: 290–91)

Indeed, branch banking took advantage of a *geographical* structure of banking that had been developing for a couple of decades. "As agriculture based on irrigation developed and the petroleum and lumber industries became big businesses," writes Mansel Blackford, "the capital and credit requirements of Californians soared." Consequently, most of the new banks that arose in this context were situated in the agricultural interior and Southern California. "By 1905," Blackford continues, "the assets of banks outside of San Francisco rivaled those of the metropolis" (Blackford, 1977: 96).

The Bank of Italy entered California agriculture at a time of exceptional growth and specialization. One must not suppose, however, that Giannini acted as he did solely to resolve the contradiction between rural scarcity and urban glut. Rather, he took advantage of it, evolving a sophisticated strategy of simultaneously concentrating and redistributing money capital. On the one hand, Giannini specialized in the purchase of already existing, but often weak, rural banks whose presidents, or other officials, he sometimes retained as branch managers (James and James: 1954). On the other hand, branch banking, Giannini style, was extraordinarily well suited to financing the *production of diverse crops grown in different areas and harvested at different times*. According to their own specializations and to their situations with respect to the expansion of operations, growers needed capital (and labor) at different times, and, as follows from the disunity of production and working times, they tended to need it in lumps rather than continuously through the seasons. (These relations are abstracted and presented in figure 2.3.) Meeting these needs was a hardship for independent country banks, but not for banks that could channel funds from branch to branch as needed (Dowrie 1930).

Put another way, the separate disunities of production and working times that accrued to individual crop regions across the separate spaces of "naturally given" differential rent were a jumble of space-time fragments passed on to individual local banks precisely as . . . a jumble of fragments. Yet, considered together, these space-times comprised year-round demand for credit—a longer season of demand than anywhere else in the United States (Valgren and Engelbert 1922: 5–6). There was the potential to coordinate these space-times, to synchronize working and production time disunities as they were further expressed across a vast landscape of differential rents, if only a high level of capital mobility could be achieved. This is what was finally realized on a grand scale by the Bank of Italy. (To greater and lesser extents, some of the large farm companies bought farmlands in various

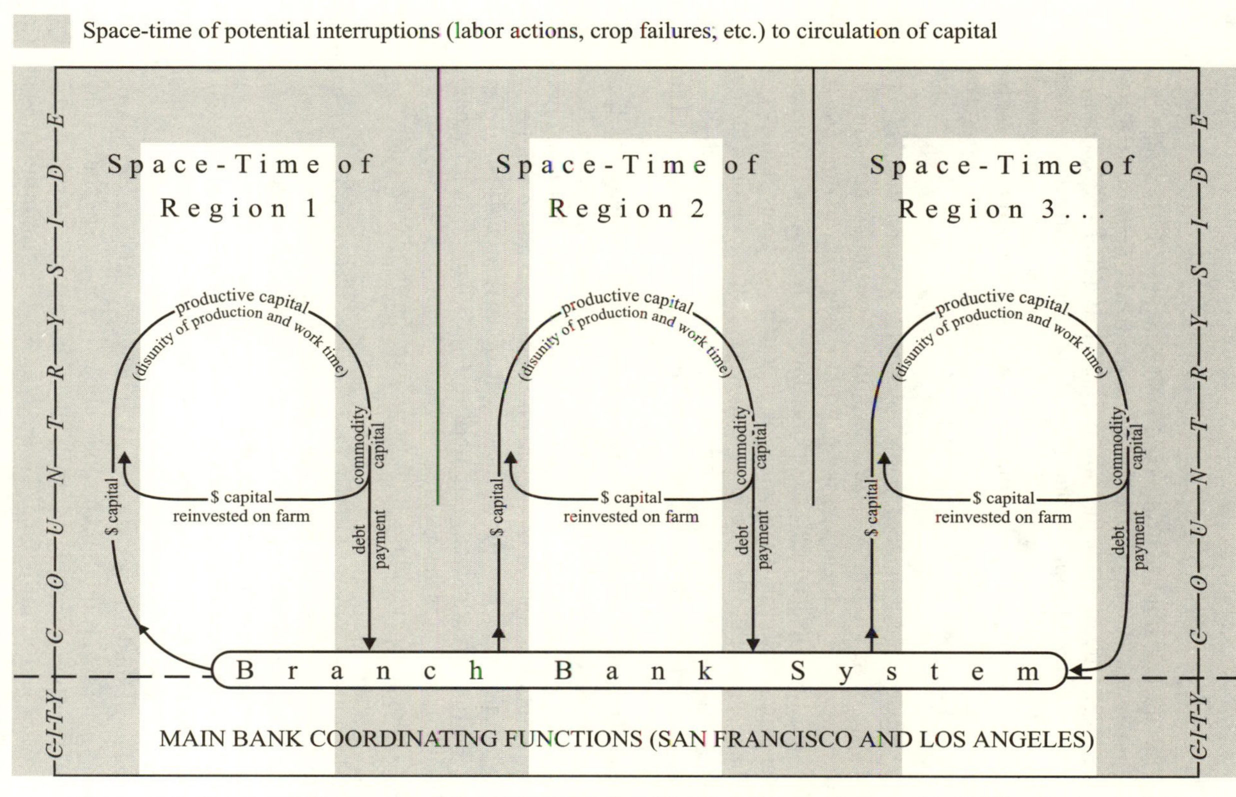


Figure 2.3. Seasonal Turnover of Capital and Labor/Capital Contradictions in California Agriculture.

parts of the state in order to accomplish similar types of coordinations [e.g., Dickason 1983].) Giannini's competitor in Los Angeles, Joseph Sartori, saw that the benefits of branch banking redounded to the state. Without branch banking, not only was there a seasonal demand for credit sales that strained local banks but also

> when the peak of this credit-demand load is over there is a very considerable time in many communities in which the banks have difficulty in finding good local investments for their funds. During these slack periods they resort to commercial paper, generally purchased upon the recommendation of their city correspondents, and to bonds. Most of this commercial paper and bonds comes from outside the state of California and the local bank, to the extent of its investments of this character, is not supporting the local community or the state. (Sartori 1923: 10)

This was very much the Bank of Italy's voice on the matter, too, though through the other side of its mouth, homage was paid to accumulation pure and simple: "Yes," the Livermore branch reported in a 1919 issue of *Bankitaly Life* (the bank's in-house, employee magazine), "Livermore farmers have larger crops and are getting better prices than in many years. Our currency has been piling up so rapidly that we have been at our wits' end as to how to keep it in proper shape. The old method of wrapping currency by hand seemed to offer no relief, so in our extremity we engaged a hay baler, which we will keep in commission until the harvest is over" ("Livermore" 1919: 17).

One must not suppose that branch banking's achievement was flawless, nor that such "harvests" could be baled without incident. On the one hand, as Don Mitchell has argued, the fact that rural social relations comprised highly mobile labor armies who assembled in large concentrations at harvest times presented a near constant potential for militant labor resistance (Mitchell 1996). On the other hand, agriculture's tendency toward hard-to-regulate production schedules occasionally erupted in crises that were passed on to financiers, as happened to heavily indebted raisin growers and the Bank of Italy in the early 1920s (James and James 1954).

Giannini's initial move out of San Francisco was into neighboring Santa Clara Valley in 1909. At the same time, the Bank of Italy was moving south and east into the San Joaquin Valley towns and cities: Fresno, Madera, Merced, Modesto, Stockton. It moved north to the truck and vine crop region in the Napa and Sonoma Valleys. From a precarious foothold in Los Angeles, the bank opened branches in Ventura, Riverside, and the Imperial Valley (after the war). Displaying great shrewdness, Giannini made sure that in the town where each branch was located there were local stockholders of the Bank of Italy, a local advisory board, and local employees. Moreover, the Bank of Italy chose the most specialized agricultural regions in the state, ones where the financial barriers to entry were high for the individual but where fertile fields awaited the bank. If Giannini's junket through California signaled rural California's greater access to credit, we might recall that the obverse was its growing indebtedness. The banner years of the world war had growers expanding their acreage and irrigation facilities by borrowing from local banks. On top of the ascending mortgages were high interest rates. Although the average rate was 7.6%, 43% of California's farmers paid 8% and, in isolated locales,

12% (James and James 1954). Into this credit-debt structure the Bank of Italy inserted itself. When Giannini opened his first branch in the San Joaquin Valley, at Merced in 1916, he responded to the prevailing high mortgage rate by offering a lower one. And where a local bank's loan resources might be monopolized by the bigger farms, the Bank of Italy steered a course to the smaller farmers, realizing that these relatively untapped sources would bring large returns collectively. After a single year in Madera, the Bank of Italy garnered approximately 75% of the accounts of the small orchardists and vineyardists. In general, 60% of the increase in the bank's deposits during the war came from local institutions that it had purchased. Giannini extended his investments "downstream" of the farm, too, financing local canners and packers, especially in the San Joaquin Valley. Previously, local banks could not carry such companies because their seasonal requirements did not dovetail well with the banks'. They were forced to look to larger city banks until the flexibility of the branch bank system offered an alternative.

Giannini preferred a certain type of farmer to complement his geographical strategy: "business-minded farmers who regarded agriculture as a commercial pursuit rather than a means of subsistence" (James and James 1954: 81). A net of debtor-discipline was cast over the "borrowing farmer." Debtor farmers were required to stick to a budget and record their expenses. As James and James note: "Behind every budget was a watchful Bank of Italy man . . . to see that the borrower lived up to his contract," which incidentally carried with it object lessons in efficiency and farm management (1954: 251). The new mobility of capital heralded by branch banking represented a contradiction from the point of view of farmers who were used to playing off the differences between larger, more distant banks and smaller, more local banks. As we have already seen, farmers came to depend on buying short-term loans from local banks based on nothing more than their word that they were good for the debt. Local banks agreed to the terms because of their familiarity with the locale and with the debtors. With the spread of branch banking out of San Francisco (and Los Angeles) came the spread of "city methods"—that is, banking by the book (Agricultural Economics Staff 1930: 51–52).

Let us pause for a moment to take stock. Banking strictly by numbers, in whatever form—branch banking or not—represented a definite form of class struggle, replete with labor discipline and value appropriation, which at least one bank official, a vice president of "one of the largest banks in San Francisco," recognized right off: "No bank which wants to maintain its solvency will loan for even [a year] . . . on farm mortgage security. . . . What the bank wants is to keep the borrower working" so that the "worker" *keeps* borrowing—for a year at a time, perhaps, but also for year after year (Chenowith 1923: 4–5; see also Roemer 1982).[8] The loan comes very close to representing payment of a piece-rate wage. To the extent that this is so, the farmer may be a wage-paying industrial capitalist at harvest time but now a proletarian at the beginning of the season. Though hardly seeing the situation in quite those terms, the editors of the *Pacific Rural Press*, for example, understood quite well that the rhythms of circulating capital had gotten out of sync with the rhythms of farming and that therein lay a form of destabilizing exploitation. In one of many editorials about the farmers' quest for credit, they quoted approvingly of a Minnesota congressman who argued that "There is 'immediate, imperative, and conclusive necessity of setting up permanent credit machinery,' of such character as to conform to the farmers' turn-over and of sufficient flexibility to meet the requirement of different localities and commodities. The credit should be extended 'for a time sufficient to enable payment to be made out of the earnings of the farm, without frequent renewals, which add to the expense of the borrower in fees and commission.'" Quite unexplained is what it means to be a "'farmer borrower'" in the first place (*Pacific Rural Press*, Vol. 102 [September] 1921: 252).

As capital circulates through different hands, the banker's class location must alternate, too. The banker (enabled by the disunity of production and working times, among other things) is both rent-seeking money seller and industrial capitalist. These alternating roles are, of course, not merely oscillations but potential contradictions. Insofar as the banker is a *piece-rate–paying* industrial capitalist (who extracts surplus in the form of interest-laden debt at the end of the farmer's term as industrial capitalist), there is a *check* on the farmer as industrial capitalist. But the more the farmer can accumulate and can come to own land, the greater the potential that the rents sought by banks will be reduced. These contradictory and alternating roles, which see farmers and bankers as variable capitalists (and, no less, proletarians as variable capital), are not things and essences in themselves but are the effects of circulating capital, of the capital that these actors circulate.

As the Bank of Italy made its geographical move into the valleys, it also entered an international space of commodity distribution and consumption that had been refined by agricultural cooperatives over the previous decade.

> By the time the Bank of Italy entered the valleys, selling activities had reached a higher stage of comprehensiveness, scale and complexity in California than elsewhere in the United States. . . . By 1920, California growers were operating approximately twenty-nine co-operative fruit-marketing agencies, twenty field-crop organizations, five poultry organizations, and ten dairying and livestock organizations. The Bank of Italy did not hesitate to put its swelling resources behind this system which was already attracting Eastern banking interests. (James and James 1954: 89)

While the largest share of California produce was consumed domestically, markets were cultivated in the East, Chicago and New York being the important nodal markets. Foreign exports also figured strongly. Barley was shipped to London, much as wheat had been in the 1880s and 1890s. Europeans relied on California for prunes. Beans went to Cuba and Puerto Rico and rice to Japan.

In 1919, the Bank of Italy sold loans totaling nearly $75 million. Over half of this was bought by farmers, packers, and canners, but purchasers also included farm-equipment manufacturers, farm-tool supply houses, and loan companies whose own collateral included cattle. In the next decade, Giannini became the most heavily invested banker involved in California agriculture and the largest holder of irrigation district bonds. When California's population surged, revitalizing the home market for produce, he extended credit to pay for farm, crop, and irrigation expansion. By 1930, his investment in farm mortgages alone topped $71 million and involved one in every eleven farms. California capitalism gave birth to a number of spatial strategists, who would see the landscape physically re-engineered toward the ends of economic growth. What Giannini did better than any of them was to spatialize capital itself more efficiently than ever before, making it supremely mobile from one place to another within his fiefdom, bringing it more into alignment with the sophisticated production and labor regimes that rural California had become.

## Conclusion: Reading the Landscape of Fictitious Capital

Human beings exploit nature in all sorts of ways. It hardly seems possible to imagine otherwise. The transformation of nature, though it takes place under all manner of conditions and through all manner of socially embedded practices, is an absolute requirement for the production of anything. Agriculture is merely a case in point, whether it's a matter of soil and water being disturbed, plants being specially selected, or wood and metallic ores being turned into farm implements. When agricultural production is organized along capitalist lines, these truths remain, though they are much reworked over time (e.g., Goodman et al. 1987). But when capital—which, admittedly, always already embodies previous rounds of transformed nature, so defying the simple opposition I am making here—confronts nature in agricultural production, it is not just a matter of vulgar extraction. I have argued here that while capitalist society, through its agriculture (*inter alia*), commodifies and exploits nature directly, it also exploits the very conditions whereby nature poses interruptions or "obstacles" to its exploitation. (Shall we say that different forms of capital confront different manifestations of nature?) These so-called obstacles that slow the valorization of productive capitals on the farm—whether due to the disunity of production and working times or to nature as space, which impedes the efficient mobilization of capitals over time—open up temporal and spatial channels for the extraction of surpluses by means of fictitious values and fictitious capital.

Where one form of capital seeks to gain from transformations of nature, in another form capital extracts profits based on nature's resistance to being transformed. This apparent opposition is, however, a single process. Again, production and the credit system develop together. The direct transformation of nature entailed in agricultural production is impeded by nature, while it is the purpose of the credit system to jump (as much as is possible) those very impediments and put capital back into production—a process that is one and the same with using those very impediments as a means of appropriating values.

Through these social relations and transactions, worlds of meaning are also constituted. Systems of representation (e.g., mortgage and crop loan contracts, bond issues, *money*) are of course fundamental to the historical elaboration of capital circulation. But, given that this essay has been concerned with plotting out a particular nexus between capital and nature, I want to close with some thoughts about how the circulation of capital appropriates and activates—I will not say *invents*—specific meanings for nature.

In deed and word, bourgeois society has proposed that nature is, among other things, a great fruit waiting to be plucked and plundered. Conversely, it has told us that nature is less to be picked apart than it is the great binding force that helps to resolve the contradictions between fragmented capitals. No great leap of imagination is necessary to see that the American West has been a great repository of meanings along these lines (e.g., Worster 1985; Cronon 1991), just as it has seen in material fact the westward tilt of fictitious capital. These representations of nature—there are, of course, many more in number and kind than I am eliciting here (see Hyde 1990, 1996, for recent statements)—devolve to the social fragmentations from whence they arise. All appeals to nature—or capital—are situated.

So let us consider just one example through which we might trace a discourse of nature and its appropriation through production and the credit system. San Francisco's Anglo and London Paris National Bank will serve the purpose. Yet another important legacy of Gold Rush days, the bank had become an enthusiastic broker and promoter of irrigation district bonds by the early 1920s. Here are three passages from one of the bank's publications promoting the sale of the bonds (Adams and Bedford 1921):

> Irrigation in the Modesto district has . . . been the agency which has transformed a vast, rather tiresome stretch of grain fields, broken at only infrequent intervals with semi-occasional roads, unadorned farmsteads, and precise fences; a country producing only hay and grain into pleasant communities of homes, trees and green fields, peopled with home-building farmers, devoted to the production of a wide variety of farm production. (21)
>
> [O]ver 20% of the bond issues of the two districts [Modesto and Turlock] are owned within the districts. In other words, these farmers have, by the very fact of their increased prosperity under irrigation, been able to buy upward of $1,000,000 worth of their own obligations, and have been so well satisfied of the worth of those bonds that they have no hesitation in putting their money into them. (47)
>
> The borrowed money becomes a part of the [irrigation] industry's productive capital. . . . The installation of an irrigation system is a capital investment such as an industry might make—and results directly in the creation and addition of new wealth to the security back of the debt. (70–71)

In these passages, we have moved from a representation of locally transformed nature, vested in a rather standard bourgeois depiction of domesticated rural landscape, to a rhetoric (codified simply as "the borrowed money") of the geography of fictitious capitals over supra-local space. That is, local nature paired with local labor and local investment is brought into tension with nature-as-space paired with outside investment of outside savings to be used in the purchase of bonds. What sort of tension is this, why is the bank eliciting it, and what authorizes the changed meanings of nature from local resource to abstract supra-locality?

In the first passage, a basic transformation of nature, irrigation, is linked to yet other transformations, yielding a distinct cultural landscape. From irrigation flows that which is good, that which is orderly and pleasing to look at, that which is not prodigal, vagrant, or migrant. As local society continues to yoke nature (e.g., water to land), it brings nature to order, and so brings itself to order. In the second passage, agency as local is further specified. The figure "over 20%" stands in defense of charges commonly leveled against abstract financial mechanisms: their impersonality, their disregard for the individual and community, their exacting pounds of flesh. "Over 20%" cannot mean that *these* irrigation bonds represent economically and geographically distant, unimpeachable, and uncaring powers. Most of all "over 20%" indicates local faith in the local. But, for the third passage, the meaning of the landscape is now less that it has been domesticated and more that a people have been domesticated by their land, yoked to that land, working to yield returns for other investors. And so, the inevitable sales pitch, where "over 20%" now must mean "nearly 80%" left over for investors ready and able to extract value from the disciplined farmer. The very idea of the local, apropos community and landscape, is erased. What is local in the third passage is merely the anonymous accumulation of capital fixed in place. What is asserted is that the rationality of finance capital should remain paramount and that "spatial substitutions" be capable of mobilization across distances.

Two master narratives suture these passages together—one on the romance of local investment in and accumulation through nature, and one on the increasing rationality and geographic reach of money over space as a way to mobilize savings. "Over 20%" signifies that local moneys can be turned back into the point of production, proving that capital doesn't have to wander. But the notion that the locals have tapped into a sure thing sells that sure thing to the outside investor, thereby reinscribing the notion that money travels—and does the job it does best when it travels (otherwise there would be "only 20%" left for outsiders to buy). The first narrative tells what money might do while the second admits what money must do, because space must be kept active and on call. But the first narrative also tells us that the farmers cannot turn their own capital over fast enough to purchase all of the bond issue. (The bond issue signifies, prima facie, both a failure of nature and a promise of nature.) Their own transformation of nature has not yielded enough to be sustained as a self-expanding system of transformation. Nature has in a sense led the district's farmers to overaccumulate periods of slow turnover. The second narrative tells us that investors thereby have a prime opportunity. But it is not so much the direct transformation of nature that constitutes that opportunity. Rather, the investors rely upon a broadly heterogeneous space of "second nature," the geography of human-produced differential rents—sites of individual capitals in particular locations, circulating along varied timelines and producing unique "needs" and "yields"—now reified, commodified, and put into service (see Marx, *Capital*, Vol. 3; Harvey 1984; Smith 1985; Lefebvre 1991). This "second nature"of course describes the space in which investors themselves are located and not only the space occupied by the farmers. The investers' site, too, is a site of capital circulating along *its* timeline, out of which surpluses are generated, potentially overaccumulating and restlessly in search of productive harbors. Local landscape is not forgotten by this more abstract space, however. In fact, it becomes more important than ever. Should the rural district fail to make good on the bond when it comes due, there has at least been a steady accumulation of fixed capital in the district. In sum, the much-romanticized living labor, which actively yoked first nature to its tasks, can potentially be scooped up as capital's rich, second-nature topsoil—dead labor, transformed nature, the "security back of the debt."

It is no coincidence that a San Francisco bank would be a major purveyor of irrigation district bonds. Part and parcel of the second nature produced under capitalism is the historical development of the city-countryside contradiction. It is in the city that the largest masses of labor congregate and that the largest masses of capital accumulate. I have already made the point that the branch banking system of the Bank of Italy was a means of speaking to this contradiction. The Bank of Italy geographically redistributed a portion of the total money capital in the state during a period when the agricultural economy was perched to be the Silicon Valley of its day. But one of the historical hallmarks of California agriculture, aside from these credit mechanisms, was the fact that California farmers *did* amass wage labor.[9] In order to develop the argument that capital has circulated through the farm in a number of important ways, I have bracketed off that fact. While the next chapter is still concerned with staying on the trail of circulating capital, it will let the brackets fall away.

# 3

# Toward Rural Realism

## *Variable Capital, Variable Capitalists, and the Fictions of Capital*

"The way to get farm labor is to get it. Get it where it is to be had. Get it just as you would any other commodity."

—A California farmer in *The Pacific Rural Press*, 1917 (quoted in McWilliams 1939: 174)

### The Way to Get Farm Labor?

It is 1917 . . . or 1893 . . . or 1921. No matter. So long as we understand that the social relations of the wage have gripped California agriculture, let us venture a few simple abstractions.

In the act and time of labor, the bodies of wage workers circulate capital *and* momentarily trap it. Waged laborers, as variable capitals/quasi-commodities in farm production, become temporarily joined to the productive capital of the farm on all sorts of scales. During select portions of the year, a single grower might purchase dozens of other people's body-time, directing labor power toward sowing seeds, coordinating irrigation flow, thinning crops, climbing ladders, or picking fruit. Over an entire crop region, thousands of these bodies will repeat these acts in uncounted combination. They will become extensions of thousands of farm tools and machines, while tools and machines will become extensions of thousands of bodies. In a single year, throughout the San Joaquin Valley, Southern California, the Imperial Valley, legions of bodies will tramp the ground that feeds the roots; they will temporarily interrupt sunlight as they lean over and work their fingers through stems or vines to find ripe berries, harvest grapes, or cut asparagus. Sometime during the heat of the day, these legions will pause for some food and drink. A portion of agrarian capital will come to a halt.

Employed as variable capital, a body, in the singular and plural sense, becomes a *geographical* space for circulating capital, no less than a crop district, an irrigation network, or even a branch-banking system. Yet, circulation must pause for these bodies, as it must for crops in the ground, irrigation canals under construction, or seasons of price deflation. As we saw in the previous chapter, there simply is no circulation without a barrier to circulation. The laborer becomes possessed by capital but also possesses, moves capital forward, but derails it, too. This is what a circulation of capital means. The farmer buys the commodity labor-power, it being necessary to reserve a portion of capital for the purpose. The laborer's work thus *becomes* capital's time moving forward *and* standing still. The worker stoops to labor and stops to eat, sleep, live, think, and, as histories of California farm labor show, question the terms of the capital embodied in them. A worker is a supple, moving, willful Euclidean point. A cog? Perhaps. A striker? Perhaps that, too. That is, contrary to the California farmer quoted above, who insists that labor is a commodity like any other, the capitalist sooner or later confronts the totality of the means of production; confronts not just (for example) the price of crop mortgages, or the cost of water chugging toward the ditch, but also the variability, the willful humanity, of variable capital.

If only it really *were* that abstract, that clean. Regardless of whether farm employers could have treated labor like any other commodity, they in fact treated labor *unlike* any other. In their quest for a constant supply of commodity-labor, farm employers subjected "their" variable capital to extraordinarily discriminating and difference-making practices. The hallmark of these practices was the channeling of agricultural labor into racialized labor markets, whose definition depended upon a political-legal-cultural process of racial enforcement. Though Euro-American ideas about race and race-based practices were neither wholly circumscribed by capitalist social relations nor invented whole cloth by "white" farmers, farm production was an important site for the reproduction of racial practice. Consequently, workers' *experience* of race (or of the process of being "race-d"), and of class, could easily be mutually reinforced (see Almaguer 1994). The combination of the abstract relations described above and of a racially discerned labor market could not be better described than in this 1903 press release from two secretaries of the biethnic Japanese-Mexican Labor Association:

> It is just as necessary for the welfare of the valley that we get a decent living, as it is that the machines in the great sugar factory to be properly oiled—if the machine stops, the wealth of the valley stops, and likewise if the laborers are not given a decent wage, they too, must stop work and the whole people of this country [the sugar beet region of Ventura County] suffer with them. (Quoted in Almaguer 1994: 193)

Labor *is* a commodity. It is variable capital in production joined at that moment to circulating capital. The difference between oil and Japanese and Mexican farmworkers, though, is that oil can't think about what it's like to grease the wheel or whether or not to grease it at all.

This chapter explores discursive connections, made by white Californians, between class and race.[1] These connections, I argue, constituted a particular discourse on circulating capital, during the period when the dominance of grain production had given way to irrigated specialty crops. The chapter offers first a brief "stage-setting" history of California farm labor. The discussion is developed as a twin theme: one, the more or less steady evolution of the wage relation in California farm production; the other, the periodic destabilizing of actual social relations on the ground, partly through the succession of minority-farmworker groups alternately employed by and routed from California agriculture and partly through labor's own agency and organized labor's response to that agency. After discussion of these "ever-new, ever-same" features, I move on to a longer critique of white representation. As part of this critique, I introduce one particularly rich example of the discursive production of race in California agriculture. This example, from a standard farm-management textbook, illustrates well how the concept, or even an ontology, of race was joined to, and operationalized through, a highly detailed division of labor, itself operationalized by an overriding concern for how commodified labor power impinged upon the efficient circulation of agrarian capital. I then consider some of the ways agriculture was talked about in the white Californian imagination, in non-fiction and fiction, as a result of agriculture's contradictory location. By "contradictory location," I refer to a clash between a social vision wherein agriculture was argued to be a mechanism for moving surplus wage earners into small-farm ownership and a different vision wherein agriculture was legitimated as a major employer of wage labor for the sake of circulation. Agriculture's contradictory location, I argue, produced a distinctive rural realist discourse and a particular social character, the capitalist laborer.

## The Ever-New, Ever-Same, 1: Continuity of Wage Labor and Changes in the Wage Labor Market

By 1924, waged farm laborers comprised the majority of all persons earning an income in California agriculture. Over 62% of California's farms employed hired labor, making California in this regard the highest-ranked state in the nation (Taylor and Vasey 1936; *Economic Trends*). A virtual constant through years of amassed landholding, subdivision, and reamalgamation of farm properties, of revolutions in commodity regimes, and of the movements of fictitious values and capital was the presence of migrant labor as a class unto itself. Although wheat producers ultimately managed to discipline their reliance on this labor by mechanizing plough and harvest operations, specialty crop producers deepened their dependence. (It was only during the 1940s and '50s that mechanization would really get off the ground, and even then, certain of the most important crops were unaffected.) Year after year, farmers renewed the supply of harvest labor, wondering about it, worrying about it, but ultimately talking themselves into it.

Beginning with the so-called Dirty Plate Route, which seasonal workers followed as they crisscrossed Miller and Lux's Central Valley fiefdom, migratory labor was in fact essential to the entire agro-industrial complex, from railroad building to irrigation-system construction to canning and packing (see especially McWilliams 1939 and Daniel 1982; also Taylor 1945; Taylor and Vasey 1936; Jelinek 1982; Jones 1970). Up through the 1920s, the largest pools of migrant labor recruited into California agriculture comprised workers of Asian and Mexican ancestry. Disrupting this pattern, yet constituting it just the same, was the repeated tendency of the white working and middle class to agitate for racial or ethnic exclusion when a non-white population showed signs of advancing toward leasing farmland or buying property outright. Yet, once a group was largely routed from the fields, a new class of non-white farmworkers—Japanese, "Hindustani," or Mexican—would be installed, each at the receiving end of finer and finer racialized discernments, as to skills, motivation, discipline, and so on.

In agriculture, California's Chinese population was the first to take the blow of exclusionary legislation, in 1882 and again in 1888 and 1893, though the 1879

State Constitution itself contained anti-Chinese provisions. Chinese workers had been the first major group that white growers had recruited. As ex-miners or contract laborers in other industries, they were hired first by the Central Pacific Railroad and then by the Southern Pacific. After their railroad work was through, farmers and land developers hired them for reclamation and irrigation work in the Delta—where the Sacramento and San Joaquin Rivers joined—and for similar work in other regions. Laboring primarily on small farms, they were well ensconced as skilled laborers in orchards, vineyards, and vegetable farms by the 1880s. Chinese workers appealed to their farm employers because by the time they arrived at the work site, they had already been organized into mobile work gangs by labor contractors. The appeal also lay in the fact that Chinese workers excelled at exploiting themselves, cheaply performing tasks that others avoided (see Chan 1986). As Sucheng Chan shows, however, this was not the whole of it. The Chinese in California ultimately became an important presence as tenant farmers in their own right during the 1880s. Insofar as this was the case, she argues, it was the tenant system itself that at times allowed large landholders to keep their land (Chan 1986: 320). It therefore could not be that cheap Chinese labor categorically aided land monopoly and prevented unemployed white workers from gaining access to California farmland, as went late-nineteenth-century anti-Asian sentiment.

Exclusionary legislation, which dramatically cut the numbers of Chinese farm laborers, was the culmination of xenophobic groundswells that had been fomented by California's working and middle classes for some years. The migrant-worker question developed early into a vociferous debate, each side of which was taken up along complex class lines both in and out of agriculture (Taylor 1945). In favor of plentiful numbers of Chinese fieldworkers were large landholders and operators of large farms. Grangers and small farmers, who had to compete with the cheap labor advantage of their large farmer counterparts, strongly opposed the migrant class. To this camp were added after 1885 increasing numbers of settlers from the East looking for work. With more popular support than any other group, Denis Kearney's urban-based Workingmen's Party of California was perhaps the most vocal opponent of the Chinese. Merchants tended to be divided on the issue, but again along lines of class and space. Larger merchants in the cities, like their landowning counterparts, favored the Chinese, perhaps being motivated by their trade with Asia and their propensity to hire Chinese servants. According to one large farmer, smaller rural merchants were confounded that the Chinese would not buy the same things that were needed by whites. Chinese workers, during their peak years, supposedly sent $10 million worth of remittances out of the state, according to McWilliams (1939). Therefore, these merchants, too, opposed the Chinese. California's middle class, or at least middle class by persuasion, were stout opponents as well. San Francisco's popular periodical the *Argonaut* editorialized that a loud cry against the Chinese was coming

> from that intelligent middle class who do not desire to see a landed aristocracy and a pauper peasantry spring up in this country; from that middle class who don't own miles of the public estate, who don't own water, gas, and railroad monopolies . . . From that great middle class who have developed the resources of the country, who have made the wilderness a smiling settlement, who have built cities, who, in short, are the backbone of this or any other country. (Quoted in Taylor 1945: 222)

What this voice of "middle class" nativism did not admit was that the small growers of specialty crops—labor-intensive crops—were also in need of the migrant worker, but because these growers had to compete with the large ones who hired the bulk of migrant labor, they were the most vociferous agitators for exclusion. In sum, to say that the Chinese "entered" California agriculture is too neutral. Before they even got there, they were despised by certain groups of "white" Californians. Hustled out of the mines and then out of San Francisco, "thousands of Chinese were literally driven into the agricultural districts at a time when the large growers were beginning to demand a large supply of cheap labor" (McWilliams 1939: 70). Anti-Chinese agitation reached a pitched level in 1893 when riots and violence against Chinese Californians broke out all through the agricultural valleys—in the fields near Fresno, at Tulare and Visalia, in Redlands, the core of the citrus area of Southern California. Driven into the fields at first, they were now driven out, back toward the cities or out of the country altogether—but certainly not before having been a major force in California's transition to specialty agriculture. "They were a vital factor," Carey McWilliams asserts, "one is inclined to state *the* vital factor, in making the transition possible." It was the Chinese who "actually taught their overlords how to plant, cultivate, and harvest orchard and garden crops" (McWilliams 1939: 67–68, 71; also Chan 1986).

After the Chinese were largely excluded from California's migrant-labor force, white workers gained a greater share of the rural labor market. At the same time, however, farm employers, especially sugar beet producers and refiners, had also begun to recruit Japanese workers. Already experienced agriculturists, Japanese farmworkers' numbers grew, just as it appeared that white workers might win wage concessions from their employers (McWilliams 1976). After first working in small numbers in the fruit harvest in the late 1880s, Japanese laborers numbered 2,000 by 1890. In 1900, there were 24,000. By 1910 (Japanese immigration was suspended in 1908), the population had risen to about 72,000 (about equal to the Chinese), 30,000 of whom worked in the fields, especially during the cultivation and harvest periods of sugar beets, hops, and strawberries (McWilliams 1939). Determined to gain a toehold, Japanese workers actively, competitively, bid for an unrivaled position in the farm-labor market. Skilled, knowledgeable, and efficient organizers of their own labor power, they in fact understood how to work the game of capitalist-driven agriculture and race construction. Underbidding the prevailing cost of labor power and thus pitting themselves against other racialized groups of workers, they anticipated the employers' game—for as virtually every labor historian has noted, among the strategies farm employers used to keep wages down in the first place was to tease workers in a crowded labor field into working for less. In a stunning turnaround, once Japanese workers achieved a dominating presence, they pressed for a larger share of circulating capital. "By 1907 their labor enjoyed a scarcity value and they were the highest paid farm-labor group in the State" (McWilliams 1939: 110–11; see also Daniel 1982).

Because they demanded higher wages, Japanese workers lost the support of many of the large growers, who were their staunchest champions. These new social relations made safe passage for the Alien Land Act of 1913, which was designed to halt Asian land acquisition. The Act begrudged the fact that Japanese Californians had become landowners in increasingly large numbers. (This law was reactivated in 1919 and added to in 1924 by Federal restriction on further immigration.) On these grounds, both large and small growers had taken up hostilities against the Japanese. The former were threatened because Japanese landownership cut into the farm-labor market. The latter group resented Japanese farmers for owning or operating land in highly valuable irrigated sections of the state, land for which these farmers could afford to overbid whites on land-leasing arrangements (McWilliams 1939). Still, all was not quite so clear-cut, as white and Japanese farmers found ways to resist. For example, there were instances of white landowners having helped Japanese farmers evade the alien land laws, especially by encouraging the Japanese to in fact expand their *leased* acreage and go in for so-called cropping contracts. Through these contracts, white landowners essentially re-theorized the agrarian wage relation (see the previous chapter) and declared the Japanese to be employees paid with crop receipts (Azuma 1994). Such landowners, like those who leased to Chinese farmers, thus had a mechanism to keep their holdings intact.

Copresent with the Japanese were "Hindustanis" recruited from Canada. While never having numbered more than about 5,000, they ultimately labored through large areas of the state. They worked the fruit orchards, vineyards, and vegetable farms of northern California before dropping south of the Tehachapis by 1909. Once there, they would usually work the melon and cotton crops in the Imperial Valley and then circle back to fig orchards and vineyards around Fresno. By 1920, Indians, too, had been nearly displaced (Liebman 1983; McWilliams 1939). For a time, Japanese, Chinese, and Indian labor overlapped. This situation was used to advantage by employers, who, as just noted, effectively put different groups in competition with each other, establishing "different wage rates for each racial group, thus fostering racial antagonism and, incidentally, keeping wages at the lowest possible point" (McWilliams 1939; 117–18). Indians soon showed signs that they too were moving into ownership status; the Alien Land Act was written for them as well.

As the Asian presence waned, a new wave of white workers was recruited into the fields during the ten years before the world war. But because *of* the war, industrial capitals entered a boom period, as would California farms, and were able to attract white workers back to urban centers for higher-paying manufacturing jobs (Liebman 1983). It was this shifting labor market, first Asian exclusion and then the recruitment of white workers out of agriculture, that laid the groundwork for the large immigration of Mexican agricultural workers. Though Mexicans had long been farmworkers, especially in Southern California, white growers now went after them with all the gusto previously reserved for Chinese and Japanese workers. Immigration restrictions and qualifications, such as the literacy test and the head tax, were lifted for Mexicans who intended to work in agriculture. These conditions extended into the 1920s. Though Mexican workers were joined by Filipinos and by white workers (no surprise regarding the latter, given the contraction of the post-war economy), Mexican workers outnumbered them all (Liebman 1983; McWilliams 1939; Selvin 1966). Between 1914 and 1930, some 150,000 Mexicans were the mainstay of a cheap mobile labor force. In the minds of employers and the agricultural press, what distinguished them from their earlier counterparts was that they could be more easily repatriated and had less inclination to move into farm ownership north of the border. After the world war, it was hoped that these transnational workers would enter silently a convenient and manageable cycle: recruitment into the fields, followed by repatriation, followed by re-recruitment the next season. That, at least, was the popular myth. In actuality, it was not unusual for one half to two-thirds or more of the relief budgets of rural towns to be spent on Mexican migrants during their off-season (McWilliams 1939). Local governments were thus compelled to absorb the social costs not only of the agricultural wage but also of agriculture's production and working time disunity.

## The Ever-New, Ever-Same, 2: Resistance and Reaction

In 1914, the California Commission on Immigration and Housing (formed in response to the Wheatland riot—see below) sent a twenty-two-year-old investigator, Frederick Mills, out into the agricultural valleys to live the life of the itinerant worker and report back on working conditions. Among the jobs he took was in an orange-packing house as a "rustler" carrying packed crates.

> Each box weighs 70 lbs. From 500 to 700 are carried in a day. I worked at this till 9 P.M. Friday night with two hours off for meals. By the time I finished my feet were blistered, my hands were torn, my arms almost numb, my back aching, and each of my thighs with a red hot sear across it where the edges of the box rubbed. I no longer wonder why there are so many I.W.W.s. (Quoted in Woirol 1992: 28)

The years leading up to World War I indeed saw active IWW (Industrial Workers of the World) organizing in California's fields. But by that time, there had in fact been a long history of labor resistance and organization of one form or another in California—ranging from labor contracting systems, in which labor contractors negotiated minimum wages and working conditions below which workers would not sell their labor, to walkouts and strikes. In 1880 and 1884, Sucheng Chan recounts, Chinese harvest workers went out on strike in Santa Clara and Kern Counties, respectively. When the effects of Chinese exclusion began to take hold, moreover, these workers became so dear to their employers that they were able to bargain for higher wages for years afterward (Chan 1986: 332–30). Whether labor actions took the form of sporadic resistance on isolated ranches—especially characteristic of the pre-1930 era (Daniel 1982)—or more-organized labor-contracting systems and unionization drives, the history of variable capital is ultimately that it is *variable,* undependable, liable to unleash its agency. That is, variability lies not only in the fact that labor power is commodified and extracted out of creatures who are more than this labor power, who are living human beings off the job, but also in the fact that they remain living human beings *on* the job.

Yet, the powers arrayed against farmworker humanity, let alone agency, were at times formidable. And they included those which came from the ranks of labor itself. During periods of labor militancy, growers renewed their hostilities toward labor and effectively banded together to brutally challenge organized resistance, time and again (Mitchell 1996). Organized labor (that is, unions other than organized farm labor) responded with ambivalence at best (Daniel 1982). Carey McWilliams insists that labor organizers found out early that farmworkers could only be organized with great difficulty. In our terms, the way agriculture was structured in time and space through production and working time disunities was inherently an obstacle: Production was scattered over thousands of square miles, and the majority of workers were only called upon for a short duration at any one site. Labor actions consequently tended to fall apart after harvest (McWilliams 1939). (As Don Mitchell shows, though, it was also precisely the combination of this mobility over space with the fixity of labor camps in space that proved an essential enabler of worker militancy in the first place [Mitchell 1996].) Still, the distance that the most powerful urban-based organized labor groups kept from farmworkers is not to be explained by the spatially influenced difficulties of organizing. The American Federation of Labor, for example, which was then America's largest working-class organization, feared alienating farmers, a historically important ally of the urban industrial working class.[2]

The efforts that the AFL made to organize migratory labor were brief and inconsistent (Daniel 1982). At least partially sympathetic with their rural comrades and inspired by the 1901 draymen's strike in San Francisco, the AFL-affiliated California State Federation of Labor helped organize a farmworkers union, whose sole demand was a $2 per day wage. This local, established in San Jose in the spring of 1903, was followed by others around the state. Up until 1913, a series of federated farmworker unions was formed, only to be disbanded (McWilliams 1939). But during those ten years, the AFL shifted its emphasis anyway, away from organizing workers in the fields—this it left to the despised Industrial Workers of the World—toward relying upon government for some sort of palliative legislation that would mandate fairer treatment of farmworkers (Daniel 1982). In so doing, the AFL retreated from the struggle to directly alter the flow of capital in farm production and instead caved in to the politics of regulation.

Worse, back in 1903, the AFL had an important chance to throw its muscle behind other organizing efforts when the Japanese-Mexican Labor Association (a union that gave the lie to unbridgeable ethnic antagonism) called a sugar-beet workers' strike at Oxnard, in Ventura County. The strike proved to be a major victory against a powerful, grower-affiliated labor contractor. But when Samuel Gompers had the choice to let the JMLA into the AFL, he would do so only on the condition that Asian members be excluded. The JMLA refused and soon disbanded (Almaguer 1994). These were complicated racial politics. As Tomás Almaguer writes, "Gompers's attitude toward the Japanese branch of the JMLA clearly illustrated that white working-class racism was not a monolithic structure impervious to differences among California's racialized ethnic groups. To the contrary, important differences existed in the way white Californians at different class locations viewed and structured their relationships with the racialized ethnic populations in the state" (Almaguer 1994: 204).

Racial hatred blended seamlessly into the general hostility of the AFL toward workers who were considered to be among the "unskilled." Perhaps if the AFL had had the same "appreciation" for the range of skilled work actually performed in the fields as that held by farm employers (see the next section below), they might have felt otherwise. But, it is more likely that racism would have blinded organized labor anyway. A plethora of back issues of the *Labor Clarion* bears this out. With virtually no sense of irony, the *Clarion* could insist:

> We, of the white race, have built up with infinite toil . . . a civilization founded on democracy. We cannot continue as a democracy with people of

> a different purpose in life . . . just as clubs vote out those who are of different habits and thoughts, so this great Caucasian club of ours must vote out people who are not clubable . . . This is a question of race preservation. Nations that have been tainted with the admixture of men of different life and ideals have lost their cohesion, tottered and fell; and the battle ground of the nations today, where the great race question must be fought out and settled, is California, where the Asiatics compete in our labor markets, lowering our standard of life to theirs, which is on an infinitely lower scale. So California demands the exclusion of Asiatics, exclusion total and complete, as the only solution. (Duxbury 1913: 13)

The Alien Land Act was not enough. The *Clarion* argued that this was merely a protection for capitalists. Asians, denied access to land, would simply flood the cities where they would underbid whites in the labor market. The *Clarion's* depraved commentary (not at all surprising to scholars working on this period of American history, but which nonetheless appears with such dizzying regularity that it never ceases to amaze) was not reserved for the "Asiatics" alone. Other issues of the paper complained about "Hindu labor." "No one except a few greedy exploiters of labor have any inclination to allow California to be flooded by the hordes from India." They "come from dirty haunts of poverty and vice of ignorance and servility," driving down wages, adding to an overcrowded labor market, and bringing "detestable personal habits" ("Hindu Labor" 1913: 8). Similar complaints were made against immigrants from southern and eastern Europe ("Labor and Immigration" 1913: 8). Despite the *Clarion's* strong words, it really had no policy other than trying to keep job competition down.

> The problem of congestion which is found today in San Francisco and Los Angeles demands immediate study. The solution here lies in getting the foreign residents in the congested districts out on the land into suburbs or into farming regions. Two factors aid in the plan. Many of these city workers were farmer folk at home in Italy or Hungary. Their residence in the United States has also, in many cases, been long enough to allow a savings bank account to come into existence. They are then likely material for missionary effort. An agricultural survey of the lands of the State suitable in price and fertility for colonizing schemes for these partly Americanized immigrants would be then an important prerequisite for this plan, and such a survey should be therefore one of the first labors of the commission. ("Immigration" 1913: 5)

Apparently, almost any sort of apartheid or removal effort would do. Even the back-to-the-land ethic could serve nicely.

Unlike the AFL, the IWW, who would be forcibly ejected from the fields for their efforts, made serious attempts to organize farmworkers, even the "foreigners." In 1913, the very year that the *Clarion* was getting its vitriol into print, a series of brief but violent skirmishes erupted in Wheatland at the Durst brothers' hop ranch, where IWW organizers had arrived a few days before to organize a protest of the working conditions—9 toilets for 2,800 people, no drinking water in the fields, wages that fluctuated from day to day. It took riots and four deaths on the Durst property to generate the first state-sanctioned, formal inquiry into the working conditions of migrant laborers. In this sense, Wheatland was a watershed event. For a brief spell, before the world war dissipated concern for rural labor and absorbed white workers into manufacturing jobs (Wheatland coincided with the period during which more than the usual number of "white American" itinerants were working the fields in California), Californians who had not known better became aware of the conditions that agro-industry had wrought (McWilliams 1939; also Mitchell 1996).

Although Wheatland in fact gained the IWW some sympathy in California (see Parker 1920), it was short-lived. During the war, in 1917, an IWW cannery strike in San Jose and crop sabotage around Fresno, presumed by growers and police to have been instigated by the IWW, provoked a series of crackdowns by federal law enforcement. Dozens of IWW organizers were either run out of the fields or tossed in jail. Federal agents were installed in several farm communities, and wages were suppressed throughout the war, which were banner years for growers (McWilliams 1939; Daniel 1982; Mitchell 1996).

As the above examples demonstrate, control over the farmworker was not hegemonic. (Indeed, see González [1994] on landscape and everyday life in Southern California's citrus worker villages. Leonard [1997] is also suggestive.) Nor was it particularly easy for farmers to coordinate their labor purchases (Vaught 1995). But in response to labor resistance, which would increase even more in the 1930s, California farmers would redesign agriculture's relations of production so as to better regulate the circulation of agrarian capital at the most fundamental levels. Increasingly after the turn of the century, therefore, farmers gathered into powerful regional and crop specific associations. (Their goal was not to address labor alone but also to respond to cycles of overproduction and competition amongst themselves.) Through mechanisms such as labor exchanges, labor bureaus, and labor pools, farmers met to estimate labor needs, fix wages, and arrange for farmworkers to arrive in the fields or canneries at the required times. With the aim of staying ahead of farmworker discontent, relations between individual farmers and wage employees were disciplined through and mediated by the suprabourgeoisie rather than by individual farmers (Selvin 1966; Fisher 1953). With the blessings of the State of California and local governments, efforts to discipline labor extended into the very homes of migrant workers, as labor camp improvements—which, it was hoped, might make for greater contentedness—were dreamed up (Mitchell 1996). More regulated labor markets and home places could not conceal the California that Don Mitchell calls the "beautiful and the damned."

## Racializing the Working Body and Multicultural Racism

There is little dispute, if any at all, that particular racial constructions accompanied the succession of ethnic minority farm laborers in California agriculture and that these constructions were broadly accepted by Anglo-European California (Almaguer 1994). On the one hand, we may see in these constructions that the rhetoric of racial difference and inequality had simply made the westward journey along with the "Anglo-Saxon." On the other hand, these racial constructions were yet another instance of how race was reinvented through quite specific milieus (especially class-laden ones) (see Horsman 1981 and Saxton 1990). In this section, I wish to touch on *discursive* constructions of race in which race was essentially defined vis-à-vis "white American" perceptions of work performance within capitalist social relations on the California farm. I want to state at the outset that while racial categories existed outside capitalism and certainly outside agriculture, it is also true that capitalism and agriculture were among many sites where race was made and "racializing" performed. The "racializing" process required that the race-d person be seen as *doing* (or not doing) something. (Following Omi and Winant [1986], I see "racialization" as a process whereby attributes of race are extended to specific relationships and acts, not just to inert body features.) The general point I want to make is that agriculture—capitalist agriculture, in the form of waged bodies—was an opportunity to further (and further *specify*) the idea and practice of race: Without it, in other words, race would have meant just that much less.

Within the logic of racialization, the race-d one must be ascribed an act to perform. White farmers not only claimed that Chinese, Japanese, Mexican, and Filipino workers were *historically* essential to agricultural production but also typically argued that they were *inherently* distinct in their ability to perform certain kinds of work. Quite often, paired with this disciplinary perception of what race-d workers were good for were certain negative capacities. Differently race-d workers were alternately "childish," "tricky," "lazy," and so forth. These ascriptions were, however, complex and contradictory. They were attributes that supposedly both befit workers for the work they were hired to do and constituted actions that also had to be disciplined in order for work to go ahead. They were the primitive forces or raw materials to be restrained in order for appropriation of labor power to proceed. Put another way, specific work to be performed was in some sense conceived as a mitigation of the very racialized traits that befit the laborers for the work in the first place, or, if not conceived as ultimately mitigating, particular work would elicit the silver lining of these negatively ascribed workers. The "childish" would become loyal, the "tricky" astute, and so forth. It is hard not to see this exchange in baldly deconstructionist terms: Because there would be no way within the logic of race to supersede racialized *difference*, ultimate mitigation would have to be endlessly *deferred*. Difference marks the race-d laborer with a potential good that can never really matter. It is a good that befits him for his very difference. Though labor would dignify race-d work, dignity would never be full. And good thing, too. In tautological fashion, it was partly by virtue of the construction of a supposedly naturally given racial hierarchy and of racialized labor capacities that capitalist social relations and specialized work details were themselves justified in California agriculture. Capitalism could be considered legitimated, brought into being "naturally," because of the supposedly inherent racialized capacity for different kinds of work. The defense of racialization was thus a de facto defense of agrarian wage labor.

The primary conceit of the racializing process was that the effective circulation of different agrarian capitals would be circulated better through one kind of race-d body than through another. This construction may be seen best by example. One of the most thorough expressions I have come across is R. L. Adams's *Farm Management* textbook for "student, investigator, and investor" (Adams 1921). A professor of farm management at the University of California, Berkeley, Adams covered every conceivable topic from farm prices, capital outlays, and sources of financing to crop characteristics, tools and machinery, and labor. "Each man," he advises in his labor chapter, "can do but a certain amount of daily work . . . Beyond this he must call in others to help him; and if his be the guiding hand, his success in getting the work done will be in direct proportion to his ability to get the best from his men . . . No one," he cautions, "has a moral right to demand that the laborers under his direction shall work at a rate that will impair working power, but with this limitation the manager has a right to expect the best service the laborer can give" (Adams 1921: 518). What a laborer can "give" depends, in the most minute detail, upon the group to which he belongs: white, hobo or tramp, Italian and Portuguese, Negro, Mexican, Indian, Japanese, Hindu, or Chinese. Adams's instructions for the care and handling of these groups occupy several pages.

While some abbreviation of Adams's field guide to California labor is warranted, it entirely defeats the purpose to compress the details too much. Note below that in nearly every case (except the first) where Adams discusses "white labor," some negative trait was—under the "guiding" hand of the employer or farm manager—the very raw material that made that labor worth employing. The trait is, again, a potential good that marks the race-d worker's very circumscription as race-d. These traits defined race-d workers' difference just as it deferred their dignity: Workers could only really excel at being their race. Through the very work given them they might prove their limitations.

In Adams's reckoning, the category of *white* labor—in which he includes the Irish, Swedes, Norwegians, Danes, Germans, Poles, and Austrians—is the "best" one can get. Coming from "good old farming stock," they are "as a rule steady, reliable, kind to stock, and familiar with farm operations." Unfortunately, he notes, these men have a tendency to go into business for themselves (519). From here, given the usual scarcity of these workers, the choices are all downhill.

*Hobo* or *tramp* labor, "when white," typically feels above farm work. Many are intelligent and educated, Adams says, but many, too, are weak and "mentally defective." Most will work for only two or three weeks, never on Sunday, and often only want a few hours of work per day. If pushed to work hard, they will easily quit. "Yet they can be held to the daily quitting time, although if over-time or extra work is attempted, a clear understanding must be had and extra money be paid." They are typically "well acquainted with the kind of work they hire out to do, and can accomplish more if allowed to select the method" (520).

In contrast, *Italian and Portuguese* laborers "make some of the best ranch help now available" and "seem to have an inborn love of farming." They are, however, "rather sensitive and inclined to be emphatic in their likes and dislikes. They won't tolerate abusive treatment . . . [but once] the employer secures their respect and esteem, they will work well and steadily" (521).

In contrast again are *Negro* laborers. "The colored man—the mainstay of southern farming—is characterized as home-loving, peaceable, easy going, gregarious, sometimes shiftless, always good natured and affable." These laborers make "good hand workers, e.g., in hoeing, planting, weeding, clearing land. They take readily to handling horses and mules. Their best work is done in the warmer sections, as they dislike the colder climates and higher altitudes" (521). "All require much patience," however, "as they are careless in reporting broken machinery, are notorious prevaricators, and constantly annex to themselves such minor things as chickens, lines from harness, axes, shovels, etc." It is best to "(a) have very little to do with the men other than to outline the work and see that it is carried out; (b) assign a stated amount of work for the day and when completed call it a day letting the worker have any extra hour or two to himself, for the negro works better for this 'tasking' him . . . than by set hours." Adams also warns against both being overly appreciative and not keeping faith with Negro workers. Though they are "erratic, irregular workers," "slow and inclined to loaf," they are, "for people who understand them . . . good workers when kept under proper supervision" (522).

The common *Mexican* laborer "is usually a peaceful, somewhat childish, rather lazy, unambitious, fairly faithful person. He occasionally needs to be stirred up to get him to work, but if treated fairly he will work faithfully. . . . When held in not too large numbers or worked in competition with other races, they prove willing and fairly reliable help." Mexicans are adept at many sorts of tasks: thinning sugar beets, teaming, range riding, pick and shovel work, fruit picking and handling, and cutting corn. Though they are "fairly good with machines," they "are not particularly adept at milking or handling complicated machinery." Adams recommends treating them with patience, letting them live on the farm or nearby, encouraging marriage, and "arranging for contract or piece work when practicable and if understood by the men, rather than by day labor" (523).

*Indian* laborers make "satisfactory teamsters and harvest hands," but their numbers are limited. "The full-blood Indians are usually to be preferred to the halfbreeds . . . [and] as a rule are not particularly steady, but given a manager they like, they will prove to be faithful, loyal, and willing" (523).

*Japanese* workers, though "not mechanically inclined . . . are good hand workers, especially at squat labor such as cutting asparagus, truck gardening, berry growing, sugar beet thinning and topping, melon picking, gathering walnuts, and for picking, sorting, and packing of various deciduous and citrus fruits." Adams notes that they do not usually work on livestock or grain ranches. The Japanese are "tricky in regard to contracts" so that "provision should be made when starting a piece of work to hold back a portion of their pay pending completion of the job" (523–24). The language barrier puts the employer at a special disadvantage: "if he tries to deal directly with individuals of a large crew . . . many of them can not, or will not, understand orders given in English." The Japanese are studious and smart, they "work best in their own way and if they know how to do certain work, they should be given an opportunity to do it by whatever method they are used to pursuing" (524).

*Hindu* laborers, of which there are many sorts—"the Mohammedans are preferred to the other natives of India"—are among the least desirable. "In their lean, lanky, enervated condition they lack muscle, will power, and energy." However, they "try fairly hard." This makes them good, for hand labor in beet, celery, and rice cultivation, or in "other work where hand labor is needed in abundance" (524).

Adams notes while there is little *Chinese* field labor anymore, what exists is slow, set in its ways, but "very reliable and trustworthy." They work well in groups and "are content with much to do and little to say" (524).

What farm employers do with all this information depends, of course, upon which farm tasks need doing.

> The general farmer needs steady, year-round men willing and able to do the variety of work incident to the production of stock and crops, to be supplemented in times of harvest or other "peak load" needs by additional

> hands for temporary use. The farmer tending toward specialization, like dairying, fruit raising, sugar beet production, or field crops such as grain or hay or beans, requires a type of labor able to do just the kind of work necessary to successful production in his particular industry.
>
> A dairyman wants men all the year . . . An alfalfa hay producer wants husky men . . . The fruit grower . . . needs men to prune, spray, cultivate, and irrigate. For picking up prunes or walnuts, any labor can be utilized and so school children, Indians, and whole families of unskilled and inexperienced people are found to be satisfactory . . . Irrigating requires men who know how to apply water properly . . . [Poultry] work consists of much detail and requires a man who not only can do the work but is quiet and gentle with the fowls. The sugar beet grower requires men able to do the hard, monotonous backbreaking work of thinning the growing plants, and pulling and topping the mature crop. (525)

The traits of race are here vividly extended into the structure of production (i.e., the coordination of production- and working-time disunities), while the structure of production was a means through which race could be codified. And that toward very, very quotidian ends: Would it be better for the *general* farmer who needs consistent year-round help to hire a white tramp or an "Italian and Portuguese"? Should the *specialist* sugar beet grower with need for *strong backs* hire a "Hindu," or would the capital be squandered? One need only check the field guide. Moreover, since different crops have different socially necessary labor times and differently race-d classes of labor have supposedly different capacities, the farm employer could check the guidebook to know just how many workers of a particular class to try to obtain and for how long. Thinning a hundred acres of sugar beets takes 20 to 30 of the right kind of workers 2 to 3 weeks, Adams says. Harvesting a hundred acres of asparagus takes 20 to 30 of the right kind 6 to 8 weeks. Given that crops came to maturity at different times in the various places where they were grown—sugar beets were thinned in Southern California in February and March and in Northern California in March and April—this too would have had to enter into the farmer's choice of labor (526–27).

It is doubtful that any farmer could have fulfilled all of Adams's recommendations in practice, but the delineation of this grid of time, space, and race-d labor power—a grid of flexible production and accumulation—is a powerful example of discursive construction of race in the context of acts of agricultural production and efficient circulation of farm capital. We should not miss the peculiar significance of the body within the grid, though—especially the importance of racialized difference. As we've seen, capital circulates through the waged body, the inefficiencies and restrictions of which threaten to stall circulation. This is indeed a unifying theme in *Farm Management*. But recall how the process begins: The problem of the body starts with the farmer himself, who hires workers precisely because his own body would otherwise give out on a daily basis and bring ruin to the farm. The farmer's money must then take over where his own labor ends; it must be plowed into the labor power of his workers. In the blink of an eye, a signal transformation occurs. The body, once the subject of the farmer's own hard work, now becomes the object of a class obsession—the natural limits of labor power. In Adams's text, this general truth about labor power and its constraints takes on the distorted form of an absurdly retentive, racialized bestiary. In other words, all that proliferating detail about the races, the myriad discursive constructions of the racialized body, are the offspring of something that is anything but prolific; they are intimately tied to the fact that the physical body, unlike the cultural, discursive body can be "constructed" only so far. Isn't this the discursive body's raison d'être, though? The restrictions of the laboring body seem to have an outlet in a sort of cultural, discursive abandon. In short, the competencies of workers' bodies, grudgingly acknowledged by Adams, have thoroughly to do with the incompetence of the farmer's body. The farmer negotiates this tension with his money, which embodies his incompetence, yet potentially makes up for it. What becomes of his money—its alienation, and distribution as wages—is one and the same with his racializing the limits of others' labor power. Race is a way of talking about how farm capital will be distributed and labor disciplined; it is a mode of planning expenditures and compensating for having to spend. With his money, the farmer-employer can make up for his own lack, and in the same breath imagine the lack of others, so as to not overspend. Without these expenses, he would have no reason, at least in this instance, to worry about race. Money and race are quite particular constructions here. For Adams, money is the white man's reward and the white man's burden.

Production, capitalist social space, class, and race, as Adams's textbook attests, were the constituents of a rich imagination of which there were numerous formulations. In Howard Baker's California novel *Orange Valley* (1931), capitalist production and its social space not only make use of race but also originate it.

> The fruit tramps, as they were called, would come into the San Joaquin valley in the fall to pick the navel oranges; they would move on into Southern California for the winter oranges; they would come back into the San Joaquin valley for the spring valencias; and then, pausing perhaps to chop cotton, they would drift up above Sacramento for the peaches, and they might go on up into Oregon to work in the apples before they came back into the San Joaquin. They were, for the most part, farmers from the eastern border of the Rockies—farmers who had become disgusted with their land and who had loaded their wives and children and belongings into the car and driven west. Once in the West they would continue to drive, the car becoming older and older as the seasons went on, their children becoming wilder and wilder, and as their wives died off they would intermarry until finally they had become almost a race in themselves. (191)

Baker's and Adams's accounts are different in purpose, but what makes them of a kind is the notion of the embeddedness of race in other social structures that both allow a race concept to take on meaning and, by the same token, make meaning for other structures—class, place, and so on. Reflecting on what his own grid of labor, space, and time might mean, Adams invokes a distinctively racialized *multicultural* agriculture. "All this," he observes, "shows what a great variety of men is needed to meet all farm needs. Agriculture as it stands today represents the cosmopolitan effort of representatives of many nations, so many in fact that to list them would include almost all that have experienced much emigration—China, France, Germany, India, Italy, Japan, Mexico, Portugal, Russia, Sweden, and on around the globe" (525). There is something almost poignant in the alphabetical ordering of these countries. After the previous discriminating exercise,

Adams seems to balk at wanting to slight anyone. His is a vision not of racial exclusion but of rigorous and emphatic incorporation—where everyone does, in fact, have a place. It is a vision of hyper-divided labor, of racialized skills from around the globe which have come to America, and especially California, where they all come together. In return, Adams would offer these workers a fetishistic view of their role: Their race-d difference is worth it, if not essential, when cosmopolitan efforts are at stake. But virtually nothing is said about anyone's troubles. Farmers, lest their farm capital circulate poorly, were not to "tolerate talk or preaching by discontented individuals." Chinese labor "is now a thing of the past." Labor has no history. It's simply there now for the buying, a commodity like any other. Even though race was a primary means of making labor a commodity *unlike* any other, it was nonetheless an ideological mechanism for thinking that it was.

## Toward Rural Realism: An Agrarianism without Illusions?

> The truth is that multitudes of people would cut and run from the cities within a week if they had the money to finance a farm. ("The Back to the Land Problem," *San Francisco Examiner,* October 5, 1911, quoted in Requa and Cory 1919: 6)

> The vicissitudes of pioneering are now so well understood that the home-seekers are avoiding them. "Let the Company do it" appears to express the general view of the new comers. (A statistician at the United States Reclamation Service, quoted in Requa and Cory 1919: 2–3)

Adams's views of the agricultural labor market aside, one of the interesting aspects of *Farm Management* is that it signals the prevalence of capitalist agriculture with so little ado. The purchase of credit and labor power are treated in full, and the farmer is given guidance every step of the way. Yet, this book is perched on the crest of decades of struggle over meaning and practice in the California countryside. The book is, let's say, triumphantly "neutral": It simply does not see itself as discursive, sided, bounded. And why should it? After all, the thing for Adams was the farm, its efficient management, and the turnover of circulating farm capital. That Adams does not frame this book in any other way (other framings, as above, lead right to this one) is a good expression of its role as discourse: It never conceives that the social relations and economic realities it describes could be otherwise. (Indeed, the talk of radical hoboes was not to be "tolerated.") Again, such a conception was not its task, one might object. But this was *itself* a position that has to have been made, an opening that has to have been presented. And presented it indeed was: by the management- and investment-minded students, investigators, and investors (read "farmers") for whom it was written. The book materializes a particular audience that was years in the making, just as the potentiality of an audience "produces" this book. (It should also be said that the book was intended to *make* these audiences as business-minded as Adams felt they needed to be.) It is this quality of constructedness that we want to get the sense of. From our own vantage point, it is relatively easy, for example, to see that the inscriptions of race in *Farm Management*—and the *Labor Clarion*—are historically rooted. And we could point to the ideological presence of this to the extent that the book does not question these inscriptions—*any more than it does the embeddedness of California farms in capitalism.*

Yet, this embeddedness, labor-power purchases inclusive, was also a historical-geographical artifact, as we have already seen, and so *too* are the ways of talking about it. That is, it is one thing—and very important at that—to examine the "race-ing" of the labor market, but it is also worth asking what meanings attached to the fact that farmer-capitalists needed to buy labor power at all. One such meaning was to simply avoid the issue. For Adams, given the farmer's need to hire workers and given a labor market of different, race-d skills, certain sorts of hiring outcomes ought to be sought by the farmer-employer and other outcomes avoided. In other words, it may have been difficult to get labor, and it may have been difficult to get credit, but it was not an issue for Adams that one *must* get those things. The only issue about race that is at all explored is how to ensure that race-d bodies interrupt the circulation of capital as little as possible. Hence, the given of race mapped perfectly onto the given of capitalism on the farm.

The year that *Farm Management* was published, something of a different order was heating up in the pages of the *Pacific Rural Press.*[3] There, the editors' backs were up against the wall as readers wrote in their concerns over white workers released from a downsized post-war economy. Though the embeddedness of farms in capitalist economic structures was not so much the issue, the place of white workers within those structures was. White subscribers pushed the *Press* to confront directly the fact that capital's race-ing of the labor market was forcing the differently race-d workers of California agriculture to compete against each other. Their point was that the labor market *should* in fact remain racialized: "White" work should prevail. From Adams's management text, one would have no idea that this might emerge, since the thrust of his message was that these races were good for distinct sorts of tasks. (Not that there weren't areas of overlap between what one race and another were good for, but Adams's was an exercise in *distinguishing* among these groups, such that competition among them would not enter into the calculus.) It is important to note that white *farmers* were among those who wrote in, also something that one would not expect after reading Adams.

"Say!" one farmer from Fresno wrote, "won't you please discuss for us the present California rural labor situation touching upon the living conditions foisted upon the native, indigenous laborer?" From an economic point of view, at least Adams's economics, it ought not to have mattered which race was hired, only whether the right race was hired for the particular work needed. The editors of the *Press* had a fine line to walk. And they did it with aplomb, managing both an argument for why this farmer needed to be patient and why it could not *be* that farm wage labor was an issue. "Let us do all we can lawfully to stem the Asiatic tide and to reduce our dependence upon such a labor supply," replied the editors. "But no such processes will produce a sufficient native labor supply in this state for generations to come." The problem, they said, was that most "natives" coming to California from other states were "those who desire to buy labor rather than to sell it." While this might eventually induce more "native" job-seekers, it would be in their nature to want "to work for others as a way to provide for their own independence later." A "native" labor supply thus was not going to answer for a permanent labor supply ("Why not more native laborers?" 1921: 148).

When the editors mentioned doing what could be done "lawfully," they may have had in mind an incident in Turlock (Stanislaus County) in which "non-resident white farm hands," angry at being underbid in the cantaloupe harvest, "emptied the Japanese dwellings at Turlock of their contents." Japanese residents were herded into waiting trucks and taken to the train station, where passing trains were flagged down to take them on board. Policemen knew of the raid but did nothing to stop it. A crowd gathered to cheer the raid on. After making sport of the whole "picturesque" affair, and pointedly remarking that the Japanese returned while the white workers soon left, the *Press* commented that "the white laborers had a right to ask their price but they had no right to interfere with those who would do it for less or to interfere with the grower paying less" ("Editorial" 1921: 109).[4] The circulation of growers' capital was the issue here:

> The grower has put all his savings and earnings into his farm and probably is paying interest on deferred payments; he has done full obeisance to money lenders to get in his crop and has pledged his sacred honor to merchants who have provided him with indispensables while the crop has been growing. His chance to redeem his promises and obligations lies in the profit he can make on the crop . . . In the face of such obligations and dangers, who has a right to dictate how he shall do his business or make it impossible for him to do it lawfully in accordance with his best judgments of its requirements? Certainly not gentlemen of touring proclivities, who have not stake in the community; who will undertake none of the burdens and sacrifices of creative production on their own account; who too often do not even wish him well while they work for him . . .
>
> We would be happy if there were not a Japanese in Turlock or anywhere else making it harder for proper California white laborers to achieve the success which such people are aiming at. But we have not enough of the right kind and therefore we should treat fairly the right kind of Japanese we already have while we are insisting that we shall not have more—in the hope and belief that decent white people in sufficient numbers will perceive the opportunity for maintaining themselves in California as a white man's country. ("Editorial" 1921: 109)

Rights fall quite clearly with the grower, with the unimpeded circulation of farm and lenders' capital. This is what makes the race-d labor market desirable; that is, farmers could force workers to compete against each other while rendering that competition irrelevant to workers and denying any agency when the consequences erupted.

But if the non-American workers were reviled by the *Press* and its readers alike, and if the right kind of "natives" was too good for wage work in the fields, as the *Press* had reported, what would be an agreeable, lasting solution? For this question, the *Press* had no answer, except that as long as capital and proper white labor (the type willing to bide its time until farm ownership) were not devalued and demeaned, there could be no real harm. "As for a 'permanent labor supply' for farming; that is, one generation begetting another with no outlook except that of service for others—it is not an American state of mind and will probably be latest of all to appear in California" ("Why Not More Native Laborers?" 1921: 148). Ten years later, novelist Howard Baker was considering that it might just be in California that such a "race" would appear first.

One of the intriguing things about the race-d labor market was that its discussion among white Californians seems to have been a way of both broaching and avoiding discussion of capitalist practice in agriculture. In Adams's case, he avoids dealing with the consequences of different labor markets being pitted against each other. The idea that white workers would form the basis of a *permanent* labor supply, as discussed in the *Pacific Rural Press,* was ignominious. This implicit admission—that an agriculture that structurally necessitated demeaning positions had been made—could only be resolved if the people doing the work were seen as the ones "permanently" outfitted for it. Non-white workers were so constructed, and when they were perceived (by the employing class) to have fulfilled that role, they were actually defended, if not a little ennobled, on the basis of the values that any bourgeoisie would understand: the defense of circulating capital. True colors were shown in the process. In the minds of white Californians, the contradictions of the race-d labor market that emerged in white unemployment were only rarely viewed as revealing a contradiction of capital itself. It wasn't Japanese workers who put white workers out of a job, it was the opportunities and constraints of booming-busting economy. The president of the Commonwealth Club of California, Beverly Hodghead, writing in 1916, put it this way, "We come to wonder in these busy times what is the real basis of prosperity; whether it is war or agriculture" ("Land Settlement in California" 1916: 370).

What were the chances that the surplus white population actually could matriculate into farm ownership status and thereby ostensibly stabilize their economic position? Whatever the chances were exactly (they were not high), the State of California decided—during the heyday of IWW activism and war-time growth—to see if they might be increased. Goaded by Wheatland and heartened by rising farm prices, the state gave the go-ahead for a study on small-farm settlement. On the eve of the Wobblie crackdown in 1917, the newly formed Commission of Land Colonization and Rural Credits was given a $260,000 budget to set up a land-settlement program with which it hoped to keep native white farmers and laborers in the countryside, so as to prevent overcrowding both in the urban labor market during the war and in the rural labor market afterward. The Commission wondered, in the words of the San Francisco *Examiner* quoted above, whether "multitudes of people would cut and run from the cities within a week if they had the money to finance a farm." The state aimed to find out. The first settlement was set up under the guiding hand of *the* heavy hitter in land reform, Elwood Mead, author of the popular book *Helping Men Own Farms* and someone whose nativist politics were right in line with the state's. The Durham colony, in Butte County, sprawled over some 6,000 acres of Sacramento Valley land. It was divided into 110 farms of 8 to 300 acres and 32 smaller farms set aside for itinerants to buy. Subdivisions were quickly bought up with low-cost credit. Things appeared to have gone well enough that the next year the state gave $1 million for a second, larger settlement at Delhi, in San Joaquin Valley's Merced County. In a number of respects—community life, cooperative marketing and purchasing—the two colonies were pronounced a success. The problem, however, was that Durham and Delhi were founded during an inflationary period. Once prices began collapsing, the settlers were left with little income to make payments on their $200-per-acre land purchases. The state itself had no more money left in its allotment, having spent in the first place $90 per acre for the land and another $90 per acre for water.

By 1921, voters proved less willing to continue funding the projects. In that year and again in 1923, they rejected the bond issues that would have kept the communities afloat (McWilliams 1939).

From-the-ground-up agrarianism on a small scale and as a policy for land and social reform was thus abandoned. (For a general discussion of yeoman-based agrarianism in California, see Pisani 1983; 1984). Beneath this abandonment lay an important change, which made the settlers' debts during a deflationary period and voters' unwillingness to fork out more cash only one part of the picture. A very important fact about the California economy during the 1910s was that it was moving away from its reliance on agriculture. This gave the agricultural establishment something to really think about. Between 1900 and 1914, capital invested in manufacturing had quadrupled (Nash 1964). Economic diversification meant that there were more outlets than before for the investment of money capital. Agriculture had to remain competitive if it was to attract investment, and with a more diversified economy, there were more examples around to think about how to do it. It was not as if there were a massive flight of capital out of agriculture. Rather, the more capital-intensive agriculture got and the more indebted farmers became, the more the bourgeois leadership—what Donald Worster calls a "class alliance" of bankers, agribusinesses, and engineers—called for farming to be organized along the lines of the modern industrial corporation (Worster 1985). (As agribusiness's movers and shakers looked back at this period, this was just what they recollected about it. Recall Charles Teague's reminiscences in the previous chapter.) The diversification of the California economy provided numerous corporate models upon which comparisons with agriculture could be made. The railroad had always been big business, and by the 1910s, petroleum was headed in the same direction. And aside from these giants, the chartered corporation, in many sizes, was on the rise, more popular and visible than ever (Blackford 1977; Nash 1964).

In consequence, it turned out that the Durham and Delhi colonies were backed by only one kind of agrarianism, the kind based on the idea that it was people who were supposed to go back to the land and, with some assistance, be put on the track toward lasting prosperity. Another formulation was agrarianism as an investment strategy for large private capital, whose rules and social relations would be absolute. Here, *it was capital that needed to go back to the land.* People would simply aid in that effort.

A more utopian comment on these trends could probably not be found than that elaborated in *The California Irrigated Farm Problem,* a book-length study written in 1919 by two engineer-apologists for corporate efficiency—H. T. Cory, the talented, former Southern Pacific employee who had bailed out the Imperial Valley in the 1905–1907 flood (see chapter 6) and M. L. Requa, a prominent engineer turned financial consultant, who had cut his teeth in mining. "The same ability," they begin, "that has . . . guided the great corporations must aid in solving the problem [of feeding the growing population and making farming more intensive and scientific]; the same financial institutions that have poured money into other channels . . . must in the final analysis supply the capital that will make possible the proper development of the farm." What they had in mind was not some small-farm idyll. Rather, they proposed that "the large business enterprise" would be able to farm "thousands of acres in the most efficient and scientific manner, with accurate cost data, and a distributing system adequate to care properly for the products produced. From a purely investment basis there can be nothing more attractive" (Requa and Cory 1919: 22).

What would it take in the year 1919, Requa and Cory ask, to start an irrigated farm project and make it a paying proposition? Their answer, the summation of the "unanimous opinion of experts" (98), is fraught with a new language of efficiency, discipline, management, and paternalism. It is well worth pausing over excerpts from their proposal, in order to appreciate what a dramatic difference there is between this document and the agitation for massive state supports stirred up by Elwood Mead.

On the "necessity for large capital":

> It is not possible to successfully undertake any irrigation development project in California without command of very large capital. . . . [I]t is necessary to control a large acreage of land in order that the cost may be within commercial limitations. It is also necessary that this work be done with the greatest rapidity possible, owing to the interest charge that will be accumulating from day to day. (98–99)

Here, Requa and Cory address the developer, not the ultimate cultivator of the land. The irrigated farm project will be undertaken not by the farmer but by the middleman, and it will be tied from the start to the constraints of a credit system in a capitalist economy. The necessary large capital to get started is something to be advanced, something one must have access to, not the amount one already has to invest. Debt comes very close to being the first and primary means of production.

For this reason, the turnover of capital needs to be as rapid as possible and must not fall prey to a hodgepodge of land sales:

> The land and the water can be guaranteed; the costs of joining them definitely calculated; but no one can promise with certainty that the buyers will be forthcoming. Herein is the weak link in the chain, and in order to make the project complete without possibility of failure it is necessary to plan and carry out the farming of a large part, if not all, of the land purchased. (100)

The circulation of capital mandates a definite social relation. The project must be a large farm *before* being sold off in parcels. "Whether such a unit should eventually be cut into small farms and sold *is for time to say*" (106, emphasis added).

> There is nothing revolutionary in such a proposal. In California the Kern County Land Company has over 70,000 acres in alfalfa, and has one field embracing over 12,000 acres. James Irvine farms over 70,000 acres in Southern California and there are numerous vineyards and orchards of thousands of acres. (100–101)

The large farm is here read as a continuing and venerated tradition. The Commission on Land Colonization notwithstanding, Requa and Cory glorify the large farm. This farm can be made to pay, they assert, through proper management—in other words, through the same "application of methods that have made the great corporations successful":

> Consider the farm as an industrial plant. . . . The demand for the product must constantly increase, and obviously prices must, in the long run, ad-

> vance. . . . Properly handled, the proposal is free from governmental attack. From its very nature the agricultural industry must enjoy the maximum degree of freedom from the restrictions under which the great corporations have been laboring. (101–2)

The farm is said to be not just a *kind* of industrial plant; it is the industrial plant par excellence. For this reason, Requa and Cory imply that the U.S. Reclamation Service's 160-acre limitation on federal projects (i.e., the "governmental attack" in the quote) is fallacious and off the mark. On the industrial farm, there would be no "plant hazards," no "plant obsolescence;" with crop rotation and well-maintained ditches and dams, deterioration would be negligible. Factoring in depreciation and upkeep, Requa and Cory add, this sort of farm would cost less than the rolling stock of railways and be more profitable.

On other kinds of farms, the problem was that they were run inefficiently by "the inefficient":

> A little thought explains this. In the cities the inefficient gravitate into the ranks of some branch of the industrial army and are directed, superintended, disciplined, forced into rigid routine, and constrained. In the country they are independent, reporting to no one, receiving no orders and few suggestions; following their own inclinations and judgments, except as they may be led thereby into such hopeless disaster as to lose their plants [i.e., farms] and be cast into the wage earning class. The wonder really is . . . that so large a proportion are able to keep their plants at all. It speaks volumes as to the profitable nature of the industry itself. (103)

Here, they imply that inefficient farmers *ought* to be disciplined into rigid routine and that farm failure is purely the responsibility of the individual—the changing structure of agriculture would seem to have little to do with it.

What, then, should one do if in possession of a large tract of irrigable land? Rather than *speculating* in it—in other words, selling it off to a bunch of individuals who would make a few improvements and resell it piecemeal to bank-mortgaged consumers—developers should *invest* in the property. How better to do this than to convert the land into a large, scientifically and expertly managed farm, hiring as wage laborers people who would otherwise be "illy able financially and probably mentally" (112) to manage for themselves a small farm. The model for the new agriculture, then, is the corporate one. But it is not even that simple, for by the time we have reached the end of the plan, Requa and Cory's rhetoric brings us full circle to a more people-centered orientation. The "Syndicate Farm" is in fact the path "back to the land":

> The true solution follows from the following facts:
>
> 1. Many people with very little capital and experience in irrigated farming are really obsessed with the desire to own and live on a California orchard and vineyard, or small farm.
>
> 2. Some of these live in crowded American cities and towns, some on American farms, and some in Germany, Italy and Portugal. The first two classes particularly would be affected greatly by pioneering hardships. The third class would probably have to be, for a period at least, guided and directed in the methods applicable to California conditions and given considerable advice for several years after coming to California.

3. Few of all these people could even consider buying land or would be sufficiently responsible or trained in the business to justify leasing to them.

4. All would gladly pay considerable in excess of the market price, everything considered, for a farm in complete cultivation, all pioneer work done—civic centers, marketing agencies, social life, etc.—and make the first payment by a proportion regularly held out of their wages over a period of several years. During this period they would also be being trained in the business, and the good sifted out from the useless and indifferent.

5. In farming, as in other lines, there is a marked tendency for men to do as their neighbors, resulting in local overproduction of one crop this year, underproduction next year, etc. Prices depend upon supply and demand, and a central *czar-like* corporation, strong financially, could steer a far more profitable course than a lot of unorganized, or even wonderfully well organized, farmers in the matter of crop selection and marketing, just as well as in construction, buying, etc., etc.

The conclusion follows that the best plan is to buy the land; put water on it; build all roads, civic centers, packing houses, etc.; establish an efficient marketing organization; attract and hold the best class of labor by a combination bonus-reserve system; farm all the land as quickly and intensively as possible . . . ; as bonus-reserves become large enough to justify, lease small acreages to each good man . . . and have such leases contain option for purchase on easy terms.

Such procedure would have several distinct advantages. It would provide a selected lot of settler, which, together with the *subconscious control* afforded over the men, would practically entirely prevent failures on the tracts. *This is a feature of vital importance.* Next, it would insure high prices for lands sold, and entirely eliminate the selling costs. . . . It would do away with all the hardships of "pioneering," and result in producing model communities—physical and sociological—quickly, with little or no economic waste. By buying additional land from time to time to replace that sold, the Syndicate Farm would continue as long as desired, and at the same time be generally regarded as an effective "back to the land" . . . agency as much as a Syndicate. (112–15, emphasis added)

Note that there is no mention whatsoever, in item 2 above, of Asian and Mexican laborers who are already in California agriculture. Many of Requa and Cory's suggestions are beguilingly similar to practices that were simultaneously being tried at Delhi and Durham. But, nearly every planning mechanism that the state put in place would, in Requa and Cory's arrangement, be supplanted by the market. The market would even accomplish the dirty work of labor discipline, separating the efficient from the inefficient. The large farm modeled after capitalist social relations would not be a transitional structure in California agriculture, according to Requa and Cory, but an essential institution out of which small farms might be hived off, with the large czar-like farm as a sort of company store selling small acreages at premium prices.[5]

In certain respects, Requa and Cory's recommendations were based on real and known elements of 1910's capital-intensive agriculture: thousands of small farms, but concentration of landownership; wage labor on the farm, but not all earmarked for farm ownership. That they should embrace these aspects of California agriculture and not condemn them seems to be a bold move. But it is not bold at all considering the question they really had in mind: How should capital be used, and what social relations might be appropriate for its use? In this, they were really no different than the editors at the *Pacific Rural Press.* But Requa and Cory did go a step further. The *Press* saw farmers as capitalists inviolate. Requa and Cory would rather not have so many little capitalists scurrying all over the place—California needed fewer, more coordinated capitalists. They wanted an agriculture that would really pay. They were less concerned with farmers' weakening position in a diversifying industrial economy (i.e., declining purchasing power) and more concerned with moving industrial capitals onto the farm, where, under proper management, it could thrive even better than in urban factories. All "natural obstacles" aside, they wanted to redeem agriculture for investors and to make it the best investment that could be made.

## Variable Capitalists All: Capitalist Laborers and the Fictions of Capital in Country and City

What I have named rural realism finds its place somewhere between Requa and Cory's vision of capital as the prime mover on the land and Elwood Mead's vision of hard-working, white, family proprietors. Indeed, these visions are already combinations of each other. Requa and Cory sought legitimacy for their plan by making allowances for family farms through bonus-reserves. Elwood Mead knew full well that family farmers, if they were to be an inviolable, white-California institution, needed investors (the state in this case) and *needed to be good investors* of loan capital once in possession of it. In rural realism, no vision of agriculture prevails unless it is also a vision of circulating capital, but no vision of agriculture as circulating capital prevails unless it leaves room for an alternative social relation outside the industrial norm. Where exactly does this leave the California farmer? This is a contradiction, I would say, that stalks every text we have looked at thus far, and more.

In Jack London's back-to-the-land novel *The Valley of the Moon*, Billy and Saxon, a white working-class couple, who tire of endless rounds of battle between capital and labor in Oakland, California, set out to find a small farm and independence. With Billy picking up seasonal farm work here and there, they "tramp" (the verb is significant for it defines their class position in the countryside) all through the Bay Area's rural hinterland to find their land. But the self-made vision that Billy and Saxon have in mind gets dispelled. At the end of the novel, Billy is given these instructions: "You must use your head. Let others do the work. You must understand that thoroughly. The wages of superintendence are always larger than the wages of the laborers. You must keep books. You must know where you stand. You must know what pays and what doesn't, and what pays best. Your books will tell that" (London 1913: 179). The denouement nicely defines California agriculture's contradictory location that I raised at the beginning of this chapter (and put in slightly different words in the paragraph above), that agriculture is figured both as the means for wage workers to move into ownership status and as the mandate to become an employer of wage workers. Here are two wage workers, then, who will be moving into farm ownership and who, by virtue of the search for maximum turnover of their capital, are about to become employers of workers themselves.

Quick to fetishize the country life, to put the representation before the real, Jack London whispers not a word as to the irony that, in his formulation, California agriculture can't absorb all the Billys and Saxons of the world, just this Billy and this Saxon (or who knows how many more before there's no one to do the work anymore). The searing class analysis with which the novel begins ends as a perfect formula for how class gets its start. What allows this contradiction to stand? It is not only the countryside fetish, which does indeed have real force in American letters, but the peculiar cultural location that rural realism gives the farmer. I would suggest that the contradiction stands because the alternative that agriculture offers to the industrial model is that *the wage worker has the opportunity to become the capitalist who still remains a laborer.* Billy does still have to work, after all. The advice he gets is overstated, for he controls his capital by "using" his head and "keeping" books. (We may draw this conclusion because of what Billy himself learns to think of as the real model to follow: the "Chinks" and "Portugeeze" that he both reviles and admires, because they have used their heads *and* hands to create fabulously productive and remunerative truck farms on farms smaller than the 160-acre homesteading norm.) Rural realist discourse about the California farmer is a discourse about a hybrid beast who emerges out of the circulations of capital—a laborer who in possession of money becomes the capitalist who, still tied to a division of labor, remains a laborer.

Circulating capital makes not only for vulgar, basic economic exchanges, then, but also for exchanges of social and cultural locations. But this involves not just capitalist-laborer farmers, for circulation, as the first two chapters discussed, ties the countryside to the city, where other workers, quite remote from the farm, may through the aegis of circulation also enjoy their status as capitalist laborers in the agrarian scene.

Let us look at three pieces of short fiction published in 1891 (Ten Broeck 1891a, 1891b, 1891c). These are of particular relevance here for three reasons: (1) They describe the development of rural California through the optic of urban-based investment. (2) They plot circulation through very specific class-, race-, and gender-located functionaries. One story features women from the working and middle classes; another is populated with "uneducated" male factory workers, while the third concerns a group of upwardly mobile, young, white male professionals. (3) They were written for and published by the Occidental Fruit Company, a short-lived, San Francisco–based developer of agricultural land in the San Joaquin Valley (A. H. Ten Broeck, who wrote the stories, was a company officer and stockholder).[6] The stories were essentially niche-market advertisements for the company's stock, but they were advertisements that have to be read as stories.

The first story, "A Bright Idea and What Came of It," introduces two "bright and attractive young ladies"—Catherine Peabody, a "descendant of the best New England ancestry" recently arrived in California, and Rica Holmes, daughter of a California pioneer, "a lively, impulsive girl, without much education, but brave and ambitious" (6). Peabody works as a teacher and Holmes as an employee of the United States Mint in San Francisco. It is Peabody who brings up the subject of what they ought to do with their savings. "'Investment?'" Holmes replies. "'Of course you have more to invest than I, but I have given up trying to save money; not that I ever tried very much. . . . [O]nce in a spasm of recklessness I concluded that the miserable little four per cent which it brought me did not begin to pay for the self-denial'" (4). Peabody replies that she has found out about a "'plan by which even small savings may be so invested as to produce in the aggregate a very handsome return'" (4). This investment is in the production of California fruits. "'[H]ere is a prospectus of a corporation which sells shares of stock payable in installments, and you may have as much or as little as you wish or can pay for'" (5). Peabody assures Holmes that they do not have to actually perform any labor—"'The work is done for us by thoroughly competent and reliable men'" (5). The women decide to gather a group of their friends to purchase a block of shares large enough to give one of them a seat on the board of directors. The first meeting of the group is a lesson to the majority about investment in stocks. Peabody is the spokeswoman:

> I have here . . . the announcement of a business so planned and organized as to render it available, not only to the rich or to men of business, but to those of small means, to clerks, artisans, laborers, in fact, to all who have saved a little money or are earning more than sufficient to meet their daily wants. . . . Each share of stock in this company represents one acre of the best land to be obtained for the purpose, planted to grape vines or peach, plum, prune or pear trees, and in full bearing. . . . Such land will pay from year to year a good income on a valuation of from five hundred to a thousand dollars an acre. (7–8)

When several of the women voice suspicions, Peabody convinces them that there really is no risk involved at all. The project's success is assured because the "'directors are men well known in the business world'" and because similar businesses are prospering elsewhere in California (9).

After the "hen convention" breaks up, the women are described as carrying on, over the next several days, with a "great deal of buzzing . . . wherever two or three were gathered together during the next few days." "A week later the pretty parlor was filled with an eager and excited group . . . and it was not late when the assembly took on the appearance of an orderly business meeting" (11). After five years, the investments have produced palpable results. Peabody and Holmes, the latter to wed "a young man of standing, character and good business prospects," have purchased a house in Mill Valley, a small satellite town of San Francisco (15). Another of their group has become widowed but lives comfortably with her children on the dividends of her investment. There is, too, in the conclusion of the story, the suggestion that what started as one small, isolated circuit of capital has now ramified, for the initial investments made by the women have generated an income that has been invested in other financial institutions. "The savings-banks and building associations have not been neglected, and other enterprises of a similar nature to this we have been depicting have been promoted" (14).

The next story, "How They Did It," begins with a conversation among some employees of "——— Iron Works." As in the first story, one character, having caught wind of the Occidental Fruit Company, asks another whether he has been saving any money. Both agree that the savings they do have draw only a small interest in the local savings bank but that at least those savings are secure. "The same evening the back-room at the grocery store, which served as a sort of club-room, was filled with the usual crowd from the Works." One of their number, Watson, describes the "proposition" to the gathering. After emphasizing that the men behind the fruit corporation are all of good standing, he notes that "'The clerks in the office [of the Iron Works] and some of the foremen in the different departments are going into it, and there is no reason why those of us who have the money can't do the same'" (3). The same protests raised in the first story are brought up again and subsequently, similarly, argued away: the success of other land development and farming companies—proof that the "general attention is turned in that direction" (3)—will assure the success of the company they are interested in; no other investment is both as safe and as remunerative as investment in California agriculture; California has yet to begin to saturate the ready market for fresh and dried fruit. Unique among the three stories, this one has characters—honest Hans Kruger, an unnamed canny Scot, an unnamed Irishman (father of seven), and a slur-speeched drunk named Hanks—who speak in "dialect." Dialect serves not only to mark the advertisement as a "local color" story. (This is an important move, though, for in appropriating a popular style, the company identifies its story as a "story" to be read. The advertisement can be hidden behind the very form it takes.) Dialect also codifies the very social and economic space where surplus funds are available. It signifies both deficit of education and surpluses of capital that *both* need to be disciplined. That the dialect can be represented at all signifies in a quite material way that Occidental knows of a particular market to target. These characters are available not only for representation but also for their surplus consumer dollars.

Unlike the first story, though, there is an opportunity for the men who do not have savings to invest to work as laborers in the fields owned by Occidental. This is especially appealing to Hanks, the drunkard. Watson explains:

> "They want men on this land. They will give you $30 per month and board. You have clothes enough to last a year or more. Go up there and subscribe for five shares of stock. I know you have a little money, but if you hadn't I think they would trust you if you are a steady man. Knock off drinking, and at the end of a year you will have five shares of stock, probably paid for, and just as much money left as you would have had here. If you are the man I take you for, you can get a job as foreman the second year, and can take five shares more, pay for them and have something besides. Then your fortune is made, for after that you'll have your dividends, and with what you will earn you can soon have a ranch of your own."
>
> "Betchyer life I'll do it," said Hanks. "I allers did have a hankerin' after the soil. Where's the recruitin' ossifer?"
>
> And he did.

This passage has a special meaning, which traces back to the story's opening dialogue. Two factory employees have begun to talk about saving money, when one says, "'I've been thinking of a plan that Watson was speaking to me about the other night. He has got hold of a prospectus of some sort of a co-operative company that has bought a big tract of land, and is planting it out in trees and vines . . .'" His coworker cuts him off. "'Don't think I want to turn farmer. I know a sight more about blacksmithing . . .'" The first character replies, "'[T]here is no occasion for you to turn farmer. You can stick to your forge, and have some one who likes it to do your plowing and pruning'" (1–2). There is more than a hint that working the land would be a regression for these characters—it is already a kind of penalty for the drunkard and would smack of a return to escaped origins for the rest. The city is decidedly their best alternative. For the purposes of the story, it has to be their best alternative since these characters are the producers of urban surpluses that Occidental seeks to redistribute into its own operations. What the characters need to be convinced of, then—and they are at the end—is the *homology* of city and countryside that takes place on the level of circulating capital.

The last story, "Over a Late Cigar," is set in San Francisco's Union-Pacific Club, "that locally-famous and aristocratic rendezvous of the gilded youth of the metropolis of the Pacific Coast" (1). The by-this-point familiar announcement of the Occidental Fruit Company's prospectus comes from an unlikely corner in the person of Mr. Gregory Henderson, the most gilded of the gilded bunch, who spends his time in stuporous anticipation of his trust fund. We catch him in the middle of a tirade against Jack, one of his associates.

> You've no business to follow my example, I tell you. I have nothing else to do, and if I had I wouldn't do it. . . . As for you, old fellow, you will be crawling down to Pine street about ten o'clock with a splitting headache and an awful uncertainty as to where the cash is to come from to pay for all this . . . [Y]ou're a fool, and there are a dozen other just like you in this room. . . . What business have Smith and Jones and Brown and Robinson to be here playing poker and bucking the tiger? Where do they get the money to pay their losses? As for me, my old father made enough, and tied it up, too, where I can't touch the principal. . . . But when I think of you young men in California, not only throwing your money and yourselves away on this cursed round of dissipation, but throwing away glorious opportunity of developing the grandest country the Lord ever made, as well as making no end of money for yourselves, it simply puts me in a rage. . . . Some of you fellows might handle the world's supply in many different lines, might control commerce vaster than we have yet dreamed of as possible, if you would only leave off being idiots and begin to be men. (2–3)

Once again, the suggested means toward that end is investment in Occidental, for there is "'more wealth in California's soil than has ever come from her mines or ever will'" (5). Henderson gives the example, learned while on an excursion to California's fecund Central Valley, of "'a little man, better known in San Francisco as an M.D. than as a land sharp'" (4), but who "'has successfully floated no less than half a dozen'" agricultural corporations (6). It is with this recounting that Henderson exhorts Jack and his kind to "'Make your own capital'" (4) by purchasing stock in Occidental. To not do so, or to not invest in something that "'has for its object the progress and development of his own section,'" would be "'criminally negligent'" (6).

The promotional fiction of the Occidental Fruit Company imagines many social spaces as one through the medium of money. The characters are identified through their distinct but signature domains: women gathering in the domestic parlor; working-class men loitering in the back room of the neighborhood grocery; young, mostly upper-middle-class men (a rung or two below the trust fund) assembling at the club. All of these domains are, moreover, leisure domains, antithetical to labor and the workplace. By their very existence, they signify the probability of surplus, the something extra that, although created out of production, has not returned to production. These domains serve to map out the itinerant geography of money. Just as people idle in the spaces of leisure, so their money takes leisure in the vaults of their savings banks. Occidental's aim is to bring cash that has thus far circulated only inefficiently in the banks into more efficient, because more profitable, circulation.

A covert but overarching plot cumulatively builds as all the stories' characters "discover" the investment opportunity. The meta-narrative, however, is that a corporation trying to raise capital has discovered them. Money (i.e., the corporation) seeks people out and routs them from their customary positions of leisure. (I will say more on this below.) Money, in other words, has no signature space: It brings both the city and the countryside into a unified circuit of capital, it lays claim to all social and cultural space as potentially its own economic space.

While celebrating the union of city and countryside, the stories also celebrate the fact that the investors need not leave San Francisco in order to enjoy rural fruits. Why would they want to leave, when their money can leave for them? Like the California farmer, they can be capitalist laborers, working and circulating their money through workers. But if it is possible for laborers (all but one of the Union-Pacific Club boys are still laborers) to also be investors, the stories are not in the business of exposing *how* investment and labor are integrated in the lives of individual worker-characters. They certainly come to the reader as thinking and acting subjects, but in political economy, they are also means of production. We ought to ask, that is, what the story allows these characters to be? What does it allow them to think? They are put in situations where they think about a process in which they do not see themselves. A whole vision of the capitalist economic formation is laid out before these fictional workers, but it is represented in a way that discourages their self-identification as workers who embody someone else's investment. They have no way to get out of this loop, only a way to explore and move back and forth amidst the circuitry of finance, production, and consumption. Indeed, for strategically symbolic reasons, the promotional narratives must contain the characters' identities in their social spaces of leisure. For precisely there may they identify themselves with their own consumption dollars and then move on to think of themselves as capitalists with capital.

Consider, too, that each story appeals to investors in the Occidental Fruit Company on grounds that have to do with specific class and gender concerns. Here is containment, and predation, of another kind. In the first story, for women with a small savings to invest, the returns on their investments will lessen risks that women, in particular, face. One woman is saved from destitution when she is widowed. When another wins a husband, it is implied that her extra income has boosted her into a class position suitable for marriage to a man of "standing." The returns to still another character are a substitute for her not having snagged a husband at all: Where a husband might have provided her with an income, her investment in Occidental now ensures that she lives in a "comfortable house on an eligible lot in the Western Addition [of San Francisco]" (14). Whether a woman is single or betrothed, debutante or spinster, wife or widow, she potentially has a need that money can fill and men cannot. If she courts no one or nothing else, she must court money. If she is eligible to no one else, she is eligible to money throughout every phase of her life, to the degree that the ways in which she needs and uses money are represented as definitive of the kinds of broader relationships with society that the woman as individual can expect, or is constructed to expect, to have. As for capital, it is necessary that woman reinvent herself in terms of her economic potential. She must be disabused of the notion that she will be taken care of by anything else but money.

For the ethnically diverse men of the second story, Occidental appeals to them because they have wives and children to provide for. (Women, it will be recalled, don't save, because they can't stop spending.) Unlike most of the women in the first narrative, these men are fully aware of the imperative to save money. If Occidental's job in the first story was to educate women as to how much *more* isolated and alienated women ought to feel, then in order for Occidental to be convincing to working-class men, it must lord over them the sense of isolation and alienation that they already have. "'How's a fellow going to save any money these days,'" asks one man, "'with strikes, small wages, sick wife, and all?'" (4). As far as their construction as working-class males goes, what is at risk is that they could lose what they already have, which is to say that it is familiar to us that they should possess the "things" they do. For the women of the first story, risk is less a matter of loss and largely a matter of not attaining everything that they might. Money, as I have suggested, substitutes for this, but given the range of women characters we encounter, we might expect that women have everything or nothing at all. More to the point, perhaps, is the extent to which the women are defined more in terms of gender and the men more in terms of class. Readers of the Occidental stories are meant to understand that most of the women's need for money stems from who they are as a gender; whereas, the working-class men's need for money stems from who they are as a class.

The last narrative relies for its meaning on the gendered identities and forms of economic consciousness constructed in the first two narratives. The emasculated men of the Union-Pacific (emasculated because they, too, can't stop spending), immersing themselves in rounds of dissipation and, fittingly enough, talking "Over a Late Cigar," are like many of the women in "A Bright Idea": Both groups lack economic consciousness. Once this consciousness is accessed, however, the consequences for each group, could not be more different. The gilded lads have only to shape up, dry out, and survey the land, and the continent will be theirs. That it should not be anyone else's (neither the women's nor the working-class men's) constitutes the "moral" grounds of Occidental's plea for "gentlemen" to invest. Where the women and the working-class men need to stop throwing away their money so that they can secure their class position (they are to be capitalist *laborers)*, the lads need to stop throwing away their class (they are to be *capitalist* laborers).

Another point might be raised about this last narrative. Why should it be that the character with the news about the Occidental stock is someone who doesn't need it himself and who, in fact, explicitly tells us that he's not going to bother with it? Whereas the authority of the narrator in the other two stories serves to buttress the selling points, the authority of this main character who stands in as the narrator (the third story is nearly all monologue) would seem to be suspect. He's got money, and he's obviously a loafer. What will prevent the young men who are being urged to make money from becoming loafers too? Has not Occidental incriminated itself by stating explicitly that money corrupts? If so, and if that is not a desirable effect, then how much money is too much? The ideological work of the stories is to never answer that question. It is instead to only identify where money has not yet been made; to go about colonizing those locations; and to shift the terrain of our interrogation to the notion of California's "development."

But there is essential ideological work also being done on class. How much money is *too much* might be difficult to define, but how much is *enough* is another question. "Enough" is the amount required to ameliorate class distinctions altogether. (Remember, the workers in "How They Did It" are on the threshold of disaffection from the California dream.) *The whole point of the stories is to critique the idea of pure class locations and to present this critique to labor.* In these stories, that is, pure laborers must suffer (Hanks might "turn farmer") and pure capitalists like Gregory Henderson are insufferable.[7]

Occidental was not alone in this ideological gambit. Consider the California Board of Bank Commissioners. "We do not think the depositors in savings banks, as a general thing, appreciate the importance of their influence in our social economy." The Commissioners go on to quote approvingly from a report on savings banks in New York:

> Whatever the purposes of the founders of savings banks in their inception, in their result, as a practical fact to-day, they have outgrown their early distinctive character as charitable institutions, and take their place proudly in the front rank among the great powers of the social state. . . . In the old systems of public economy mankind was divided into two classes, the capitalist and the laborer, but through the agency of savings banks, in later years, our political economy must be written anew, for behold, the laborers have become the capitalists in this new world! Thirty-one millions [of dollars] of the earnings of the poor are loaned to the rich on bond and mortgage in this state. . . . Savings banks are revealed as a sort of cooperative union of the industrial classes. Their savings aggregated as capital minister to public enterprises, and these public enterprises demand laborers for their prosecution, and thus return to labor in the form of wages what they have borrowed from it in the form of capital. . . . Other "unions" are formed as combinations of labor *against* capital, but here is a combination of labor *and* capital. The former seeks to control the price of labor by arbitary [sic] dicta; the latter affects the price of labor, favorably, through the operation of natural laws. (California Board 1880: 18–19)

The only problem, noted the Commissioners, was that California savings banks habitually accepted exceptionally large deposits from single individuals, thus putting at risk the other depositors should those individuals falter or withdraw their money. The only other problem, according to the captains at Occidental, was that banks weren't circulating savings capital aggressively enough.

Clearly, a similar rhetoric drives the narratives of Occidental, which combine to make a single story about how the "needs" of a particular company to accumulate capital coincide with the needs of a diverse set of individuals, defined by the class and gender locations of those individuals. Counterposed to social divisions, in other words, is the unity of money as a system that finds ways to appropriate across all divisions simultaneously. Money is the imagined community and is the medium through which trans-class/gender/ethnicity community formation becomes imaginable by bourgeois inductive reason: Various economic "needs" and wants, including Occidental's, are represented as autonomously arising, rather than as outcomes of the way that capital is produced and distributed in the first place.

## Coda: The Labor of Fiction

In what sense, though, does it matter that these advertisements are presented as stories? That is, in Occidental's ad-fiction, we have an intersection between company talk and literary structure. What difference do they make to each other? In answer, I'd like to venture four speculations.

1. Commodity producers depend upon their ability to manufacture or identify a consumer's sense of deficiency, which the purchase of commodities promises to overcome. This *is* the act of turning people into consumers. The Occidental stories identify some of those deficiencies and describe how they might be overcome, in the process identifying the sort of reader they are looking for. This construction of an "implied reader," as Wolfgang Iser calls it, is carried to its very limits (Iser 1974). What is essentially one story about the "community" of money is divided into three, each one populated by characters meant to correspond with the category of reader that the characters themselves represent. Thus, the structure of the advertisement imposes itself upon the structure of the story: The population of implied readers are the very characters that populate the stories. And any gap between reader and character is occupied by, and only by, the commodity.

2. Realist and, especially, local color, regionalist conventions of late-nineteenth-century literary representation, whether found in William Dean Howells or Sarah Orne Jewett, are potentially compatible with the aims and strategies of making a sale. The key idea, if we follow Richard Brodhead's history of the period, is of ineluctable differences of types and classes of American people (Brodhead 1993). Characters in the novel and in short fiction—strongly identified by their differences, along class, ethnicity, and gender axes—represent the very types of individuals whose savings Occidental wants. There is, in other words, a hugely enabling commonality between the literary imagining of "local" characters—that is, characters of difference—and the market identification of potential consumers. Just as Occidental conceptualizes unique sorts of purchasers and reads them through literature's logic of locality, different demographic groups are asked by Occidental to imagine the alternative circuits into which their earnings might enter. (Is there not more than a rhetorical parallel between Occidental's characters of difference and Adams's laborers of difference? To capital, each group is articulated to a double strategy: to amass as a "first cut" and to differentiate as a "second cut.") The efforts that Occidental made in ferreting out these consumer groups, whom it urges to purchase stock, have, moreover, a parallel in Occidental seeking to put their money in a place where they would not have thought to put it. Occidental has sought a monetarily undeveloped cohort in order to develop an undeveloped place. Nineteenth-century literature, with its emphasis on the different figures of everyday life, as well as the figures who represent those differences, has already done parallel work of theorizing about the structures of consumption based upon class, ethnicity, and gender.

3. Late-nineteenth-century authors strove to write fiction that had the aura of the true, the honest, the authentic (Borus 1989). Occidental had something like the very same task—to convince readers that what the characters experienced, they could experience too. Occidental plays with that boundary. Its promotional literature must actually be more real than actual *literature*: "While the reader may look upon this as a fancy sketch, there is nothing in it which is not authentic; the

examples given are from actual experience; what has been set down here has been done and can be done again" ("A Bright Idea," 15). But, the stories get to be more real, in the first place, only by occupying the space in which actual *literature* seeks to be, and convey, the "real."

4. The stories construct parallels between reading and investing one's money: Each of these activities is framed in opposition to labor. If reading can only occur at the *end* point of labor, and is made possible by laborer-readers having labored for leisure time, the Occidental stories situate reading as a crucial *beginning,* one through which the worker gains access to the sphere where money is produced without having to labor. Put another way, where money makes reading possible, reading makes more money possible. But reading is also an ideological divide that can hide capital's recuperation of surplus value. If reading (as leisure) and labor (as the production of surplus value) are mutually exclusive, then investment that is spun out of acts of leisure-reading is a way for capital to recuperate those energies into the formation of more surplus value. Marx would remind us that in leisure labor reproduces itself. The commodification of leisure is then a strategy by which capital can cash in on what is ostensibly "downtime." In exchange for reminding workers that leisure hours are not really their own (characters' signature spaces have been invaded; readers have been given an advertisement in place of a story), Occidental proposes a method for workers to profit from their own production of surplus value. But they are never to equate, as the stewed and pickled Hanks surely never will, labor performed and surplus value produced. Investment, in the narratives, constitutes a separate economy, wholly unconnected to labor. The function of the ad, prior to inducing the sale of stock, is to commodify the act of reading. If the only gap between the characters and the implied reader is occupied by the commodity purchased by the characters (and not yet by the reader), then the first step in bridging the gap is to commodify leisure, reading, itself.

Rural realism, I have been arguing, is the discursive terrain that grew out of incommensurate agrarian visions, one that placed agriculture within the firmament of circulating capital and one that named it as an alternative to social relations of industrial capitalism. The figure of the capitalist laborer is a construction that allowed these divergent visions to combine. The Occidental stories are interesting, I think, in that they extend that figure to the urban realm, which is then figured as a source of capital for agricultural investment. They provide, on the one hand, a good example of the land-development companies that regularly appeared in the late nineteenth century, precursors to those that would sell their wares later on the bond market. But, they are, on the other hand, highly instructive of how accessible literary tropes were for economic plots. (In the chapters that follow, this is made abundantly clear; as is the reverse—that literary devices were convenient tools for scolding capital for its excesses.) Capitalist laborers in the Occidental narratives were inextricably imagined through particular enabling literary structures, just as Adams's constructions gain their authoritativeness in the pages of a textbook, or just as the *Pacific Rural Press,* as the *press,* always constructs its position as the last word.

The figure of the capitalist laborer is a figure with a gaping hole in the middle, however. There is one question that refuses to go away. Why couldn't farmworkers, like the city workers in the Occidental stories, also be capitalist laborers? The answer, perhaps, is that the capitalist laborer, constructed out of rural-realist discourse, is subject to the constraints set by that discourse. In the white bourgeois imagination, or at least that faction of it concerned with issues of class mobility, we might say that the California farm was supposed to be different. There was not supposed to be a permanent wage force in California agriculture, or at least it was not supposed to be white. The *Pacific Rural Press* practically balked at the question of a permanent labor supply: Certainly, white labor would not stand for it, and non-white labor seemed to tolerate it only on a permanent *trial* basis. It was a necessary evil, which if remedied would compete with white farm labor for capitalist-laborer status. Non-white labor was only with rare exception supposed to be upwardly mobile. Signs of farmworker upward mobility were countered more than once by exclusionary legislation. Another answer may simply be that it is useful for a capitalist society to be able to offer contradictory locations, to offer a change of roles, with respect to circulating capital, without a change in mode of production and in the basic rules of surplus value creation. It is useful to be able to address class differences not through changes in the rules of production but through the mechanisms of circulation and through the production of cultural "welfare"—through stories we can tell each other about our chances, our achievements, our dreams for a better competitive edge. Let us say, however, that it was not useful *enough* to extend that vision to non-white others in California in the places where their labor power was purchased on the color line.

What makes Occidental's fictions unique among those that I explore in part two is that they were specifically intended to sell something. They exist in the last instance only to sell. If the novels that I engage later are not advertisements in the strict sense, the Occidental stories no less suggest a tendency of the novels, which are not so much promotion pieces as they are promotional. Fiction need not be an advertisement, need not be corporate authored to advance the platform of agro-economic accumulation. While I hasten to add that arguments for agro-economic growth were highly varied and launched by many individuals and groups whose specific interests and class positions made them contradictory, in the main, such growth was the platform upon which the novels stood. *Then* followed the questions of means and distribution of wealth, of agency and access in the structures of rural society that the novels explore.

But while there was such an evincing of concern with the sources of social and economic value, the Occidental narratives and the novels, as I hope to lay out, bear out the historicity of that concern. For example, what marks the stories by Occidental in particular (and some of the novels I treat later) is the overriding ideological, rhetorical emphasis on money as a nearly autonomous social force with tremendous powers. This very emphasis allows us to historicize them. For soon came a time when there was not enough money in the right places and at the right moments for it to be so vested. Although the Occidental stories were published in 1891, the company did not actually incorporate until 1904, apparently having had to ride out the 1890s depression. As if this were not enough, though, the incorporation papers filed by Occidental with the State of California bear a stamp that tells us that, in the fall of 1906, the company's charter was forfeited for failure to renew the business license, due most likely to the San Francisco earthquake in the spring of that year (Occidental 1904).

# PART II

# EXCAVATING GEOGRAPHICAL IMAGINATIONS

### Many Countrysides

The stories published by the Occidental Fruit Company suggest that representations of the countryside, the city, and capitalist economy are refracted by the forms that representation and discourse take. In the following chapters, I wish to explore these relationships much more closely, focusing on the California novel and developing the argument that it matters that discourse was shaped within novels and through certain sorts of plots.

Human geography, I will be arguing, also matters. Most of the remaining chapters present some episode of regional change within California and then a reading of two or more works of fiction. Regional transformations of economy and society were not simply the background to these novels, however. They were the crucibles in which were formed the discourses to which the novels give expression. The difference in putting it this way is that California literature can be seen as a historical, geographical artifact itself. This argument has an important repercussion for what we do with a novel. It is less important here to evaluate the quality of a work on the basis of whether it tells the truth about some historical event, or whether it sells as highbrow literature, than it is to see the discourse within the work as a historical, socially produced "event." The novel and discourse, then, while situated, are not true-or-false. They are always true, and cannot be otherwise.

Because it is a purpose of the remaining chapters to particularize in various ways the basic trends set forth in part one, let us now quickly bring these into view. The development of irrigation, though it came in fits and starts—having been interrupted by the 1890s depression—marked a radical change for rural California. It enabled farmers to convert their land to specialty crops (although as Ellen Liebman reminds us, it did not dictate that they would convert). It made farming possible where none had been before, on millions of acres of arid and semi-arid land, yet also reinforced the imperative of the market and the commodity. Irrigation required unprecedented amounts of money and finely tuned financial mechanisms. Although it made small-scale agriculture and subdivision possible, it also raised the cost of doing business, a change that was also due to the need for a seasonal wage-labor market. Irrigated agriculture tended to be a labor-intensive agriculture. To feed this need, California relied upon an international division of labor that connected the west coast of the United States to Asia and Latin America. California agriculture was not simply a matter of farmers' needs, though. The very seasonality of agricultural production times drew forth the credit industry, especially the state's bankers, who were able to insert their capital into the seasonal production and working time disunities. In this way, farmers and farms were quite rigorously employed *by* creditors for circulation of their capital. Farmers came to rely on these sorts of creditor investments, such that they expanded their production during periods of rising prices and easy credit, only to feel the pinch during periods of economic crisis—not only in the 1890s depression but after the world war. As agriculture came to depend more and more on the purchase of a whole constellation of inputs—such as water, land, credit, fertilizer, nursery-stock, specialized tools—the stability of middle-class and poorer farmers, and working- and middle-class access to farming, were steadily threatened with erosion. Thus, despite some movement toward democratization of landownership early in the irrigation phase, including the movement of Asian farmers into farm-owner or operator status, land and water fell back under the control of concentrated economic power in the 1910s and '20s. Concentration of powers extended even into the cooperatives organized by many of California's specialty-crop producers. Despite wholly new methods of credit and distribution, which eliminated the role of powerful middlemen-merchants, a power structure dominated by the large growers remained intact. The existence of wage labor, the periodic instability of the smaller farmer, and the dominance of the large farm operators contributed to years of debate about what sort of social relations ought to prevail in rural California. Yet, despite these fluctuations and social costs, the aggregate of agricultural production and productivity in California soared. It was during these decades between the 1880s and 1920s that the San Francisco Bay Area and Los Angeles both solidified their roles as centers vital to rural development and faced each other as major competitors in financing, food processing, and shipping. As capital poured into Southern California after the collapse of the rancho economy, San Francisco kept a cautious eye on its new competitor (even as San Franciscans were early developers of the region). Unevenness thus came to be expressed in a north/south divide, with the financial establishment of each city seeking to develop the agricultural trade. Moreover, although the cities of San Francisco and Los Angeles entered into a shared social division of labor with rural hinterlands, which was of fundamental importance to each of them, they each also entered into new states of tension with those hinterlands—especially as the search for larger urban water supplies extended farther into the countryside (this will be the subject of chapter 7).[1]

In greater or lesser detail, chapters 4 through 7 take up these themes. Typically, each chapter focuses on a particular moment of capitalist development (usually some crisis that turned a spotlight on the contradictions of high-stakes agricultural development) and the manner of its representation.

In the San Joaquin Valley, taken up in chapter 4, large landholdings were generally the rule. These were established early, partly during the Mexican period, then especially after U.S. conquest in 1848. The process sped up during the 1860s, with state land disposal and the accumulation of capital from gold and silver mining during the 1850s and early 1860s. The large landholding pattern, dominated by the Southern Pacific Railroad and a handful of powerful merchant-growers, was challenged in 1880 by a group of settlers who had squatted on railroad land in protest of the company's title. Violence erupted in the spring of the year at Mussel Slough (Tulare County) when government agents attempted a court-ordered eviction. Although in the immediate vicinity of the incident, large ranches had been broken up into smaller holdings, "Mussel Slough" became synonymous with small farmers' struggles against land monopoly and graft. The inescapable conclusion was that the countryside was as much a scene of struggle with capital as the city.

As described in chapter 5, capitalist social relations entered Southern California along a different course. There, even until statehood in 1850, practically all land was held by Mexican land grantees and used primarily as pasture for a cattle and sheep economy. Following drought and legislation that gnawed away grantee land ownership, Anglo Californians swiftly accumulated enormous quantities of this acreage in the 1860s and 1870s. But the crucial capitalist moment—one centering on the buying and selling of real estate—came after the collapse of the cattle era in the depression of the 1870s. Mass Anglo-American settlement, following the completion of two transcontinental railroad lines to Los Angeles, ushered in a period of frenzied real estate transaction in 1887–88. Land was commodified extraordinarily rapidly. In a decade, it passed from rancho to real estate to orange grove. In the process, thousands of Mexican inhabitants were proletarianized. If in the San Joaquin Valley it seemed that the smallholder could barely get a toehold on the land, in Southern California the market became glutted. Southern California became the scene of a ruralized urbanization, a rush of simultaneous town founding and orchard planting. When it became clear, however, that the nascent fruit economy could not support so many settlers and consequently that there were more sellers of land than buyers, the bottom fell out of the land market. The critics of the 1880s had to face the contradictions of real estate: Though it was an essential capitalist institution that forced a reshaping of the region—cheered by the pundits of manifest destiny—it was no substitute for real agricultural production in the sectoral switch out of a cattle and mining economy.

When the wave of Anglo expansion reached the Imperial Valley, in the southeast corner of the state, the half-dozen Native American groups who claimed this desert region were quickly and unceremoniously rousted out. Occupying a portion of the desiccated Colorado Desert, below sea level, the Imperial Valley was in name and fact an irrigation and real estate scheme (the largest of its kind in the country) organized by engineer-capitalists who called themselves the California Development Company. The aim of the project, discussed in chapter 6, was to sell land and water to a "white" settler class of small farmers who would also be sold hundreds of thousands of acre-feet of water imported from the Colorado River. After a few successful years, the scheme slipped into crisis when the Colorado rampaged into the valley in 1905 and created the Salton Sea (which still sits just inside the southern extreme of the state, swollen by toxic irrigation runoff). The Southern Pacific Railroad stepped in, took over the California Development Company, and, with its own engineers and millions of its dollars, put the river back between the banks. In an era of heated public debate over who should be in charge of a public good like water, the entire episode proved to many observers the primacy of private capital over the resources of the federal and state governments. But it also proved to the agricultural policy establishment, from the head of the United States Reclamation Service on down, that irrigated agriculture had no place for the poor farmer.

Behind these three regional cases was a general expression working its way through the California economy: the economic use of space to absorb capital and relieve pressures derived from the boom and bust nature of capitalism. Large capitals entered the San Joaquin Valley because land purchases there helped to absorb California gold and Comstock silver fortunes. The accumulation of Comstock silver and San Joaquin wheat fortunes, and the decline of hydraulic mining in northern California, redirected investments to Southern California. And, in turn, Southern California real estate money flowed east to the Imperial Valley once the depression of the 1890s had turned around. None of these places developed *wholly* through these particular regional capital transfers (other transfers from other regions—Midwest to Southern California, for example—and the local accumulation of local capital were vital also), but these transfers were nonetheless indicative of capital's geographical imperative. Lest it be overlooked, there was also such a thing as too much capital tied up in particular locales. For example, it is quite possible to argue, and I do (following Richard Orsi's historical analysis), that the railroad "octopus" written about by Frank Norris at the turn of the century had been struggling to come to grips with over-accumulated potential values: land *granted* to it that nonetheless developed skyrocketing opportunity costs unless it could be subdivided and sold.

As surpluses of capital were produced and mobilized for investment, the California economy was reinvented in a new guise and through new places. (The effects of this process were, not surprisingly, recursive. As Southern California's economy grew, for example, it competed with San Francisco for a slice of the San Joaquin Valley trade. The increase in agricultural production in each region, moreover, was an increase in the pressure that all felt to develop and maintain export markets and turn over capital as quickly as possible.)

As treated in the novels covered in chapters 4 through 6, conflicts between city and countryside typically revolve around control of rural surplus values. In the hands of Frank Norris, for example, the San Joaquin Valley is a great battlefield for the control of agricultural modernization. For the writers who turned to the Los Angeles basin, though there was a much more interlocked geography of urban and rural land use, conflict is registered in much the same way. In the Imperial Valley novel, there is perhaps a different emphasis, in that agriculture, though it relies on urban sources of finance, is also figured as an economy that will give rise to a desert urbanization. But the thread that runs through all these episodes is that while farmers may be threatened at times by powerful urban actors, the agricultural economy itself is not; it is the prize. Chapter 7 turns this theme on its head.

This last chapter addresses developments in the early twentieth century that led urban growth coalitions in Los Angeles and San Francisco to turn to the same resource base upon which California agriculture came to depend, water. Along with the Mussel Slough episode, the 1880s land boom, and the Imperial Valley flood, the San Francisco–Hetch Hetchy and Los Angeles–Owens Valley controversies are classic episodes of Californiana. Shortly after the turn of the century, each of these cities sought to increase its water supplies by leapfrogging to the Sierra region for its bountiful snowmelt which collected year after year in its permanent streams. Though the two cities were successful, they fought protracted battles. In the novels that treat of these events, I argue that we see something new in California's literary history: that capital is producing or has produced surplus agricultural landscapes that it can do without.[2]

## The Trials of Capital and Narratives of Social Space

California rural realists, as I will call the novelists, looked to these critical moments of regional restructuring as reference points for their own representations of capital and its social/spatial relations. Contrary to "the fall into Eden," as David Wyatt (1986) has put it, California writers are marked *not* by having had unmediated encounters with "natural" landscape, but by having approached land, or nature, with preconceptions of what the natural was—a space of economic and social conflict—and was to serve—the troubled concerns of an anxious, white bourgeoisie.[3]

My contention is that the rural realists were both enabled and constrained by California's restructuring and its production of nature.[4] That is, just as these writers' purpose was (among a great many other things) to theorize those processes and their effects, the class- and race-based nature of the processes and their effects secreted, to use a favorite word of Lefebvre's, their purpose. The choice of settings and the decisions about where to geographically locate characters evidences an engagement with how capital was pressing into new spaces and then transforming them. These novels show capital *in terms of* its spillage into new rural frontiers, and they show these new rural frontiers *in terms of* capital mobilization. It is because of these writers' willingness to share in the bourgeois engagement with these dialectical conceptions, I think, that the San Joaquin Valley of 1880, Southern California of 1890, and the Imperial Valley of 1905 were popular subjects of choice for novelists who wrote about rural California before the 1930s. I say that these writers' engagements were essentially performed as bourgeois engagements: private property and private accumulation are never once questioned. Indeed, all questions derive *from* these values.

Let us seize on this business of ruralized capital and capitalized ruralism, for it is what marks these novels as written in the rural realist vein. To construct a narrative out of the rural realist stance is to ask a number of questions: What happens to capitalists when they go rural, and *oughtn't* something happen to them anyway? What happens to rural areas when developed by capital, and *oughtn't* something happen to them anyway? What should remain the same and what should be different, and who and what should change in the process? These are all questions that drive the plots of the novels. Yet to categorize this literature as bourgeois is really not enough. The world of the bourgeois is very much a world of difference. Rural realism as developed in the novels suggests that there might be something transgressive about capital's spillage and that there might also be something good about it, something good for capitalist culture and practice and perhaps something good for nature, too. The potential for transgression and change is developed in a plot device employed by every one of the writers: the plunging of some faction of capital into crisis and darkness. Almost never is it a case of this literature swooning over every economic upswing. Capital must have gone to court to prove its case. It's *exchange value v. use value*.

Typically, the novelists placed two groups in opposition. On one side was an alliance of agrarian idealists—farmers and irrigation engineers and/or enlightened financiers who hoped that their irrigation projects would provide farms for the landless. On the other side were usurious middlemen and capitalists—ruthless city bankers or corporations who extracted profits from the countryside and claimed market rationality as justification. Much of the time, though not always, mediating the two sides was an incipient feminism (see chapters 5 through 7)—female protagonists who had double identities as avatars of the contested arid regions and shrewd muses of capitalism. Typically, exchange value wins, but it is figured as the victory of the locale against a non-local competitor. In this way, exchange value is figured *as* use value through the medium of locality fetishes.

The primary arenas over which these actors clashed were the nascent spaces of agricultural production. Carved out of the state's dry regions, these new agricultural hinterlands were nonetheless tied to cities via real estate interests and flows of money. In these spaces, particular questions had to be resolved. Who would control the new region, farmers or middlemen? Would it matter that land, the immutable and idealized wealth of the countryside, was also real estate that could be alienated like all commodities? And questions of money: Who had it and who did not, who wanted it and why? These were central, too. The contradictions of these new spaces filled up all of the novels and created the dilemmas of character and situation that the novelists attempted to resolve with a flexible, agrarian ideology, a dual rhetoric about capital and nature.

As agriculture became more expensive and rationalized, novelists (and journalists and boosters) wrote about the new "scientific agriculture" and the new "businessmen farmers," trying to contain within a single ideological framework the economic imperative of agriculture, as well as a hoped-for rural simplicity. The operative idea, I think, was that of redemption. It was expressed along two axes.

### *Rhetoric One: Capital Redeems Nature*

This rhetoric posited that the state's "arid wastes" actually desired to bear fruit, in a sense that conflated sexual passion and economic passion. In this rhetoric, progressive financiers investing in canals and dams would supposedly make up for nature's deficiencies. The profit motive and the capturing of nature by capital, especially during expansionary episodes, could then be said to be necessary to and functional for the production of the rural. This economic rhetoric, moreover, borrowed the familiar rhetorics of patriarchy and colonialism in order to make chaotic economic relations seem more familiar, and natural.

### *Rhetoric Two: Nature Redeems Capital*

This second rhetoric, associated more with responses to periods of local capitalist crisis, posited that in nature, *because of* nature, an altogether new society would emerge—a white, democratic socio-economy, full of opportunity and free of monopoly capital. The new "natural" economy, unique to the arid regions and reformer of crass capital, would be an antidote to economic turmoil and monopolistic corruption faced by society elsewhere. This alternative rhetoric, which (like the first) devalued and displaced the non-Anglo Other, was an idealization that failed to acknowledge the inheritance and reproduction of power relations within the new economy.

Because the rural realists were attuned to the transitional nature of the capitalist economy, as it moved in and out of crisis, both rhetorics were often found in the same novel—which is to say that narrative fiction *is suited* to this purpose.[5] In chapter 3, I introduced the figure of the capitalist laborer as the figure who lives out the contradictory location of agriculture. I believe we ought to view the rhetorics above in a similar sort of way, for they too mark a contradiction solved by agriculture. Agriculture represents capital mending nature and nature mending capital. (The capitalist laborer is the capitalist mended by his labors and the laborer mended by his capital.) Nature needs capital so as to complete its nature. Capital needs nature so as to reproduce itself.

## The Narrative of Social Space in Rural Realism

These introductory notes have claimed that the dynamic nature of capitalist development propelled economic expansion into new spaces: the San Joaquin Valley, Southern California, and the Imperial Valley. The land-extensiveness of the economy, which for most of the period under study was led by agricultural production, created a powerful industry oriented toward real estate, land subdivision, and control over water resources. In order to interpret the importance of this fact to literary production—to, as Michaels says, map the reality in which literature finds its place—let us reconsider the argument of literary critic and historian Walter Benn Michaels. He asserts that it is moot to debate whether late-nineteenth-century American novelists were for or against capitalism, since there was no place in which they could be said to be beyond its reaches and which could provide some neutral standard for evaluation. The novelists, their works, and their protests were already part of the given social relations. Well, yes and no. There is space, literally and figuratively, to explore. It makes a difference what kind of process these novels see capital in.

I think a crucial point is that often these authors see capital expanding to the point of its own possible dislocation and dispersal. The rural realists used the spatial dynamism of capital to socially and culturally re-situate their characters. The frontier of capital is, in a sense, a space of skepticism. Whether it's bankers and real estate developers who move into new territory or local farmers who may or may not see the benefits of banking, characters are forced into social networks otherwise peripheral to them. The implied reading, I would argue, is one that indulges in a certain skepticism about capital while at the same time giving capital a kind of reprieve. Capitalism is allowed to be seen as chaotic, alienating, elusive, and riddled with crisis, while nature is eternal, holistic, and morally empowering. But by this very logic, *the union with nature is the path back to capital*—though now a cleansed and tamed capital, shorn of crises stemming from debt, bankruptcy, or overproduction. These rural realist resuscitations are etched into the classic California "chronotopes" (Bhaktin 1981): the irrigation ditch, the orange grove, and, we can now add, the office of the avuncular banker, the marvelous earthworks of the engineer.

The contests that run through the novels—variously between financiers and farmers, between good financiers and bad ones, or between effective civil engineers and engineers manqué—all take place in the context of capital's economic expansion into new territory. The same goes for transformations of character, of financiers who become farmers or farmers who become real estate developers. Along with the spatial expansion of capitalism comes a reformulation of agrarianism. Here I disagree with Henry Nash Smith, who did not take his discussion of "virgin land" far enough west. In California, when agriculture failed the capital-poor and the landless, the dominant agrarian thinkers gave agriculture over to the capitalist laborer, the yeoman capitalist—the myth of the garden did not disappear, but it was boldly altered to suit new class alignments between financiers and the investment-worthy growers and farmers. Agrarian ideology became more flexible according to the economic and geographical restructuring of agriculture, and rural realists were drawn to this transformation as to a new cultural oasis.

The trials of capital entertained in these "economic novels" (to borrow Taylor's [1942] phrase) are the explorations of an anxious culture. No author wrote into their novel an escape from capital. What each did write in was the bourgeois notion that culture and capital could be prized apart and kept separate so as to make certain wishes: Without praising money, can't we still legitimate capital? Without saying that everyone should speculate, can't we still heroize speculators? Without retreating into isolation, can't we still romance the local?

Few people, I imagine, really want to read most of these novels anymore, but the separation anxiety behind those questions still has its way.

# 4

# Mussel Slough and the Contradictions of Squatter Capitalism

In the early 1870s, the San Joaquin Valley was among the first of California's agricultural areas to be singled out for extensive commercial potential. In books and pamphlets by the Central and Southern Pacific Railroads and by local boards of trade, the valley's hundred-mile-wide, five-hundred-mile-long corridor was praised for its endless pastures and vast acreages of grain (e.g., Hittell 1874; Nordhoff 1872; Orr 1874; see also Starr 1981 and 1985). But in nearly the same breath, the authors of these tracts expected that bonanza farming and stock raising would not last forever. In isolated pockets, such as Mussel Slough near the southern end of the valley, in the Tulare Lake Basin, there had already begun more intensive agricultural practices based on irrigation.

Through the remainder of the decade and into the 1880s, Anglo-Californian boosters interested in seeing the San Joaquin Valley become densely settled grasped at every improvement, every homestead, farm, and town, as proof that—after the setbacks of drought, flood, and mined-out veins—California was finally coming into its own (Preston 1981).[1] Attention thus began to shift away from the grain kings and baronial ranches toward a more intensive development process: incoming settlers and the growth of a local labor market; subdivision of the large estates; and the extension of the railroad—the single largest private landowner in the state—southward through the San Joaquin Valley.

In the booster's mind, these forces ought to have worked happily together. But in the spring of 1880, a bloody confrontation erupted at Mussel Slough. The result of a dispute between the railroad and a faction of squatters over land titles and prices, "Mussel Slough" quickly became a rallying cry of anti-railroad factions throughout the state (McKee 1948). While descriptions of the event would soon be found in nearly every general history of California, as indeed they are still to be found,[2] Mussel Slough has become legend, especially through Frank

Norris's 1901 novel, *The Octopus*. Less well known, but instructive for the contrast it offers, is William Chambers Morrow's *Blood-Money* (1882).

At the time he wrote his novel, William Chambers Morrow was an antimonopolist writer of small note. (In the 1890s, in a turnaround for which I have no explanation, he would become the chief of the Literature Department of the Southern Pacific Company!) With less of the historical distance evident in *The Octopus*, and asserting a different political agenda than Norris, Morrow drew up an impassioned indictment of both the Southern Pacific Railroad and the corrupt San Francisco power structure that he argued formed the very basis of capitalism in California. His novel rails against the yielding of agrarian capital to urban industrial capital. But, as we'll see, an analysis of what his characters actually do and say reveals that his message has less to do with the particular corruption at the root of capital than it does with a critique of money's much more general corrupting powers over virtually every class, working, middle, or ruling, and in virtually every spatial domain, from city to countryside. Not unlike the Occidental stories, *Blood-Money* speaks to the negotiations involved when one is to have neither too much money nor too little.

If Frank Norris, who had himself written one of the most money-obsessed novels in American fiction, *McTeague* (1899), were to have commented on Morrow's work, he would have likely thought the effort a quaint first cut. In *The Octopus*, the distribution of powers under capitalism may well produce corrupt actors, but capital itself is no more corrupt, nor corrupting, than a sack of wheat. This, at least, seems to be the perspective of *The Octopus* twenty years after Mussel Slough. Norris based his account on information contained in the files of the San Francisco *Chronicle*, material from the Mechanics' Library, and agricultural data that he gathered at the Santa Anita rancho near Hollister, a ranch town at the base of the coast ranges east of Monterey (Rice et al. 1988; Deverell 1994). Norris, like Morrow, indicted the railroad and the entire urban power structure *and* strongly implied that farmers and squatters were also responsible for the events at Mussel Slough. However, his more grandiose aims (at least as vested in his main character, Presley, an aspiring young writer) had to do with reconciling the capitalist economy to the natural laws of which it was the supposed outward manifestation. As I make clear toward the end of this chapter, these aims involve *The Octopus* in numerous excursions into capitalism's contradictions.

Each novel has in common a view of Mussel Slough as an episode symptomatic of the *structuring* of California's rural economy. Each sees that a distinct phase had been entered into in California, with an urban power center as a cultural and economic dominant. Any lessons that a more simple agrarian existence might have to offer are simply struck dumb by this massive transformation dating back to the Gold Rush. Leo Marx, in an unparalleled study, *The Machine in the Garden*, has provided what has probably been the most enduring optic through which to thematize this cultural moment, this striking dumb (Marx 1964). Marx provides a breathtaking cultural history of what he calls the "interrupted idyll," a reverie that appears in numerous works of American literature (not to mention a wide range of Western classics) in which contemplations of nature and its bucolic manifestations are rudely halted by the sights and sounds of technology and industrialization. As Marx shows, *The Octopus* has a paradigmatic example in Presley's witnessing of a gruesome slaughtering of sheep in the path of an oncoming train. In Norris's treatment, however, I will want to argue that the interrupted idyll comes full circle and then goes through the looking glass. If, at the beginning, Presley occasions his own rustic contemplations, by the end, these are occasioned secondarily, through primary thoughts about the process of industrial capital accumulation itself. Presley's struggle to understand the very painful social dislocations and contradictions of capital, in other words, brings about a new horizon of meaning for nature. As Presley erases the distinctions he once drew (or at least entertained) between capital and nature, he reinscribes the values of bourgeois ways of seeing.

For now, it is enough to begin with the proposition that Morrow and Norris play with notions of rural innocence and agrarian idealism, only to challenge their utility. It was not simply the idea that the city siphoned off rural surpluses that interested them. The point seems to be that the making of rural social relations was not all that different from the making of industrial urban economy and society. Due to sensibilities that were apparently much more regional in scope (and even global in Norris's case), these writers invented characters who deal with the fruits of rural labor having become money, rootless and free to circulate across geographical and social boundaries according to abstract sets of laws.[3] The implication for the experience (or the representation of the experience) of the rural was definitive: For farmers to struggle to transform nature was simultaneously to struggle with capital, both their own and that of external agents.

## The Commodification of Mussel Slough: Railroad, Speculators, and Squatters Converge in the Tulare Basin

Until 1870, the Mussel Slough country, fed by the Sierra-born Kings River, was like much of the surrounding area (the Tulare Lake Basin)—a cattle-raising outpost limping through alternating years of drought and flood. Though some farmers had begun experimenting with wheat production, the building of the Southern Pacific into the Tulare Lake area in 1872 was the real catalyst. Farmers in the Mussel Slough district, to which the Southern Pacific extended a branch line in 1876, were among the first to take advantage, augmenting pasture and grain land with alfalfa and corn (Preston 1981). Irrigation, which had begun in fits and starts before the railroad arrived, soon became a central fact of life. By 1879, the area served by irrigation from the Kings River comprised 62,000 acres—the total acreage for the San Joaquin Valley at the time was only 189,000. By 1912, these numbers were, respectively, 629,000 and 1,739,000 (Rice et al. 1988; Maass and Anderson 1978: 147).

The Southern Pacific's expansion was both anticipated and reviled (see Deverell 1994). It was a powerful rival of the stagecoach business, it forced towns to compete against each other for a railroad stop, and it typically demanded a subsidy from the counties and towns it proposed to pass through. For example, the company's request that Visalia—the largest town in the Tulare Lake area and in the San Joaquin Valley, aside from Stockton—pay the railroad to pass through drew bitter protest. In response, the railroad simply avoided communities like Visalia and constructed a direct line through the more remote parts of the valley, planning to build its own towns along the way and develop brand-new agricultural potentials. This is precisely what lay behind the railroad's extension into Mussel Slough, where it founded the new towns of Hanford and Lemoore (Rice et al. 1988; Preston 1981).

The railroad had extraordinary and unrivaled power to quite literally make place and to "take advantage" of the farmers and merchants who proposed to take advantage of the railroad. This point is well worth pausing over. In a very real sense, the Southern Pacific produced the very consumption matrix necessary for the sale of its two major commodities. One of these commodities was the land granted to the railroad by the state (federal and local). Obviously, these millions of acres of land to sell could spur agricultural production (and possibly land subdivision) and, consequently, spur demand for the railroad's second commodity—the journey to market or to processing plants of various kinds. That is, the railroad commodified the very distances it traversed in pushing out to the periphery. Marx (Karl, not Leo) simply calls this singular commodity produced by the transport industries "change of location" (*Capital*, Vol. 2: 52). But more than selling just change in location, the particular historical advantage of the railroad over, say, stage companies was that it sold that change of location as an unprecedented form of time-space compression (Harvey 1989), the significance of which was, under competitive conditions, a reduction in capital's socially necessary circulation time. If the railroad could transport goods more efficiently, that is, then the turnover of capital would be speeded up, too. Moreover, even though the "change-of-location" industry under capitalism often involves a different set of actors from those whose products are transported, it is an extension of production processes, per se, and in qualitative terms no different from when a worker moves a commodity-in-the-making from one part of a factory to another. The commodity has not really finished being made until it is in the consumer's hands. "Within each process of production," Marx writes,

> a great role is played by the change of location of the subject of labor and the required instruments of labor and labor-power—such as cotton trucked from the carding to the spinning room or coal hoisted from the shaft to the surface. The transition of the finished product as finished goods from one independent place of production to another located at a distance shows the same phenomenon, only on a larger scale. The transport of the products from one productive establishment to another is furthermore followed by the passage of the finished products from the sphere of production to that of consumption. The product is not ready for consumption until it has completed these movements. (*Capital*, Vol. 2: 150)

The change-of-location industry is much more than just transportation. It is the production process itself, extended and reproduced over distended geographical space. Marx continues: "The transport industry forms on the one hand an independent branch of production and thus a separate sphere of investment of productive capital. On the other hand its distinguishing feature is that it appears as a continuation of a process of production *within* the process of circulation and *for* the process of circulation" (Vol. 2: 152). Given these supple, relational definitions, producers would view the transport industry as one of their means of production, whereas the transport industry could legitimately view the disparate locations from which goods originate as its own means of production. The transport industries sell change of location, but in the process, they produce Location writ large, the sum total of individual sites of circulation which variously coordinates and contradicts those constitutive sites.

As David Harvey (1989) notes, Norris latched onto a very similar insight and used it to fashion an exhilaratingly holistic, if socially murky, analysis of the California economy, pushing his images to the point of imagining a new culture of instantaneous, dramatically recursive effects. In the superheated chamber of *The Octopus,* the total of all circulation in California is subsumed in the single Location of the beastly railroad. The repercussions are manifold. Urban consumption structures, for example, have immediate consequences in the countryside: Norris's paupers starve *while* the bourgeoisie eat their fill. The reduction in circulation time thins out and dissipates the boundaries between the rural and the urban, producing a second nature which now imposes its own rules and substitutes for those of primordial nature. The change-of-location industry comes to dominate all industry in California, Norris suggests. It is really the only industry there is.

But Norris exaggerates. There were industries other than the railroad. By the end of the 1870s, Tulare County's population had more than doubled, going from 4,500 to 11,300 in a decade. This is hardly a startling county-wide figure, but Mussel Slough was the focus of most of this growth. It became one of the state's earliest regions of small, irrigated farms (Rice et al. 1988). Unlike other portions of the San Joaquin Valley, where large-scale speculative land developers (apart from the railroad) limited access to land, farmers seeking homesteads were able to get a strong toehold in the Mussel Slough area. These new landowners formed cooperative, mutual irrigation companies, combining their water rights, capital, and labor (Rice et al. 1988; Maass and Anderson 1978). Those who belonged to these companies took shares of stock, for which they not infrequently paid in kind with their labor. The stock was assessed according to the cost of building and maintaining the canals, with the right to divert water depending on the number of shares a farmer had. Local capital and local labor were thus crucial to these companies' survival (Maass and Anderson 1978).

Not that this guaranteed their success. Farmers sometimes were unable to keep up their payments, and when their shares were forfeited, there was often difficulty finding other buyers. By 1881, in fact, nearly a third of the People's Ditch Company stock was returned to the company (one of three companies in the vicinity of the town of Hanford). Even with water-company stock only semi-commodified, however, 37,000 acres were being irrigated in the Mussel Slough country in 1879. This was a substantial portion of the Tulare Lake area's total acreage (Maass and Anderson 1978: 197). These local circuits of water development become an important, if little-recognized, feature of Norris's novel. But it was really land that galvanized Mussel Slough's opposition against the railroad.

Before 1870, the federal government still held much of the land around Mussel Slough. In the early 1870s, homesteaders acquired it with land scrip for, at first, 45 cents per acre. But these costs rose as soon as it became clear that the railroad and incoming buyers would combine to make intensive agricultural production a reality (Maass and Anderson 1978). In this way, by the end of the decade, an acre of unimproved farmland was going for 10 and 20 dollars (Rice et al. 1988).

Most lands in Mussel Slough that had not been owned by the federal government were granted to the railroad. These consisted of odd-numbered alternate sections extending out to ten miles from each side of the rails, between the towns of Goshen and Huron and serving Hanford, Armona, and Lemoore en route (Rice et al. 1988). Before the railroad actually received title to this land, however, squatters moved in to occupy it. The company offered to sell the property to them, but there were considerable misunderstandings over the price and over whether the railroad's title to the land would be legally binding. This last point devolved from the fact that the railroad had actually built track through an area other than that proposed in its charter. The uncertainty in the company's ownership of Mussel Slough land led directly to a very active and acquisitive squatter movement (Rice et al. 1988).[4]

Only a minority of the squatters in Mussel Slough were actually "homesteaders." Instead, an economy of squatter capitalism grew up around the speculative values of railroad land, which, it was thought, might never be patented to the railroad. John Doyle, an Indiana transplant, was one of those who risked everything for the speculative spirit. Motivated by the news of the railroad's troubles, in 1871 he sold his farm farther to the north in the San Joaquin Valley and moved onto "railroad land" at Mussel Slough. Self-admittedly a squatter, Doyle spread the news that the railroad's title was flawed and then established a real estate business on that basis. Partly through his promotional efforts, squatters' numbers amounted to hundreds by 1875. Buying and selling claims on railroad land, they traded at premium prices ranging from $500 to $1,000. By 1880, these speculative claims, in the words of one local individual, were "'the principal stock in trade in the Mussel Slough country'" (Rice et al. 1988: 221).

Under Doyle's leadership, a number of individuals tried to obtain titles without having waited to see if the railroad claims would clear. These attempts failed. Arguments that they should be granted access through federal preemption and homestead laws were rejected by the local land office in Visalia. Similar arguments presented to Congress failed, also. Through the 1870s, Congress had been establishing precedents for not recognizing squatters' claims (Rice et al. 1988).

When the railroad's claims were finally confirmed, a large faction of squatters, including a militia, organized into a Settlers' Grand League to thwart attempts to dislodge them. Short of eviction, the league was concerned that the Southern Pacific would proceed with the sales of its land by cutting deals with individual squatters or that it would sell land to outsiders. When the railroad did begin to sell land and install new occupants, the league retaliated violently against the new owners (Rice et al. 1988). The league also feared that when the railroad came around to setting prices for its newly patented land, the prices would be too high for the league's liking. In the interim (and even after prices were announced), most of the squatters stayed put, perhaps in hopes of forcing a bargain (Showalter 1969).

The Southern Pacific was not anxious to stir things up. In fact, it was having some troubles of its own. On the one hand, the railroad's objective was to see California develop quickly and peacefully. It had already demonstrated that land sales were a primary mechanism toward this end. (While it professed to have a preference for the small buyer, it was not above making single sales of 15,000 to 30,000 acres to make the land go quickly [McAllister 1939].) In the Mussel Slough area, it charged prices similar to that of unimproved government land, which was being sold for as low as $2.50 per acre; and throughout its domain, it facilitated land transactions by selling low interest credit (Rice et al. 1988; McAllister 1939). On the other hand, the 1870s sorely tried these efforts. Financial depression in the middle of the decade slowed real estate business down. [5] The railroad's land sales dipped accordingly. In the late 1870s, drought added yet another deterrent to the railroad's efforts to attract buyers (McAllister 1939). Not wanting to make times harder for itself, the railroad actually avoided applying for patents in instances where squatters' claims might have been considered legitimate.

When news of the railroad's asking prices—$10 to $20 per acre—reached the Settlers' Grand League in 1878, members were furious. They were willing to buy the land at previous government prices and would even pay for the land at current prices, minus the value of improvements. But $2.50 per acre was still their ceiling (Showalter 1969). They contended that land values in the area had been raised not by the railroad's presence but by their own irrigation improvements. Richard Orsi has shown, however, that these improvements were much more extensive on non-railroad land, the implication being that the squatters were trying to benefit from neighboring economies. Moreover, the railroad's prices were consistent with the speculative buying and selling prices of Mussel Slough land, on which some of the squatters themselves had been speculating throughout the 1870s (Rice et al. 1988).

Alarmed at both the continued vigilance of the opposition and declining sales of land in the Mussel Slough area, Southern Pacific decided, toward the end of 1878, to file lawsuits against the squatters. About half of the 500 or 600 squatters responded by signing contracts with the railroad: the company still preferred land sales rather than forced evictions. Numerous other squatters were convinced by the Grand League to await the outcome of cases then being tested in court. When the first decision came down, in 1878—*Southern Pacific Railroad Company v. Pierpont Orton*, heard in the U.S. Circuit Court in San Francisco—the judge ruled to uphold the railroad's title (Rice et al. 1988).

Although the Southern Pacific's president, Charles Crocker, had little sympathy for the squatters, Leland Stanford, another of the "Big Four," was aroused to their side—perhaps not a little motivated by political ambitions. He decided to meet with the Grand League and, in early March 1880, reached an agreement with Doyle and Thomas Jefferson McQuiddy, president of the League, to try to secure reduced prices. The understanding (according to the squatters) included the deduction of $400,000 from the value of the lands being contested, in recognition of irrigation improvements that had been made. The accord was not as firm as the squatters thought, though, and accusations of breaches in the agreement soon erupted. When Stanford was unable to convince Crocker of the efficacy of reducing the land values to meet squatters' demands, little more could be done. Land agent Jerome Madden informed the squatters that they had to either buy or leave, and gave them ten days to decide (Rice et al. 1988; see also Showalter 1969).

As leaders of the Grand League rallied support for their cause against the railroad, outside purchasers—men such as Mills Hartt and Walter Crow who would become embroiled in the Mussle Slough shoot-out—waited impatiently to be put in possession of their newly bought acres. Hartt was informed that on the morning of May 11, 1880, a federal marshal would be arriving to ensure that he, Crow, a man named Phillips, and several others finally would be able to take possession of their land. That same morning, the Grand League had scheduled a mass protest in the town of Hanford (Rice et al. 1988).

When May 11 arrived, the federal marshal, Alonzo W. Poole, accompanied Phillips, Hartt, and Crow to the farm of Henry Brewer, who along with John Storer was cultivating wheat on 320 acres of adjacent land. It was this adjacent acreage that the railroad had sold to Crow. When they reached Brewer's, approximately four dozen armed men arrived, too. News had traveled fast that a marshal was in town. Poole walked over to the group of men, informing them of his intentions, leaving his companions behind. A group of the armed squatters broke away and surrounded Poole's companions, and one of the squatters engaged them in argument. When one of the horses in Poole's party reared, several men began firing their guns. A volley of fire then erupted, and though it ceased quickly, six men were killed. Crow escaped but turned up dead later, apparently having been spied by another troop of squatters (Rice et al. 1988).

News of the event reached the east coast within a few hours. In Tulare County, condemnation of the Southern Pacific was the rule, yet there were major newspapers in the state who denounced the squatters (Rice et al. 1988: 233). But these denouncements were short-lived. Mussel Slough came to be venerated by farm, labor, and anti-monopoly civic groups as a site of anti-railroad martyrdom. Eventually, eleven men, among them Doyle, McQuiddy, and Patterson, were indicted. Five were convicted of obstructing the federal marshal and served a lenient eight-month sentence in San José. McQuiddy, who eventually escaped and then had the charges against him dropped, was nominated for governor in 1882 by both the Anti-Monopoly League and the Greenback Party (Rice et al. 1988).

Residents in Hanford had no unified plan of action after the battle. The Grand League continued to press potential railroad-land buyers not to negotiate with the railroad, and the railroad continued suing until every squatter was slapped with an eviction suit. Quietly, negotiations took place between many of the squatters and the railroad, which resulted in Charles Crocker lowering land prices by 12.5% (Rice et al. 1988). By about the same time the following year, practically all the railroad's land in the Mussel Slough area had been purchased or was being occupied under a lease arrangement. Meanwhile, the U.S. Supreme Court agreed to hear three of the resisting settlers' cases on appeal. Again, they were defeated, the last case being lost in 1883. And although most of the settlers gave in to the railroad, or left Mussel Slough, some still occupied railroad land as late as 1887 (Rice et al. 1988; Showalter 1969).

## *Blood-Money* and the Anatomy of Development

At first glance, the significance of the Mussel Slough struggle, for Morrow's *Blood-Money*, is that there can be no celebration of capital, no praise for speculation, no possibility for the local. That is, on one level, *Blood-Money* has no truck with the sort of rural realist inquiries I laid out at the end of the introduction to part two. Yet, in a more layered reading, I want to pursue the novel as *quintessentially* suspended in rural realist webs. For one thing, *Blood-Money* centers on the farmer as the best and final locus of moral reasoning in the context of capital's predations. It is farm society, and especially marginal farmers, that must grapple most with capital. And they do so in two senses: capital as an external encroachment and capital as something they desire. This is established through the book's unifying plot device concerning a stolen inheritance, which was supposed to have been passed on to the main character, John Graham. The loss (theft) of this money, a very tidy $22,000 farm profit earned by Graham's father, stirs the son's desire for it and thus leads him into questionable ethical territory. For here is this young laboring farmer now distracted by the promise of a quick fortune. The sin for which he must suffer is that he is prepared to throw over the ethics of laboring should he recover the money. Aside from establishing these issues, however, I want to identify a number of narrative asides that throw into question whether Graham should get the punishment that the novel metes out to him. In true rural-realist fashion, the novel is neither wholly comfortable with the farmer's "humble station" nor wholly convinced that money can sustain the quest for a meaningful life.

*Blood-Money* is constructed of three interlaced plots, one that builds toward the Mussel Slough incident, one that involves the stolen inheritance, and one that traces the troubled prenuptial period of the young Graham and Nellie, his betrothed. The story opens in the mid-1870s. We are introduced to John Graham, a financially struggling, somewhat naive Mussel Slough farmer working railroad-claimed land. An inexperienced young man, whose father was murdered when he was still a boy, Graham one day receives an anonymous letter, penned (unbeknownst to him) by one of his father's murderers. The letter informs him that $22,000 in gold, buried at a site just north of Tulare Lake, is his for the taking. His grandmother tells him that the money belonged to his wealthy father, who seventeen years before was robbed and murdered on his return from San Francisco. The money was the profit from the sale of some cattle and land. (Thus *Blood-Money* invokes the turnovers of capital that accompanied and furthered agricultural change, but it stalls that turnover in order to open it up to question.) When Graham goes to recover the hidden coins, he discovers that someone has gotten there first and taken the money. His fiancée, Nellie, urges him to keep looking, but his grandmother pleas with him to stay home and keep working the farm.

Graham cannot stop thinking about what has happened. He recalls that the same year his father was killed, two wealthy men (the Webster brothers) had supposedly been murdered in the same area. He locates the "graves," only to find that the coffins had been filled with wood and stones. His curiosity now on fire, he sets off for San Francisco, where he meets a private detective, J. V. Covill. Graham does not know that a sideline of Covill's is to snoop for the railroad.

Covill has been instructed by a Judge Harriot to trail Graham, apparently to protect the railroad's interests. A capitalist with substantial landholdings, who also has ties to large corporations, Harriot believes that the militant squatters at Mussel Slough have baited Graham with the letter—first, in an attempt to eventually convince him that a railroad sympathizer killed his father and, second, to get Graham to do their bidding when the need arises. Covill is instructed to provide John with misleading information in order to get him out of the way. While John is busy with his doings in San Francisco, Mrs. Harriot looks after Nellie, buying her loyalty with the gift of a gold bracelet and seducing her into San Francisco's elite society. This drives a wedge between Graham and Nellie.

Curious as to what lies behind his orders, Covill gets on the trail of the author of the letter, whom he discovers to be some man called Harris. Covill soon tracks

Harris down on the east side of the San Francisco Bay "begging a living among the comfortable homes that nestle cozily in the foothills east of Berkeley and Temescal" (107). Covill disguises himself as a tramp in order to gain Harris's confidence. Together, they make their way to the San Joaquin Valley and on to the banks of the San Joaquin River. That night, while Harris sleeps at the riverside, Covill climbs up an embankment and rolls a heavy log on top of him, leaving him for dead. Harris regains consciousness, however, and escapes by amputating his own leg. His sanity already in question, he loses his mind almost entirely because of the ordeal.

Having returned to Mussel Slough for lack of money, Graham learns that an undercover railroad agent has been in the district appraising the railroad land that the squatters have been occupying. We are given to understand that the history of this land under their occupation is one of transformation from dry cattle pasturage to wheat, irrigated alfalfa, and well-watered orchards and vineyards. The squatters, pressured by the mortgage debts they have incurred in transforming the desert into valuable property, decide to organize. Graham joins them at a meeting in Hanford.

Several years elapse.

The story picks up again in the spring of 1880. John and Nellie have drifted apart as a result of her association with "that society of California whose standing is on a basis of money" (146). She tells Graham that through her connections she can get him a job on the railroad. John, having taken up the cause of the Mussel Slough farmers, will have none of it. He lectures her on the corporation's oppression of the poor farmers, and its power over the courts, the government, and the legal system: "'I fear that . . . [blood] must be spilled before the people are sufficiently aroused to the danger that assails them—the danger of cold, cruel, grasping money'" (150).

One day that spring, Graham discovers a one-legged man (Harris) by the side of a road that runs through Mussel Slough. Ignorant of Graham's identity, Harris begins muttering about having been chased for twenty years for something he once did. Graham feels such sympathy for the man that he takes him home to be looked after. But when Harris sees Graham's grandmother and hears of the discovery of the Webster brothers' fake graves, he collapses, only to blurt out the next day, "'My brother stole the money! . . . He knew I wanted to restore it to Graham's boy. He has hounded and hunted me all these years and wouldn't let me earn an honest living'" (177). That same day, news reaches the settlers that a federal marshal has arrived in the area to enforce settler evictions. Morrow goes on to describe the violent events at "Storer's ranch."

After the shoot-out, Graham goes to San Francisco to find Nellie. There, all the principals of the story converge. Graham finally discovers that Covill is a railroad detective. Harris, also in the city, is overheard by Graham demanding $22,000 from another man. Not realizing that this other man is Judge Harriot, Graham figures out that these two men were the Webster brothers who killed his father, stole the money, and supposedly died.

> Twenty years ago you [Harriot] and your brother [Harris] . . . murdered my father in the San Joaquin Valley, and buried his money under Lone Tree. . . . You . . . heard that your brother was determined to restore it; and then you

> . . . dug up the money, and took it away like a thief. . . . You were a rich man already, but that didn't satisfy you. You must rob a poor young man and a helpless old woman of what belonged to them by right. . . . You never knew that I went down to the bottom of your grave and found your coffin filled with sticks and stones instead of your worthless carcass. . . . Your spies were watching me, and they soon informed me that I had come to San Francisco and applied for a detective. It was then that you sent this miserable fellow to me, to throw me off the track, and beguile me with false theories. . . . You knew well enough that your brother would learn that Lone Tree had been robbed of its treasure, and that he would know you had committed the robbery, and that he would seek me and tell all. It was then that you decided upon a desperate plan . . . to murder your own brother. . . . You fooled even Covill, who never suspected until this moment that you are the brother of the man he tried to murder. Covill, you ought to be thankful to me for opening up to your gaze such a grand opportunity for blackmailing your worthy employer. (224–25)

In a last flash of insight, Graham also understands that his split with Nellie had also been engineered by Judge Harriot.

Also in San Francisco is Graham's grandmother, who has come to plead with one of the railroad men to let her remain in her house. Unsuccessful, she returns to Mussel Slough, where her possessions have just been thrown into the road and new occupants installed in the house. Her grief soon kills her.

Unfazed by Graham's accusations, Covill and Harriot continue their assault against Graham. They have him arrested on a trumped-up robbery charge, for which he is sentenced to a year at San Quentin. Nellie, embarrassed and ashamed, comes to visit him in jail once she learns how she and John have been used, though sometime back she had begun to see through the manipulations of her new friends. Quitting their circle, she begins piece work as a seamstress. The two lovers reconcile and marry in the jail. Here the story ends. There is no implication that Graham will ever get his inheritance money back, that Covill and Judge Harriot will be found out, or that Graham will serve anything less than the full sentence for a crime he never committed.

## The "Silent Obstacle": The Social Relations of Money's Signifying Chain

Obviously, money has many significations and makes multiple encroachments in Morrow's novel, but there are two fundamentals that make these cohere. One is that money lies behind the surface of daily life, the other is that money itself hides something. The narrator speaks to the first of these:

> [T]hat man is a fool who undertakes to run against the power of money. He finds himself encountering silent obstacles that he cannot understand. In California, a rich man is powerful, because as a rule his interests are common with those of other rich men. The community of great interests operates to the strengthening of the power of capital. This is a condition existing everywhere; but nowhere is it so great as in California. The reasons are quite plain. . . . The two great interests in this State are production and transportation. The great productions are those of agriculture and mining. Transpor-

> tation is consolidated into one set of men, and the other interests are scattered among in-numerable individuals, who are not organized. But many of these producers are extremely rich, and many of them, as individual persons, are strong enough to embarrass the operation of the transportation monopoly. The poorer producers are not. Hence it becomes necessary for certain favors to be shown the rich producers, and certain other favors are granted in return. . . . [T]his community of interests is strong enough to bring considerable discomfort to a man whose only means of earning a livelihood is that which capital offers to labor. . . . [N]ot only is there a community of interests between capital and capital, but capital occupies a position in which it can extend minor favors to thousands and thousands of poor people, ambitious persons, politicians, and political leaders, and the many hundreds of thousands who are natural sycophants, and whom small favors will win. It is such as these also that the influence of the corporations can extend in advancing or hindering the interests of others. (85–86)

*Blood-Money* pulls no punches—clearly this is not the Bank Commissioners of California speaking. To live under capitalism, according to *Blood-Money's* narrator, is not to live in a world of reciprocal social relations but in a world of hegemonic capitalist agency. Because of the book's outcome, we are encouraged by the author to agree with the Judge's pronouncements.

The notion that the class power of money is what really lies under the surface of things (Graham's $22,000 inheritance is buried in the ground; class power over money is hidden in faraway San Francisco, and so on) has its corollary in the idea that money itself hides something—that it might force some other reality to go into hiding.

Consider that Graham is motivated by a quest for money that he never obtains, even though it actually belongs to him. In the process of searching for buried money, money (its absence, actually) buries the true Graham. Graham allows this to happen because of a willful act of misconception about where it comes from. It does not, as it were, grow on trees. What Graham does not understand is that labor is the reality that makes money. Graham's grandmother asks him—before he begins his search for the stolen money—"'Ain't you afraid that we can't make enough to live on, and that we might lose the place, if you quit earning anything?'" (32) In fact, Graham *fails* to be afraid, and this failure causes his grandmother's death. His infraction is that he fetishizes money as a thing to be desired in its own right. What he is supposed to have known is that money is a hollow representation of something more real, that is, hard work, labor. Money, when worshipped, allows a veil to be dropped over its own basis in labor.

Morrow suggests that money is peculiar in that it has the property of becoming detached from the social relations that gave rise to it, only to reemerge within society as an object of intense desire. That much unifies *Blood-Money's* characters. There is a basic division, however, in how the costs of that desire are distributed. Unrelenting desire for money is supposed to corrupt the soul. But *if* that desire is managed properly and intelligently, then it appears that one can gain and retain enormous wealth and power. After all, Graham falls, not Judge Harriot. *Blood-Money* thus courts an ideology that it at first set out to dismantle.

When he finds out in the letter that he is heir to a pot of gold, Graham is psychologically altered and bodily infected: "He gasped for breath at the prospect of a wonderful fortune so suddenly brought within his grasp—a fortune greater than that ever pictured in his day-dreams, dazzling in its splendor, overpowering in its magnificence, and *lifting him far above the surroundings of his humble lot"* (11, emphasis added). In his sleep, he is disturbed by "unpleasant dreams, wherein blood and gold were mingled—as nearly always they are" (18). When Graham locates the right tree and discovers that the money has been stolen (again), he becomes obsessed. "The entire face of nature and the whole expression of home were changed to him" (22). The real Graham dies, as "the poison boiled in his blood and made a madman of him" (25).

A more extreme version of the blood-money-madness equation is the episode where Harris is forced to amputate his own leg in order to free himself from under a tree trunk. Like Graham, Harris has been exposed to "that corrupted life-center that sends poisoned blood through every artery of the State's body" (109). This is the blood that has infected Harris's body and which must be drained.

> [T]hat part of his leg beneath the heavy mass was curved downward, and crushed flat upon the hard ground. In addition to the transverse fractures already mentioned, the bones were split longitudinally into innumerable splinters, the sharp ends of which protruded through the badly lacerated flesh.
>
> The blood spurted freely.
>
> [As he tried to pull out from under the log] protruding bones, forced back by the straightening, cut still longer gashes in the flesh, and divided the muscles into shreds . . . With a powerful mastery of self that is possessed by few natures, he put forth every stupendous effort of a strong will, and brought his reasoning faculties under control. This effort was combated by involuntary movements of his muscular system in rebellion. There was a spasmodic action in the throat, much like that produced by sobbing. . . . There was a sudden jerking in the muscles of the spine, extending upward, and drawing his head forcibly back. . . . [A] thought, sudden, ghastly, and revolting . . . stole upon him, and stabbed him unawares.
>
> It was the idea of self-amputation. . . . The sufferer had no anaesthetic, no drug for producing coagulation, no amputating knife, no saw, no threads with which to tie up the arteries, no appliances for stitching, no lint, no bandages. He had only his pocket-knife.
>
> [After an agonizingly painful amputation] a sheep-herder found him sitting on the bank of the river, nearly naked, and covered from head to foot with blood. His eyes rolled wildly, and he grinned and gibbered and chattered—hopelessly insane. (132–44)

The amputation (described in detail as painstaking as the predations of capital) forces out the "poison" blood, but it does not cure Harris. Instead, the poison is simply brought to the surface. Harris must be "covered from head to foot with" it so that the reader may face him for the first time as the person he became once he was driven by money lust. *Blood-Money*'s business is not to forgive sin but to reveal it. Recall that Graham, also, is not returned to good society simply because he realizes his errant ways. Only Nellie seems to walk away unscathed, *seems* being the key word. She walks away only to become John's domesticated wife, even though "by nature she was qualified to become a dashing woman of the world, courting admiration, conquering hearts, and trampling under foot everything that opposed her wishes" (30). Family and domesticity are her reward *and* punishment for having not succeeded in her aspirations (30). Just as punishments are certain, so it would be best to not sin in the first place.

*But just how is the lust after money to be avoided?* In fact, it is built in to what the novel imagines as perhaps an even greater transgression than crass desires for dollars: the prevention of economic gain. Here, the narrator describes the farmers' transformation of Mussel Slough:

> [S]urely human avarice should not mar this handiwork of God, and lurk in the darkness, like a thief, and set man against man, and neighbor against neighbor, and husband against wife, and father against son; and lay traps, . . . and trip the unwary, and make cowards of brave men and rob the poor, and hinder the thrifty, and cajole its misguided friends—surely these noble plains, lying under the full light that pours straight down from heaven, should not be cursed with the hand of the rich on the throat of the poor; with the robber rolling in princely wealth. . . . Can a man raise wheat? Well enough; for the ground is rich and the soil is deep. Can he sell it? Well enough; for a hungry world holds out its hand for the harvest from these plains. Can he reap a profit? Why not?—for cheap is the land, and little is the work that this paradise demands. *Does* he reap a profit? God, no! for his costs are weighed, and his gains are pared to the quick. (73)

The passage begins with a list of all the social inversions that blood-money wreaks. Man fights man, husbands wives, and so forth. But then we read on until we get to the fact that what smarts so much about the money grabbers' abuses is that they prevent farmers from grabbing money, for *cheap is the land and little is the work that this paradise demands.* It is a tragedy that the squatters lose, because they would not have had to work so hard in order to reap profits—but can it also be immoral of Graham to have left home because he did not place work on a higher plane than easy money? The meta-transgression effected by capitalist social relations appears to be that it prevents individuals from transgressing where they have the opportunity. I am not arguing that Morrow, or the novel, necessarily intends this to be so. But I am arguing that this is a slippage, an aporia, produced by one ideology (let's say a minimally monetized agrarianism) having run up against another (that of rural realism which leans toward monetization). Graham is not supposed to leave home for easy money, because he is supposed to be a hardworking farmer. This is what farmers do. But what is farming in California? It is business. It defines a market for the farmer's own investment, and it is embedded in larger markets. If the land is cheap, and the labor minimal (a fiction, of course), then the profits are assured, unless something intervenes (which it has, in the form of Judge Covill, the railroad, etc.). But what this passage lets us get a glimpse of is that the Mussel Slough farmers have already intervened in their own identification with agrarian innocence. So now, it seems the real question is, If nature is ripe for the picking by capital-oriented farmers, then why should not farmers be ripe for the picking by industrial capitalists? For whom is the San Joaquin Valley fair game, and why?

In other words, perhaps it just does not matter that Judge Harriot walks and John Graham serves time. Perhaps the San Joaquin Valley and Mussel Slough are fair game for whomever can legally claim the land as property. Though *Blood-Money's* ideological contradictions (as above) do not prevent such a reading, the novel does mark out a more furrowed cultural terrain. At least for some characters, let's say the sort of characters who would most likely be morally engaged by a reading of Morrow's novel (an implied readership of "real world" Johns and Nellies), the quest for money is posed as an enormously risky proposition. *Blood-Money* fosters an ethos of moderation, probity, and balance. Although money is a necessary evil, one should have neither too much nor too little. If one can get money, it should be obtained through honest labor, though it is nice if one's labors are neither too hard nor too easy. (As one farmer tellingly asks: "'Why is it that land is given in unlimited quantities to rich men and corporations, while we poor devils have to pay for it *and live on it*?'" [121, emphasis added]. Think about poor Hanks's fate in the Occidental stories.) As for the stolen inheritance, then, and why the Harris brothers left it buried in the ground for so long, rather than just spending it as soon as they robbed and murdered John's father—the narrative demands this turn of events. This is what marks the narrative as being about moral dilemmas and not only about circulating capital. The gold has to have been kept in the ground long enough for Graham to become an adult who can desire it, but ultimately it has to be kept from him because it represents to him a totally unearned increment. It represents the chance that he could become the capitalist laborer, or even the capitalist, without ever having to think through the costs.

## The Country and the City: From Transgression to Similitude

I have argued thus far that to some extent the blood-money in *Blood-Money* is everywhere at once: "Location," to harken back to my introductory remarks, is what structures the little "locations" that would do somewhat false battle with it. Paralleling this discourse about the geography of money is an overtly supportive discourse around space, which *to a point* reinscribes the differences that the monetary discourse fudges.

We can begin with the two primary social-spatial orders, those of the countryside and the city. Let us follow John as he begins his journey to San Francisco, to find the solution to the mystery of his father's murder. The significant thing here is the ease with which he finds his way.

> He crossed King's River, skirted the northern shore of Tulare Lake, crossed the parched desert beyond, penetrated the Coast Range, emerged on the western side through Pacheco Pass, entered the broad, beautiful valley between the Coast Range and the Santa Cruz Mountains, turned northward, passed through Gilroy and San Jose, skirted the Bay of San Francisco on the west, and arrived at San Francisco, three hundred miles from home.
>
> It was the first time he had ever seen a city; yet so even was his organization, and so readily could he adapt himself to circumstances, that he was not seriously, if at all, bewildered. He asked necessary directions in an easy manner, and had a straightforward way and a dignity of bearing that won him respect. He felt at home in any street, and found his way without difficulty or embarrassment. Two weeks ago he could not have done it. (58–59)

Graham's trip to the city is then followed by a different party's excursion to the countryside around Tulare Lake. "A few days after Graham left for San Francisco, a merry party of pleasure seekers left the railroad at a station in Tulare County, and from persons living there, with whom arrangements had previously been effected, procured large wagons, in which to take a trip to Tulare Lake" (70). The leader of this group is Mrs. Harriot, a "woman of unusual strength of character . . . [with] a certain steely look in her eyes—a certain dangerous and uncompromising coldness" (74–75). Like Graham, she is eminently adaptable to new environments. "She displayed an unobtrusive but surprisingly accurate knowledge of all the common affairs of every-day life, under many of its varied aspects. She was as much at home on the plains as she was in her reception room in San Francisco. She knew the name of every weed and flower . . . She was familiar with the mountains . . . She had a quiet, dignified air, that commanded attention and respect" (75).

What has to be noticed here (because the *narrator* insists on it) is that John and Mrs. Harriot are so extraordinarily at ease in spaces that ought to be alien to them, given their accustomed haunts. Accounting for their ease are the powers with which each of the characters are vested. "'We have on our side right against might," Graham says, "justice against infamous wrongs, honesty against theft, industry against robbery, hunger against a feast'" (149). Conversely, Mrs. Harriot has the power of money on her side. She is a walking gazetteer, an expert at things rural and natural, because it is the business of money to know about and transform these things. Yet as with "cheap land" and "little work," there is a slight hitch. Graham's confidence in the city is something he never would have had "two weeks ago" before he learned about the pot of gold. Graham has to have been inflamed with the desire for money in order to call forth city/countryside differences. The value of the rural is here not so much the opposite of the value of the fiscal as it is supplemental to it: When John seeks to protect the rural, he seeks its surplus values. John Graham and Mrs. Harriet are emboldened by the same thing.

By contrast, what would it be like to enter the city without a care for money? John's grandmother is that figure. In her own efforts to save her home from foreclosure, she makes her way to the mansion of one of the "Big Four":

> An idler at San Francisco might have seen . . . a feeble, tottering old woman, . . . slowly picking her way along the noisy streets. The idler might have seen at a glance that she was frightened and shy, and not in the least accustomed to the bustling crowds that hurried past her. . . . [After obtaining directions to the mansion,] he might have noticed the infinite pains that she took to follow the directions closely, and the repeated failures that she made, and the many apologies that she offered for troubling people so often. (206)

Hardly the self-confident traveler that John is, her alienation in the city is total. "'Do you want money?'" she is asked by a servant when she finally reaches the "rich man's house." "'Money!'" she answers, "'No; I want to see . . . [your master] . . . I have come to beg for my home. They are going to turn me out'" (207). At the same time she is turned out of the rich man's house, her possessions are being removed from her own house in Tulare County. She arrives back at Mussel Slough only to discover that a "great change had taken place there. She saw all her household goods in the road, where they had been recently put. And they were all covered with dust. . . . She hobbled to the door, and there she was met by a man whom she had never seen. If John had been there he would have recognized in the intruder the man who discovered him digging for the treasure at the foot of Lone Tree" (211).

What the grandmother does not perceive is that the very making of Mussel Slough *is* the "change that had taken place there" or, at least, is continuous with the fact that change has been pervasive since Mussel Slough's inception as a "settled" area.

The narrator tells us, "It was only a few years ago that this vast garden was a desert wilderness, scoured by bands of cattle, horses, and hogs; and the land was of little value to any one" (181). The Mussel Slough pioneers are the ones responsible for making no place into a place. They create something distinctive out of an indistinguishable wilderness, turning nature into culture. This very production of place threatens to slip away into a very different meaning altogether. For, eventually, it reinstalls a kind of sameness. We may go back to Graham's initial difficulty with finding the "Lone Tree" near which the pot of gold is supposed to be buried. "There seems to be in California a fashion of naming every isolated tree 'Lone Tree'" (13).

> . . . and it has come to be so that, in the minds of local geographers, there is much doubt as to which Lone Tree is the only original Lone Tree of early local history. As the new order of things has come about under the natural operation of the laws of progress and civilization, it would be hardly just to attach blame to anybody, or to assume that the unknown writer of the letter might have kept himself informed in contemporaneous history so that the identity of the only original Lone Tree should not be swallowed up by the tendencies of advancement toward multiplication. . . . Indeed, as Graham was comparatively a stranger in that particular section of country, he had to learn, by hard experience, that Lone Tree, for all he knew, might exist at intervals indefinitely all over the world. (14)

Although quests for capital redeem nature—Mussel Slough has been produced out of nature's wilds—these sorts of quests implant a Lone Tree everywhere that they are embarked upon. There is no way around the fact that *as Mussel Slough developed, it developed in relation to Development.* In Morrow's novel, productions of spatial difference under capitalism emerge only through processes that produce sameness. Culture becomes a wilderness within second nature. What does the novel think of this? This is hard to say, for it is caught between wanting to decry commodification, on the one hand, and wanting to lovingly describe it, on the other. As the title suggests, money draws blood and is blood.

### *The Octopus* and the Bourgeois Sublime

Like *Blood-Money*, events in Norris's *The Octopus* conspire toward the Mussel Slough incident. Also like *Blood-Money*, *The Octopus* engages capital as a moral terrain only to then pull back from this engagement. The latter novel pulls back much more definitively, however, at least from the point of view of its main character, the aspiring writer Presley, and his (in)famous statement that all things work toward the good. In the following discussion, I argue that representations of scale are essential to Presley's "findings" and to what I also argue is a core contradiction: When viewed from enough distance, all manner of events and details that might be cared about are rendered moot by Presley, even though, it is through the same narrative tactic of shifting scales that the novel finds a way to care about anything at all. Once we get the details, the local hardships at Mussel Slough, it is extraordinarily difficult to see them as irrelevant. Indeed, the joke is on Presley. For despite its ostensible object, wheat production in California, *The Octopus* allows the undergirding structure to show through: In the very evocation of the empire of wheat, Norris sows the idea of its demise. The novel is persistently concerned and intrigued with the constant transformation of California agriculture through the aegis of circulating capital. With this comes, on the one hand, the asserted irrelevance of particular events, like Mussel Slough, individual corporations, like railroads, and single economies, like wheat, and, on the other hand, transcendence into the bourgeois sublime: transformation and circulation as ends in themselves.

## Spectacles, Landscapes, Bodies: Spatializing Capital

As a visitor to the countryside from the city, *The Octopus*'s protagonist, Presley, is the eyes and ears of the reader. What we know, we know through him—and what we learn is largely through his peregrinations over the landscape, from the ranches of Mussel Slough to the town of Bonneville, the city of San Francisco, and back to the one ranch, where Presley stays as a guest. No mere observer or visitor, he is a presence who spatializes economic and social relationships for us. As true of the beginning of the novel, when he conducts a bicycle tour of the extensive Los Muertos ranch, as it is true of the end, when he boards a merchant ship stuffed with wheat, where capital goes Presley follows.

Taking up nearly all of the first chapter of Book One is Presley's bicycle tour around El Rancho de Los Muertos and Quien Sabe Rancho, into Guadalajara, and back. In the very way that Norris structures this chapter, social and economic space is made paramount. We meet all the major characters in their relationship to the landscape at particular moments in their working day as Presley encounters them: the Hoovens, tenant farmers for the Derricks; S. Behrman, railroad and real estate agent; the Derricks, a great wheat-farming family and lessees of Los Muertos; Dyke, an engineer for the P & SW, recently fired from his job; Annixter, the brains behind the Quien Sabe ranch; Vanamee, an itinerant shepherd. We are led to understand that there is a division of labor within the ranch and that the ranch is situated within a functioning hierarchy of places: ranch, service towns, and San Francisco. Together, these constitute a spatial division of labor, an interconnection of working elements spread out geographically and making the geography through which their interconnections are enabled in the first place. The novel's attention to class divisions tells us that this division of labor is an unequal division of powers. *The Octopus* comes with a frontispiece map, which graphically illustrates the forces that intersect at the ranch and its environs—the ranch seems to be comprised of these intersections (see also Wyatt 1986). The bicycle tour is more than a neat plot device that introduces us to the characters and what they do: it makes space itself a character, which, like other characters, changes over the course of the novel.

Space is, in fact, Presley's would-be intimate. He seeks to know its dimensions and his limits within them. (In some sense, Presley is a free-floating representation—he is the one character who tries out all sorts of rhetorical formulations for how to describe space and what space means. He is the signifier cut loose by a shifting reality, the one who seeks a return to his signified. When Presley thinks he has found his signified at the end of the novel, readers may understand this as yet another of his interpretive steps. But we shall come to this later.) At first, Presley grasps space as simply a view of the landscape. "As from a pinnacle, Presley, from where he now stood, dominated the entire country . . . [C]lose at hand . . . was the seed ranch. . . . Beyond that was the Mission itself. . . . Farther on, he could make out Annixter's ranch house. . . . Far to the west and north, he saw Bonneville very plain. . . . Others points detached themselves, swimming in a golden mist" (45). Suddenly, something dawns on Presley: Why stop at the "golden mist"? "Beyond the fine line of the horizons . . . were other ranches, equally vast, and beyond these, others, . . . the immensities multiplying, lengthening out vaster and vaster. . . . As from a point high above the world, he seemed to dominate a universe, a whole order of things" (46–47). But, of course, Presley does not dominate space, for at this point of exhilaration it inebriates him (like money inebriates John Graham in *Blood-Money)*. Presley expands within space (or fantasizes such), only to face the fact that it contains him. He has for the moment reached too far. It is instructive that the narrative's next foray into the spatial wilds is through the "eye" of the ticker in the office of wheat rancher Harran Derrick. Here, we are no longer distracted by Presley's ambitions to exceed the limits of global space. Instead, we simply have a device produced by capital, for capital.

> The most significant object . . . was the ticker. . . . The offices of the ranches were thus connected by wire with San Francisco, and through that city with Minneapolis, Duluth, Chicago, New York, and . . . most important of all, with Liverpool. Fluctuations in the price of the world's crop during and after the harvest thrilled straight to the office of Los Muertos, . . . Quien Sabe, . . . Osterman's, and . . . Broderson's. . . . The ranch became merely the part of an enormous whole, a unit in the vast agglomeration of wheat land the whole world round, feeling the effects of causes thousands of miles distant—a drought on the prairies of Dakota, a rain on the plains of India, a frost on the Russian steppes, a hot wind on the llanos of the Argentine. (53–54)

*Almost in answer to Presley*, the ticker signifies (as Frederic Jameson has more recently written [Jameson 1984]) that capitalist space on this grand scale cannot be *seen*, it can only be represented. But such a representation is only possible if capital produces the mechanisms for its own representation. There will be no successful representation from "above" or "outside"—only a representation that is of the capitalist industrial juggernaut. The ticker achieves what Presley cannot yet achieve.

Although they fail him, Presley's strivings after space have important repercussions.[6] They confirm for him that the quotidian features of life in the Mussel Slough district—the ranches, the dry stubble of wheat stalks, the ranchers' struggles with railroad freight rates and property claims—are "a mere array of accessories—a mass of irrelevant details" (46). But in a novel whose business has been with details for dozens of pages, including the languid tracing of Presley's move, how can this be so? That is, Presley's view must be tested. We need an image now of distortion and invasion—not a grandiose vision of "second nature," but a competing image of totalizing forces. The test comes almost immediately as one of the P & SW trains comes roaring from out of nowhere and erases Presley's fantasy. Suddenly, we understand the difference between Presley ruminating about the irrelevance of lives and the obliteration of life. The difference eventually comes to fruition in a third image of totalizing space.

Book Two opens with another sort of tour of the countryside. Lyman Derrick (son of the rancher Magnus Derrick and a new Railroad Commission member who is to represent the ranching interests) is seated in his San Francisco office looking at an official railway map of California:

> The whole map was gridironed by a vast, complicated network of red lines marked P. and S.W.R.R. These centralised at San Francisco and thence ramified . . . to every quarter of the State . . . a veritable system of blood circulation, complicated, dividing, and reuniting, branching splitting . . . laying hold upon some forgotten village or town, involving it in one of a myriad branching coils, one of a hundred tentacles, drawing it . . . toward that centre from which all this system sprang. . . . It was as though the State had been sucked white and colourless, and against this pallid background the red arteries of the monster stood out, swollen with life-blood, reaching out to infinity, gorged to bursting. (288–89)

The rhetoric is similar to Presley's perception of the landscape around Mussel Slough—details are obscured by vastness. But here, we see scale and space being *produced* in a vivid, if gothic, image of creative destruction. There is nothing *given* about economy here. As in *Blood-Money*, the railroad has gone out and extracted what it wants by having built a circulatory system that both creates and renders powerless "forgotten" villages and towns. The language of subsumption, of the whole state of California being transformed into food for the production of the monster, pervades the passage. Norris not only evokes the spatialization of capital, but implies that California is the single location for and as capital. (It is an image that draws the extremes out of Marx's discussion of the "change-of-location" industry and leaves out anything dialectical.) With this image, the rhetoric of scale has been reversed. At first was the endlessness of the landscape as a romantic visual given that made the ranches appear small. Now at last we see that it is the railroad that makes space in the first instance.[7] Whereas Presley *renders* small detail irrelevant, the railroad has the power to produce scale in the first place.

The ultimate totalizing gesture of capital (again, as in *Blood-Money*) is its absorption of the human body. Capital, we see, moves through every conceivable spatial scale: the global, the regional, the local, the individual ranch, and bodies, which by the end of the novel start dropping like flies.

In the aftermath of Mr. Hooven's death at Mussel Slough, the female members of the family wander up to San Francisco, where each is handed over to the sort of fate that only the railroad can construe. The hop farm that might have supported Hooven's survivors has been crushed by the market. The elder daughter Minna, forced to find some way to support herself, is recruited into prostitution—"Where was that spot to which the tentacle of the monster could not reach?" (589)—while Mrs. Hooven and the younger daughter, Hilda, wander desperately through the streets of the city. Norris handles this section with brutal economy in a series of passages that alternate between a feast at the house of the P & SW's vice-president and descriptions of a progressively weakening Mrs. Hooven. It is a representation of simultaneous gluttony and starvation: "Turning toward the wife of the Railroad King, he said: 'My best compliments for a delightful dinner.'———The doctor who had been bending over Mrs. Hooven, rose. 'It's no use . . . she has been dead some time—exhaustion from starvation'" (613; 590–613 for the whole sequence). The juxtaposed images are such as to suggest that Mrs. Hooven herself has been eaten; and not by the revelers, but by the railroad.

Consumption is S. Behrman's fate, too. Toward the end of the novel, Behrman, who has been climbing up the economic ladder as a real estate agent and grain dealer, is overseeing the loading of wheat into the hull of the merchant ship *Swanhilda*, when he loses his balance and tumbles in. His cries for help are drowned out by torrents of grain, which gradually engulf and drown him.

Perhaps the ultimate incorporation (because he lives on as pure labor power) into the vast envelopment of the grain economy is suffered by Magnus Derrick, former head of Los Muertos and known to all as "Governor." Once evicted from his ranch, he is given a desk job for the P & SW. "Magnus was sorting papers. From the heap upon his left hand he selected a document, opened it, glanced over it, then tied it carefully, and laid it away upon a second pile on his right hand. When all the papers were in one pile, he reversed the process . . . only his hands, swift, nervous, agitated, seemed alive" (622–23). The railroad has broken him so completely that only bodily motions are left, and even those are repetitive and thoroughly useless. Their precision, however, describes the very economy that *The Octopus* seeks to evoke. Magnus's job mimics circulating capital and all the images of origins and return in the novel: of the wheat encircling the globe, of the forces of supply and demand pushing grain in one direction and pulling it in another. Still, we could return to Presley's question, Do these details matter? If things/people are rendered moot through being subsumed by the railroad, isn't there a point at which subsumption comes at too high a cost for the railroad itself?

The absorption of these bodies by capital is, to my mind, one of the more perplexing aspects of the novel—perplexing because it gives us something to think about concerning the way Presley figures capital. By the very end of the novel, with Presley prattling on about all the good that comes from evil and about how good outcomes cancel out tragic ones, he has distanced himself again from detail, from body dramas and micro-spaces, back up to that larger scale of global production and distribution, a better "reality" from which to gain perspective. But those dead or barely animate bodies trip Presley's logic. If the laws of capital work toward the good by balancing death with life, wouldn't it be more to the good if the fullness of human life were preserved in the first place? (A supposed law of nature that reveals the mechanisms of a social construction, in other words, must be tested by supposing alternate social constructions.) Mrs. Hooven, Minna, Magnus, Behrman, not to mention those killed at the Mussel Slough battle—contra Presley, what is wrong with the gears of capital that they would grind these characters up? In the next section, I argue that the bestiality and monstrosity of the octopus have less to do with its inevitable consumption of *everything* than with the fact that its circulation of capital has begun to slow down. It can still engorge, but it cannot disgorge on its own terms. In a manner of speaking, these bodies are not ground up by capital so much as they are representative of capital beginning to get stuck.[8]

## Accumulation Crises: "The New Order of Things" versus Squatter Capitalism

Over and against Presley's sublime view of capitalist absorption is a pervasive subtext of crisis not easily resolved by his argument for the "larger view": "all things . . . work together for good" (652). For one of the themes of the novel is that with integration of California's economic activities, and the restructuring of the economy from mining into agriculture, comes a fundamental vulnerability. As Harran Derrick ponders: "Everything seemed to combine to lower the price of wheat. The extension of wheat areas always exceeded increase of population; competition was growing fiercer every year. The farmer's profits were the object of attack from a score of different quarters . . .—the commission merchant, the elevator combine, the mixing-house ring, the banks, the warehouse men, the labouring man, and, above all, the railroad" (56).

There is also an undercurrent of the making and unmaking of places as the economy is restructured: "Presley went on . . . wheeling silently through the deserted streets of the decayed and dying Mexican town. . . . There was no business in the town. It was too close to Bonneville [the new railroad town] for that. Before the railroad came, and in the days when the raising of cattle was the great industry of the country, it had enjoyed a fierce and brilliant life. Now it was moribund" (20). (Many commentators on *The Octopus* have noted the pure fiction of Norris having placed Mussel Slough on the Mexican border [e.g., Wyatt 1986; Deverell 1994]. In my reading, it suits perfectly the novel's aim of sifting through the rhetorics of time-space conquests.) Capital's production of scale is thus not just about the tying of one place to another. It is about selective and uneven development. Try as it might to make all places alike, to make them serve its own ends, fissures in the accumulation matrix have opened up.

The railroad is pitted against the farmer but is responsible for an overproduction of space, which has lowered the price of the commodity upon which it depends. In the following passage, the industrialist Cedarquist provides the analysis:

> All our California wheat goes to Liverpool, and from that port is distributed over the world. But a change is coming. . . . Our century is about done. The great word of the nineteenth century has been Production. The great word of the twentieth century will be . . . Markets. . . . Population in Europe is not increasing fast enough to keep up with the rapidity of our production. . . . *We*, however, have gone on producing wheat at a tremendous rate. The result is over-production . . . and down go the prices. The remedy is *not* in the curtailing of our wheat areas, but in this, we *must have new markets, greater markets*. . . . What fatuous neglect of opportunity to continue to deluge Europe with our surplus food when the East trembles upon the verge of starvation. (305–6)

Cedarquist worries that capital is being poured into a landscape that simply can't absorb all the capital being put into it. Rather than adjusting production, however, the solution in his mind is to produce yet more space for capital's absorption. As Norris builds up the theme of crisis and change, though, there is not much reason to think that Cedarquist's solution would be anything but temporary, if even that.

In fact, the theme of the temporary and contingent builds steadily through the novel's six hundred pages. One of the first commentaries comes from Magnus

Derrick's wife: "This new order of things—a ranch bounded only by the horizons, . . . a principality ruled with iron and steam, bullied into a yield of three hundred and fifty thousand bushels . . .—troubled her . . . The direct brutality of ten thousand acres of wheat, nothing but wheat as far as the eye could see, stunned her a little" (60). What Norris calls "the new order of things" is not only the existing form of wheat production in the San Joaquin Valley but also the near certainty that other, more competitive regimes will pass it by.

Attentive to this possibility, Annixter strives to keep the ranch as up-to-date as possible. In college, he had taken courses in "finance, political economy, and scientific agriculture." But this was not enough. He went back and took a degree in civil engineering, and "then suddenly he had taken a notion that a practical knowledge of law was indispensable to a modern farmer" (24–25). Annixter has also installed telephone cables for instant communication among all the distant buildings and fields that constitute the ranch. Still, his efforts cannot forestall a new wave of change.

After the battle has taken place, many of the ranchers are evicted. S. Behrman takes over and picks up where Annixter left off. He introduces the steam-powered harvester and consolidates ranch operations: "Never had Los Muertos been more generous, never a season more successful" (615). With the steam harvester, ranch hands can sack grain at unprecedented rates. Behrman also eliminates the middlemen in the sale of the wheat. "The new master of Los Muertos had decided upon accumulating his grain in bulk in a great elevator at the tide-water port, where the grain ships for Liverpool and the east took on their cargoes. To this end, he had bought and greatly enlarged a building at Port Costa . . . and to this elevator all the crop of Los Muertos was to be carried. The P. and S.W. made S. Behrman a special rate" (618). S. Behrman is to sell his harvest direct to the Famine Relief Committee, a charity founded by San Francisco's upper-class women who were galvanized by the poem that Presley had finally managed to write, "The Toilers." Behrman also remodels the ranch buildings "at length, to suit the larger demands of the New Agriculture" (632–33). These remodelings are traceable to what the narrator calls "the New Movement, the New Finance, the reorganisation of capital, the amalgamation of powers, the consolidation of enormous enterprises" (104). In Norris's novel, the "new" wheat farming constantly becomes the "newer" wheat farming.

Yet, there are currents of agricultural change that threaten the wheat itself. At key points, specialty agriculture makes an appearance. For example, when Dyke is fired from his job as an engineer for the railroad, he goes into raising hops. And according to the wife of Gerard, the railroad's vice-president: "'We get all our asparagus from the southern part of the State, . . . We order it by wire and get it only twenty hours after cutting'" (611). Then, later, Presley encounters Cedarquist, who has gotten out of the iron works business. He mentions in an aside to Presley that his wife had raised the money to display at the "Million Dollar Fair" a "figure of California—heroic size—out of dried apricots" (648). These signs of things to come are summed up by the journalist Genslinger when he makes what I would argue is probably the book's major revelation about the California countryside: "'Telephone, safe, ticker, account-books—well, that's progress, isn't it? Only way to manage a big ranch these days. But the day of the big ranch is over. As the land appreciates in value, the temptation to sell off small holdings will be too strong. And then the small holding can be cultivated to better advantage. I shall have an editorial on that some day'" (451). Indeed, by Norris's writing of *The Octopus*, that is precisely what was happening, and as if to reinforce it, the buying and selling of subdivided agricultural lands is a business in which Norris's ranchers will have an interest: "'As soon as the railroad wants to talk business with me,' observed Annixter, 'about selling me their interest in Quien Sabe, I'm ready. . . . I'll bet I could sell it tomorrow for fifteen dollars an acre, and if I buy of the railroad for two and a half an acre, there's boodle in the game'" (97).

Norris further underscores the point that rising land values and agricultural modernization are at issue by repeatedly mentioning the irrigation ditch at Los Muertos—in which Magnus and Annixter have invested five thousand dollars. Near the beginning of the novel, we learn that the ditch is an "important" feature of the ranch. Later, when the ranchers prepare to meet S. Behrman and the federal marshal, they discover that as a defense the "irrigating ditch was a natural trench, . . . crossing both roads as Hooven pointed out and barring approach from Guadalajara to all the ranches save Annixter's—which had already been seized" (510). After the conclusion of the battle, Norris denotes the skirmish as "the tragedy of the fight in the ditch" (532), "the affair of the irrigating ditch" (536), "the fight in the irrigating ditch" (561), "the welter of blood at the irrigation ditch" (651). He fastens on that detail, singling out not the ranch, but that into which the ranchers' capital had been sunk and that which made the ranch modern and signaled its potential conversion out of wheat. The railroad fights less against the squatters than it does against progressive, cutting-edge investments in "earth capital": the irrigation ditch. The wheat economy and the railroad's lumbering circulation now appear as the real squatters.

Threaded through Norris's undeniably powerful evocations of the wheat economy is a quieter but insistent refrain about the wheat itself being born of processes that will prove its undoing. Out of this refrain emerges an image of capital cannibalizing its progeny and subverting its conquests. It recklessly does away with the bodies that it once forced to articulate with its project of grand incorporation. (Or it incorporates them in a distorted way, substituting gruesome trophy kills for maximal appropriations of labor power.) These disparate images of excess and waste are stunningly brought home in the book's final passages.

Recall that Presley, having done everything he could (and nothing) in the San Joaquin, decides to take passage on the merchant ship loaded with S. Behrman's wheat. Behrman himself lies entombed in grain in the ship's hold, and Presley takes in the sights from the bow, ignorant of Behrman's fate. The ship itself is headed for India, the wheat having been purchased by a charitable organization to aid in famine relief (an irony I shall come to shortly). For Presley, all is now right with the world: "Annixter dies, but in a far distant corner of the world a thousand lives are saved" (652). (Note that this statement displaces Presley's earlier class critique made in strikingly similar terms: "because the farmers of the valley were poor, these men were rich" [608]. With the displacement, it's simply as if Annixter had not died; he is merely substituted—but then, because he is substituted, the "rich" need not be accused of anything.) Presley seemingly believes that he has finally merged with the grand scheme of incorporation in which capitalist equations of supply and demand reveal themselves as the very laws of nature, of FORCE, as it's called, in which life follows death.

By a fuller reckoning, though, *nothing* is right with this picture, for Presley is sailing away not so much with what capital incorporates but with the entities (including Presley himself) that it has cast off and written off. It has cast off Behrman, who threw all his chips into a wheat economy whose days are numbered (by the coming kingdom of apricots). And, indeed, it has cast off Presley, whose famous poem, "The Toilers," garnered him instant fame but only by virtue of the fragmented and distorted meanings created in the mass market.

> Presley's Socialistic poem, "The Toilers," had an enormous success . . . It was promptly copied in New York, Boston, and Chicago papers. It was discussed, attacked, defended, eulogised, ridiculed . . . Editorials were written upon it. Special articles, in literary pamphlets, dissected its rhetoric and prosody. The phrases were quoted,—were used as texts for revolutionary sermons, reactionary speeches. It was parodied; it was distorted so as to read as an advertisement for patented cereals and infants' foods. Finally, the editor of an enterprising monthly magazine reprinted the poem, supplementing it by a photograph and biography of Presley himself. (394)

Like the wheat, the poem suffers from its own multiplications.[9] The more it is (re)produced, the more meanings accumulate and thus can never return back to Presley in usable, gratifying form. Dismayed, Presley appears to have given up writing and representation for something more real: the wheat. But capital has also cast off the wheat. For the wheat in the hold is excess supply, charity, being sent to an area of excessive, impoverished demand, which cannot pay for the wheat. The wheat is an overaccumulated commodity, a representation of invested capital that will never turn over. A transaction has been made that could only have been made if the economy were *not* functioning as Presley represents it. There is, in fact, no causal connection between Annixter and the others dying and thousands being saved. Behrman comes in possession of the grain and then sells it to the charity, which then donates it. Annixter did not have to die in order for this transaction to be made: The charity could have bought it from him instead of Behrman, had he remained alive. That the wheat is given as a donation is a sign that there is more in supply than in demand (if demand is figured as that which can return capital to "itself," which non-paying, starving people cannot do). Starving people will get the grain not because the wheat economy is working but because it has begun to cease working. If starving people do get fed because a group of capitalists can afford to put capital into circulation without getting a return on it, in the world of supply and demand this is more a cost to capitalists, not something they can afford. Free food for the millions is perhaps simply a sign that there may be no other market for the commodity than this false one, but this just signals the problem in Presley's market. Or, free food may be a sign that the capitalists have already accumulated enough capital (having already fed, which they indeed have) and let a portion of it go out of generosity, in which case their generosity is not really generosity but a form of payment due to starving people (Indians, not Mrs. Hooven). If free food really is a sign of actual good will on the part of people managing to separate themselves from the interests of their capital, then the abstract, de-personalized law of supply and demand is not quite the force for good that Presley would believe it is. Instead, investing *people* with goodness takes away from the law of "supply and demand" the property of justice that, Presley argues, inheres in the law. Where wheat once enjoyed being the pinnacle of economy, in this last image it suffers at the hands of economy.

## Bourgeois Discourse and the Uses of Nature

*The Octopus* strains against the rural realist discourse that it erects. It offers image after image of ranchers frenetically strategizing how they are going to turn over their capital, and it shows them struggling not to lose their capital to the production process directed by the "change-of-location" industry. As we've seen in *Blood-Money* and *The Octopus,* the Mussel Slough ranchers mostly fail in this endeavor. The railroad manages to absorb their individual circulations into its own master circulation. But given this, and the discussion just above, how are we to be prevented from reading the farmers' failure as also capital's failure to share its bounty?

Recall that *Blood-Money*'s answer to this question is to challenge the ethics of bounty hunting. The development of local places ultimately involves courting "Development." Capital redeems the desert but plunges those it touches into murky waters. The novel offers no believable way out of the problem, partly because it is mesmerized by it.

Presley is also mesmerized but wants to trick the trick. He insists on a double reading of nature and capital, one that renders the whole question of redemption and ethics moot. In an exchange that proves key to his rationalizations, Presley listens intently to the head of the railroad, Shelgrim.

> "The Wheat is one force, the Railroad, another, and there is the law that governs them—supply and demand. Men have only little to do in the whole business. . . . If you want to fasten the blame of the affair at Los Muertos on any one person, you will make a mistake. Blame conditions, not men."
>
> . . . [Presley concludes that f]orces, conditions, laws of supply and demand—were these then the enemies, after all? Not enemies; there was no malevolence in Nature. Colossal indifference only, a vast trend toward appointed goals. Nature was, then, a gigantic engine, a vast cyclopean power, huge terrible, a leviathan with a heart of steel. (576–77)

The hegemony of industrial capital over the Mussel Slough farmers, though they are themselves party to capitalist strategies, is neutralized. Nature does not have to redeem capital because capital is already natural, and nature is already capitalistic. Nature is not a *place* that existed before Mussel Slough was settled; it is a process that brings Mussel Slough into being. Presley's gambit is that he has rendered it impossible to separate capital from nature. He trusts in a fine line (or no line?) between exploring what sort of discourse might be good for California agriculture and exploring why California agriculture might be useful for bourgeois discourse. It seems to me he invests that trust in the argument that the ebbs and flows of circulation, supply, and demand are equally evident in the production of a nature-centered commodity. That is, just as it is natural that wheat is sown and harvested, that fields are fallow and full, so it is natural that the politics of global demand will even out the politics of global supply: to spatially encircle the globe with commodity fluctuations is akin to, *and an extension of*, the temporal cycles of nature. Nature/Capital figured on, and as, this grand scale means that what ends up "over there" *might as well be* "right here." The world, in the bourgeois sublime, is configured as a single place, a single Location, without difference and heedless of complaint.

# 5

## Realty Redux

### *Landscapes of Boom and Bust in Southern California*

#### Where Is Southern California?

> Of all the booming booms in the booming city of San Bernardino, the boomiest boom is the boom in the Heart Tract, the garden spot of the Beautiful Base Line. Fourteen prizes aggregating $16,000. First 30 lots, $750; remainder, $850. Buy now and make $100.
>
> —Advertisement in the September 1887 issue of the San Bernardino *Times* (quoted in Netz 1915–16)

> [M]ore fortunes were made in California lands and real estate than in gold mining.
>
> —A. M. Sakolski (1932: 256)

"Southern California" did not always exist. It was defined in the acts of regional capital accumulation and intensified real estate sales. Charles Nordhoff, for example, did not know about "Southern California" when he published one of California's most popular guidebooks of the post–Civil War era, *California: For Health, Pleasure, and Residence* (1874). To this New York newspaper editor lured west by the Southern Pacific Railroad (see Starr 1985), Southern California was simply whatever lay south of San Francisco. Not that this was negligible. "In fact," Nordhoff reported, it was "the Italy of this continent; its equal climate, its protection from cold by mountain ranges, its rich soil and healthfulness, give it a place alone among its sister States" (Nordhoff 1874: 172). Nordhoff extolled the "shrewd" citrus growers around Los Angeles, but his definition of the region also included the Salinas Valley, well to the north, and the San Joaquin Valley, isolated from Los Angeles by a rugged stretch of mountains. As yet, the southern San Joaquin Valley still belonged to San Francisco: "Immense tracts of fertile land, with abundant water for irrigation, lie here awaiting settlement and occupation, as public or railroad lands. A number of San Francisco capitalists have bought up 10,000 acres of 'swamp land,' including part of the town of Bakersfield and Kern Island" (Nordhoff 1874: 225).

By the time Walter Lindley and J. P. Widney published their own guidebook, *California of the South: Its Physical Geography, Climate, Resources, Routes of Travel, and Health-Resorts* (1888), few could have held to Nordhoff's amorphous distinctions. Widney and Lindley, both physicians, saw Southern California as considerably smaller than what Nordhoff had written of. But the point in shrinking the region was to see it less as a periphery and more as a center vying with San Francisco for importance.[1] Widney's half of the book is particularly telling. For one thing, by 1888, the climate had shrunk. California south of the Tehachapis Mountains now had its own "belt" of weather embracing "what is distinctively known as Southern California . . . that portion of the State lying south of the transverse chains of mountains just mentioned" (Lindley and Widney 1888: 13). To Widney, the climate north of this belt and on up to California's border with Oregon was as much a single entity as Nordhoff had said all of California south of San Francisco had been. Apart from climatic determinism, of which Widney was an ardent proponent, the real point was that San Francisco's commercial hegemony in California was coming to an end.[2]

"About the year 1875," Widney reasoned, "a great change set in" (Lindley and Widney 1888: 52). Commerce began slipping from the grasp of San Francisco businessmen, shifting south along the coast to Los Angeles, new center of a booming regional economy. Widney, who was also a real estate speculator and booster (see Starr 1985), stressed that by the time of his writing, Los Angeles already had its own rail connections to the east and that these passed over smoother grades and through territory less interrupted by unproductive land than was the case to the north. San Francisco could not boast of such advantages, nor could it compete with the appeal of the southland's balmier temperatures and its attraction to "the best and most highly-cultivated elements of older communities [from the East]." These elements would only improve over time, as "the power of climatic surroundings" worked its charms on "race-development" (Lindley and Widney 1888: 61, 64).

The question of Southern California's whereabouts, as proposed in the two guidebooks, reveals the shift in point of view as capital began accumulating in the southland. But the change was more than just a matter of perspective, or of language. These books were intended to promote and sell a product: land. The more money and Anglos spilled over the Tehachapis and poured in from the east, usurping and then transforming the cattle and range economy of the rancheros, the more "Southern California" was given a definite shape. Drawing attention to the land, and what that land would do when water was brought to it, was accomplished in part with the production of an increasingly specific geographical image.

When we say "Southern California," therefore, we refer as much to a particular historical-economic geography as we do to a real place. The point of this chapter is to investigate that geography. It begins with a discussion of land commodification and economic change in the 1870s and early '80s. This discussion lays out the conditions that enabled what California historians have dubbed the "boom of the eighties" in 1887–88. The boom was a brief but extraordinarily important land (and water) rush that set the tone of Southern California's development for decades. The second half of the chapter is a reading of five novels written about or in the context of these few years of boom and bust in the Southern California economy. (I move through four of these works fairly quickly, just to impart a sense of the plot devices used and the cultural logic driving them. I spend much more time on the fifth, and most popular, of the bunch, Stuart Edward White's *The Rose Dawn*.) I argue that these novels "theorize" the meaning of the boom and bust of the late 1880s along two axes (both, of course, in the rural realist vein). One of these critiques the idea of speculation, of profits without production. This critique typically consists of a narrative that calls for a return to prosperity through agricultural production. The other, conversely, is concerned about giving capitalist speculative practices an "out," by narrating the boom as something that speeded up the Anglo-American takeover of Southern California.

## From Ranchos to Real Estate

The core area of rapid transformation from ranchos to real estate in the post-Mexican period is what I will refer to as Southern California. The area can be thought of as a roughly bounded, very elongated wedge, excluding San Diego, which was an outlier of the boom. One side begins on the coast at Point Conception and heads east to Santa Barbara and Ventura, up the Santa Clara Valley and across the ridges of the San Gabriel and San Bernardino Mountains, to the base of Mount Gorgonio. Here are the headwaters of the Santa Ana River. The second side begins at the river and follows it downstream southwestward to where it disgorges near Newport Beach. The third side follows the coast back up to Point Conception. This triangular area includes mountain canyons where water was impounded for irrigation and hydroelectricity, belts of foothills which are fortunate enough to collect substantial moisture, and semi-arid but fertile coastal lowlands and inland valleys—most especially the Los Angeles and Santa Ana Basins.[3] I will argue (as others have) that, from a social and economic standpoint, the single most important factor in this region was the monetization of land transfer. Monetization was an all-encompassing process that resulted in Mexican land loss and economic displacement. Central to the process were the 1851 Land Act and a serious drought in the 1860s (Cleland 1951; Camarillo 1979).

Except for the higher mountain reaches, the vast majority of Southern California was covered by hundreds of thousands of acres of Spanish and Mexican land grants held by a comparative handful of grantees. Under the Land Act, passed during the year following statehood, all holders of grants were forced to verify to the U.S. government's satisfaction the legitimacy of their titles. Although the majority of the grants were eventually upheld, the land cases crawled through the courts for some thirty years. The litigation fees, the running back and forth between Sacramento and the south, and the taxes levied by the new American rulers gradually eroded the Californios' monopoly on the land. In Los Angeles County, for example, one in ten of these landowners was bankrupted. Moreover, expenses incurred in complying with the Act were often met by selling portions of the land grants. In the same county, 40% of Mexican-granted land was disposed of in this way, usually for very low prices (McWilliams 1973). Also during the 1850s, the rancheros cycled through a boom and bust in the cattle industry: the mining economy in the north provided a sudden, large market for southern beef, but as better breeds and more efficient marketing were gradually established in the San Joaquin Valley (due especially to Henry Miller and Charles Lux) and other places in the north, the bonanza prices that southerners had enjoyed plummeted (McWilliams 1973; Dumke 1944; Cleland 1951). Between the court and tax expenses and the loss of the northern market, the cattle economy was ill-prepared to face a killer drought in 1863–64.

The decimation of Southern California's economy in the 1860s was especially noticed by San Francisco capitalists who reshaped the economy during the next decade. "Comstock millionaires and wealthy retainers of the Central Pacific Railroad," Mike Davis writes, "began to buy up the bankrupt ranchos of the South" (Davis 1990: 107, 108). The story of the lands of Don Abel Stearns, owner of seven ranchos in the San Gabriel and Santa Ana Valleys, has become archetypal. To compensate for the loss of his cattle to drought, he put 200,000 acres of land on the market. They were sold to the Los Angeles and San Bernardino Land Company, actually a syndicate of San Francisco capitalists, for $1.50 per acre—a total outlay of $300,000. The resale of this land inaugurated the 1860s land boom and netted the company $2 million (Guinn 1915–16; Cleland 1941). Davis notes that "Within a decade of the breakup of the Stearns empire, virtually every major land grant . . . had been alienated to Northern California interests" (Davis 1990: 108).

While anxiously awaiting the arrival of the Southern Pacific Railroad, the small city of Los Angeles was meanwhile developing as a pole of accumulation in its own right. In the early 1860s and continuing into the mid-1870s, silver mining in Inyo County kept millions of dollars of bullion moving through Los Angeles. It was to preserve this trade, but also to spur real estate development, that the city's elite lobbied hard for the extension of the railroad (Davis 1990; McAfee 1968).[4]

In the 1870s, large amounts of Southern California land were already on the market, ready for sale by either landowning Californios or individual real estate syndicates. In various locations throughout much of the region, large acreages of this land were bought up by consortiums of various kinds for conversion to agricultural colonies (see Madison [1990] for an excellent recent discussion). Stimulated by the forthcoming rail connection between Southern California and the eastern states, founders of these colonies subdivided large tracts into parcels of five, ten, and twenty acres. Their purposes varied from the strictly pecuniary (i.e., blocks of real estate offered to whomever would buy) to the expressly cooperative. The availability of farming land influenced the location of the colonies, but the lands that were for sale usually existed near urban cores, which have persisted up to the present (Nelson 1959). The colonies drew not only farmers, but lawyers, doctors, teachers, mechanics, craftspersons, and businesspeople (Winther 1953). Riverside (founded 1870), Pasadena (1873), Pomona (1876), Long Beach (1880), Ontario (1882), and many other Southern California communities all began as colonies. Together with the growing fortunes in Los Angeles, they were integral to the productive base upon which the boom of the 1880s rested.

### The Boom of the 1880s

Similar to the flurry of land sales in the late 1860s, the boom of the 1880s had three geographical centers, places of intensive subdivision and inflated land values: Los Angeles, Santa Barbara, and San Diego.[5] Of the three, the primary nexus was Los Angeles (Dumke 1944). In part, the boom was a reflection of economic resurgence, especially a relaxation of credit restrictions, after the 1870s depression. (Not to be discounted either is that land titles had, for the most part, been cleared, per the 1851 Land Act.) But, it also had a base in local production and trade, in Los Angeles and in surrounding agricultural districts. Thus, farm profits were important in announcing the successes that could be had on Southern California land. Indeed, the area was already becoming known as a center of orange production in the 1870s (Dumke 1944; Cleland and Hardy 1929). Investments in citrus, and grape, production helped boost the value of farmland. Ten-acre to forty-acre fruit farms went for $150 to $200 per acre in 1880—up tenfold from the previous decade (Netz 1915–16). These successes, as well as various amenities—health, climate, hotels—were vigorously promoted by the Southern Pacific Railroad, local newspapers, and advertising pamphlets distributed by local governments and private business.

The most proximate cause of the boom, however, was a rate war between the Southern Pacific and the Santa Fe railroads—the two transcontinental lines with terminals in Los Angeles. The completion of the Santa Fe in 1887 triggered deep fare reductions, which in turn set off a frenzy of buying and selling. The boom peaked during the summer months, when $38 million worth of real estate transactions took place in Los Angeles County. One way to see the boom is that, while production and credit had been for a time reasonably well coordinated, the *expected* rate of turnover accruing to land speculation in 1887–88 fatally outpaced the circulation of capital in actual production. As an early historian of the boom has written: "All legitimate buying and selling of real estate was now forgotten, all standards of measurement and comparison were flung aside. A wild enthusiasm and passion for speculation broke over the country and for a brief period the most restless excesses were committed. All values were merely fictitious" (Netz 1915–16: 57). When the boom collapsed, only a few banks failed since most had acted relatively conservatively. And although undeveloped "developments" and broken fortunes lay strewn across Southern California, dozens of subdivisions survived intent on further economic expansion.

The rate war between the two railroads arose over Santa Fe's determination to break the Southern Pacific monopoly in California. (The companies focused on the Midwest, especially Illinois, Iowa, Ohio, and Missouri. Recent hard winters, declining grain prices, and farm consolidation and mechanization were push factors encouraging some Midwesterners to look elsewhere to live.) To travel from the Mississippi Valley to Los Angeles, passengers usually paid in the neighborhood of $125. When the Santa Fe completed its line in 1885, the company offered a fare of $95. The two railroads kept their rates competitive until the beginning of March 1887. On the fifth of the month, they slashed their fares. On the sixth, their largesse overflowed. The fare between Kansas City and Los Angeles fell that morning to $12 . . . $10 . . . $8. "Then," as Dumke explains it, "the Southern Pacific, through some apparent misunderstanding, underbid itself, cutting to six dollars, then to four.

Finally, shortly after noon, the Southern Pacific announced a rate of one dollar. . . . For approximately a year . . . fares remained below twenty-five dollars to Missouri River points and did not soon regain their former heights" (Dumke 1944: 24–26).

With Los Angeles at the center of the land boom, it was also Los Angeles whose capital financed most of the boom towns of the countryside. The city's land brokers organized the biggest auctions. And Los Angeles excursion trains were the primary vehicles used by purchasers of both town and country property as they shopped for real estate (Dumke 1944). Outside the city, in the surrounding valleys and basins, there were several nodes of development: the San Gabriel Valley–Pomona–San Bernardino–Riverside corridor, the San Fernando Valley, and the Santa Ana Valley. Before the height of the boom in 1886–87, each area held within it seeds of development on which the boom capitalized. The largest magnet of boom capital was the San Gabriel Valley corridor, which included Pomona and Ontario and continued east to San Bernardino and Riverside. Here, where town founding was as important, or more so, than farmland development, much of the subdivision followed rail lines, for already the Southern Pacific's tracks laced through the area. (This was a crucial factor in making the boom a region-wide phenomenon.) In addition, alluvial fans plump with groundwater, and occasional surface streams coursing over the landscape, provided water that made for a number of successful agricultural colonies, such as at Pasadena, Ontario, Riverside, and San Bernardino. Their existence spurred further sales of agricultural real estate. The boom in the San Fernando Valley, which primarily consisted of farmlands, was spurred by the Southern Pacific and the town of San Fernando. The Santa Ana Valley boom was based on the previously established towns of Anaheim, Orange, and Santa Ana and the farms that were giving the valley a reputation in fruit growing (Dumke 1944; see also Robinson 1939; Nelson 1959).

Before and during the boom, water was speculated upon together with land. Most water development projects were undertaken by real estate dealers and developers for whom land sales and water supply were inseparable. All over Southern California, the boom, or the easing of credit that immediately preceded it, accelerated irrigation development through the formation of private companies—the Los Nietos Irrigation Company, the Agricultural Ditch and Water Company, the Arroyo Ditch and Water Company, Alhambra Addition Water Company, and dozens more. In Santa Ana, irrigation companies brought irrigated acreage—from 6,400 acres in 1879 to 15,000 in 1888. Also in 1888, in Anaheim, the Anaheim Union Water Company was irrigating 7,000 acres of vineyards. These water developments, based in older communities, were repeated in the newer colonies of Etiwanda and Ontario. In the San Fernando Valley, the boom was given a jump start by three water companies, all adjuncts to land development—the San Fernando Land and Water Company, the Porter Land and Water Company, and the San Fernando Valley Improvement Company. Before 1880, water development in the San Gabriel Valley was only gradually being commenced by undercapitalized ditch companies or, occasionally, by associations of water rights holders. Then, between 1880 and 1902, fifty-seven irrigation companies appeared. Thirteen of these were formed in the early 1880s with the rise in land values, and a dozen others sprang up during 1886–88. Developers, encouraged by the economic development in the wake of the boom, continued forming these companies until there were thirty-two more by 1902 (Dumke 1944). During this period, competing claims over water were a frequent occurrence, sometimes erupting into armed conflict (Clark 1970). One of the water projects repeatedly noted at the time was the construction of Bear Valley Dam in the San Bernardinos, on land purchased by an engineer and his business partner (a coupling that would be noticed in more than one Southern California novel). Nearly four thousand acres were sold to them by Los Angeles landowners and seven hundred acres by the Southern Pacific. Built in 1883–84, when credit was easy to obtain, the dam supplied water to a number of boom colonies through the engineer's Bear Valley Land and Water Company. The value of a share of the company's stock rose from $25 in 1884 to $225 in 1887 (Dumke 1944: 236–37). Dumke notes that the rapid development and mobilization of water resources put pressure on the existing water rights legislation. The passage of the Wright Act in 1887 (see chapter 2), Dumke observes, was associated with the great boom and was "stimulated largely by southern irrigators like L. M. Holt, J. De Barth Shorb, and Judge North of Riverside" (Dumke 1944: 241).

In all the areas touched by the boom, rural and urban, the process of buying and selling was more or less similar: Few land purchases were cash sales; most land was bought on contract and credit. The method varied according to the size of the purchase. Properties bought by syndicates and intended for subdivision were paid for with a 25% or 30% down payment, to be followed by semi-annual payments. Individual lots were sold for a small down payment followed by monthly payments. Options, which were purchased for speculative purposes, were also plentiful. These were small payments on a property made to delay actual purchase for a sixty- or ninety-day period. Typically, a person or consortium with limited capital would by an option, then start a rumor that the property was to be improved. The option could then be sold for a substantial profit (Netz 1915–16).

By the spring of 1888, a glutted market, declining land sales and values, a poor showing of winter tourists, the tightening of credit, and a rise in interest rates spelled the end of the boom. Of all these factors, the credit policy of the region's banks was perhaps the most immediate and powerful force to bring the boom down. Historians have pointed out that because banks acted conservatively as the boom began to crest, they suffered only minimally when the land market crashed. Even as the boom was building in the mid-1880s, for example, banks steadily decreased the amount of loans. In July of 1885, for example, loans extended by Los Angeles banks comprised 80% of deposits. By January of 1888, they made up only 28% of deposits (Netz 1915–16). The restriction of credit was also accompanied by higher interest rates, which further protected banks from failure (Dumke 1944). Tight credit meant a scarcity of money with which to pay obligations once they became due. Rather quickly, panic struck and everyone became a seller. Property values rapidly depreciated. As Netz wrote, "There could be no permanent prosperity by the rich coming here and laying out townsites, and building hotels without really producing anything" (Netz 1915–16: 66).

## Results of the Boom

Though there was no "permanent prosperity" in the boom itself, it left an indelible imprint on many areas of life in Southern California—population, capital expansion, town growth, irrigation, labor policy, social geography.

The boom years brought tens of thousands of tourists and new residents, many from the Midwest, to Southern California. In 1870, fewer than 6,000 people lived in Los Angeles; still only 11,000 by 1880; yet by 1890, there were over 50,000 permanent residents. Although Los Angeles's population growth was more pronounced than surrounding areas, substantial increases were recorded through much of the south between 1880 and 1890, even accounting for the thousands who moved away after 1888 (see Dumke 1944: 278, for exact and estimated population figures). The incoming tide meant more than just greater throngs on the street or at the railroad depot. The profits that came back to Los Angeles investors were, from a geographical standpoint, largely new money, for land was mostly being bought up by newcomers (Dumke 1944: 264–65). In ever-expanding waves, Mike Davis adds, during the 1860s, 1870s, and 1880s, migrants "transferred their savings and small fortunes into Southern California real estate. The massive flow of wealth between regions produced population, income and consumption structures seemingly out of all proportion to Los Angeles's actual production base" (Davis 1990: 25).

The value of land and improvements increased by as much as 500%. Los Angeles and two of its tributary counties, Orange (carved out of Los Angeles County in 1889) and San Bernardino, were the undisputed leaders. The value of their real estate between 1880 and 1890 climbed from $12 million to $64 million. Property improvements rose from under $4 million to $20 million (Hinton 1891: 87).[6] During the boom decade, most of the land speculation had an urban focus, with $34 million worth of mortgages on town and city lots. With $27 million worth of mortgages, however, rural acreage was no mean runner-up (Dumke 1944: 267).[7]

For all the boom's urban foci, agriculture was still the basis of the Southern California economy when the collapse came. This remained the case until after World War One (Nelson 1959). Essential to this fact was that sales of farm property (and the intent to sell farmland) during the boom spurred investments in irrigation. For example, irrigated acreage served by the water systems in and around the Santa Ana Basin (the eastern section of what I have called the San Gabriel Valley corridor) grew many times over between 1880 and 1890. Riverside jumped from 5,000 to 10,000 acres; the Gage Canal and North Riverside Canal from nothing to 25,000 combined; Pomona from 1,000 to 12,000; Ontario and Etiwanda from nothing to 8,000 combined; Cucamonga from 2,000 to 10,000; Bear Valley Reservoir from nothing to 18,000 (Hinton 1891: 87). Irrigated agriculture underwrote industrial growth, too. The majority of new industries had a basis in the new utilization of agricultural products, such as the fruit-drying plants that sprang up around Glendale. Towns and farms in Los Angeles and the other boom districts were knit together into a single economy—a multinucleated region of over forty new satellite settlements. By 1887, towns from Ventura to Pasadena and San Bernardino, from Anaheim to Riverside and Colton, were all linked to each other, to Los Angeles, and to San Diego by railroad (Dumke 1944).[8]

Acutely aware that the boom had given Southern California a tremendous jump start, local capitalists once again turned their attention to competition with San Francisco. They saw an opening in Los Angeles's incipient labor movement. If they could nip it in the bud, advantage was theirs relative to union-strong San Francisco. Certain of the city's developers, businessmen, and bankers—men such as *Los Angeles Times* owner and real estate speculator Harrison Gray Otis—formed the Los Angeles Chamber of Commerce and, later, the Merchants' and Manufacturers' Association. In alliance with the transcontinental railroads (the largest landowners in Southern California), they organized an anti-union drive, mobilized to get picketing outlawed, and inaugurated a prolonged era of open shop. They believed that a source of cheap labor had to be kept on hand if Los Angeles was to once again attract investment. Labor historian David Selvin notes that the leading burghers in the Los Angeles Chamber of Commerce hoped to "build a vast agricultural-industrial empire. The more perceptive—later, even the less acute—saw that a large pool of cheap labor would help Los Angeles prosper at the expense of the relatively high wage, increasingly unionized economy of San Francisco." In fact, Los Angeles's economy was already dependent on the cheap labor provided by thousands of newly arrived Anglo, Mexican, and Chinese workers (Selvin 1966: 29; see also Davis 1990; Starr 1985; McWilliams 1983).

Into the early twentieth century, the Los Angeles Chamber of Commerce probably gave more thought to labor structures in Southern California than did early historians of Southern California. For years, it was a tradition in historical writing to give short shrift to changes in Southern California's social geography and the division of labor that followed the arrival of the Anglos (e.g., Netz 1915–16; Dumke 1944). To Dumke (as to Nordhoff, Lindley, and Widney, two generations before), the boom "wiped out forever the traces of the Spanish-Mexican pastoral economy." This accomplished, "the American citizen built his trolley lines, founded his banks, and irrigated his orange groves. The boom was the final step in the process of making California truly American" (Dumke 1944: 275–77). His intimation that the Spanish-Mexican citizenry simply disappeared denies a broader social geography that had been in the making since the 1860s.

The demise of the pastoral economy and the entrance of capitalist social relations signaled by statehood was a two-sided affair. On the one hand, Mexican Californians were overwhelmed by droves of Anglo immigrants. There is some truth, therefore, about what Dumke says. On the other hand, Mexicans did not just disappear. In the wake of land loss and political disenfranchisement, Mexican society was reshaped by the barrio and proletarianization (Camarillo 1979; see also Almaguer 1994; Romo 1983; Griswold del Castillo 1979; Heizer and Almquist 1971).

Mexican pueblos established before the American takeover of California often became the core of the segregated barrio. In Los Angeles, for example,

> The vast majority of Spanish-surnamed property owners, and approximately 70 percent of the total Chicano population . . . , inhabited two enclaves in the city. The larger one corresponded to the core area of the original Mexican pueblo in the central part of Los Angeles adjacent to the plaza; the smaller was located in an area just south of the old pueblo. During the late 1880s Chicanos continued to be highly segregated in the old pueblo area . . . and in the less segregated area to the south. (Camarillo 1979: 118)

In some places, however, pueblos were effectively destroyed. For example, in San Salvador, a Mexican-dominated area near San Bernardino, the two existing pueblos disintegrated at the same time that enforced changes in the mode of production began. Ranching and farming became impossible when access to grazing lands was denied and fence laws enacted. Mexicans gradually moved away to Riverside, Colton, and San Bernardino, leaving the area they left behind to more of the same: absorption "of San Salvador land . . . into the encroaching farms and ranches of Anglo owners" (Camarillo 1979: 122).

The formation of a Mexican wage-working class—especially in the lower strata of the capitalist labor market, where they joined, and then eclipsed, Native American and Chinese workers—was a direct parallel to barrioization. Mexicans worked the semi-skilled and unskilled jobs in both the tourist-, construction-, and (nascent) manufacturing-driven economy of the towns and the agriculture-driven economy of the countryside. By 1880, the scenario was nearly complete. The vast majority (60%–80.9%) of the Mexican workforce were employed in unskilled jobs, whereas unskilled Anglo workers comprised a small minority (8.9%–13.5%) of the Anglo labor market. "As the economy changed from one based on cattle raising to one tied to large-scale capitalist agricultural production and urban development," Camarillo writes, "Anglos successfully entrenched themselves as the dominant political and economic force in the region" (Camarillo 1979: 132).[9] Incorporated into the Anglo project of inventing "Southern California" was a racial division of labor. After the Southern California Chinese dwindled in number, Mexican Californians labored in the fields, towns, and cities of Southern California. Mexicans (especially women) worked the canneries and packing sheds of the "new" agriculture. Mexican workers graded, picked, and shoveled the streets of the modern transportation network; they dug ditches and hauled material required by the utility companies.

The boom of the 1880s and the Anglo-dominated social and economic relations of later decades did not wipe out Mexican Californians. In fact, they depended on Mexican labor—and then reinstalled (sometimes with the help of the Mexicans themselves) Mexican culture, or the "Spanish" culture of the Mexican landed class, in commodified form.[10] Historian Kevin Starr has vividly documented the emergence of the Southern California "mythology" (Starr 1985). The formulation was predicated on an obsession with health, assured prosperity, and the enshrinement of the mission and rancho past. California as a place where the invalid could attain health, or where the healthy could remain healthy, was stressed in countless pamphlets and books. These texts plied readers with the stark differences between the crystalline atmosphere of California and the asthmatic summers and pneumonic winters of the East. The romance of the missions, catalyzed by Helen Hunt Jackson's 1884 novel, *Ramona,* fed into the image of California as a pulmonary oasis. Jackson intended that her book would forever testify to the Anglo land grab and the consequent injustices done to Native Americans and Mexicans. Instead, it was remembered as "a celebration of Southern California as a sunny arcadia"—a place that would yield the vigor, the social and domestic refinements, and the sophisticated culture of Mediterranean civilization (Starr 1985: 62; also Walker 1950). In a message to Midwestern farmers, *California of the South* states the idea succinctly: "Orange-culture naturally develops the finer qualities of humanity to a higher plane than that of corn- and hog-raising" (Lindley and Widney 1887: 241).

For their largesse and hospitality, the old rancheros were fondly recalled by Nordhoff, Lindley, and Widney, and in countless other contemporary narratives. But they were faulted for their shortsightedness and lack of pecuniary know-how. "Spanish California," Nordhoff wrote in the decade before the boom, "did not belong to the nineteenth century, and the railroad will, in a year or two, leave no vestige of it this side of the Mexican border" (Nordhoff 1874: 245). Of course, given the near simultaneity of barrioization and romanticization, it was precisely the vestiges that would be turned into some of Southern California's most precious commodities.

To have romanticized the past in the act of erasing it was a dangerous thing to do, however, in the context of boom and bust. For what else was boom and bust but a kind of self-erasure? (Of the one hundred or so towns platted by developers in Los Angeles County between 1884 and 1887, sixty-two busted [Nelson 1959: 85–86].) And what sort of pecuniary know-how was that? That, at least, was what California writer Charles Dudley Warner wanted to know after the boom. In 1890–91, he published a series of articles in *Harper's Magazine*, later collected into his book *Our Italy* (1904). With full cognizance of the busted boom, he wrote, "I wish there might be something solid in [the] expectation . . . that this may be a region where the restless American will lose something of his hurry and petty feverish ambition." Perhaps, he mused, the American in Southern California "will take, he is already taking, something of the tone of the climate and the old Spanish occupation." Yet, anxious to venture too far in this direction, he adds: "But the race instinct of thrift and of 'getting on' will not wear out in many generations. Besides, the condition of living at all in Southern California in comfort, and the social life indispensable to our people, demands labor . . . demands industry." Lest the original point be forgotten, though, he asks again, "Is it altogether an unpleasing thought that the conditions of life will be somewhat easier . . . , the race having reached the sunset of the continent?" (Warner 1904: 320–21). Warner's musings betray not a little anxiety over just what this boom and bust meant and what sort of ethnic relations were the right ones to proselytize about. The interesting move, for our purposes, is that Warner simultaneously summons *and* erases the supposed values of the old "California Pastoral" (Bancroft 1888). The goal is to be like the old "Spanish" occupants and better than them at the same time. To quote Warner again: "Orderly, contented, industry; increasing its gains day by day, little by little, is the life and hope of any State" (Warner 1904: 342; also Henderson 1994a). It is precisely this sentiment that drove a generation of fiction writing about the boom to speculate on agriculture as the seat of the new prosperity.

## The Southern California Boom Novel

> Q-u-i-t b-u-y-i-n-g? May I be eternally scorched if that isn't strange talk.
>
> —Theodore S. Van Dyke (1890: 135)

> I can not tell why, but I despise this country. . . . It has no past, its future reveals nothing but an ignominious scramble for dollars, its politics are odious and its population mongrel.
>
> —Charles Dwight Willard to Harriet E. Willard, Santa Barbara, February 20, 1887 (quoted in Orsi 1973: 37)

The economic mechanism for the transformation to what Kevin Starr calls the "bourgeois utopia"—indeed, its very basis—was real estate. In as little time as a generation, Southern California was converted from hundreds of thousands of acres of land-grant ranchos to hundreds of thousands of acres of resaleable rural and urban property. The boom and bust of the 1880s and the notoriety gained thereby sent this fact home to a congeries of writers and major eastern publishers competing for the Southern California story into the twentieth century—Frederick R. Sanford, *The Bursting of a Boom* (1889); Theodore S. Van Dyke, *Millionaires of a Day* (1890); Horace Annesley Vachell, *The Procession of Life* (1899); Frank Lewis Nason, *The Vision of Elijah Berl* (1905); Stewart Edward White, *The Rose Dawn* (1920).[11]

Real estate in these novels is figured as a fulcrum for a wide array of transactions. It is not just an object, property to be bought or sold; it is a social relationship that draws forth class, gender, and ethnic distinctions, metes out penalties and rewards, and in the end contrives the downfall of its abusers. At the same time that the real estate economy is figured as something necessary and desirable to engage in, it is also a hurdle of sorts. The novels try to work out a contradiction in the land commodification and development process, between land and water as a farmer's means of production and land and water as developers' means of extracting rents without, moreover, having to produce anything themselves. The plots that were devised to explore and settle this contradiction are what I shall call rural realist narratives of production. These narratives decried the wave of speculative investments that capped the founding of "Southern California." They consisted of tales that shifted the center of economic activity away from nonproductive, speculative economies toward productive ones.

However, the production narrative hesitated to be critical of capitalist social relations per se, since they had everything to do with making Anglo "horticulturalists" new landowners and water-right holders. Those aspects of the new social relations were decidedly encouraged and directly related to the formulations worked out in what I will call rural realist identity narratives. The brow-knitting contradiction of boom *and* bust, in what was supposed to be an economy superior to the Mexican Californian one, was smoothed over by Anglo-izing processes of land transfer and cultural change. Desired social ends retroactively diminished, or even justified, risky economic means: Real estate was thus figured as a harbinger of a new Anglo identity for Southern California.

## The Rural Realist Production Narrative

The Southern California production narratives actually tend to focus on the financial circuit "upstream" of the farms (i.e., the realm of illegitimate speculative profits). Presumably, it was enough to simply use the farm as a solid, reified, and dependable "backstory." This is true of *The Bursting of a Boom* (1889), *Millionaires of a Day* (1890), and *The Vision of Elijah Berl* (1905). Only *The Procession of Life* (1899) dares to spend much time on farm settings, and even then circuits of finance capital are crucial to its plot twists. A fifth novel, *The Rose Dawn* (1920), works at both locations, devoting space to both farms and financiering and the conflict between the two. (I will discuss this novel in the section on the identity narrative, since it nicely illustrates the ideological interdependence of production and social identity themes.)

In *The Bursting of a Boom*, Warren, a young New York lawyer and society man, sets out for Ventura to see if he can "manage the boom" in the Santa Clara Valley, northwest of Los Angeles. For this purpose, he has sunk two-thirds of his capital into the Oakdale Land and Water Company, a syndicate that intends to lay out town and farm sites and develop a water supply. Warren knows nothing about the agricultural potential of the tract; he only knows what his partners have assured him, that real estate values are jumping.

Mollie, to whom he has become increasingly attracted, is contemptuous of this wealthy young man's pretensions of making money without working for it. In her view, "'it certainly takes no great amount of education to delude poor unsophisticated Easterners into speculating in real estate'" (97). The narrator chimes in, "It never dawned upon even the shrewdest, keenest, and most far-sighted of these speculators . . . to stop long enough to ascertain if there was any reason that a city *should* grow up where they had located this new town site" (109). The boom goes bust, and the Oakdale Land and Water Company folds because it had been formed too late in the boom-bust cycle. Warren loses the bulk of his fortune in the crash; but as far as Mollie is concerned, his loss restores him to his proper place.

Gradually, Mollie has been realizing that her and Warren's personalities actually are well suited to each other. Three events irrevocably win her over. One proves that Warren is a man of action, not just of ideas. This occurs when he rescues her from her runaway horse. The second is the fact of his financial loss. This puts him in harmony with the requirements of gender. Had he retained his fortune and therefore been able to offer her unending prosperity, she would have been deprived of her very identity, because the best—and only—thing she can do is to "aid him in his conflict against trouble, and assist him in turning defeat into victory" (234). The only troublefree relationship, that is, is a relationship with troubles to be worked out. And what is the ideal location for them to work things out? Says Warren, "'I own a fine piece of ranch property here, just outside of the city limits. It is a good property, well stocked with fruit-trees and nuts, all in bearing condition'" (247). His financial loss, which (surprise!) left him with only this one piece of property, also synchronizes with the post-boom developmental bias. Warren needs to work, the country needs to be worked. The third event, then, is that he decides to rent out his New York home, live and work on the ranch, and practice law. Mollie, a New Yorker herself, who had come to tour California with her aunt and uncle, makes a similar renunciation: "'I have eaten the lotus and I have forgotten my old home'" (248).

According to *Millionaires of a Day*, Warren's story is the story of many foiled speculators who remained in California. Usually read as a satirical commentary on boom methods to sell town sites, Van Dyke's book is really a booster's plug for the countryside, which "right now is on the eve of the biggest boom it ever had—a boom of raising good stuff and plenty of it to sell to those who can't raise it" (200). Seasoning his book with references to the superiority of California resources over eastern ones, Van Dyke, also a promotional writer and newspaperman, advises that "One half the money spent in mere convenience for future tourists if put into the development of water and railroads to open the interior and connect its different portions would have made the country the richest in the world" (126). More rounds of land commodification are definitely *not* what Van Dyke fears. Quite the opposite. The boom provided not the opportunity to critique the plunder but an occasion for his own promotional enthusiasm for reorienting it. "Thousands of people supposed to have seen something and been somewhere were acting as if money had just been discovered on this earth" (125). Now the question was not how they were acting but where they were acting:

> In the little glade at the base of the hill, where mighty live-oaks nod over wavy swells of ground clad in wild-oats, foxtail, and ivy, where the yelp of the coyote still wakes the cool silence of the nights and the wild-cat lies in the edge of the lilac and manzanita to spring up the hare that plays along its edges, is the cottage of the man who but three years ago required a special bookkeeper and stenographer and typewriter to attend to his private accounts and correspondence. (192)

The speculators who bottomed out discovered the thousands of acres available in the uplands. Such men now make more money on their forty acres than when they had controlling interest in the land corporations. In this version of the production narrative, illegitimate real estate economy becomes legitimate when linked to production—when circulation is tied back to the turnover of productive capital.

A more complex story of land speculation is *The Vision of Elijah Berl*. Elijah Berl, a New England émigré to the San Bernardino area, feels called by God to reclaim the desert. Yet his feelings are conflicted: "'If I can only do this, it means fame and fortune to me . . .'" (19). To this end, he enlists the aid of Ralph Winston, an engineer who cut his teeth on northern California hydraulic mining operations. Elijah's proposal appeals to Winston because it speaks to his own professional calling: "The building of a great storage dam in the mountains, the laying out of canals should lead the stored waters to the sun-parched deserts; this was an engineer's work" (5).

Elijah and Ralph, intent on stirring up a boom in orange cultivation on the outskirts of Ysleta—a fictional boom town at the base of the San Bernardino foothills, east of Los Angeles—form the Las Cruces Irrigation Company. They bring aboard businesswoman Helen Lonsdale to manage the company office. Like Ralph, Helen is a northern California émigré who grew up in the mother lode and drifted south with the decline of mining in the north. Together, they are figures for the southward tilt of California's economy. Elijah is smitten with Helen because of her business acumen, her independence, and her interest in Las Cruces's work. Helen is everything that Elijah's wife, Amy, is not. Amy is less than taken with the whole enterprise of Southern California and, because of this, she is deeroticized by Elijah. "'It's these miserable orange trees. I wish oranges had never grown in this country. . . . You look at the mountains and the springs and the orange trees, but never at me'" (17–18).

Anxious to realize a profit before the boom collapses, Ralph recognizes that the company needs quick and heavy financial backing. After some negotiating, Ralph and Elijah convince an investor named Seymour to put up $100,000. Helen does not want to be left out of the venture. With $5,000 to invest she proposes buying up five thousand acres from a Mexican land grantee and setting up a separate land company. The settlers on this land would buy their water from the Las Cruces company, thereby increasing the profits of all the investors.

The plans are threatened when a speculator tries to cash in at the Pacific Bank in Ysleta, instigating a run on the bank. Amidst the panic, Elijah arranges privately with a bank cashier, T. J. Mellin, to embezzle $50,000 of Las Cruces funds. Elijah is going to use the money to set up another land and water company, figuring that he can use the profits to pay back the money to Las Cruces before it is missed by Seymour. Mellin sees an opportunity to make some money of his own. He forces Elijah to take out a mortgage, which will have to be publicly registered, in order to buy for an exorbitant sum the charter to establish the new company. When the mortgage is publicly posted, Berl's shady dealings are revealed. Seymour decides that there is no point in prosecuting Elijah because had he not withdrawn the money, the Las Cruces funds would have disappeared along with the failed Pacific Bank. But Elijah, in spiritual ruins because his "vision" required him to act like every other boomer, wanders off into the desert. There, he is rescued and cared for by another outsider, a local Mexican rancher. Still, he slips further toward mental collapse.

Convinced that everyone is against him, Elijah decides to sabotage the Las Cruces dam project, which, along with aqueducts and canal works, is now completed. Up at the dam, a christening ceremony is about to begin when Helen spies Elijah at the gates of the waste weir. He has jammed the mechanism that opens the gates. In a last ditch effort, Helen finally persuades him that, unscrupulous dealings and all, events have come out in his favor. Frantically, Elijah succeeds in opening the flood gates but is swept down the canyon in the torrent of water. The book closes a few years later with a look at Palm Wells, the bungalows-amidst-the-orange-groves farm suburb spawned by the Las Cruces company. Here in Palm Wells is the new home of Ralph, Helen, and their baby.

*The Vision of Elijah Berl* reinforces the same themes of *The Bursting of a Boom* and *Millionaires of a Day*—that is, the failure of characters who engage in unsavory business practices and the importance of agricultural production once the boom has collapsed. Both Warren in *The Bursting of a Boom* and Elijah are faulted for trying to make money from idle speculation. Warren is restored when his effect on the world is based on action. Similarly, Ralph—an engineer—ultimately gets the credit for the irrigation works and reaps the rewards as a landowner. Elijah, self-centered and dreamy, meets his end. These novels celebrate the production side of the economic equation, the back-to-the-land atonements for the crime of 1887–88.

If the rhythms of boom and bust as fed through social and sexual reproduction are thinly veiled in *The Vision of Elijah Berl* and *The Bursting of a Boom*, they are writ large in *The Procession of Life*. In this novel, there are two sisters, one an "idler" (Esther) who marries a "worker" (Jeff) and the other a "worker" (Martha) who marries an "idler" (Guy). The point of these pairings is clearly put by a question that Esther asks her husband: "'[W]hat should have happened if I had married Guy and you had married Martha[?] I suppose Nature is the only honest matchmaker. If the idlers intermarried, and workers only mated with workers, the world would soon be divided into two distinct races—those who did nothing and those who did everything. The one would be wiped out by inanition and the other by exhaustion'" (233). Here, family equations are also class equations. But Esther is not talking about capitalists marrying laborers. In reality, Jeff and Esther each come from wealthy stock.

Esther's mother is appalled that her daughter would give up her independent means and submit to becoming a farmer's wife. Jeff has alienated himself from his family's wealth in order to earn his own livelihood on the farm. He soon learns that hard work alone cannot keep Esther and him in room and board. Jeff has a rough time of farming precisely because his occupation is not immune from economic crisis. We are informed that his wheat ranch, La Carisa, nears failure because this is an era of high mortgages for farmers and of declining wheat prices. When Esther's mother comes to the realization that a marriage can be successful even when financially wanting, she saves the farm by paying off Jeff and Esther's mortgage just before foreclosure. Then Jeff's father dies, leaving him $250,000. (*Contra* John Graham in *Blood-Money*, Jeff may keep the money as a reward for the labor whose value he well understands. Jeff has already renounced easy wealth, whereas Graham destroys everything by leaving in search of it.) Jeff decides that since wheat will not pay, he will set up an experimental farm in order to prove that Southern California's future lies in orchards, vineyards, and stock. Here is repeated the same theme common to all the production narratives, the transfer of idle capital into real estate and then back into productive capital. The theme is carried through in that figure we have seen already, the capitalist laborer, here in the guise of Jeff.

Jeff does what Esther needs to appreciate more—work. The argument is solidified at the end of the novel. Guy, who is Esther's parallel insofar as he is also an idler, comes to a sudden realization after nearly leading his marriage to ruin:

> This was the lotus-land, so called. What message had it for him? A message of peace? Yes, but not of rest. From the tiny blade of grass pushing upward to light and sunshine to the stupendous ebb and flow of the ocean, was not the eternal energy made manifest? And was he created to stand aloof, an idle spectator, a mere time-killer? Not so. He rose to his feet and drew a deep breath. "By God!" he exclaimed, "I will work, too." (318–19)

Guy thus takes Esther's notion further. Idlers should not just marry workers, they should become workers.

In the production narratives, the spotlight is turned away from the financial circuit of the economy and pointed instead toward production on the farm. One could say that the plots of these novels are just tracing out the boom and bust cycle in order to buttress the notion that Southern California's economic well-being was linked to its agricultural prosperity—that these two things were one and the same. But, more so, the logic of the production narrative is that it is wrong to think that money can beget money without producing something in between. Still, there is something bothersome about this aspect of the production narrative, because the plots of these novels, in fact, say that speculative practices actually *are* the leverage for agricultural development. They also say that the actions of the practitioners of speculation are punishable (especially in *The Vision of Elijah Berl* and *The Bursting of a Boom*). They want to have their cake and eat it too. Producers are shown as de facto needing the money that speculators pour into the economy, but these same speculators are then judged on the producers' terms, for these are the fiat terms of the narrators.

## The Rural Realist Identity Narrative

Woven through the production narratives we have just examined are concerns about the ethnic identity of Southern California. For example, in *The Bursting of a Boom*, the narrator warns that the "Spanish," an "ardent and impetuous race," must be approached carefully because of their "fiery temper and hot prejudices." After breaking up a fight between a young Anglo and the son of one of the few remaining Spanish landowners, Warren cautions, "I would invite your attention to the fact this is now a civilized section; the laws now have a force out here, and the sentiment of the people endorses this love of law and order" (142). The ranchero past, it is strongly implied, has come to outlive itself—in Nordhoff's words, Mexican Californians are not of the nineteenth century. In another version, especially in *The Vision of Elijah Berl*, there is the belief that a divine hand has been arranging affairs to the benefit of the newly dominant Anglo immigrants. Alternatively, as in *Elijah Berl* and *The Rose Dawn*, Mexican and Anglo Californians are waged in outright struggle, as competing members of the bourgeoisie. Whoever can "do" real estate best wins, even if the game is a little crass. Although all of the boom novels implicitly offer one or more of all these formulations, the quintessential one, and most popular of its time, is *The Rose Dawn* (1920). Written with hindsight on the 1880s boom, its author credits Sanford's and Van Dyke's boom novels as influences. *The Rose Dawn* offers a synthesis of the narratives of production and identity, giving equal weight to the struggles between a land grantee and the speculative interests that try to ruin him.

Like *The Bursting of a Boom* and *The Vision of Elijah Berl*, *The Rose Dawn* concerns manipulations in the real estate and land development industry, but it explores much further the conflict between residual and emergent social formations in Southern California. The final book in Stewart Edward White's trilogy of California novels, its characters are directly or indirectly involved in the transition of the ranch lands around Santa Barbara into an irrigated region. The characters are related to each other in terms of the economic interests they represent. One set of characters revolves around Colonel Richard Peyton, the owner of a large, old ranch who clings to the traditional social and economic order of cattle and pasture and tries to prevent the sale and subdivision of his property. Another set of characters is the father and daughter team of Brainerd and Daphne. Brainerd is a widower who farms a section of land that used to be owned by Peyton and that sits in the middle of Peyton's ranch. These characters are opposed by a third set—a transplanted, retired eastern businessman and developer, Patrick Boyd, and his son, Kenneth. Peyton clearly represents the passing rancho economy. Brainerd and Daphne represent Southern California's future as an intensively farmed, irrigated region. Boyd represents the urban-based power of real estate. The plot that draws these characters together concerns what land use will replace the old rancho economy. Once it is clear that Colonel Peyton is out of the way, that his real estate machinations are no contender in the battle against the Boyds, the battle is primarily fought between Patrick and Kenneth. That is, the novel is concerned with shedding a critical light on capitalist practices, depicting them as consisting of a range of possibilities. Patrick is motivated by a pure capitalist logic and Kenneth by respect for tradition, for local ways, and for long-term goals taught to him during his romance with Daphne.

## Colonel Peyton and the Rancho

The novel opens in the mid-1880s with Colonel Richard Peyton surveying (Presley-like) the grounds of his 30,000–acre Rancho de la Corona del Monte, which, together with the neighboring Las Flores rancho, is the last anchor of genteel "Spanish" culture. Situated to the north of Los Angeles and bordering the town of

Arguello, in fictitious Arguello County, it is a classic Southern California setting, sandwiched between the mountains and the sea.

Before financial troubles beset him, Colonel Peyton had been the crown patriarch of Arguello, a society that had come to be defined by its intermingling of ranch, hotel, and town life. Ethnic displacement and proletarianization are well in place. In Peyton's employ at the ranch are multiple generations of loyal Mexican ranch hands and in the house itself a faithful Chinese cook. Peyton owns the two tourist hotels in town—one, a comfortable establishment for tourists who stay through the winter and that he personally oversees; the other, geared to working- and middle-class visitors. Not yet hit by the boom, the region is nonetheless beginning to see more and more tourists remain in the area, buying 20–40 acre plots, planting Bahia navel oranges, discovering irrigation, and making a little money for their efforts. As the Colonel makes his rounds about Arguello, he is recognized everywhere and is given access to any place of his choosing, from the wealthy homes of the Arguello elite to the office of the First National Bank president, Oliver Mills.

Like many other past and present owners of ranchos, Peyton has overborrowed on his property in order to have the necessary cash to live day to day and to support his hotels. On this occasion, he needs a loan of $15,000 for the Fremont, his luxury hotel. Although Mills is concerned that the hotel already carries as heavy a mortgage as it can support, he loans the money anyway but on condition that the Colonel sell a piece of his property in order to repay the note in thirty days. Mills warns Peyton of the danger of the situation, explaining that through this very process the ranchos have been divided up over the years:

> "Some day when you get time I wish you would go over to the courthouse and look over the tax lists of the outside property for years past. It would open your eyes. First lists were small and all Spanish names. Then they became larger, and alongside of each Spanish name appeared one or two American names. As time went on the lists grew longer and longer, and even the few Spanish names became fewer and the American names more numerous. Now how do you account for that?"
>
> "The big ranchos were divided up, of course."
>
> "Yes, but why? Not one of the those old Spanish holders would sell an acre. I'll tell you how it happened in one word—mortgaged! In the case of the Cantado in the south, old Pancho borrowed twenty-five thousand dollars. The interest was high and was compounded every month. Before the matter was settled Pancho owed nearly three hundred thousand and lost the whole ranch, just on the basis of that original twenty-five thousand—that's all he ever really got for it." (71)

Mills announces that very soon even Las Flores—whose Don Vincente is a close friend of the Colonel—will be foreclosed unless an interest payment can be made. Loathe to see Las Flores obliterated, the Colonel makes a loan to Don Vincente. Peyton subsequently goes to a Los Angeles bank for a loan to cover his loan from Mills. Then, in order to raise more cash, he sells his stock in Arguello's own First National Bank—and all this away from Mill's prying eyes.

The Colonel's efforts prove fruitless against the downsizing and managerialism that lay siege to the indebted properties. After a couple of years, First National forecloses on Las Flores and replaces Don Vincente with an agent of the bank.

The Colonel's own pyramiding debt forces him to trim back his operations. He sells his hotels to a real estate syndicate, which in turn hires a professional manager to run them. The Fremont is now a "very perfect machine for comfortable living while away from home: it was no longer a home itself" (229). As the Colonel economizes (and it is his wife, Allie, formerly protected by the Colonel from the ranch's economic troubles, who teaches him how to scale back), the ranch's link to the town gradually corrodes. Without hotels to run, the Colonel and the tourists no longer know each other. Eventually, the Colonel is forced to let more and more of his ranch hands go. The result is a smaller but more efficient operation. The Colonel is able to hold onto his ranch for a while longer.

## Patrick Boyd and Real Estate

While the Colonel attends to his affairs, Patrick Boyd mingles with other eastern and midwestern capitalists who spend the winter months at Peyton's Fremont Hotel. Unlike these other capitalists, Boyd is alert to the economic potential of the area, especially the potential for anyone who owns real estate. "'[You] can stick a railroad up the coast, and bore a tunnel in through these mountains here for water so you can irrigate the way they've begun to do at San Bernardino, and cut up these big ranches into farms with water on them, and—'" Boyd is cut short and silenced by his cronies' laughter (100). But the narrator picks up the argument: "The vision, genuine though narrowly commercial, that had made him what he was, pierced the veils of apathy behind which Arguello slumbered to a sense of the rose dawn of a modern day. Now, suddenly, there on top of the mountain he came to a decision" (100). Promptly, Boyd sets out to learn—from everyone and anyone, from the bootblack to the banker—what makes Arguello tick and how he can wake it up. His first stroke of luck is to acquire from a broker, Ephraim Spiner, the First National Bank stock that Colonel Peyton had had to unload. This purchase "at once gave him considerable influence in the management [of the bank], should he choose to exert it" (104).

Boyd increases his influence at the bank and plans a massive development project consisting of a whole series of horizontally and vertically linked projects. The first stage in his plan is to modernize the town so as to later boost land values. In order to finance street improvements, he fixes the election of the Arguello town council so as to ensure that the council will assess property owners for the cost of paving. He sets up the Western Construction Company, purchases quarry land on the outskirts of town, gets a contract to pave the streets, and leases his own quarry to the company. And he pays extraordinary rates for advertising the Western Construction Company in the local newspaper in order to ensure favorable editorials on all the recent civic improvements. Later, he gains a seat on the board of directors at First National, thus gaining a "birds-eye-view of the affairs of the county" (208). Sardonically, the narrator adds that Patrick Boyd does not do all this for money, but "to see Arguello wake up and be somebody: for he loved the valley between the mountains and the sea as only an Easterner transplanted to California can love" (208–9).

When the transcontinental railroads begin a rate war, a real estate frenzy breaks out in Los Angeles. Boyd travels to that city to observe how the boomers and speculators operate. He returns to Arguello with two convictions. "The first was that this epidemic was sure to reach Arguello sooner or later. . . . The second was that until the boom broke, and until genuine prosperity had had a chance to struggle to its feet after being knocked flat by the explosion, his irrigated twenty-thirty acre farm scheme was as dead as a Pharoah. Few people were thinking farm" (263). Boyd initiates the boom in Arguello by subdividing some of his land in the foothills and having it sold off by a boomer who comes up from Los Angeles. Soon, the boom hits the town full force. Only the Colonel and Brainerd isolate themselves from all the activity. The one part of Boyd's scheme that does not work out, however, is purchasing from Colonel Peyton a hundred acres adjacent to the town. The Colonel refuses to sell. Nonetheless, Boyd, who keeps his shrewd wits about him during the boom, makes a fortune.

When Boyd senses that the boom is reaching a critical peak and therefore is in danger of collapsing, he gets the First National Bank to cut back on its loans and to make loans only on pre-boom land values. The boom collapses, but the banks remain open. There is a quick recovery: "Men talked in terms not of profits, but of production. And Patrick Boyd knew that at last the time had come for him to put forward his old scheme of irrigated small farms" (285).

The vast acreage of the Corona del Monte, now the last of the original ranchos in Arguello County, becomes more important to him than ever before. For Boyd's scheme takes a new turn. His idea is to impound water in the mountains above Arguello, generate electricity, and then irrigate thousands of acres across the foothill region. Because Corona del Monte is close to town and of exactly the right topography, Boyd goes at the rancho with a vengeance.

He invites William Bates to town. Unbeknownst to anyone in Arguello, except Boyd, is the fact that Bates is one of America's most powerful capitalists. Bates's manipulations nearly rule the stock market. His operations cover two continents. His wealth is uncounted. Boyd secures Bates's commitment to finance the keystone of the project, the purchase of Colonel Peyton's mortgage and consequent control of his property. The only problem is that the Colonel will not sell, having no desire to see Arguello "develop." Otherwise, the other aspects of the plan—buying mountain land, water rights, options, and rights of way—will be easily accomplished. Undaunted by the Colonel's refusal to sell his property, Bates himself goes to the Colonel and tries to scare him into selling the land by informing him that, otherwise, Patrick Boyd will order the bank to foreclose on the property. The Colonel is thunderstruck—and so is Daphne, who overhears their conversation. She breaks off her romance with Boyd's son, Kenneth, assuming that he is in on his father's scheme to take over Corona del Monte. Kenneth is quickly able to set things aright with her, having convinced her that he is as confused as she and the Colonel are about what his father has been up to. Their worries are not enough, though.

Bates and Boyd have already been east to arrange the financing (incorporating a new company in New Jersey). Upon his return, Boyd convinces the directorate of the First National Bank to foreclose on the ranch to let him personally take it over. Boyd has in mind the total eclipse of Peyton, the "obstructive old fool." In his mind, it would not be too difficult, for "to the new population, the dwellers on the prosperous, smiling irrigated farms; the thousands who must flock to this garden spot of the world, Patrick Boyd would be what he was—leading citizen, public benefactor, bringer of prosperity, the man with vision who had seen and brought in a new era. Outside the bank building he paused to light a cigar" (317). Soon, the whole town learns of Patrick Boyd's intentions. Almost down to the last individual, the townspeople are appalled. This includes Kenneth, who is incredulous at his father's proposal:

> "I've got water rights in the Sur staked out and tied down. All that is necessary, my engineers say, is to do certain tunnel work and build certain dams. I've got, or got options upon, rights of way for pipe lines or ditches. We can bring water enough down to irrigate an immense area of land. In addition when Arguello outgrows her present water supply—as anybody but these moss-backs here could see is bound to happen—we'll be in shape to step in. Also we're figuring on some scheme to generate electricity—possibly by a series of reservoirs at different levels so as not to waste the irrigation water. It's a big proposition! . . .
>
> "The big money, though, at the start is from this Peyton property. . . . That's where you come in, Ken: that's your part of it. . . . Without you the scheme wouldn't have been considered." (328–329)

Kenneth tries to explain to his father what the ranch means to Colonel Peyton and what the Colonel means to the community. His father is impatient, though, and tells Kenneth to grow up and act like the businessman his father is grooming him to become.

## Brainerd and Daphne, the Experimental Farm and Realty Redux

Brainerd and Daphne eke out their subsistence, trying to ignore Colonel Peyton's regular ministrations. (Though the homestead is smack in the middle of the rancho, a sign of the rancho economy's certain end, there is no animosity between the ranchero and the smallholder.) Such is the state of the farm when Patrick Boyd's son, Kenneth, meets Daphne.

Kenneth finds in Daphne a kindred spirit. He is captivated and challenged by her naturalness; while she is artless when it comes to social conventions, she has a deep, intuitive intelligence. She "seemed to possess an astonishing local knowledge of things that grew or moved out of doors" (146). (Earlier, the reader has learned that she is conversant with tree spirits.) Through Daphne, Kenneth meets her father. Brainerd is independently minded, believing that people should make their own decisions and earn their reward through hard work, as exemplified in his experiments with irrigation. He echoes Patrick Boyd in telling Kenneth that cattle ranching is bound to pass, that its "'place will be taken by agriculture and horticulture'" on Southern California's arid lands (201). (Fittingly enough, Brainerd's farm has its beginnings as a 160-acre homestead, which through an unusual loophole sits at the center of the Rancho Corona del Monte. The suggestion is that just as the Colonel's ignorance of the Anglo capitalist economy dooms him, his Mexican-granted ranch harbors the means of its own destruction by a venerated American institution.) But unlike Patrick Boyd, Brainerd has no desire to gain riches through speculative practices. Brainerd's philosophy resonates with Guy's conclusion in *The Procession of Life*: Everyone should work, even the leisure class. Brainerd is all production. "'The ideal job,'" he lectures Kenneth, "'is one that produces something either in the shape of material products or some service needed; and at the same time gets us something beside money'" (200). Kenneth is impressed with Brainerd's approach and walks away thinking along new lines about his career; indeed, he begins to consider even having a career.

Kenneth formulates his own plan. He convinces his father to capitalize Brainerd's experimental farm to see if it would work on a large scale. Patrick Boyd insists that they take a business approach. Kenneth (like Billy in Jack London's *Valley of the Moon*) is not to do any of the physical work of farming (advice which he later rejects, also like Billy). Rather, he is to be a manager.

> I will furnish sufficient money to develop Mr. Brainerd's property along the lines he has laid out. You are to see that the property is developed, under Mr. Brainerd's supervision and advice. You are, however, to have charge of all details of hiring and firing men, of buying necessary supplies and all the rest of that, of attending to the details of housing and feeding your help, and all that sort of thing. . . . Lay out the work for others: and see that it is done. (224)

Patrick's idea is not so much that Kenneth remain on at Brainerd's place but that he learn from his experience and then apply it elsewhere. Patrick believes that farming is a business like any other business, and lessons learned will translate into other enterprises. Patrick has an ulterior motive, as well. For while Kenneth is managing Colonel Peyton's ranch, his father wants him to report in secret on his progress and on the Colonel's operations, too. Perhaps Kenneth will figure out how to make such a large-scale outfit pay better than the Colonel has managed. Perhaps, since his position at the bank gave him knowledge of Corona del Monte's finances, Patrick Boyd can buy a section of the ranch, a partnership with the Colonel, or the ranch in its entirety.

Backed by Patrick Boyd's capital, the success of Brainerd's farm is overwhelming. "It had changed its very appearance. The sage desert had been pushed back: and the gray Old Man brush had given place to flourishing citrus trees. The dry, powdery hard pan from which it had wrested its desiccated existence had turned into a brown, moist productive soil that justified the visionary dream that it was richer than the bottom lands" (235). Kenneth and Brainerd's success convinces Patrick Boyd that, indeed, riches are there for the taking, especially at Corona del Monte. Divided into twenty-acre, irrigated farms, it could bring the owner considerable wealth. "The strip nearest town would be a veritable gold mine when people discovered, as discover they must, that here they could live in beautiful flower-smothered homes, under the fairest sky in the world—and make a living doing it" (236). The narrator tells us that similar experiments in irrigated farming are cropping up all over Southern California. With the growing number of tourists each year, "People gradually ceased thinking so much of what the soil could produce and began to figure what someone would be willing to pay for it next year. From that to speculative buying was a short step" (241).

But Kenneth devises other plans. With the help of the *Sociedad*, a group of local ranchers who are friends and supporters of the Colonel, Kenneth poses as his father and buys the Colonel's mortgage himself. He obtains the money partly from an inheritance left to him by his mother, partly from the *Sociedad* members, and partly from the Colonel's Chinese house servant, Sing Toy, who solicited money from his friends in Arguello's Chinatown. Kenneth and Daphne plan to marry, but, as she reminds him, there remain some weighty details to be worked out. They still have to make a going concern of the Colonel's ranch. They still have to meet interest payments. They still must repay the *Sociedad* and half of Chinatown. Thus arrives Daphne's moment. She evidences more concern with the business details of the ranch than does Kenneth, who would rather let well enough alone.

Daphne dashes off to the Colonel, lest he think that the ranch's new owner, Kenneth, is yet another malevolent force. Daphne convinces the Colonel to allow Kenneth to become his junior partner. The Colonel's only stipulation is that they leave the ranch intact for as long as possible while he is alive. Afterward, they can subdivide and develop as they wish, he does not care. Ironically, Daphne's plan that Kenneth become a partner in the ranch suits the Colonel's own plan to bequeath Corona del Monte to Daphne.

The novel closes with a description of Arguello County in 1910, twenty years after the principal events. Enormous changes have transformed the landscape and the characteristics of the population. There has been a large influx of money, cars, and all sorts of urban improvements. The historical past exists only in fragmented, poorly understood form. As the county has urbanized, people have failed to appreciate the uniqueness of the region, as fads and fashions from the outside have consumed them. Bungalows and orchards cover the landscape in "what was apparently one endless orchard. Miles and miles without distinguishable boundaries" (364). On the network of roads that connect the orchards, convoys of "Orientals" on bicycles shift from field to field. The orchards, though owned by distinct individuals, function as a unit. The produce is cooperatively packed and marketed. "It was all very simple. Each owner of a bungalow did as much or as little work as he pleased. He was credited with what he did and was charged with what he got; and his fruit was sold for what it was worth. . . . [I]t is the usual thing in the fruit belts of California" (365).

The wide-open range land of Corona del Monte has passed into orchards, too. Kenneth and Daphne, now worth millions of dollars, still live in the old ranch house—but as capitalist laborers—and through a mixture of new and old features have preserved some of the flavor of the old days. They consider themselves farmers, like their neighbors, and choose to keep a distance from fast-paced, fashionable Arguello society. The water development that William Bates and Patrick Boyd had planned came off a success, and instead of purchasing the Colonel's ranch, they were able to acquire Las Flores from the bank. The only drawback was that they had to await further transportation developments for their profits to come through, since the property was in an outlying area. In the end, then—because with the Mexican economy gone, there is now enough space to achieve it—everything worth changing gets changed, and everything worth saving gets saved. And none of these appeasements cost capital anything. But as it turns out, there was actually very little worth saving anyway.

As an identity narrative, *The Rose Dawn* saves the ranch from the predacious Patrick Boyd, but *still* the ranch becomes the center of a thriving, modernized Anglo rural economy, underwritten of course by the surplus values extracted from the labor convoys. The heart of Peyton's ranch is sacred, yes, but rancho economy is a thing of the past. In the logic of the romanticized past, this dialectic of preservation and change at the ranch is allowed to stand only because it marks the contradictions that constitute it. That is, Stewart Edward White cannot *not* be at odds with his own story—the story of the extremes of capitalist development in Southern California. He has produced a narrative uneasy with the pace and social consequences of change, so he romanticizes the ranchos. But just as he regrets their passing, he charges them with being at fault to begin with. Don Vincente and Colonel Peyton try to play the mortgage game but allow their towering debt to get the better of them. The only way to resolve this unease with change, and the sacrificing of those who do not keep up with change, is through fetishizing place: through claiming that because Peyton's *house* still stands, some synthesis has been achieved. (Note, however, that Patrick Boyd does get his hands on the non-Anglo ranch of Don Vincente.) Daphne and Kenneth, on the one hand, and Patrick Boyd, on the other, may thus coexist in their separate places at the conclusion of the book.

It is instructive that Patrick Boyd's punishment is not meted out in economic terms, like every other speculator in the boom novels. He is not killed off, like Elijah Berl, nor does he turn to farming, like Warren in *The Bursting of a Boom*. White's narrative allows Patrick Boyd to carry out his real estate activities, making them culturally permissible by rewriting their geography and doing it in a way that suggests just how essential land commodification and development have been and will be. The core of Corona del Monte is preserved as a historical landmark that gets it value, its moral power, by being a reminder of the social and cultural integrity of an imagined past, which has of course *passed*. Capitalist development meanwhile marches on. Part of the ranch romance is that the rancho economy, while having certain aspects worth emulating, was not really an economy at all, at least not a modern one.

## Conclusion: Production, a Necessary Evil

In the second volume of *Capital*, Marx writes of the circuit of money capital (M . . . M') that "exchange-value, not use-value, is the determining aim of this movement." From this perspective (and for Marx, the circulation of capital is always a matter of perspective), he argues that "the process of production appears as merely an unavoidable intermediate link, as a necessary evil for the sake of money-making." Every now and then, this awareness—that is, this perspective on capital from the point of view of the circuit of money—erupts like a blinding flash of insight: "All nations with a capitalist mode of production," Marx says, " are therefore seized periodically by a feverish attempt to make money without the intervention of the process of production" (*Capital*, Vol. 2: 56). Periodically, something that is structurally built into capitalism—the inevitability of having to build something, having to reserve a portion of capital for the sake of production with which to beget more money—reaches a (il)logical end: the forsaking of production itself. What an alien concept this is to Brainerd, who lectures Kenneth on the value of forms of production that get us "'something beside money.'" And how easily the concept comes to Patrick Boyd, who minimizes production as much as possible in order to stoke the money furnace.

The production and identity narratives of the Southern California boom novels display the bourgeois anxieties that accompanied capitalism's reshaping of

Southern California. These narratives do not want too many "feverish attempts to make money," but neither do they deny the structural necessity of money. The production narrative exposes the contradiction (the boom and bust) of real estate and finance capital in order to put renewed emphasis on production as the real source of value in the region. But the identity narrative is a salve for the fever; it celebrates the rapid process of land transfer and cultural change that real estate sets in motion and that furthers Anglo aims. That is, contradiction *in* the economy and legitimation *of* the economy go hand in hand.

For the novels I examine in the next chapter, I want to take up a theme that has been building in this one. Aside from acquiring land and water as means of production, what is at stake in California is no less than the basic social structure of "civilized," "racialized" life—the restitution of the Anglo family and its gender relations. The boom novels, we have seen, are filled with characters whose familial, gender, and economic identities intertwine as they make their way toward founding family farms. Because the family farm and its prosperity are the basic unit of the agricultural "utopia," it makes sense that the novels are also stories about families. But they are stories about families in a very particular way. At times, they give us family farms that eschew old family ties for new ones—for example, in *The Rose Dawn.* They give us wives who compete with potential mistresses—in *The Vision of Elijah Berl*, for instance, and, as it turns out, in *The Procession of Life.* And they give us children from fragmented and troubled families who go on to make families of their own—for example, Daphne and Kenneth in *The Rose Dawn.* In short, when the novelists set their characters down in the incomplete landscape of post-boom Southern California, they also embroil them in intra-family tumult. They like the broken or threatened marriage and betrothal. They like orphans and single-parent households. They practically exalt in riven filial relations. Rarely is a complete family at the center of affairs, although by the end of the novels, new families are often assembled. More often than not, that is, families do not make farms, farms make families. What are these mutual incomplete/complete relationships about?

# 6

# Romancing the Sand

## *Earth-Capital and Desire in the Imperial Valley*

### The Problem

> The artificial control of moisture supplies the basis of absolutely scientific agriculture. The element of chance is wholly eliminated. Man asserts his control over the forces of nature.
>
> —William Elsworth Smythe (1909: 20)

> Hard upon the heels of a philosophy which glorifies success must follow a philosophy which rationalizes failure.
>
> —Lucy L. Hazzard (1927: xix)

Before the current era of water management in the American West reduced water flow at the mouth of the Colorado River to a trickle, there were two options for the river as it neared the end of its run: either proceed toward the Gulf of California or at the last minute reverse direction, swing north across its own delta, and plunge into a below-sea-level, exitless trough called the Salton Sink (Waters 1946; Kniffen 1931–32). Most often the river ran Gulf-ward, but periodically, under high-water conditions, it disgorged into the Sink, turning it into the inland Salton Sea. The last time of note that this happened was in 1905. This would not have been so much of a problem had not the American West's largest private irrigation and land development venture to date been busy reclaiming the Salton Sink with Colorado River water in order to turn it into a vast inland, agricultural oasis, which the developers took to calling the Imperial Valley. Because of the flood, which required many months of Herculean effort to control and a sizable amount of capital from the Southern Pacific Railroad, the Imperial Valley became a lightning rod for debates over the ideals, practices, and intersections of capitalism and agrarianism as they were taking shape in the rural arid West.

Historians of water development in the American West have long recognized that irrigation was a means to an array of ends: inflation of land and crop values, increase in crop acreage, urban expansion, land speculation, and, not least, the implantation of the nuclear family and expansion of the Anglo-Saxon race. These ends—as writers such as John Walton, Donald Worster, Donald Pisani, and, from an earlier era, Walter Prescott Webb have reminded us—were themselves articulated through many legitimating practices, not only political speeches, proposals for legislation or newspaper editorials, but also advertising rhetoric and the plots and characters of western fiction (Walton 1992; Worster 1985; Pisani 1984; Webb 1931).[1]

This chapter follows in the footsteps of these multi-dimensioned accounts. It begins with a discussion of the Imperial Valley's development by the California Development Company (CDC), the private outfit that began developing the Valley at the turn of the century. It goes on to examine the debate surrounding the causes of the flood, which devastated thousands of acres of farmland, and the changes in promotion rhetoric emanating out of the Valley, as the CDC yielded control of its irrigation facilities to the Southern Pacific Railroad. A discussion of the enormously popular novel *The Winning of Barbara Worth* (1911), by Harold Bell Wright, follows. Supplemented by readings of passages from a second Imperial Valley novel (*The River* [1914], by Ednah Aiken), this discussion centers on the legitimating discourses surrounding the capitalist development of Imperial Valley irrigated agriculture. I am concerned with eliciting one theme in particular: Legitimating discourses had a way of collapsing in on, or, if you will, deconstructing, themselves. For example, the argument that irrigation was "natural," or a completion of nature, only called attention to the deficiencies of nature in the West and the hardships of living there. The alternative argument—that irrigation was a wing of capital capable of creating and preserving desert economies—drew attention to the uncertainties that the circulation of capital introduced. The argument that irrigation would domesticate the desert wilds reverberated with contemporary struggles over gendered divisions of labor and the meanings of domesticity. In short, the act of legitimation was a venture into unsettled rhetorical and ideological territories. It helps, therefore, to think of the production of water resources not only in terms of the transformation of nature into "earth capital" but also as a deeply contested and fettered cultural production.

## Engineers and Entrepreneurs

Even before the flood, it was the Imperial Valley's misfortune to have begun in false starts. In 1891, an aspiring land developer, John Beatty, lured the civil engineer-cum-investor, Charles Rockwood, to the banks of the Colorado River with the intent of irrigating a part of northern Mexico. As law permitted, Beatty filed a claim on enough of the river's flow to irrigate hundreds of thousands of acres. Rather than Mexico, however, Rockwood convinced Beatty that the Salton Sink was a better target. The steeper grade from the river to the Sink meant that canals could be gravity fed, and there were thousands of acres of public lands that settlers could take up at nominal cost through the Homestead and Desert Land Acts. The idea seemed sound, but potential investors were extremely difficult to find in the depressed middle 1890s. This was a time for capital to retrench, not to venture without good cause. After Beatty himself bowed out of the project, Rockwood purchased his former associate's share, including the critically important water rights, and reorganized the concern into the California Development Company (CDC). Rockwood met with investors and bankers from Chicago to New York and London, and still, he could only scrape together a few thousand dollars (Rockwood 1909; Cooper 1968).

Finally, he netted two of the most skilled men then developing rural land in California: George Chaffey and Anthony Heber. Chaffey was a brilliant engineer-capitalist who, with his brother, built a fortune around the success of irrigation colonies that he developed near Los Angeles in the 1880s, notably Ontario and Etiwanda (Kershner 1953; Alexander 1928; Dumke 1944; McWilliams 1983). Heber was the Chicago agent of the San Joaquin Valley-born Kern County Land Company, a concern begun during California's wheat days and which profited immensely from land and cattle holdings and extensive shipping activities in California and other western states (Rockwood 1909).

Chaffey had the financial muscle to stand the CDC on its feet. With the worst of the depression over, he raised $150,000 (partly his own money and partly loans he secured in Los Angeles) (Kershner 1953). Rockwood, goaded by Chaffey's insistence that settlers be found immediately, carved out a subsidiary, the Imperial Land Company. Headquartered in Los Angeles, the company surveyed and promoted Imperial Valley lands and expedited the process of filing on government land. (In 1901, Chaffey and his son also formed the First National Bank of Imperial. Chaffey was positioned to not only back the CDC but also to sell credit to farmers and any others who would need what the CDC had to sell.[2]) Once they filed or purchased land through the company, claimants were bonded to buy stock in one of the seven mutual water companies that the CDC had organized. Further solidifying the Imperial Valley's essentially Southern California roots, Chaffey picked his friend L. M. Holt to head the Imperial Land Company. Holt was a boosterish newspaper man who had cut his teeth in Riverside, a premier citrus center at the eastern reaches of the Los Angeles-San Bernardino corridor, where the two had worked together in the 1880s. There, two decades before they joined again in Imperial, they had devised the water arrangement that they would reprise in the mutual water companies formed by the CDC (Rockwood 1909).

Rockwood, Chaffey, and Heber's vision for the Imperial Valley was that it should give rise to a population of thousands of middle-class small farmers, who would feed themselves and countless others (Heber 1904). For decades, the issue of how to wrest agriculture away from the control of land barons had preoccupied the popular press in California and aroused sympathy for the anti-monopoly movements and squatter uprisings that had appeared sporadically since the 1870s (see chapter 4). Because it was expected to raise land values and thereby encourage profitable subdivision, irrigation was thought by many reformers to be the simplest solution to the problem of land concentration that California's renowned political economist Henry George so sharply articulated (George 1879).[3] Well apprised of the situation, the CDC asserted itself as a rational capitalist firm devoted to bringing the old notion of a prosperous yeoman West to fruition. Yet, the reverse was perhaps more true. The legal basis of a yeoman West—that is, access to very cheap land and water—promised to bring to fruition a rational, capitalist firm.

## Producing the Imperial Valley

By 1900, the lineaments of the irrigation system had taken shape. Following Chaffey's plan, water was diverted just 600 feet north of the Mexican border. Laborers with mule teams and dynamite dug a canal southward over the border into Mexico and joined it to the dried-up Alamo River. The Alamo, a tributary of the Colorado River in the delta, was appropriate because it bent northward, going back over the border and into the Salton Sink (Heber 1904; Worster 1985). In order to obtain the right to carry water through Mexico, a subsidiary company was chartered there and Mexico was promised half of the water. The possibilities this situation offered were seized upon by American capitalists, most notably the Los Angeles financial giant Harry Chandler, who bought 800,000 acres of land in Mexico—acreage that would eventually be watered by the Imperial Valley's own irrigation system (Harding 1960; Cooper 1968; Tout 1931).

Within two years, the CDC completed 60 miles of canals. By 1903, 25,000 acres were under ditch; by 1905, 120,000. The ranks of the white population swelled from 2,000 to 14,000 (Harding 1960; Cory 1915). And in the process, some 1,200 Native Americans were driven up into surrounding higher country, although later they would be drafted to help repair the flood damage (Trava 1987). All during these transformations, the irrigators labored under a cloud. The Colorado River was known by them to be wildly erratic on occasion. Moreover, greater crop acreage meant more silty water and more clogged ditches. Bypasses would have to be cut, and cut again, straining the CDC's finances and laying a foundation for disaster (see Cory 1915, Worster 1985, and Starr 1990 for more detailed, but still succinct, accounts of the flood).

In the fall of 1904, Rockwood ordered one such bypass south of the border. This new cut was done quickly, without adequate reinforcement. Rockwood's purpose was to evade the United States Reclamation Service, which was looking to gain ground in the valley by prohibiting CDC water diversions on the U.S. side. The bypass proved fatal. Late that year, in December, high waters came down the river. By August of 1905, the Colorado was roiling into the Imperial Valley. By autumn, the cut widened to a mile, keeping an infantry of Indian, Mexican, and itinerant white laborers busy sandbagging, rock dumping, and willow-mat building. The CDC was completely overwhelmed.

The Southern Pacific Railroad, owner of new branch lines in the Valley and of thousands of land-grant acres, moved to protect its interests. It loaned $200,000 to the CDC to help cover the costs of the flood-control effort, in exchange for control and management of the failed company. The task of managing the gutted CDC fell to one of Southern Pacific's executives, Epes Randolph, who subsequently brought in a top-notch civil engineer, Harry T. Cory, to close the break. This Cory did, with Taylor-istic efficiency, turning the vicinity of the flood into a hive of dredging, filling, and strict labor discipline. An electric plant was built so that work could proceed night and day (Holt 1942). He directed workers to erect work camps and had them regularly policed. Indian men were Cory's preferred labor force since they could be paid less than both American whites and Mexicans and because Indian women supplied their food (Cory 1915).

After spending over $3 million of the railroad's money and working at the task for over a year, Cory's charges turned back the river. It was November 1906. The next month, the Colorado flushed away another section of levee; and it was three more months before Cory gained the upper hand again, this time having finished a 10-mile-long, rock-faced levee. The results: The Salton Sea had risen 100 feet, wiped out $750,000 worth of railroad track, required the relocation of 67 miles of track, and delayed freight shipments all over the West. Flood waters had destroyed 3,000 cultivated acres and 10,000 uncultivated acres, ruined crops over an even larger area, and driven away many farmers (Cory 1915; Harding 1960).

But instead of tumbling into oblivion, Imperial stepped up the development process. By 1910, 200,000 acres were soaking up Colorado River water, and in the next nine years, this figure approached half a million (Worster 1985; Cory 1915; McWilliams 1979). The expansion of the Valley's economy, like its very emergence before 1905, was driven by a number of intersecting developments. Although a downturn in the national economy took hold almost immediately after the flood, it was Imperial's good fortune to be shielded from the full force of the financial panic and, moreover, to benefit from newly rising crop prices and land values. Because water flowed, local burghers—such as William Holt, owner of banks, real estate, public utilities, and newspapers—were assured of continued credit from Los Angeles. In fact, while Holt secured several million dollars from his associates on the coast, other capitalists in Los Angeles fought vigorously with him to win more direct control of the Valley's economy (Holt 1942).

### What a Difference a Flood Makes

In the early years, both before and after the flood, the presence of corporate capital (i.e., the California Development Company and the Southern Pacific) was the most hotly contended issue in the Valley. At the center of this debate was the fact that the Imperial Valley had come to be perceived as something of a test case for both large-scale irrigation and the prospects of the small-scale farm in the arid West. Who, then, private capital or the state, could bring these prospects to fruition, and relatedly, who should bear responsibility for the flood?

The conflicting stances on corporate capital, the state, and culpability for the flood are distilled in the statements of two people in particular: Elwood Mead and Harry T. Cory. Mead, whom we met in chapter 3, was the career advocate of government-sponsored irrigation projects and small-scale farming in California (see Kluger 1970 and Pisani 1983). Writing in 1915 about the flood and its aftermath, he was shocked that the federal government had early turned its back on the Valley and let it drown and was incensed that absentee speculators had acquired large quantities of land. According to Mead, irrigation should have led the way back to the family farm, but instead its management in the Valley had put that dream in grave danger. The caprices of the private sector, Mead argued, made irrigation too expensive. Therefore, the federal or state government should have undertaken the project at a cautious pace and extended low-interest loans to farmers (Mead's comments appear in Cory 1915).

In fact, the federal government *had* created a role for itself such as Mead had argued for, but its agency, the Reclamation Service, had lost its bid for the Valley very early in the game. The Service, born in 1902, was a mere fledgling when the CDC was enjoying pre-flood success. Made bold by its mission, the Service planned to oust the CDC and take over its irrigation works. It circulated an old Department of Agriculture report that had pronounced the desert infertile, thereby scaring away prospective settlers and stalling CDC-bound credit from Los Angeles banks (Rockwood 1909; Cory 1915).[4]

At the same time, the Service threw its weight behind a settler organization that was agitating for a Reclamation Service buyout of the CDC and all its water works. In response, the CDC moved the main water diversion point to south of the border. Done in haste, this new diversion point was the very one left unprotected by a headgate, and that brought disaster. The CDC's argument, therefore, made some sense: Far from crippling the progress of irrigated agriculture, private capital had itself been crippled by an overzealous government agency. Elwood Mead overlooked the fact that the federal government had tried to bully its way into Imperial and ended up an object of scorn. At the time, in fact, Heber had expressed his willingness to sell the CDC to the Service if only he was offered a fair price (Heber 1904; see also Holt 1907).

Cory, the Southern Pacific civil engineer, took a different tack. Assuming that massive flooding, at one time or another, was inevitable, he doubted that the government had the immediate resources to respond. With so much capital already fixed in place across the West, only the railroad was positioned to transport labor and equipment, to obtain the lowest prices by buying huge quantities of flood control materials (rock, lumber, etc.), and to quickly finance these operations without putting a strain on local resources (Cory 1915).

There was, after all, no easy answer to who should shoulder responsibility. Mead, Heber, the Reclamation Service, and Cory could disagree all they wanted over what caused the flood, but the more important question, as all knew, was, Did saving the Imperial Valley from the flood's rampage, itself save anything? A fact that none of these agents could change was that an irrigated farm was beyond the reach of anyone who did not already have some money to invest in one (although Mead would soon oversee State of California attempts to reverse that fact at the Delhi and Durham colonies).

Agriculture, especially its incorporation into an economy of speculation in rural lands and waters, was not going to be an alternative to capitalism, but a version of it. And yet, as we saw in chapter 3, this did not spell the end of agrarian fantasies. Agrarian notions were too tenacious and flexible, too capable of being appropriated and transformed, to come to quick ends.[5] This does not mean that easy rhetorical work was involved. For, combined with a certain reverence for the so-called frontier—such as that celebrated by Frederick Jackson Turner (1894)—the yeoman interpretation of American history was like a cultural brick wall that, as Harry Cory would readily assent, had to be either dismantled, redesigned, or relocated in order for the Imperial Valley to make cultural and historical sense. In fact, Cory did readily assent to something very like this in his 1919 manifesto (again, see chapter 3). The Valley finally got water, but the accompanying social structures and institutions were distinctively not those of the small-farm empire.

Once it became clear that irrigation was an especially capital-intensive undertaking in the Valley, it became more attractive to the economic elite and their supporters to engage in a rhetoric that would help protect the economic gains that had been made.

### Imperial Valley Representations, 1: Promotion and Its (Dis)Contents

While Cory was definitely much more interested than Mead in defending capitalist actors in the Valley, capitalist views of Imperial Valley land and farm development were not predetermined by class location alone. Not only was the flood serious business, but as we have seen, it changed the face of capital's presence in the Valley once the CDC took its fall and was displaced by the railroad. Meanwhile, the bourgeois perspective was, for a time, open to different ideas.

Before the flood, the Imperial Land Company, under L. M. Holt, was the CDC's promotional body. Holt, also a rancher in the valley and a CDC stockholder, published and distributed booklets that celebrate the desert's redemption by corporate capital. Typically, the photographs in these publications, with titles such as *From Desert to Garden*, *From Worthlessness to Wealth* and *Imperial Valley Catechism*, depict Imperial Valley crops—especially cotton and sugar beets on the experimental farms operated by the Imperial Land Company and milo maize and alfalfa for the booming cattle and hog business. Or the photographs are of foreshortened views of railroad tracks and canals, whose sharp diagonals converge rapidly toward the horizon. Either way, the images "argue" that capital has conquered the desert and, in so doing, has redeemed it. Other photographs push this rhetoric further. They show clusters of isolated buildings and vast expanses of desert. Here, desert is not so much desert as it is the vast space of real estate, ready for purchase at low prices. From past production to future consumption, Imperial Valley was being "written" and historicized in one way: Its only fulfillment could be that given by its designation as a commodity. In these views, nature is no opposition to capital, it is always already claimed by capital. The written portions of these booklets follow suit. They sing praises to the private corporation turning "worthlessness" into "wealth," a perfect vocabulary to describe the progression of visual images from raw desert to farm cornucopia. But again, the text smacks of an even more entrenched meaning. To speak of worthlessness being turned into wealth is to attribute a value to worthlessness. To even utter "worthlessness" in this context is to venture a preemption in which speculation lays claim to what has not yet been produced. Above everything else, however, the affordability of it all is stressed. And that affordability, the argument went, translated into family farms surrounding a middle-class constellation of churches, schools, and small businesses (Imperial Land Company 1902a, 1902b, 1904).

When the Southern Pacific took over the California Development Company after the flood, it brought its extensive experience as a promoter of agricultural lands. In the 1880s, the railroad had embarked on a massive campaign to sell its arable land. Its literature then was not unlike the Imperial Land Company's. It argued that farm and land ownership could turn tramps into dutiful citizens (see Orsi 1975). But after the flood, the Southern Pacific held suspect the vision of Imperial Valley as an oasis for all comers. Public land had become scarce in the irrigated portions of the Valley, so it would no longer guarantee the price of irrigated land. Although it wanted badly to sell acreage, Southern Pacific defended itself with inscrutable logic: "Land gets its value from the interest it will pay on the investment, and from the demand. Somebody wants it, and the price advances"

(Passenger Department 1908: 13). Farmland is not just an *outcome* of invested capital (the Imperial Land Company's view), it is now totally *subservient* to the actual and potential capital that would circulate through it.

The Imperial Valley now clarified for all who may have doubted it that irrigation was a capital-intensive, capital-circulating undertaking, the burden of which had to be borne by or shared by the farmer. This was a situation fully realized in 1905 by William Ellsworth Smythe, founder of the journal *Irrigation Age* and a promoter second only to Elwood Mead in his missionary zeal to see arid America settled:

> There is one warning which should be sounded for the benefit of a certain class of settlers. The man who attempts to make a home on the primeval desert, even with the free land and the best irrigation and drainage facilities, requires money to make a successful start. . . . [T]he average man will need capital in order to bring his farm to a paying stage. This capital he cannot borrow until he gets title to his lands, and he cannot get title until he completes payments for his water rights, ten years hence. There is no way in which these payments can be commuted. (1905: 303)

Agents of the Southern Pacific called for intelligent, already successful, business-minded individuals. "Land gets its value from the interest it will pay," it had warned. Once again, nature and capital are less oppositional than they are synonymous. But with a twist. Here, the economy operates according to immutable laws. *It* is even more natural than nature.[6] And if this is so, then there would be clear implications for social relations in the Valley.

Instead of corporate capital as a creator of wealth-from-worthlessness whose benefits would fall to farmers, farmers must themselves have capital. The railroad is not handing anything over cheaply. Farmers are to join in the same economic enterprise as the railroad. At the same time, though, the old goal of landed self-sufficiency holds fast. The difference is that Imperial Valley farmers would be self-sufficient on the land in the same way that the railroad would be: Land would not so much generate income as it would be the material through which prior income circulates and returns in enhanced form. When we confront the language of Southern Pacific, though, we are looking not just at our familiar rural realist stuff. We are looking at the plain fact that one capitalist entity has had to bail out another.

## Imperial Valley Representations, 2: *The Winning of Barbara Worth* and the Erotics of Western Conquest

> Commodities borrow their aesthetic language from human courtship; but then the relationship is reversed and people borrow their aesthetic expression from the world of the commodity.
>
> —W. F. Haug (1986: 19)

In spite of the subtitle—*The Ministry of Capital*—Harold Bell Wright's wildly popular, relentlessly Anglo-Saxonist *The Winning of Barbara Worth* is not quite the article of faith it would seem. (Or at least it must turn somersaults to turn out as such.) The idea of capitalists vigorously going at it forms a large part of Wright's narrative, but it is also cause for the narrative to keep its "ministers" at a distance. Capitalists may have an important message for would-be farmers, but seeing them practice what they preach is not a nice sight.

Published in 1911, *The Winning of Barbara Worth* entered the ranks of the top five national bestsellers of 1900–1930 (Weeks 1934). (It was subsequently made into a feature-length film in 1927, with Gary Cooper in his screen debut and with some early, spectacular special effects. The film was financed by A. P. Giannini, whose bank was a major backer of California agriculture, as we've seen already [Nash 1992; James and James 1954].) A very successful novelist by 1911, Wright's previous three books had sold half a million copies each by 1910. "His books were awkward, mawkish, and ingenuous," popular cultural historian Russell Nye writes. "His characters sermonized, his plots creaked, and he repeated all the melodramatic clichés—rascally villains, pure heroines, suffering orphans, unbelievably virtuous heroes—but the public forgave him all his flaws" (Nye 1970: 39). Actually, Wright helped in that last endeavor. The new novel had a $75,000 advertising budget, a generous bit of self-promotion given that the author held half interest in the publishing firm that produced his books (Nye 1970). Wright was also a sometime minister and horse rancher who had settled for several years in the Imperial Valley, circulating among the Valley's elite and befriending the Holt family (Hart 1950; Starr 1990). Like the promotional literature of the Imperial Land Company and the Southern Pacific Railroad, *The Winning of Barbara Worth* ranges over a field of interconnected discourses. In Wright's text, however, the rhetoric of capital and nature is joined to those of East-West difference and masculine-feminine contest. When these rhetorics are put into motion through plot and narrative, they enter an extended signifying chain through which the novel is able to stake its claims among contested representations of how capitalism works, for whom, and to what end.

In particular, Wright's narrative traces an arc away from claims that the circuit of capital beginning with finance is the source of power and prosperity, toward the claim that the circuit beginning with production on the land is such a source. But the legitimation for what makes one circuit of the economy praiseworthy or another scurrilous—a matter of some delicacy, lest the "ministry of capital" be tarnished—has much to do with the significations through which these circuits are presented. That *The Winning of Barbara Worth* offers a full-blown melodramatic romance as a subplot is especially important in this regard.[7] In the narrative of romance, heterosexual passion makes everything else that happens thematically subordinate to it. (I think this is what the novel claims for itself. I am not arguing here that the novel belongs only to this one "genre.") As we will see—and started to already in certain of the Southern California boom novels—romance centers representations of capitalist workings on production. Romance especially performs a particular kind of ideological work by turning heterosexual desire into the bedrock cause of economic growth and Anglo-Saxon hegemony. Yet, while "localizing" or temporarily diminishing and distracting from economy in that way, romance also helps the narrative secure an idealized, reconstructed representation of that larger economy in both the agrarian sphere and capitalism in general. To be "mawkish" and "sermonizing" and to write plots that "creak" may be seen less as melodramatic faults than as ideology leaving as little as possible to chance.

## The Rhetorical Circuit: The Thrill of Production and the Agony of Finance

The development of the Imperial Valley ("The King's Basin" in the novel) is plotted through the movements of four main characters. Jefferson Worth is a local banker and land developer, honest in his dealings but not above foreclosing on farm mortgages when he concludes they are delinquent. Worth's rival is James Greenfield, a ruthless New York capitalist intent on edging him out of the Basin. Willard Holmes, Greenfield's "nephew" and employee, is an eastern, college-bred civil engineer, overeducated and a little too androgynous for his new western colleagues. Barbara Worth, Holmes' counterpart, is an orphan who was found in the desert as a little girl and raised by Jefferson Worth. Her education is that of the outdoor life; her androgyny apparent to both eastern engineers and tourists.

As the novel opens, we learn that "Good Business" is the "master passion" of humankind and that Jefferson Worth is its very personification. "He was Capital-Money-Business incarnate," whom other men "set . . . apart as one not of their world" (11, 144). When Worth looked at The King's Basin, he saw its future: "an army of men beginning at the river and pushing out into the desert with their canals, bringing with them the life-giving water." Settlers would replace the "ragged patches of dun earth" with alfalfa and grain, orchards, vineyards, and groves. "Desert life" would yield to "home life." The railroad, too, would arrive and "towns and cities would come to be where now was only solitude and desolation . . . [O]ut from this . . . vast wealth would pour to enrich the peoples of the earth." To Worth, this frontier periphery would become a thriving economic center. There are no qualms about this eventuality, such as there are in *Blood-Money*—the narrator is with Worth all the way. But without the capital to achieve this transformation, no water can be brought to the desert. "Therefore Capital was master of the situation," and Jefferson Worth's role is to follow accordingly (153–54). And necessarily, the laboring class must follow too. "The new country was settled by working people of limited means," who "could feel dimly that mighty forces were stirring beneath the surface, but they could not fathom what it was all about. One thing was clear: the one thing that is always clear when capital speaks to businessmen of their class—they must obey" (331).

In no uncertain terms, capital sets in motion a process from which all sorts of social goods flow. But, as Jefferson Worth explains, this is not *why* capital does what it does. "'Capitalists, as individuals might and do, spend millions in projects from which they, personally, expect no returns. But *Capital* doesn't do such things. Anything Capital, *as Capital,* goes into must be purely a business proposition.'" Banks, for example, only benefit people by doing business with them "'on strictly business principles'" (170). The only thing that makes Worth different from other capitalists, especially Greenfield, is that instead of serving capital, he tries to make it "serve the race," the subtext being Anglo-Saxon supremacy (395). Worth's plan is to circulate a first round of capital in the form of credit sold to King's Basin settlers, until such time as the settlers' successes will support town development on land that Worth owns. As the Basin becomes more productive, the value of his property will rise, and he can extract rents on this second circuit of his capital. This is the kind of mutual exploitation between capitalists and workers that is supposed to grease the economic machine. An efficient division of labor and property is thus sacrosanct to his supply-side, trickle-down equations.

James Greenfield, who serves only "Capital," poses a direct challenge to Worth's plans. Although he invites Worth to become a partner in his monopoly, The King's Basin Land and Irrigation Company, he warns him, "'[I]f you think you can enter The King's Basin in opposition to our Company, . . . [w]e'll smash you. . . .'" (165–67). Entering the Basin solo is, of course, Jefferson Worth's own plan. So, for *The Winning of Barbara Worth*, it is not a question of corporate capital or no corporate capital, but a question of which kind of corporation. Predictably, Greenfield takes a fall when he refuses to spend enough money to upgrade the headgates of the irrigation works. When the flood arrives, the blame is his. I say *predictably* because Greenfield is obviously the straw man: In the implied reading of the novel, he epitomizes the excesses of laissez-faire economy.

Greenfield's presence and his harsh handling of Jefferson Worth raise a question. If we already know to reject an unacceptable capitalist and why, what would be necessary to consider a capitalist acceptable and why? Part of the novel's answer has to do with Worth wanting to make capital "serve the race." But what about his own monopolistic ambitions? Do any means justify Worth's ends? Perhaps they do. But the work of the novel, I would argue, is to deflect these questions by introducing new logics. If capital itself can be understood in an alternative way that makes western American economics look more legitimate than eastern ones; if the novel can successfully insist that this better capitalism intrinsically yields desired agrarian outcomes; and if the novel can, at the same time, underpin the rural economy with a romance more natural and less contrived than anything Jefferson Worth can dream up—then these maneuvers can draw capital into a cultural echo chamber in which it will be very difficult to discern which force is which and what causes what.

Let us return to Jefferson Worth to see how these significations unfold, because he is in fact their first subject. The effect of ideologically disposing of Greenfield is to cast a shadow on the agency of capital. This leaves Jefferson Worth, a "money making machine" intent on mastering the desert. But with a difference. It's not only that he would make capital "serve the race." For Worth, the circulation of money, from investment to realized profit, actually originates from somewhere other than money. "Business, to this man as to many of his kind, was not the mean, sordid grasping and hoarding of money. It was his profession. . . . The work itself was his passion" (158–59). Worth's goal is to work productively enough so that his *work* may continue. Money is the means, not the ends. More to the point, the narrative has rewritten the capitalist as the worker. The investment of money *is* the labor that Worth performs. In this circuit, his labor sets in motion all the events that beget his capital. The effect is to position him within the class of productive laborers such that the hierarchy between the financier and those "below" him is obscured and obliterated. Worth simply does what workers, or rather western workers, everywhere do.[8] The primary difference between working-class workers and him is simply that, ideally, Jefferson Worth's work is vested with the power to make sure that what he produces works.

Greenfield's transgression is not due to the flood, per se, then, but to his having put money ahead of all else. His calculus, from where Worth stands, is all wrong. More interested in the rapid circulation of his capital and with minimizing investments in production, Greenfield is socially/culturally identifiable as one who yields to the tendency to "attempt to make money without the intervention of the process of production," as Marx would say (*Capital*, Vol. 2: 56).

The same work-or-be-damned logic drives the condemnation of irrigation workers who at one point go out on strike. Even though they rebel against Jefferson Worth's inability to meet payroll, they have placed dollars before duties. Laborers may be held in contempt, in other words, for acting like contemptible capitalists. The point may be further developed by reading a passage on labor and money in a second novel of the Imperial Valley flood, Ednah Aiken's *The River* (1914). Nowhere near Harold Bell Wright in popularity (among the writers dealt with here, only Jack London and Stewart Edward White kept that company), Aiken was nonetheless in the promotional swim. The spouse of Charles Aiken, who was editor of the Southern Pacific's promotional magazine, *Sunset*, she took a Cory-like view of the railroad's role in bailing out the Valley.

As the Colorado rages on, Aiken recounts how the engineers in charge of holding the river back import American Indian labor. "The long-haired tribes . . . famous for their water-craft" work on woven mats of branches to be anchored to the riverbank in order to catch silt and stabilize the banks against further erosion. Assisting them are the "short-haired" tribes, "the brushcutters to replace the stampeding [Mexican] peons" who are being driven crazy by the noxious odors released by the "arrow-weed" plant that grows in the area (250). In the mind of one of the civil engineers, Native American laborers represent a malformed relationship between labor and money.

> It was inspiring activity, this pitting of man's cumulative skill against an elemental force. No Caucasian mind which did not tingle, feel the privileged thrill of it. To the stolid native, as he plodded on his raft all day under a blazing sky, or lifted his machete against the thorny mesquite or more insidious arrow-weed, this day of well-paid toil was his millennium, the fulfillment of the prophecy. His gods had so spoken. Food for his stomach, liquor for his stupefaction; the white man's money laid in a brown hand each Sunday morning was what the great gods forespoke. *The completion of the work, the white man's victory would be an end of the fat time. A dull sense of this deepened the natural stolidity of their labor.* (297–98, emphasis added)

Everything that is to be maligned about the quest for rapid turnover of capital is transferred to the "stolid native," who consumes his money too rapidly. Short-sighted finance capital caused the break, and here, "stolid" but short-sighted labor would prolong it. This passage, that is, is a way to bracket off some of capital's less desirable tendencies: While the flood provides good capitalists with the opportunity to show they know how to suppress the drive to rapidly circulate their capital, the Native American workers make the (ideologically) fatal mistake of acting like capitalists during the flood. Money is dirty in this equation. Whereas elsewhere in the novel money is permitted to have value and to be desired—as when one of the Caucasian characters, Senator Graves, sets out to make a fortune from buying and selling land and water in the Valley—the Native American's money is devalued by virtue of *his* wanting it and spending it. It is the way in which the native strategizes this wanting and spending that is telling. The native knows something that the capitalist knows, that it is sometimes better to withhold what you have to sell—just as Senator Graves prefers to hold out on selling his property to make more money from the eastern syndicate that wants it. *The River* would have us believe that the natives do not know how to handle money (they drink it away), when in fact just the opposite is true (they slow down their work so as to make more money). In terms of the novel, this laboring *for money* is, of course, abhorrent. And although the "brown hand" of the native is to be contrasted with the "tingling," white "Caucasian mind" that appreciates pure work, this passage darkly parallels a similar sort of rhetorical move whereby the novel rebukes money grabbers like Senator Graves by keeping them as background characters. Each wishes to obtain money while minimizing production. (If there is ever going to be a time when these narratives say that money-making values are never good, it is never going to be the Anglo-Saxon bourgeoisie that has its knuckles rapped.)

*The Winning of Barbara Worth* struggles through the same sort of balancing act when it comes to its lauded working capitalist. As it turns out, the labor of the capitalist may save Jefferson Worth from moral condemnation, but it also traps him. While he plays a decisive role as the worker who has the vision to see The King's Basin picture whole, from its primitive, frontier state to its domesticated future, Worth has only this one role to play. In fact, all the agents (race-d, classed, and gendered to a one) who are bringing about the reclamation of the Valley are restricted by the very divisions that unite them:

> Not one of them thought of the significance of the group or how each representing a distinct type, stood for a vital element in the combination of human forces that was working out for the race the reclamation of the land. The tall, lean desert-born surveyor, trained in no school but the school of his work itself . . . ; the heavy-fisted, quick-witted, aggressive Irishman, born and trained to handle that class of men that will recognize in their labor no governing force higher than the physical; the dark-faced frontiersman, whom the forces of nature, through the hard years, had fashioned his peculiar place in this movement of the race as truly as wave and river and wind and sun had made The King's Basin desert itself; the self-hidden financier who, behind his gray mask, wrought with the mighty force of his age—Capital; . . . dark Pablo, softly touching his guitar, representing a people still far down on the ladder of the world's upward climb, but still sharing, as all peoples would share, the work of all; and, in the midst of the group . . . Barbara, true representative of a true womanhood that holds in itself the future of the race, even as the desert held in its earth womb life for the strong ones whom the slow years had fitted to realize it. (289–90)

Certainly one reason to impose these divisions, and to invent characters who don't see the "whole," is to fetishize the reclamation community not as something one sees (what one sees are stark class and race divisions) but as an article of faith. The "significance of the group" is that "group" minimizes the stark social divisions that constitute it. (*The River* holds to this rule also and, as we just saw, condemns those whose "fulfillment" is heedless of the group.) These stark divisions are also grist for the most central concern of the book: the transformation of the desert and the heroizing of the right characters.

Quite clearly, Barbara—as nature—is the prize here, and for a number of reasons that will become clear shortly, none of the above characters "wins" her. Until such a character emerges, no character can be given too much power, for they are all in competition to reap the desert's offerings. Jefferson Worth may be a leader of the local financial world, but, as this and numerous passages emphasize, he wears a mask: His work as a capitalist demands that he act without apparent feeling and without displaying his interior self to anyone. He cannot win Barbara, not only because he is her father but because the work of capitalists is too abstract, too removed from contact with the land itself. Pablo cannot win her, for racial reasons, and neither can the Irishman or frontiersman, who are too brutish. The "desert-born surveyor" is too much of a father figure to Barbara, but his young assistant Abe (a character who contends with Willard Holmes for Barbara's affection) could be a good candidate. Yet there is more ideological work for the narrative to do. Abe is simply too local; and besides, he is already a convert to the project of irrigating the desert. Though Abe is a good bet, it is important to recognize that the "winning" of Barbara Worth cuts both ways. This is not just a story of who obtains access to her but of whom she obtains access to and what spaces they represent. For Barbara (as nature) is herself in competition with the menu of choices available to Willard Holmes (as productive capital), who may or may not decide to remain in The King's Basin.

Enter Willard Holmes, then, who serves a crucial role, though not without being tested on a number of fronts. The production centricity toward which the novel steadily moves is a lesson figured in regionalist, gender, and race terms. A well-bred, impeccably mannered corporation servant, who answers to his boss Greenfield, Holmes is discounted by the locals. In spite of his attempts to fit in by exchanging his gray suit for a "tailor-made outfit of corduroy," "the natives . . . accepted him with no more than passing glance as a part of the strange new life that the railroad was constantly bringing" (104). In western terms, Holmes mistakes the conditions of manhood, which are not about style and fashion but about deeds. That his career advancements were quickened through familial ties and social position are also cause for suspicion. Everything but the actual Willard Holmes made him what he is. Moreover, he cannot ride a horse. As Jefferson Worth warns Willard Holmes before Holmes defects to the side of righteousness, "We have only one standard in the West, Mr. Holmes. . . . What can you do?" (115).

As Holmes settles into his new life, he is stripped of things eastern. After various trials, "he began to sense the spirit of the untamed land and of the men who went to meet it with sheer joy of the conquest" (142). When he discovers that the joyless Greenfield tries to foul up Jefferson Worth's finances, Holmes switches affiliations to the Southwestern and Central Railroad, which puts him in charge of turning back the flood. (This is all the more significant because he had designed the headgates during his tenure with Greenfield.) Positioned now as hero, he does this job superbly, as the narrator reminds us. "The thousands of acres of The King's Basin lands that would have been forever lost to the race through one corporation were saved by another; and the man who—without protest—had built for his employers' gain the inadequate structures that endangered the work of the pioneers, led the forces that won the victory" (477). His vigor and worth now proved, Holmes can be celebrated as one of the new breed of "healthy manhood, . . . our civil engineers." And the narrative, in heroizing Holmes, lays more groundwork for valorizing the productive sphere.

As more forthright evocations of Barbara Worth and "her" desert shape the narrative, the emphasis on production takes on an additional aspect, romance. According to *The Winning of Barbara Worth,* capitalism *should* work toward the social good, but unlike *The Octopus* there is clear evidence that there is nothing *inherent* in capitalism to ensure that it will. It needs some form of undergirding when capitalist logic does not pan out, as is the case with Greenfield's disastrous withholding of funds to improve the headgate and with Jefferson Worth himself not having enough capital to shape the Basin according to his plans. The railroad, of course, has the capital to fix the flood, but it is not a local, full-service provider like Jefferson Worth. With the narrative's every wincing glance at the missteps of capital, it moves closer to offering capital absolution and consolation. In Wright's characteristically maudlin tones, we learn that something lurks in the Basin: "the dominant, insistent, compelling spirit of the land; a brooding, dreadful silence; a waiting—waiting—waiting; a mystic call that was at once a threat and a promise; a still drawing of the line across which no man might go and live, save those master men who should win the right." "Beside the awful forces that made themselves felt in the spirit of Barbara's Desert," continues Wright, "the might of Capital became small and trivial" (34, 162). Even Jefferson Worth's capitalist labors cannot be exempt from this reevaluation. Here, then, is the rhetorical switch—capital is about to become the epiphenomenon of nature, and romance will become the medium for that transfer.

## The Economy of Racial Yearning: Capitalism and Regionalism Subsumed

Nature's opposition to capital is of a curious order. Its defiance is simply an instance of desire. Nature, Wright tells us, yearns to be transformed by capital, just as capital must have something to transform. This proposition is carried forward by Willard Holmes and Barbara Worth. Nothing quite conveys the conflation of economy and desire like a few more of Wright's own passages. Willard "was held as though by some magic spell—not by the lure of her splendid womanhood, but by that and something else—something that was like the country of which she spoke so passionately." "'The desert—the mountains—the farms and homes and towns; it is all you,'" Willard confesses, "'as I came to love my work I came to love you.'" Barbara's success at seduction seduces her in return. Thrilling to the "nation-building ancestors" that she detects in him, "[s]he wanted to cry aloud with the joy and victory over barrenness and desolation. It was her Desert that was yielding itself to the strong ones; for them it had waited . . . and at last they had come." Here (with the bluntest of objects), Anglo-Saxon heterosexual desire is shaped into *the* productive force and bedrock of, ultimately, all economic value, and, further, it is definitive for Holmes's and Barbara Worth's sexual identity.

Willard Holmes's "masculinity" becomes finalized through and because of his desire, just as Barbara Worth becomes "feminine" by being taken.[9] One might say that for both of these characters, desire is the currency used to trade in their former androgynous selves. That same desire, like any currency, can only be possible in the market itself, (i.e., the mutual agreement, or rather drive, that makes the currency viable, increases the population, and expands production), which is to have its apotheosis in the Far West.

The codes continue to merge until they are drawn into a veritable black hole of cultural conflation. If we are led to believe that western women like Barbara have traits that eastern readers would consider border-crossing into the masculine, Wright assuages those regional frictions and in the process threatens to demolish the borders of regionalism altogether: The denouement of *The Winning of Barbara Worth* is that Barbara Worth is actually the orphaned niece of Joseph Greenfield, whose own brother had long ago made the westward journey, Connestoga style, only to get lost in a King's Basin sand storm. So, not only is Barbara *not* "Mexican or Indian"—Greenfield had discouraged Holmes's feelings for her on the grounds that she might be—she is yet another easterner of good breeding, like Holmes himself.

Let us take stock. Willard's coming into masculinity is, as I have noted, an easterner's westernization. Now we are to understand that the fulfillment of Barbara's femininity is a westerner's easternization. The combination of the two transformations is to be the stuff of "nation-building." Wright urges the reader to see the West as a national, domestic, and racial construct—the site not of sectionalism or regionalism but of Anglo-Saxon national unification (a narrative that is most congenial to federal-level reclamation plans). As Wright says of Holmes: "It was as if this man, born of the best blood of a nation-building people, trained by the best of the cultured East—trained as truly by his life and work in the desert—it was as though, in him, the best spirit of the age and race found expression" (476).

Western historian Patricia Nelson Limerick has noted that in the West, "personal interest in the acquisition of property coincided with national interest in the acquisition of territory" (Limerick 1987: 36). This is precisely what Wright determined the "spirit of the age" to be. Nowhere in his novel is it more evident, yet buried, than in the evocation of the irrigated landscape itself: "[T]here was more in Barbara's desert now than pictures woven magically in the air. There were beautiful scenes of farms with houses and barns and fences and stacks, with cattle and horses in the pastures, and fields of growing grain, the dark green of alfalfa, with threads and lines and spots of water that . . . shone in the distance like gleaming silver" (508). Conquest becomes scenery, existing in itself and for itself. Home building, the "victory over barrenness and desolation," in which Barbara Worth revels, is not just a vindication of male/female desire and reproduction but a vindication for the reproduction of an expanding economy, eroticized and racialized from the very beginning of the novel as "the master passion of the race."

If economic development is the offspring of heterosexual desire, the reputed guarantor of reproduced labor, then the novel's conceit would be implicit: Just as agro-economic growth depends on the conquest of space, male power advances when single women are domesticated as wives.

This conceit raises certain issues anew: what romance construed the economy to be; why romance is so central to telling an economic story; why capitalism makes romance an attractive venue for representing the economy. We must recognize first a long-running ideological development in which the American economy was seen as a form and outcome of Anglo-Saxon *passion*, an innate, self-confirming drive for dominance (see Saxton 1990 and Horsman 1981). "The race impulse was irresistible," wrote Frank Norris in 1903. "March we must, conquer we must" (Norris 1969).[10] But in the world of *The Winning of Barbara Worth*, even though the novel traffics in Norris-like images—what cultural historian T. J. Jackson Lears calls the "martial ideal"—the conquest is placed in jeopardy by the very romance that would clinch it (Lears 1983, chapter 3 especially). The narrative teases that passion, for (*and as*) economy, could go unfulfilled. The operative idea, in other words, is that the economy is reducible to passion, while passion itself, as the core of expansionist legitimation, is irreducible but must, just the same, be *made*. There is no "must" about romance in the romance narrative, nothing automatic about it. That's why the narrative exists, to make romance happen, so that in this case the proper sort of capitalist transformation can also happen. More than just grafting romance onto representations of the Imperial Valley, the Valley's very transformation occurs in romantic, Anglo-Saxonist terms.

If, as I am arguing, it is a problem for the novel that those drives have to be elicited—and necessarily so because of the romance narrative, which needs to keep lovers apart for a period of time—this points to a further problem. There is a contradiction in the novel's gender discourse when the sexual passion between Barbara Worth and Willard Holmes becomes the figure for the joining of nature and productive capital, respectively. Before the characters join up, each lives in a gender-crossed state—Barbara has too much passion and Holmes not enough; she likes rugged wear and he likes suits of corduroy; she rides a horse, he does not. She wants the desert to be transformed, and he does not know why or how. In other words, within very strictly defined definitions, she plays out his man while he plays out her woman. (We know that they were gender crossed because they re-gender in the process of romantic involvement.)

Increasingly through the nineteenth century, women had crossed over into the working spaces "officially" deemed male (Matthaei 1982; Matthews 1987). The American West was a powerful reminder of this, as Annette Kolodny has noted in her examination of western "relocation" novels (Kolodny 1984).[11] As a number of feminist's and women's histories have shown, it was not unusual that western women engaged in all sorts of economic activities, from mining and ranching to real estate and shop ownership (Myres 1982).

The presence of strong women in the West was a source of tension, however. One California businesswoman, Harriet Strong, complained in 1913 that although women were permitted to own a ranch or run a small business, "let her go into the business of incorporating a large enterprise . . . as a man would . . . and then see if the word does not go forth, 'This woman is going too far; she must be put down'" (quoted in Myres 1982: 268–69). Likewise, Charlotte Perkins Gilman, author of the widely read 1898 treatise *Women and Economics* and one-time resident of Southern California, gave qualified praise to the expanded place given to women in fiction, even, as she terms it, "reactionary" fiction. These fictional women are measured neither by looks nor by docility. "[T]hey *do*. They are showing qualities of bravery, endurance, strength, foresight, and power for the swift execution of well-conceived plans . . . and even when . . . the efforts of the heroine are shown to be entirely futile, and she comes back with a rush to the self-effacement of marriage with economic dependence, still the efforts were there" (Gilman 1898: 150–51; also see Raub 1994).

Barbara Worth fits Gilman's description well. She may be a woman of foresight and endurance, but when it comes to carrying out plans, the work of men takes over. What, then, is the purpose of having allowed her freedom when, ostensibly, it will be taken away?

Gilman's provocation about the intersection of sex and the economy points the way. A woman, she observes, "gets her living by getting a husband. He gets his wife by getting a living. It is to her individual economic advantage to secure a mate. It is to his individual sex-advantage to secure economic gain. The sex-functions to her have become economic functions. Economic functions to him have become sex-functions" (Gilman 1898: 110). The time that it takes in *The Winning of Barbara Worth* to develop the desert is synonymous with the time it takes for such a sex market to reach completion. Charles Aiken put the matter succinctly when he conceded in *Sunset* magazine in 1908 that although there was a lack of women in the Valley, they would arrive "when the men can stop from money-making long enough to build cabins" (Aiken 1908: 376). In these cultural formulations, the point at which it is permissible for a woman and a man to take possession of each other is determined by a particular point in the realization of circulating capital.

Again, we can get a firmer grasp of this by assessing developments in *The River*. In this novel, the formulation above is verified by seeing what happens when the sex market matures too early. *The River* has two women protagonists, Gerty and Innes, to Harold Bell Wright's one. Gerty, the wife of the engineer whose faulty headgate causes the flood, has a penchant for all manner of domestic habits entirely out of place on the flood battlefront. Whereas Innes dresses in a "khaki suit, simple as a uniform" (81–82), Gerty appears "in a fresh pink gingham frock, . . . dancing around the table to the tune of forks and spoons" (87). Innes works at the levee along with all the other women who forsake their domestic duties for flood control. Gerty insists that her business is to just keep her husband "convinced . . . that it is the desire of his life to support her" (118). While everyone else is obsessed with the emergency at the river, she is obsessed with what color to wear, how to redesign the work camp, and how to cook captivating meals. At the same time, it is not as if Innes has all the answers. As the battle with the river calms down, she reassesses things.

> The real work of the world is man-work; no matter how she or other women might yearn, theirs not the endurance. All they can do is negative; not to get on the track! Neither with pretty ruffles; nor tender fears!
>
> . . . Suppose she were not there, she were off building a house when he came home to find her, craving her comfort or her laurels? Suppose she had promised to deliver a plan, and that pledge involved her absence, or her attention when the world work, the man-work released him. . . . Was it still necessary for that wife to help with the bread-getting? On some women, that problem is thrust, but her college study, her later reading, had taught her that all women should seek it. An economic waste, half of the world spending more than the other half can earn! To the woman who has been spared the problem, comes the problem of choice. Has any one, born a woman, the daring to say—"I will not choose. I will take both! I will be man and woman, too!" Supposed she were not at home when he stumbled back to her! (387–88)

*Gerty*'s mistake, it now seems, is to have advanced too far too early. For this, the narrator accuses her of vanity, of placing too much value on a form of gender work that is not yet in demand. Gerty prefigures Innes's own realizations once the flood is under control. Now that the very same tasks valued by Gerty finally have a place in the sex market, vanity turns into "self-effacement" and it would be a continuation of vanity to keep doing man's work.

Although both Wright's and Aiken's novels are interested in exploring some of the outer boundaries of heterosexual gender roles, *The Winning of Barbara Worth* pushes its discussion just a little further by fraying the edges of meaning surrounding "man-work." Whereas Aiken is content to write (through Innes's character) that the men "were making her [the desert] over to their wishes, as a man makes unto his liking the wife of his satisfied choice" (235), the male power to activate productive capital in Wright's novel is subverted by his terms of romance.

Recall that the "winning" of Barbara Worth cuts two ways. Romance in Wright's novel signals a transformation of the two poles it seeks to attract. The act of conquest, when properly enacted, is made out to be consistent with, if not *subjected* to, feminine desire. In Wright's hands, we are no longer supposed to know who or which (Barbara? Willard? nature? capital?) has really won or transformed whom or what. As the market develops, we find all these subjects yielding to each other. The upshot is that unequal distribution of power between men and women and the overwhelming power of capital to reshape nature and society are obscured. It is the market itself—"Good Business"—that emerges as the victor.

The settling of gender relations into their preappointed grooves and the capitalist transformation of the landscape occur together in *The Winning of Barbara Worth* as sexual desire is sublimated toward landscape transformation and validated by it.[12] This is the end point of a rather long narrative arc, however. First came speculative investment in land, surveying, and the building of the irrigation works. Then came settlement, the building of homes, and the restitution of Anglo society and its gender appointments. But we get more than a telling of one circuit, from investment to realized profit. The bourgeois conceit of the novel is to redefine, as the story moves along, its own representations of capitalism and regional growth in order to make capitalist development an outcome of passionate Anglo-Saxon impulses to work, produce, and, by implication, reproduce. To clinch that redefinition, good capitalists double as workers, masters of nature double as servants, man doubles as woman, and woman as man. What the reader at first thinks is capital gaining dominion over nature is a fetishized nature simultaneously molding capital to its designs. But to seek these couplings is to acknowledge that an exogenous plot has brought them together. The narrative would have these pairings appear utterly natural and preordained but de facto, as a romance narrative it acknowledges their *constructed* "nature." Capital first claims nature, then invents a kind of separation from it, whose trajectory is a "reunion" with capital.

## Conclusion: Engineering Rural Realism

The enormous popularity of *The Winning of Barbara Worth* vested Wright with the cultural authority to act later as a spokesman on the Imperial Valley. In a statement of acknowledgment in his novel, he had written, "I must admit that this work which in the past ten years has transformed a vast, desolate waste into a beautiful land of homes, cities, and farms, has been my inspiration." In 1915, he wrote an essay for a promotional booklet put together by the Valley's board of supervisors. In so many words, he tells the reader about the battle for dominance of a desert region in which only the fit have survived. The Valley, he notes, is populated with farmers, not speculators; sound businessmen, not hucksters; homes and women, not lonely men (Weaver 1915). It is as if all the themes of his novel had come true in real life.

Even if the Valley was populated the way Wright portrayed it, it was becoming thick with other meanings. The very year Wright's novel was published, the Valley became the home of the largest irrigation district in the country. Its first bond issue, $3.5 million, put together in 1916, was to allow the district the means to buy from the Southern Pacific Railroad the irrigation works that had been installed by the California Development Company. Moreover, although the Valley was irrigating half a million acres and producing at premium prices some of the nation's earliest produce, thanks to its warm winters, it did not buy its own bond issue. Instead the bonds were purchased almost in their entirety by the Southern Pacific Railroad itself, thus maintaining the railroad as a major backer of the Valley economy (Cooper 1968; Tout 1931; Cory 1915).

The Imperial Valley's agriculture was a far cry from that envisaged by Chaffey, Rockwood, and Wright. Within the first decade or so after the flood, tenant farming became the norm, thousand-acre farms dominated the local economy, and Mexican wage workers were regularly recruited during harvests (Worster 1985; Cooper 1968; McWilliams 1979). As Donald Worster notes, the majority of the Imperial Valley Irrigation District's directors were drawn from banking, real estate, and merchandising. "The transformation of the Imperial Valley Irrigation District into a local power complex, immune to many residents needs," he writes, "was in large measure the achievement of a succession of hired managerial experts" (Worster 1985: 201–2). By the 1910s, it was clear that wage labor made the agrarian motor run. By the early 1920s, a third of the population comprised Mexican farm workers and their families. These workers lived in separate settlements adjacent to the Valley's towns and when at work in the fields dwelt in ramshackle housing.[13] Their presence turned a mirror on a bifurcated farm-operator class. During periods when labor was in short supply, small farmers objected that the large landowners, often absentee, could be assured of attracting the labor they needed by offering higher wages. Yet, in fear of being overrun, these same small, resident farmers opposed unrestricted immigration (Edson c. 1927).

Perhaps because agriculture itself had to be saved when the Colorado River was turned back into its channel, *The Winning of Barbara Worth* (and *The River*, for that matter) heroizes the civil engineer rather than the farmer, as we have seen in other rural realist formulas. But there is something about the civil engineer that is inclusive of the logic behind making farmer-heroes/capitalist laborers in the first place. A final question, then: Since its point seems to be to steer representations of capital toward production- and labor-centered circuits, why doesn't *The Winning of Barbara Worth* heroize a farmer as the consummate producer of value—instead of celebrating an engineer? The answer, I would argue, concerns the very tensions that capitalist laborers try to negotiate. If as capitalists they must worry about the best circulation of their capital, then as laborers they want the best returns on their work without such work being so arduous as to deprive them the benefits of capitalist status. The engineer, though, fills this void that the capitalist laborer must perpetually negotiate. The engineer is, by design, always in the sweet spot that rural realism and narratives of capitalist laborers seek to describe. Wright's novel, in fact, prefigures a similar analysis of the engineer performed by Thorsten Veblen a decade later in his essays in *The Engineers and the Price System* (1921). "These expert men," Veblen argues,

> technologists, engineers, or whatever name may best suit them, make up the indispensable General Staff of the industrial system; and without their immediate and unremitting guidance and correction the industrial system will not work. It is a mechanically organized structure of technical processes designed, installed, and conducted by these production engineers. . . . The material welfare of the community is unreservedly bound up with the due working of this industrial system, and therefore with its unreserved control by the engineers, who alone are competent to manage it. To do their work as it should be done these men of the industrial general staff must have a free hand, unhampered by commercial considerations and reservations; for the production of the goods and services needed by the community they neither need nor are they in any degree benefited by any supervision or interference from the side of the owners. (Veblen 1921: 69–70)

These words could nearly have been penned in *The Winning of Barbara Worth*. The engineer's entire raison d'être is to specialize in the maximum efficiency of pure productive capital. Shorn of the worries about the finances preceding production, the engineer does not—as rendered in *The Winning of Barbara Worth*—have the worries that the financier has. And shorn of the oppression endured by laborers, he does not suffer the aches of the working class but rather is in control of the productive capital employed through him. Technology and the army of engineers are, in addition, the forces that bring the corporation and the farmer together. The engineer's installation of an irrigated landscape was a social good from which both factions potentially benefit. The engineered landscape makes the corporation productive and, as well, can be utilized by productive farmers.

# 7

# Take Me to the River

## *Water, Metropolitan Growth, and the Countryside*

### Designer Ducts

For the moment, let us forget California and recall that nameless, unforgettable landscape—"somewhere in the twentieth century"—summoned up in Terry Gilliam's cult-film classic *Brazil.* Among the many extraordinary images is a metropolis that wears its infrastructure inside out. The film has been rolling for a few scant minutes when all sorts of conduits, ducts, and pipes that convey essential utilities begin tumbling out onto the urban surface. They erupt from behind walls and arc across ceilings in great looping swags—a Gorgon of hoses sweating, gurgling, pulsating. There is no question that the plumbing *thrives* with insistent life.

This film is a heady, phantasmagoric reminder of the capitalist polis as the accumulator of matériel, of infrastructure, *par excellence.* But thrive as it will, the hydrocircuitry also wrings the life out of the surrounding environment. Urban plumbing is the flip side of every acre of land having been scoured and turned into desert. Anymore, the rural lives on only in dreams—dreams produced from within the heart of the city itself. (In the movie, this is not only bad for the environment but bad for the dreamers.) Attempting to hide the inversion is "Central Services." Their logo is a lake of fresh, clean water sprouting a branching tree of aqueducts; their motto, "ducts in designer colors to suit your demanding taste." Central Services tends to the vast landscape of tubes and pipes, which are an essential mechanism for the maintenance of political and economic power. Those characters who understand how the plumbing works join together in an organized underground movement against political corruption. They use the urban blueprint against itself, sabotaging its hoses, turning valves on and off, in order to wreak havoc on the halls of power. Other characters, though, are doomed to fantasize a return to easier, more pastoral times in some imagined place beyond the city's reach. The film's protagonist and anti-hero, Sam Lowry, is one of these dreamers. In the movie's final frames, while clamped in the very jaws of urban machinery and corruption, he dreams of a romantic escape to a greener time, to a well-watered place of small farms and self-sufficiency.

For all its extremes, *Brazil* invites its viewers to map real histories and geographies onto it. Located only "somewhere in the twentieth century," *Brazil* is no place in particular and all capitalist, industrialized places at once. The film seems to me a provocative medium for setting out the historical, geographical, and cultural themes involved in Los Angeles and San Francisco's search for water. (Certainly it goes much further than Roman Polanski's film *Chinatown,* which, while directly speaking to Los Angeles and the Owens Valley, shares little with *Brazil's* vivid spotlight on matériel as both a sticking point for capital and politics and the essence of the finest civic achievements.) In the early twentieth century, each of these cities, hot to compete against each other and to lay the groundwork for a new century's worth of industrial and residential growth, reached out over a hundred miles to the east to augment its water supply. Los Angeles secured its source in the ranching district of the Owens Valley, an elongated high-desert basin at the foot of the Sierra Nevada eastern escarpment. San Francisco won its battle to flood the Hetch Hetchy, a remote Sierra valley high up in the Tuolumne River watershed, which was ostensibly protected by being within the boundary of Yosemite National Park. The cities accomplished these ends as much through brilliant feats of engineering as through political secrecy and manipulation.

In 1917, while in the midst of a prolific career as an essayist, a short-story writer, and a novelist, Mary Austin published a novel combining elements of the Los Angeles and San Francisco water schemes. Entitled *The Ford*, her novel shares certain elements that we have already seen in the rural realist narrative, especially a socially progressive financial circuit of capital, a development plan to unite water with parched earth, and a heterosexual romance.[1] Some of the same is true of J. Allan Dunn's *The Water-Bearer*, published in 1924. Dunn, a much less prolific novelist, explorer, and travel writer, focused on the San Francisco–Hetch Hetchy controversy, especially the corporate and engineering maneuvers of a private water company cashing in on water sales to the city during the lengthy period of Hetch Hetchy aqueduct planning and construction. Dunn's novel departs from Austin's in that his water development plans only very sketchily benefit agriculture. Both novels, however, clearly separate urban and rural circuits of capital. I argue that this constitutes a unique corner of rural realist discourse that strains the discourse nearer its limits than we have seen so far. As the subsequent discussion will show, both Los Angeles's and San Francisco's water grabs were firmly tied to negotiations between urban and rural interests in ways that illustrate the importance of one to the other. Austin and Dunn, however, merely flirt with rural economy and depict it as more or less expendable by the city, at least as contrasted to the novels looked at in previous chapters. I say *flirt* here, because agriculture is put before the reader only to show that it can be diminished in value. The novels are therefore still making rural realist kinds of inquiries: What does urban capital *do* with agriculture, and how does it confront it when the brute fact is that both urban and agricultural economies circulate capital through nature?

In these novels' portrayals, I would argue nonetheless that we have less a misconception of the importance of agricultural economy to the details of how the

Los Angeles and Hetch Hetchy aqueducts actually panned out than we have an exploration and justification of capitalists seeking efficient returns on their capital. Just the same, *The Ford* and *The Water-Bearer* are not released from certain cultural repercussions. These novels are caught where poor Sam Lowry is caught: between the two representations of nature that *they theorize* are entailed by capitalist development processes. Nature becomes both more precious and romanticized, on the one hand, and more likened to the workshop of capital, on the other hand.

## Los Angeles and the Owens Valley

Just after the turn of the century, a small group of Los Angeles technocrats and developers put together a plan to gain control of the Owens River, hundreds of miles away at the base of the Sierra's eastern escarpment, and convince voters that they should pay for an aqueduct to bring the water to Los Angeles. The plan involved dumping the water into the San Fernando Valley, just north of Los Angeles. The valley, when charged with water, would act like a hydrographic sump that could be drawn upon to feed the Los Angeles Basin. In 1913, the 230-mile-long aqueduct was completed, on time and under budget. Meanwhile, however, news of the plan to deliver water to the San Fernando Valley was leaked by a member of the Los Angeles Board of Water Commissioners to a consortium of developers, himself included, who then bought up thousands of acres of San Fernando Valley land. With water on the ground, they sold off their property at super profits.[2]

The key players were J. B. Lippincott, Fred Eaton, William Mulholland, and members of the San Fernando Valley Mission Land Company. On the surface of it, not all of these were people whose interests ought to have merged. Lippincott was the Chief Engineer of the newly created U.S. Reclamation Service, which had identified the Owens Valley as a potential site for an irrigation project in 1903. The Service promptly began informing Owens Valley farmers that a federal project was coming their way. Eaton, a former superintendent of the Los Angeles City Water Company, as well as mayor of Los Angeles in 1899–1900, had hit on the idea of going to the Owens Valley to import water to Los Angeles. Eaton, therefore, wanted to block the federal project. Lippincott, who had a private consulting business on the side that brought him into Los Angeles's inner circle of technocrats and property developers, turned out to be the man to help him. Posing as an agent of Lippincott, with Lippincott's knowledge, Eaton went up to the valley and began buying options on land and water in 1904. The next year, he went up again to purchase more options, only this time he brought a few Los Angeles bankers and William Mulholland—a brilliant, self-educated civil engineer who had gone from tending ditches to becoming the Chief Engineer of the Los Angeles Water Department. Mulholland was to study the feasibility of building an aqueduct to ship Owens Valley water to the San Fernando Valley. By the end of 1905, the city, primarily in the person of Eaton, had water rights along forty miles of the Owens River.

The San Fernando Valley Mission Land Company was now poised for pay dirt. Among its members were some of California's most powerful men: Harrison Gray Otis, owner of the Los Angeles *Times and Mirror*; Harry Chandler, Otis's son-in-law and owner of the Los Angeles *Tribune*; Moses Sherman, a Water Commissioner and former trolley magnate; Henry Huntington, creator of the Pacific Electric Railway Company, owner of vast Southern California real estate holdings, and nephew of Collis of the Big Four; and Edward Harriman, head executive of the Union Pacific railroad system. On the basis of inside information provided by Sherman (much of the evidence for this being circumstantial, Norris Hundley [1992] warns), Otis broke the story of Eaton and Mulholland's plans and, soon after, began promoting San Fernando Valley lands. Lippincott promptly announced that the Reclamation Service was no longer interested in the Owens Valley. He quit his job with the Service and took a position with the Los Angeles Water Department. Both Otis and Chandler began a campaign to convince Los Angeles citizens of the need for more water. Voters passed a $22 million bond issue in 1905 to build the aqueduct and purchase the land and water rights from Eaton.

Meanwhile, the city still had to apply for right-of-way for the aqueduct to cross federal lands. They met some difficulty at this juncture but eventually put through an appeal directly to President Roosevelt and U.S. Forest Service head, Gifford Pinchot, a champion of multi-use for national forests. With the backing of these two heavyweights, the aqueduct bill slipped through Congress. Nearly treeless lands of the Mojave Desert, over which the aqueduct was to travel, were declared national forest and thus taken out of the public domain, under which they would have been subject to homestead law. The only stipulation that the federal government put forward was that Los Angeles could not irrigate land outside the city limits with surplus water from the aqueduct. To get around this measure, the city simply annexed most of the San Fernando Valley in 1915 (the Valley was twenty miles outside Los Angeles proper). This was a double-edged maneuver, for it allowed an increase in the city's assessed valuation, which in turn raised the amount of debt that the city was allowed to carry (in the form of bond issues that would pay for the aqueduct).

The beauty of the Owens Valley caper was that from a growth standpoint, the area that comprised Los Angeles before the San Fernando Valley annexation used very little of the Owens River water for twenty years. Most of the city's draw, therefore, went directly toward irrigating the San Fernando Valley. From a rural standpoint, this fact drips with irony. While the San Fernando blossomed with water-intensive crops—irrigated land in the Valley stood at 3,000 acres the year before the aqueduct and 30,000 by 1917—the Owens Valley nearly dried up.[3] As Norris Hundley notes, the vastly productive San Fernando Valley helped Los Angeles County retain its place as the nation's first-ranked agricultural county, while, in conjunction with a new deepwater port at San Pedro (incorporated into the city by the famous "shoestring" annexation), the aqueduct's supply to Los Angeles urbanites helped the city outrank San Francisco as the West Coast port (Hundley 1992: 167–68).

And in Owen's Valley? Through the 1910s, rainfall was well above normal. Hence, after a brief register of protest by petitions and letters, in 1904–1905, Owens Valley farmers were quieted. Then in the early 1920s, drought struck. At the same time, the city of Los Angeles quickened the speed of its purchases of Owens Valley land, water rights, and ditch companies. Not only farmers were alarmed, but merchants, too. Valley residents saw "not only that agriculture would suffer, but also that city purchases would depopulate the farms, stifle local banking and commerce, and ultimately destroy the towns" (Walton 1992: 155). In 1922, citizens banded together and formed an irrigation district, hoping to put up a unified front against the city. Los Angeles tried to block the sale of bonds and, by inducing many farmers and landowners to sell to the city, stirred up deep animosity among Owens Valley residents.

Matters were made more difficult by the fact that the city refused to guarantee what its water take would be or say whether it would leave behind a guaranteed amount for local use. Added to the general post-war downturn, crisis followed: "local lending stopped, real estate stagnated save for the city's bidding, farm production dropped, and schools began to close" (Walton 1992: 158). In May of 1924, Los Angeles filed suit against water diverters north of the aqueduct; and on the 21st of the month, Owens Valley saboteurs began the first of a three-year round of assaults against the aqueduct and other city properties in the valley. During their first attack, the "Inyo Gang" bombed the aqueduct wall at Alabama Gates. Two years later, a city-owned well was dynamited. In 1927, rebellion peaked during late spring and summer. Five more sections of the aqueduct wall were obliterated; a large-diameter, water-bearing iron pipe was blown up; the intake to a power plant was destroyed; and a set of control gates was knocked out (Walton 1992).

Los Angeles endured these acts of resistance and rebellion while it tried, unsuccessfully, to get a conviction of the "Inyo Gang." It also kept buying up Owens Valley properties, thereby eroding the very base of the irrigation district. By 1926, the city had acquired 90% of the land and water in the valley.

Los Angeles was locally aided in its victory, for up and down the Owens Valley, residents were never unified on what to do about the city's junket. One faction, led by a small group of influential local businessmen, urged cooperation with Los Angeles in hopes that the city would build a reservoir that might meet the needs of all parties. Due to a bitter entanglement between Eaton, the owner of the land on which such a reservoir might have been constructed, and Mulholland, who tried in vain to get Eaton to lower his price, this option did not arrive in time to save the valley. What seemed to have crushed the already weakening revolt, however, was the collapse of Owens Valley's prominent banking family, the Wattersons. The family had vibrantly supported the revolt against Los Angeles, but when news hit of their having diverted local funds for personal gains, enthusiasm behind what had been an intense, cross-class protest movement drained from the valley (Walton 1992). As Walton points out, the agriculture stagnated. Short-term leases were readily available, but "the city also made it clear that water for irrigation was scarce and subject to cancellation or reduction from year to year. These constraints meant that production of livestock and some alfalfa were the only rational choices for the farmer" (Walton 1992: 209–10). Owens Valley land and water were accordingly de-commodified as the money ran downhill.

### San Francisco and Hetch Hetchy Valley

*Sans* dynamite, the developmental process behind San Francisco's water supply had certain resonances with Los Angeles's. The very year that the Owens Valley–Los Angeles aqueduct was finished, the U.S. Congress passed the Raker Act, which authorized the city of San Francisco to seek a new water supply in the Sierra Nevada, over one hundred fifty miles away in Hetch Hetchy Valley, Yosemite Valley's neighboring gorge.

San Francisco's desire for a publicly owned water source dated back to reaction against the first large water supply developed for the city by private capital, the Spring Valley Water Company. Spring Valley, which had been under the control of banker and all-around developer William Ralston in the early 1870s, fought the construction of a municipally controlled water system for years. In 1900, after fifty years of explosive urban growth, monopoly water rates, and vigorous campaign among proponents of the idea, a revised city charter proposed that a large, city-owned water source be found and a delivery system built. C. E. Grunsky, a civil engineer working for the City of San Francisco, suggested that Mayor Phelan look into damming the Hetch Hetchy Valley at the headwaters of the Tuolumne River—never mind, for the time being, that since 1890 the valley had been declared a wilderness preserve, enclosed within the boundaries of Yosemite National Park. Phelan tried to obtain the site for the city but the Secretary of the Interior refused. Meanwhile, through the services of J. B. Lippincott, who had not yet done his work in Los Angeles, he filed for water rights on the Tuolumne. Only after the San Francisco earthquake and fire of 1906 did the pro-reservoir forces get their break. In 1908, with nods from Roosevelt and Pinchot, the new Secretary of the Interior, James R. Garfield, gave San Francisco the go-ahead to flood Hetch Hetchy (see Hundley 1992; Nash, R. 1982; Clements 1979; Jones, H. 1965; Richardson 1959). Although Garfield believed an inadequate water supply had led to San Francisco's undoing, the fire actually could not be brought under control because of faulty water lines (Hundley 1992).

Opposition to the city's Hetch Hetchy plans immediately followed, however, and was effective enough to hold the city up for five years. The opposition came from disparate quarters. The Spring Valley Water Company fought vigorously up to the very last minute to convince the federal government that the gravel-bottomed valleys surrounding the San Francisco Bay were saturated with enough water for a million people. The groundwaters underlying the Livermore and Sunol Valleys were said to be adequate enough to assure San Francisco's growth into the twenty-first century. Hence, why go to the Sierra to import water? Ironically, the consultants that the company brought in, in 1912, to prove the sufficiency of local reserves were none other than Messrs. William Mulholland and J. B. Lippincott (Spring Valley Water Company 1912).

Allied with Spring Valley were the Modesto and Turlock Irrigation Districts, who were themselves already looking ahead to the day when they would need more water from the Tuolumne River, which was their water source *and* whose channel was their common boundary. After considerable effort involving major legal, financial, and construction challenges, the districts were not about to lose out to San Francisco's expansion. (The man who directed the districts to the Tuolumne, C. E. Grunsky, was the same engineer who would later point San Francisco upstream to Hetch Hetchy, before water was even flowing to the districts.) Both districts were established in the summer of 1887, the Modesto occupying 81,000 acres on the north side of the river, the Turlock comprising 176,000 acres on the south side. It took six years and repeated misadventure for the districts to finish building a dam (the Lagrange) in the Tuolumne's channel. A smart piece of work, it lay twenty miles to the east, tucked away in the Sierra foothills. Fifteen of those miles crossed the rough terrain that climbed steadily up from the floor of the San Joaquin Valley. This made a difficult crossing for the canal that would take water to each of the districts. Thus, it was not until 1901 that the Turlock would even gets it share of the Tuolumne; and 1903 for the Modesto district. The water came at great expense: In 1904, the districts were in debt for well over a million dollars each, and while they were capable of irrigating much, much more, they had only a combined 27,000 acres under ditch between the two of them. Much of this was in alfalfa, but here and there farmers had planted their land to grapes, sweet potatoes, figs, melons, and beans (Adams, F. 1905). Unlike their counterparts in the Owens Valley, who were much more removed from the California mainstream, the districts, whose bond sales already tied them to San Francisco investors, won several lengthy clauses in the Raker Act guaranteeing them a satisfactory amount of water. Even in times of drought, the districts would have access to water stored by the city of San Francisco (Taylor 1926).

Opposition to Hetch Hetchy also came from those seeking to protect wilderness areas. John Muir, whose passions for nature were stoked by Henry George's well-known arguments against the buying and selling of nature, teamed up with Robert Underwood Johnson, the editor of *Century* magazine. Together, they led a spirited publicity campaign for the salvation of Hetch Hetchy's wilderness scenery, which they believed would be a salve for the nation's over-worked, over-commercialized psyche. Fifteen years before, they had joined forces to become an effective voice in helping to promote the formation of Yosemite National Park, and thus Hetch Hetchy's off-limits status. They were supported in this new effort by the Southern Pacific, which wanted to preserve its tourism-based ticket sales.

In 1909, as Roderick Nash (1982) recounts, the House and Senate solicited testimony both pro and con. (For examples of these, see Parsons [1909] and Olney [1909].) The anti–Hetch Hetchy faction won a brief victory, as a majority of lawmakers were swayed over to the argument that capital had to leave room for nature if civilization was to remain civilized. Nature appreciation, they argued, was essential to the perpetuation of human health and productivity. Moreover, they pointed out, to be pro-nature was not to be anti-development. Nature could, in effect, pay its own way, bringing in a sure and steady stream of tourist dollars. Others argued in more abstract terms that in a godless, money-hungry world, nature took on great spiritual significance. The House denied San Francisco's application on the grounds that the recreational rights of the public would be otherwise deprived.

By 1913, the city decided to take its battle to Washington again, and this time the Hetch Hetchy bill passed by an overwhelming margin (183 to 43), although 203 representatives did not even vote. Construction began in 1914, and in 1923 the biggest of the dams, the O'Shaughnessy, was complete. During this second round of struggle, the Sierra Club had thought it had a friend in Representative William Kent from Marin County, since it was Kent who had presided over the founding of the redwood preserve Muir Woods in 1909. But Kent had an important seat on the House Committee on the Public Lands and wanted to use that power to stop the Pacific Gas and Electric Company's private designs on Hetch Hetchy. (Pacific Gas and Electric was also an opponent of the Hetch Hetchy reservoir.)

Even though Kent was a self-professed friend of wilderness, he thought that private utility interests had made dupes out of the nature lovers (Nash, R. 1982).

Senators who voted to give Hetch Hetchy to San Francisco did not consider themselves to be voting *against* the intangible values of wilderness but *for* thirsty mouths in a teeming city of half a million people. If anything, environmental historian Roderick Nash argues, the fight to save Hetch Hetchy was proof of the power of a wilderness "cult," which, steeled by its Hetch Hetchy fight, would then go on to ease passage of the National Park Service Act. The passion for the preservation of Hetch Hetchy increased with distance from San Francisco. Before the Raker Act reached the Senate, a hue and cry in favor of preservation arose from hundreds of newspaper editorials and letters and from several of the high-circulation magazines in the heavily populated East. Nash points out that the number of articles on the national parks published in popular magazines between September 1916 and October 1917 numbered over 300, spread out over 95 journals. This performance was nearly repeated in 1918 and 1919 (Nash, R. 1982).

When the Raker Act was passed, it was not earthquake and fire that got Washington to back San Francisco's designs. Instead, it was San Francisco's Washington lobby, masterminded back home by Mayor James Rolph, Jr. Rolph reigned at a propitious time. Taking office after the *post*-Phelan administrations, which waffled on the need for Hetch Hetchy, Rolph was able to take advantage of the fact that Franklin Lane, a crony of Phelan and backer of the reservoir idea, had been named Woodrow Wilson's Secretary of the Interior. During the first few months of 1913, Rolph went into high gear. As San Francisco historians Issel and Cherny explain, "Rolph's city attorneys drafted a bill, Democratic Congressman John Raker (another political ally of Phelan, whose district included Hetch Hetchy) introduced it, and San Francisco turned out a full force of lobbyists: Phelan and Rudolph Spreckels both went at their own expense, and Rolph, O'Shaughnessy [city engineer], city clerk John S. Dunningan, and others from the Rolph administration all made one or more journeys to Washington" (Issel and Cherny 1986: 176). On the morning of the day of the vote, December 2, 1913, senators found in their offices a "Special Washington Edition" of the *San Francisco Examiner*. It featured an illustration of Hetch Hetchy as it would appear when flooded. Expertly done, it showed a modern highway ringing the lake and towering granite cliffs all around. "Does this beautiful lake ruin this beautiful valley?" the newspaper asked of the senators. The article that followed was designed to hit every conceivable angle, from arguing that it was only the "chronic opponents" (those who opposed "Everything" all the time) who didn't want the valley flooded, to arguing that the Spring Valley monopoly deprived San Francisco of what Los Angeles already had, to making the case that the Panama Canal would be in vain if San Francisco was prevented from maturing enough to meet the expectations of those who would pass through the canal "seeking California, the new Hesperides." There was also the argument that a lake would make the valley more beautiful than it already was—so much more, in fact, that the *Examiner* wondered: If there had been a large lake to begin with, which engineers would have proposed to *drain*, then surely the nature lovers would have fought to keep it there. So why not dam the valley and let engineering imitate what nature herself had failed to do?

Since the beginning of his administration in 1911, Rolph had made the Hetch Hetchy site more acceptable at home by linking it to the much-anticipated Panama

Pacific International Exposition, planned for 1915. The Exposition had the backing of organized labor and the majority of the downtown business establishment. Rolph told them that if the Exposition was to succeed, the city would need to supplement its water supply. However, plagued by unforeseen construction difficulties and cost overruns, Hetch Hetchy water did not flow into the city until 1934, almost twenty years after the Exposition. By the time Sierra water made it into the taps of San Francisco households, some $100 million had been spent—five times that spent by Los Angeles (Issel and Cherny 1986).

Three years before the Raker Act, the bond issue to build the aqueduct had passed easily in San Francisco, but in that year voters turned down another important facet of the city's water expansion plans, a proposal to buy the Spring Valley Water Company. This proposal was rejected again in 1915, 1921, and 1927. Finally in 1928, Rolph and O'Shaughnessy got their way. Indeed, they *had* to get their way. With the city's water infrastructure owned by Spring Valley and with the Raker Act stipulating that the new city-owned system could not resell water or electric power to a private company, San Francisco was essentially forced to buy out Spring Valley (Hundley 1992). The price, $41 million, was so heavy that only a consortium of buyers organized by A. P. Giannini could afford the purchase of the bond issue. Giannini himself had already invested in several million dollars worth (Issel and Cherny 1986).

## Rural Eclipse: *The Water-Bearer* and *The Ford*

In virtually every novel treated so far that deals in depth with city-countryside relations, the city is a maker of agriculture. Although the processes entailed may be none too pleasant, as detailed in *The Octopus* and *Blood-Money*, that the city is a fundamental participant in the production of rural surplus, which is itself of fundamental importance to the city, is announced quite clearly. Agriculture is a basic economic strategy employed by the most powerful urban capitalists for the reproduction of their capital and the aggrandizement of the polis. In J. Allan Dunn's and Mary Austin's novels, this is not so. In these novels, a corner has been turned. Urban power brokers and financiers now threaten, at worst, to displace agriculture rather than mastermind it and, at best, to simply render it irrelevant to their concerns. This new rhetoric turns around the question of water development. Water development is to be managed directly by the city for the exclusive use of its own plumbing, rather than circulating first through agriculture, which would then generate surplus for larger economies. In other words, in these California novels, the city is no longer just a core economic space that seeks to articulate with, shape, or control surrounding economies, but a material, infrastructural space that competes with and perhaps displaces those surroundings by virtue of core and periphery competition over the same spoils.

In *The Ford*, Mary Austin writes a story contrasting the experiences of two California families, the Brents and the Rickarts, in the booms and busts of the agricultural and oil economies. The plot culminates in the "Tierra Longa" (Owens Valley) water and land controversy. The Brents are a family who must struggle every day to make ends meet on their Tierra Longa ranch, Palomitas. The Rickarts are a highly successful oil and real estate family. In her novel, though, Mary Austin, who was once married to an irrigation engineer and who lived for a time in the Owens Valley, unexpectedly rescues Tierra Longa from the clutches of urban conspiracy, even though Los Angeles's machinations in the Owens Valley had been well secured, and were well known to her, by the time of her writing (see Kahrl 1982). In fact, *The Ford* combines elements of Los Angeles's water grab in the Owens Valley with San Francisco's grab of Hetch Hetchy. The novel makes San Francisco the seat of urban power rather than Los Angeles, and Tierra Longa is saved from the city when the city goes to Hetch Hetchy instead. In making these alterations, *The Ford* reveals itself as much more interested in the cultural and social parameters of regional capitalist transformation.

Let us review the basics of Austin's novel. Aside from the Brents—Mr. and Mrs., daughter Anne, son Kenneth—one of the first characters we meet is "nature," in the form of the river that runs through Tierra Longa. And, alas, nature is incomplete: "swift and full, beginning with the best intentions of turning mills or whirring dynamos, with the happiest possibilities of watering fields and nursing orchards, but, discouraged at last by the long neglect of man, becoming like all wasted things, a mere pest of mud and malaria" (34). Immediately we recognize that this novel is not going to pit nature against development but is, in fact, lamenting the *lack* of nature's development in the valley.

Due to a prolonged drought, the Brents are forced to sell the Palomitas ranch to a secretive outsider, a man named Jevens, who has been making the rounds of Tierra Longa ranches. Mrs. Brent in particular is not wholly averse to this development. All around her she sees the countryside being developed, property being bought and sold, oil being discovered, and large tracts of land being subdivided into irrigated plots. Her fervent desire is to be "in" this game, to be its subject and not its victimized object—"I live in the country," she says, "but I don't have to *be* country" (52). With the proceeds from the sale of Palomitas, the Brents move to the boomtown of Summerfield and acquire a small stake in an oil concern, the Homestead Development Company. Although Homestead oil is gushing copiously, Homestead is edged out by the Rickart family's monopoly on the pipeline. The Brents' dream of being "in" fails. As the parents age, and then when Mrs. Brent passes away, little is left for Kenneth and Anne to make a go at life except for Jevens's last payment for Palomitas. Mr. Brent splits this between his son and daughter, both of whom harbor a wish to buy back Palomitas some day.

As Kenneth and Anne mature into adulthood, they find their lives increasingly drawn into "Old Man" Rickart's orbit. Like Cedarquist in *The Octopus* or Greenfield in *The Winning of Barbara Worth,* Rickart is a skilled practitioner of cash-cow capitalism: "Nothing developed far in the Old Man's hands. . . . Lands, waters, and minerals, he took them up and laid them down again, wholly uninformed of the severances and readjustments made necessary by that temporary possession" (176). Anne develops into one of Rickart's competitors. She had educated herself to be "a business woman. She had the gift of detachment; she could buy land without wanting to work it; she could buy it with the distinct intention of unloading it on somebody else who believed himself elected to work it and was willing to pay handsomely for the privilege" (178). Her goals are different than Rickart's, however. More like a combination of Harold Bell Wright's Jefferson and Barbara Worth, she is concerned with what the land itself "wants." "'I'm a real estate agent,'" she tells her brother Ken, who works in Rickart's office, "'I am one the same way other people are musicians and writers. I'm making money at it because I'm a success; but I'm being it because I like it. Land doesn't mean crops to me the way it does to you and father, it means people—people who want land and are fitted for the land, and the land wants—how it wants them!'" (199). Her brand of land commodification is vindicated by the fact that even though her job deals in a kind of "detachment" and depends upon her not wanting to labor on the farm, she brings land and laborers together. Toward this end, her business increasingly relies on cutting deals with Rickart, including convincing him to take out a mortgage on her behalf for Palomitas. Her plan is to launch an irrigation project and subdivide the area around Palomitas into small farms. Anne creates a mechanism for productive circuits of capital in which labor and production beget money, even though her actual livelihood is much like Rickart's: money begetting money.

Separate from Anne's doings and Ken's general befuddlement about things financial and capitalistic, events in Tierra Longa take a new course. Jevens (who had purchased Palomitas) and another character, Elwood, roam the valley taking out options on a number of ranches and important water rights. Rickart, too, is buying land, snatching up struggling and marginal farms. The narrator is less concerned with denouncing these acts than using them in judgment of the locals, who seem not only unperturbed but flattered to have the attention. "It gave them a feeling of opulence to see [Elwood] toss up and catch again the very source of their livelihood. And besides, he paid good money for his options" (225). Picking on the ranchers provides a rather interesting problem for the novel, however. For while Anne is upholding her agrarian end, as it were, Mary Austin cannot seem to invent a population of farmers who are willing to remain on the land in the face of a good offer to sell out. So, while Anne gets to reap the rewards of land as real estate, not so the ranchers. And if the ranchers are willing to sell, thus demonstrating the fact that they are not suited to the land in Anne's calculus (as above), then the novel ought not to worry about it: This is supposed to be a novel where people are free to practice what is in their nature to practice. Mr. Brent puts a very fine point on the issue in a conversation he has with a local political radical:

> "I've always said there ought to be a farmers' union. They are as much the victims of the Capitalistic System as anybody; they've just got to organize against it."
>
> "Why *against?*" said Steven Brent. "Doesn't the land need Rickart as much as it needs the rest of us? All this struggle—all this plotting and contriving—" He mused in his beard. "What the land needs is that we should cherish and work it. . . ." (363)

In Anne Brent (seconded here, by her father), Austin has invented a character who excels at romanticizing a certain kind of real estate business—but the laboring farmers are tired of "being country." At the end it falls to Kenneth, who remains somewhat clueless throughout the story, to idealize that lifestyle.

Eventually Anne figures out that what Elwood is after is the valley's water. She wants to be in on the plan in order to preempt Elwood and whoever is behind him. To this end, she pushes Kenneth to file for the surplus water of the river instead of just taking out options on previously established water rights, such as Elwood had been doing. Rickart, unaware of what Kenneth and Anne are up to, assumes that they are ignorant of the larger machinations—for instance, the fact that Elwood is both a representative of the Bureau of Irrigation and an agent for Rickart. Revelation follows upon revelation as a newspaper prints the story that Rickart was planning to export water from Tierra Longa to San Francisco using the cover of the Bureau to assemble land and water rights. Ironically, and implicitly by virtue of their surplus water right, Anne and Kenneth are now "in" on the plan that would take away the valley's water.

Placed alongside these two wheeler-dealers—Rickart and Anne—Kenneth cannot decide whether he is coming or going. He wants to be used by Rickart but cannot see how he will emerge to be a capitalist player himself. "His six years of working with Rickart had taught Kenneth that Business was an immense, incontrovertible Scheme of Things" (182). Kenneth, like Frank Norris's Presley, is caught between this bourgeois way of seeing and a feeling that the West is destined for some other immutable purpose.

> All the way down the valley the land had reasserted her claim to him. Under the thin bleakness of November he felt its potential fecundity, he felt its invitation and the advertisement of man's inadequacy. It came and offered itself to the hand, and yet no man had tamed it. . . . Here and there scattered homesteads tugged at the dry breast of the valley . . . and over it all the defeating, jealous overlordship of the Old Man. (225)

"[W]hat could men do," he wonders, "in a world in which lands, waters, the worth of women, had no measure but man's personal reaction. It was a moment of deep but revealing humility" (373). Certainly, these passages invite comparison with a similar theme in *The Winning of Barbara Worth*, where the "might of capital" is also humbled by the land. The difference here, of course, is that the one who has failed miserably at capitalism is the one who is humbled. There really is not much left for Kenneth to do but increasingly feel that his destiny is tied to the land. Kenneth no longer wants to be "in" but wants instead to be nurtured by the ultimate reality, the "unseen, the immeasurable" (373). From his conversion experience, he emerges a man with a plan. "'I'm done with business. From now on, I'm a producer. I shall produce'" (406). Nature, it seems, is about to save him from his capitalist aspirations, but only after Anne's own brand of capitalist aspirations saves Tierra Longa.

Anne and Kenneth eventually use the surplus water right that she had urged him to file in order to foil Rickart, who insists that the water right is his since Kenneth filed for it while under his employ. Although competition with the "Hetch Hetchy people" had motivated Rickart in the first place, Kenneth and Anne stall Rickart long enough on the surplus water right issue that the Hetch Hetchy project wins out. After many attempts to persuade them, Kenneth finally induces the residents of Tierra Longa to join him in forming an irrigation development company. The final scene has Kenneth and his love interest, Ellis Trudeau (Anne Brent's skillful though compliant office helper), meeting in a field on the Palomitas property:

> Her dress was white, and she walked as one seeing the end of the way and not the path before her.
>
> She saw him and stood still, waiting; the hem of her dress lay in the grasses, and the grasses stirred about her feet as though she had just risen,

> so blossom white and softly brown, out of the earth to be the final answer to all his decisions. (439)

It hardly needs stating that Ellis is a personification of nature, an entity that Austin had been constructing as highly feminized and eroticized. As we saw in *The Winning of Barbara Worth*, the heightened sensations to be discovered in nature open a rhetorical path to heterosexual union, and ultimately the triumph of commodity capitalism. Here, things happen just a bit differently though. In a near-perfect rural realist denouement, Kenneth's turning to nature is rewarded by capital returning to him: Kenneth learns from Rickart that the Palomitas (which Anne had resecured for the Brent family) has a rich reserve of untapped oil. Kenneth gets to be a farmer, gets to be the organizer of an irrigation company, the utility of which local farmers finally concede, and gets to be a petro-capitalist, too.

Let us turn now to *The Water-Bearer*. In this novel, a young, eastern-educated civil engineer, Caleb Warner, devises a plan to bring water to the city of Golden (San Francisco) while it waits for the completion of the Hetch Hetchy project. Caleb, whose "make-up was typically American, Yankee-American, un-marred by in-breeding" has come west to California to find his fortune. Above everything else, he wants to "be able to inaugurate some [water development] scheme, plan it, develop it, . . . dams, irrigation, power, lighting, civic supply" (18). Except for this broader vision, which he holds from the outset, he is Willard Holmes's cultural brother.

Soon after his arrival, Caleb takes off for Hermaños Valley in the Gabilan Mountains, south of Golden, on a fishing excursion. He hikes up to the head of the valley and above a waterfall finds "a wild region . . . breeder and catcher of rain, source of many waters" (4). In this place, he stumbles across the Rancho El Nido, the property of the Clintons, an "American" family of *Californios* whose lineage on the west coast dates to the 1840s. El Nido is a vestige of the old California—"The place was above all a home, long-settled, deep-rooted" (12)—but at the same time it stands for the future promise of rural California. It is studded with orchard trees—peach, apricot, almond, cherry, walnut—and contains a spring "in the exact center of the court" (12). Alfalfa and other crops grow along the banks of the river that runs through the valley. At El Nido, Caleb meets Betty Clinton, the very eligible farmer's daughter. Like Barbara Worth, Betty is a quasi-orphan. Her mother deceased, most of her life has been spent under the protection of Maria and Luis, the Mexican housekeeper and ranch hand, respectively. Also like Barbara Worth, Betty is enthusiastic about water. If she were a man, she tells Caleb, she, too, would want to bring water to the "thirsty earth or to thirsty people. To make a city grow where none has been, or render dry lands fertile" (18).

In Golden, Caleb shares an apartment with an old college friend, Ted Baxter. This pair forms another branch of the novel's economy in that they represent two distinct circuits of capital. Caleb finds that Baxter has "embarked upon the pastime of spending all the money he could get hold of in the pursuit of amusement" (30). Given past literary constructions, we should not be too surprised to find that his profession is real estate, making agricultural land deals, feeding off the market. "At present," and for no other reason than the whim of profit motive, Baxter prefers "the vineyard to the lemon grove" (45). Caleb is Old Man Rickart, Joseph Greenfield, and Patrick Boyd rolled into one. But being less of an investor than these characters and with a gadabout development philosophy, he is cast by the narrator into a deeper shadow: he has a "tendency to dissipation" (29).

Nonetheless (or perhaps quite fittingly), it is through Baxter that Caleb meets Golden's real power elite: Wilbur Cox, big landholder, mining industrialist, president of Crystal Springs water company; Cox's son, Jack, the trolley magnate in the Imperial Valley; Morse, the head of the Lumber Ring; Towle, president of the Sundown Railroad; Marlin, developer of agricultural colony lands; Lawler, oil magnate; and Winton, manager of Golden Light and Power.

Through discussions with Wilbur and Jack Cox, Caleb learns about Golden's water development history and its current struggle to compete with Los Angeles, which has recently completed its Owens Valley project. "'I need not tell you,'" Wilbur says to Caleb, "'that water is the life-blood of a city'" (67).

> "It runs in its mains, in its flushing system, as it does through the arteries and veins of a body. Over build, without water, and you have atrophy, as you cannot expect the blood that is sufficient for a child to sustain the body of a full-grown man. We know to-day exactly how many gallons per capita we must figure on for a modern city with domestic, civic and manufacturing supply. The number of gallons in our reservoirs, divided by that ratio, marks the present limits of Golden's population, of its progress. And that limit is almost reached.
>
> "If we hope to keep ahead as the metropolis of the Pacific Coast we have got to get more water. The Government Sierra project will supply that water in time—and amply—but, before we get it, our competitors may outstrip us. . . . We are in the business of conserving, buying and selling water—at a profit, as I said at dinner last night. . . . My interests, the interests of those who were at dinner. . . , not to speak of others, are centered in Golden. Our investments are large, we believe in its destiny, we have linked ours with it." (67–68)

Caleb recalls all that he had seen of the region around El Nido and the Caliente Plain that spreads out toward the bay from the base of the Gabilans. With what he has learned from Wilbur Cox, Caleb begins formulating a plan based on Hermaños Valley.

Wasting no time, Caleb conducts an extensive survey of the Caliente Plain, into which flow several of the rivers that drain the Gabilans. He concludes that the upper end of the Plain contains an underlying basin of water, and that this water is both capped and supported underneath with layers of clay, making for perfect artesian conditions. These conditions extend into the lower end of the Plain, except there the basin is capped by gravel, which purifies any surface water that percolates through. Thus, he finds an "inexhaustible, ever renewed commodity, that was as commercial as any mineral, that, conveyed to Golden, meant the assured progress of that city" (120). His plan is to impound water above the sink and regulate water flow through the gravels, down to the aquifer, and pump it to Golden. Like a one-man chamber of commerce, Caleb quivers with delight at the thought of all that water, "for incoming families, for factories, for fields and gardens, for civic use!" (129). The trick is to keep his discovery a secret from the landowners in the Caliente Plain, whose properties will have to be purchased at a low price.

All the while that Caleb is putting this plan together in his mind, something is tugging at him, thoughts of Betty Clinton and thoughts in general about love and professional success. "He was consumed with eagerness in the progress of his profession. There had been no room for anything else" (119). But, oddly, the closer he gets to his discovery of the aquifer, the promise of nature, the more his emotions will not let his male, rational self be. He is ignorant of women and love. "Until now he had scarcely speculated about it and it was strange that he should first do so seriously in the big swing of the biggest task he had ever conceived or undertaken" (134). It may be strange to Caleb, but to any reader of Harold Bell Wright, it is clear that economic passions and romantic passions are to converge and define each other. At first, this bodes poorly, because Caleb realizes that El Nido will be obliterated by his plan to flood Hermaños. Economic geography and the geography of love appear to be on a collision course. Caleb presents his project proposal to Wilbur Cox, who is duly impressed. Caleb and Cox meet with the directors of the Crystal Springs Company, whose interlocking directorate includes a familiar group of men: Lawler (oil), Winton (electric power), Marlin (colony developer), and Morse (lumber). The company accepts the project. Caleb is to receive $100,000, a post as consulting engineer, a patent on his pipe design, and credit as the project's creator.

While Caleb is on the road to professional progress, Baxter spirals downward. He squanders a large sum of money in a bad land deal and is cut off from family funds. Moreover, he has gotten one of his girlfriends, Mary Morgan, pregnant and has no money left with which to carry out his plan to pay her off and send her out of the city. Worse news is that Baxter, aware of Caleb's plans, has taken out a one-year option to buy Hermaños Valley in order to start up an agricultural colony. At this point, he inflicts the ultimate injury by convincing the Clintons that they are being used by Caleb for his personal gain.

To regain his financial position, Baxter attempts to blackmail the Crystal Springs Company. He will go public with the water plan unless the company buys the land from him after he has exercised his option on the Clinton property. Wilbur Cox is prepared, however, and exposes the option as a forgery. He threatens to expose Baxter's crime and his injustice to Mary Morgan.

Still, Caleb appears to be in a hard spot since his plans for Hermaños remain the same. This does not remain the case for long. A series of plot twists rapidly unfold. Hermaños, after all, has no suitable dam site. Caleb finds another site, one that had to be incorporated into the first plan anyway and that in certain ways is even better than Hermaños. This site is the only one that the company had not been able to secure an option on, for the simple reason that Caleb had long ago obtained it himself, thinking that he might need to negotiate for the position he presently holds. The paternalistic Cox is approving, for Caleb has shown himself to be both an engineer and a businessman. "You could have held us up for a stiff profit and that too would have been business. But your New England conscience walks hand-in-hand with your New England forehandedness" (268).

Although Caleb has still not had much contact with Betty, he realizes the "essence of it all was that Betty Clinton was indissolubly mingled with his ambitions, his victories, his pleasure, sorrow and defeat and that she could so leaven them as to make life well worth living" (277). She will want to be part of his work, too, and he thinks that she will have "ample capacity for entering into the technical side of it" (277). "The personal had entered into the mechanical" (278). He "fancied Betty and himself . . . preparing the way for the fertility and population that should follow their discovery and development of water. And Betty did not appear entirely as co-worker. He had seen something of the softer side of her that came as a revelation that warmed and thrilled him to the core" (291).

The day of the opening ceremony for the water works arrives. All is going well until Caleb is told of trouble with one of the underground conduits. He enters the conduit and suddenly hears the sound of rushing water. Someone has opened the gate from the filter gallery and Caleb is trapped. He manages to get a fingerhold on a narrow crack and hold on until the water subsides. The culprit? Baxter. Caleb climbs out, only to find Betty unconscious, her "blouse in shreds . . . skin showed where a rude hand had torn her undergarment" (300–301). She had managed, in her struggle with Baxter, to close the gate. Luis gives chase to the escaping Baxter, but before he catches up to him, Baxter collapses of a heart attack, another casualty, along with S. Behrman, Elijah Berl, and other California characters who have meddled with modernization.

Caleb, the New Englander, and Betty, the Anglo-Californian, meet up at El Nido. In formulaic fashion—though a bit more hormonal than we have yet seen—love and work, region and romance, come together in the end.

> Now he stood opposite to her, close and looking down at her upturned face. The curves of her mouth maddened him. He clenched his hands until his nails stung his flesh, hanging on to himself, restraining a desire to woo her only with kisses. His reason fought with his passion. He knew Betty Clinton was not to be won that way alone . . . He could see her sway a little and he suddenly caught her in his arms. . . . She had not resisted him. . . . "We shall go on together," she said softly—after quite a while—"always on and on, Caleb. Bringing water to thirsty places and to thirsty people? Blending work with love to make all perfect? Anything else would only mean stagnation in the end." (310–311)

Again, then, we have a novel that drops into our laps the familiar set of associations: regions, romance, and labor, with Anglo-Saxon racial purity an implied aim. (The Mexican housekeeper and ranch hand have not simply raised Betty but prepared the way for the solidification of racial turnover.) A main difference between this story and, say, *The Winning of Barbara Worth*, however, is that Betty is to join Caleb in his engineering work—a triumph for Veblen-ist engineer heroism.

We cannot, however, get away from the water-for-profit equation, which is taken just a tad further by Dunn than it is by Wright. Water for Caleb—for Golden and Crystal Springs—is the "ever renewed commodity . . . as commercial as any mineral." *The Water-Bearer* does not try to hide Caleb's thrill with commodity capital being behind water's "civic uses." The irrigation of "fields and gardens" is just one example of many potential uses; it is not singled out for special favor. Caleb's sound engineering sense opens up to him all manner of capitalist opportunities.

Let us back up for a moment, though, and examine the dynamics of the "ever renewed commodity." To do so, we need to take note of a tour of the Crystal Springs Company watershed that Caleb takes early in the narrative.

> "We have to keep the watershed private," explained Hinckley [Head Engineer of the Crystal Springs Company]. "Possible pollution is our bugaboo. So I'm going to show you, within twenty miles of Golden, a bit of California as it used to be. Not exactly primeval but relapsed into its ancient conditions . . ."

> They rolled swiftly on through a strange region and a beautiful one. The engine purred softly, the roads, well-drained, were the last word in road-building. . . . [T]here were trees, densely clustered, shutting out the sun, growing tall and healthy, oaks and sycamores, redwood, madroño, buckeye, pine and fir. Beneath them flourished great ferns. Through them Caleb caught glimpses of lakes lying far below, bits of blue far deeper than the sky they mirrored and intensified. . . .
>
> Then, as they rounded a curve something leaped from a bank, landed in the middle of the road, turned and snarled. It was a full-grown lynx . . . A quarter of a mile further on the driver braked the car . . . A doe was stepping daintily through the undergrowth to the stream. Another followed her and then another. Lastly there came a noble young buck . . . unhurried, unafraid.
>
> "Nobody ever hurts them," said Hinckley. "They all fight it out among themselves and they seem to keep the balance preserved." (76–78)

Before long they arrive at the reservoir.

> It was a beautiful sheet of water above the dam, set in the silence of a wooded cañon . . . The long lake had once been a peaceful valley, . . . a stage-road winding through it on the way to the sea, farms, farmhouses and a hamlet with a famous road-house at the Crystal Springs for which the valley was named. All these had been razed to prepare the bottom of the great reservoir, fences taken up, trees eliminated, the place devastated as the big dam rose in the great notch that formed the main outlet to the valley. (79–81)

"Does this beautiful land ruin this beautiful valley?" the San Francisco *Examiner* had asked. Well, yes and no. There are a number of salient points worth making about these passages from Dunn's book. For one, this is a narrative about what is worth sacrificing: a rural, agricultural economy. This passage is both an interruption of rural realism and an extension of the logic in which rural realism is embedded. That is, finally, agriculture is represented not as a precious link in the circulation of capital through nature but as an expendable link. Capital has taken the chance to go to nature directly. And the passage is at first suitably humbled by this. Mention is made of the well-engineered road, but the car proceeds slowly enough to allow for the observance of several species of trees, a lynx, and two deer. It's hard to say how genuine this humility is, though. The image that all is right with nature doubles as the image of the free market: Everybody fights it out among themselves, and balance is preserved in the end. The ever-renewed commodity is itself protected by ever-renewed commodification.

Read across one grain, then, capital steals nature back from agriculture and keeps it for itself. In this transaction, capital is refigured as an extension of the natural process that it has actually preserved. This leads us directly to a different grain across which we might also read the passage: that nature is also a place. And a restricted one at that. The "naturalness" of competition is of a piece with the fact that competition produces uneven development, radical discontinuity across space and time. The watershed itself is sharply bounded. A farm valley is "devastated," and El Nido is fortunately passed over, but only by luck—and largely for the purposes of romance, which will see that El Nido's daughter will go forth to (re)produce change somewhere else. In sum, nature cannot claim a territory larger than that which capitalist development allots it. Nor can El Nido.

But place and process are incongruous in Dunn's narrative. Places made through "natural" processes of capitalist competitive development contradict "nature" as an overarching place that illustrates what's so "natural" about capital. Within the terms of the novel, nature as place can only have a truncated existence: capital is destined to geographically inflict fragmentation on nature. And it is only in these fragmented spaces, or "heterotopias," Foucault would call them, that nature both compensates for capital *and* teaches capital about itself (Foucault 1986; see also Gregory 1994). Just the same, despite the unique devaluation of agriculture in *The Water-Bearer*, I would argue that we have seen this contradiction before. This is, once again, capital (the bourgeois) wanting the world both ways: Capital is poised both to wreak stunning transformations and to restore nature to its revered status. Like many of the novels I have treated, Dunn's finesses the contradiction: If land development has the power to unlock the secrets of nature, nature's secret is only that it wants to be developed. For, "anything else would only mean stagnation."

## Wither Rural Realism?

The Los Angeles and Hetch Hetchy Aqueducts were built during a period when claims to nearby waters that might have been used to supplement urban supplies were mostly taken by farm communities or resource industries of different kinds (lumber, mining, etc.). It seems almost inevitable, given the power of urban growth coalitions in San Francisco and Los Angeles, that these cities would leapfrog to mountain sources. Of course, it was not inevitable, just calculating. These cities were building a kind of *Brazil*. They were in the business of expansion and land development and, hence, were anxious to intensify their matériel in advance of growth.

In rural realist discourse, capitalist growth occupies hallowed ground. Neither Austin's nor Dunn's novel appears to want to detract from this set of values. They are each critical of forms of wanton behavior—of economic motives that have only selfish, rather than selfish *and* "civic," foundation—and in each, growth always surfaces as something for characters to rally around. It is in these novels that we can see rural realism also retreating. In *The Ford*, land developers do battle with each other but have opposing goals. Anne Brent wants to bring water, land, and the right kind of people together. Rickart wants to take that water and import it to the city. In neither case are urban and rural economies argued to be indivisible or *mutually* fated. (Urban growth certainly has implications for farming districts, but the economy of the farming district has no particular impact on urban fates.) Anne and Kenneth may have won at Tierra Longa, but there is little, if any, suggestion that the renewed rural economy there will tie back to the city in any important way. Moreover, Anne's base of operations is in Tierra Longa, not in the city where Rickart's is. In *The Water-Bearer*, it is suggested that there is something appropriate about El Nido having been spared. But just what that appropriate thing is is never adequately spelled out, except that it would be impossible to imagine Betty Clinton desiring Caleb if he had maneuvered her property out from underneath her. What saves El Nido, after all, is not the argument that its economy must prosper but the fact that there is no appropriate dam site nearby.

In like manner, rural realist romances are courted but kept at a distance. Austin brings together a young farm-minded couple, but these two are the dullest of the bunch. Any dynamism that Ellis Trudeau might have had is given instead to Anne, the political radical Virginia, and the tragic Mrs. Brent for that matter. Kenneth Brent, a failure at capitalist business practices for much of the novel, finally pulls together a water company in Tierra Longa, but as Austin has made clear, his clients (the local ranchers) are mostly stubborn losers. To work a farm is practically a consolation prize for those lacking in business vision. Romance in *The Water-Bearer* keeps a polite distance from the farm as well. An engineer and future engineer will together embark on a career of bringing water to thirsty people and thirsty places. As with the Imperial Valley novels, the engineering profession is placed in that "sweet spot" between investing and laboring. Caleb dabbles enough in investing to set the water project on its feet, and he would remain close to the ranch by virtue of his coupling with Betty Clinton—except that she decides to exchange her ranching life for an engineering one. This is fully consistent with the free-floating, non-special status the narrative assigns to agricultural economy.

All other characterizations aside, it is Kenneth Brent who ultimately thinks the one thought that establishes the theme of these novels exactly: "They were all hopelessly and scarifyingly wrong . . . the settlers of Tierra Longa. They had known that Rickart had ruined them, but they had recouped their self-esteem in the pride of having struggled with him. . . . What Kenneth had faced in the revealing years [of working for Rickart] was the certainty that what Rickart had done, he had done without thinking of them at all; he had done it by his gift of being able not to think of them" (175).

# 8

# Conclusion

California has been a site of extraordinary energies since the late 1840s. Through the shocks of the Gold Rush, the bonanzas of wheat and citrus, the regions of re-plumbing, and the armies of labor—capital has circulated in many shapes and sizes. But alongside these material routes, the wheels of commerce have trod distinctive, discursive paths. The purpose of this book has been to trace these, using as guides the insights of political economy, historical and geographic case study, and the social and economic "theories" deployed in past narratives. Over the course of a decades-long debate, California's bankers, engineers, and ranchers, its boosters, journalists, and novelists obsessed over how to plant capital in the ground and keep it moving at the same time. That is, lurking behind what may in fact be a rather familiar historical premise here—that agriculture was a key feature of the post-gold economy—is the geographical ur-premise that the "ground" in fact poses as both attraction and repulsion for capital. Each time capital reaches for the ether, for instantaneous turnovers, it eventually learns the lesson anew that it must also remain earthbound and quotidian.

Take the state's bank commissioners, whose very jobs were the product of capitalist crisis in the 1870s. "The most noticeable feature, which we mention with much pleasure," begins their report of 1881–82, ". . . is a decrease of nine millions and a half ($9,521,742) in 'loans on stocks and bonds'—principally mining stocks—and a more than corresponding increase of nearly eleven millions ($10,711,191) in 'loans on other securities'—mostly grain" (California Board 1881–82: 11). Having witnessed the reckless wane of the Comstock and the collapse of the once-unassailable Bank of California, the commissioners were delighted to see finance capital descend from the speculative heights of the mother lode. Their collective sigh of relief was certainly underwritten, too, by something a little less specific yet so pervasive as to appear self-evident: the cultural logic that agriculture has redemptive powers for capital. The peculiar significance of this should not be underestimated. When in California writers and bankers turned their expectant gazes toward the California farm, they did so not because farming was an exotic residual in an otherwise industrialized society but because all that loam and all those irrigation ditches were hothouses for greenbacks.

But precisely therein lies a conundrum.

For many of us in largely urbanized societies, the rural has stood for the remote and the historically fixed. That is to say that it is redolent of what Raymond Williams has called a structure of feeling. We admit that the countryside has changed and responded to all sorts of pressures, and that it even creates certain pressures of its own. For example, that switching of capital into grain, so vaunted by the bank commissioners, resulted in a spasm of overproduction in the next decade—the "grounding" of capital is salvation and condemnation both. We readily admit, too, that the city and the countryside have been falsely polarized. And yet, as Raymond Williams has eloquently reminded us, the rural almost always represents a place and process apart from the exigencies of modern life, even as it undergoes such thorough permutations as to defy any definitive meaning of "rural." It remains one of Williams's most powerful and resonant insights that this fixation on "apartness" often escapes notice as itself an aspect of modernity.

Like the ever-receding ideal of the English countryside described in Williams's *The Country and The City*, rural California was the locus of the most calculated and astute deployments of fiscal reasoning and power. These deployments, in tandem with the labor that gave them material life, were responsible for regional changes of lasting magnitude. While the essays here have investigated those transformations, they have also put emphasis on the expenditure of rhetorical energies directly and indirectly involved in promoting and legitimating them. So, whereas for Williams literary rhetoric about the countryside's gradual and sometimes sudden "disappearance" was drenched in nostalgia, in California representations of agriculture were more frequently joined to celebratory discourses of capitalist expansion.

The circulation of capital through agriculture, I stressed in earlier chapters, was a complex affair shaped in part by agriculture's basis in nature and capital's swim-or-sink expansionist tendencies. That agriculture's basis in nature posed different opportunities and constraints for different sorts of capitals, whose requirements for turnover were highly variable, meant that these complexities shook out differently in different locales. What actually happened to rural places could be wildly dissimilar, including revolutions in agricultural production, decimations of agricultural economies, and a range of ambivalences over the class status of agriculturists. But to understand the multiple directions that capital takes in order to gain proceeds from a nature-based economy—an understanding that our novels aim for as much as I have in chapters 2 and 3—is to begin to understand why it is that novels that would celebrate capital would so often (not always, but often) exchange farmer protagonists for protagonists from other classes. It is also to begin to understand why the acquisition of rural property, particularly land and water during a period when capital-intensive irrigated agriculture was fast on the rise, was so frequently foregrounded. To represent the circulation of capital through agriculture necessarily changes representations of agriculture.

The continuing obsession with property turnover and development, and the eagerness to divine positive meaning out of the commodification of nature, situates these works in the field of bourgeois culture. At the same time, this culture is not all sunshine and light. Capital, in these narratives, is cast into dark moments. As capital circulates over time and space, it faces challenges that are not just economic but cultural. The novels *tell* us that much, and they are, I think, direct, material manifestations of such. If, in virtually all the narratives explored here, the meaning attached to the California landscape never comes into focus, unless it is through the lenses of property in particular and accumulation of capital in general, it was also with a certain hesitancy that these aspects of California were celebrated. For the decades between the 1880s and 1920s were battered by storms of boom and bust and speculative switches of capital from one economy to another: the circulation of capital destroys and creates. It was incumbent upon rural realist fictions, which would champion capital's transformative impulses, to also try to arrange the shards of change into some "innocuous" pattern.

The writings examined here recognize quite well, for example, that in the tireless circulation of money, the propensity for capital to create landscapes in *its* image lay exposed. How much less frightening this might be if that image was clothed in heterosexual, Anglo-Saxon virilities and local emanations of capital. And how much more believable the writings could be if they defrocked non–Anglo-Saxon, non–money-savvy others. None of these novels can claim to have invented those images, but many do draw upon them. Working with such a tool kit, a continually repeated structure of feeling emerges: a simultaneous enshrinement of the past and celebration of its good riddance.

These novels were committed to making self-serving economic sense of California's social and cultural dislocations, such that we might say the bourgeois culture of making economic sense of things is itself one of the contours of bourgeois economy. The place of the bourgeois novel—of rural realist discourse—in California, as I see it, is that it never simply re-presented the economic landscape. Instead, it was part of that landscape. It was an "argument" that arose from within the very political economy through which these landscapes were produced.

This work has been concerned with the ways in which the valences of California agriculture, regional social relations, and bourgeois discourse were tethered together in the late nineteenth and early twentieth centuries through processes of capitalist uneven development. For reasons whose investigation is beyond the scope of this study, bourgeois discourse with respect to California agriculture never had access to literary writing and publishing circles like it did in that period. (There is a book waiting to be written that tells the story of what kinds of California narratives east coast publishers have looked for over the years.) Certainly, it is my sense that when it came to representations and arguments about California agriculture, the dominant novelistic "tradition" changed in the 1930s. After Steinbeck's intervention with *The Grapes of Wrath*, which came hard on the heels of unprecedented labor militance in California's fields, it is hard to imagine anything like the work of Harold Bell Wright taking hold again. John Ford's film adaptation of *Grapes*, released at the end of the world war, perhaps clinched the break. So, even though California's agricultural output, its labor army, and its water infrastructure continued to expand throughout the 1930s, '40s, and beyond, it never had a bourgeois literary apparatus like it did through the '20s. The rural realist years, therefore, stand somewhat in isolation. California capital grew older—

its mechanisms became more sophisticated, its technologies more advanced—but California novels grew wiser.

At least in some respects. Importantly, the major critical move in the agricultural novels by Steinbeck and by non-Anglo writers who were able to get their work published, especially after the war, was putting the spotlight on migrant labor. Yet, without belittling those narratives in any way, one wonders—Where are the big novels of dam building? The novels of the Bureau of Reclamation and the Army Corps of Engineers? Where is the novel of the Bank of Italy's transformation into the Bank of America? Where is the novel of agribusiness investment? Of the building of transnational commodity chains? One wants these not for more wallowing in the spectacle of capital but for holistic narratives that map out capital's troubled circulation.

For all their bourgeois sympathies, racism, and rural realist angst, the literary works studied here had a rather frightening honesty to them when it came to naming and detailing the workings of large forces and powers. Later, when resistance finally surfaced in a serious way, did something else go underground?

# Notes

## Introduction

1. I should say, when agriculture came to hold pride of place for the second time, the first being before the 1848 gold strike when California was linked to the capitalist world economy via the hide and tallow trade. See Richard Henry Dana's *Two Years Before the Mast.*

2. For an extended inquiry into the nature of uneven development, see Neil Smith's book of that name (1984); also Storper and Walker's *The Capitalist Imperative* (1989).

3. There is a large and still growing literature questioning the capitalist character of American agriculture. See, for example, Friedland (1984); Friedmann (1978); Hahn and Prude (1985); FitzSimmons (1986); Mann (1990); Goodman et al. (1987); Page and Walker (1991); and Gordon Wood's comments (1994).

4. The pioneering work of geographer David Harvey (1982; 1989a; 1989b) remains the benchmark.

5. There continues in studies of late-nineteenth- and early-twentieth-century literary realism a tendency to give privilege to the urban over the rural, as if the city was the place where capitalism was most clearly expressed (see, for example, Kaplan 1988). The problem with this view is that it tends to limit discussion of capital formations in the "periphery," which far from being functionally peripheral have been historically essential to the rise of a capitalist mode of production. Even when it does not adopt classic capitalist social relations, the "periphery" is always instructive of what capital can do and has done. We need a theory of realism, in other words, that can take account of the very different geographies found in Frank Norris's *McTeage* versus his novel *The Octopus.*

6. I have set aside theorizing the exact boundaries of these genres. To do so would be to reach into debates that are too tangential to this book's core concerns. I am reminded, too, of David Perkins's cautionary words: "[I]t seems that very different works may belong to the same genre and that a work may belong to different genres. If this is so, the actual role of genre concepts in the production and reception of works must often be less than genre theorists suppose" (1992: 80; though see Glazener 1997). Nonetheless, the codes of realism, regionalism, and romance are here taken to be vehicles for exam-

ining, in the first case, the representation of social and economic structures as processes that absorb their representers; in the second case, the desirability of the local against the supralocal; and in the third case, heterosexual desire as a prime mover. Encoded in narrative and character, these can contradict or enhance each other.

7. It is worth noting how much the impact of Walter Benn Michaels's arguments depends upon overturning in the reader's mind the radicalness of realism and naturalism. For Michaels, the naturalist or realist (having no particular stake in drawing a line in the quicksands of genre, he does not worry about which is which) mode reenacts the given problematics of American industrial capitalism. Likewise, the sentimental American literature of earlier decades did not relinquish the self to feeling so much as discipline the self (see Brodhead 1988). Michaels's and Brodhead's strategy relies on a sort of substitution: It makes a claim for a reduced dissonance between society and text than had previously been thought, and thereby implants a dissonance in the mind of the readers, who must deal with the new critical frame of reference. Yet there are, of course, texts on which critics need not have worked so hard for the particular gains they achieve—and what I am asking is what, then, is to be done with texts that are overtly ideological in ways that in other texts must be "unmasked"? Would such texts now have less appeal to the literary theorist and new literary historian? The critical unveiling to be performed in the California novels treated here is less the unveiling of a capital-friendly ideology than an unveiling of ideologies and literary codes that support *it.* It is not that there are no ideologies to be defamiliarized, but that the opening questions are different.

8. Some readers may wish to see in the discussion of rural realism in later chapters a mere repeat of antebellum tensions between Whigs and Democrats over agriculture and capitalist markets and institutions (see the brilliant discussion in Kulikoff 1992). It is undeniable that rural realist discourse engages some of the same sorts of issues, but I would argue that capital had changed too much, had become too sophisticated by the close of the nineteenth century, for the discourse of rural realism to have meant the same thing.

## Chapter 1

1. World War One spurred yet greater diversification. Shipbuilding was given a temporary boost, petroleum extraction and refining gained a firm footing, the auto and aircraft industries surged, and electronics began to stir. The dynamism of California's economic history has long been seen as deserving of special mention by economic historians. In comparison with the structure of the national economy, late-nineteenth- and early-twentieth-century California stands out in several respects. It had a higher rate of population growth and was more highly urbanized. Indigenous cheap power sources (oil and hydroelectricity) readily fueled industrial growth. These factors in combination made for a high rate of local consumption of manufactures. Still, in an overwhelmingly industrialized era, California manufactures specialized in food, forest, and petroleum products. Economic diversity, including a solid base of finance capital, and a growing population, made California's experience of national economic ups and downs peculiar. In general, while recessions came to California a little later than they tended to elsewhere, California also recovered from them more quickly. And if California went through national cycles of economic growth and decline just the same, they "have been superimposed upon an economy [i.e., California's] undergoing very substantial secular growth" (Kidner 1946: 114; see also McLaughlin: 1938).

2. The development of the American West at large as capitalist development has in the past decade begun to receive more attention (even if the idea has long been around especially in local and industry studies [for a recent example, see West 1993]). See, for example, William Robbins (1994) and Richard White (1991). Perhaps more than any other historian in the last decade, it has been William Cronon (1991) who

has garnered the most attention for arguing that the West's capitalist development was inseparable from the command and control functions of key localities, in his case Chicago.

3. A number of factors combined doomed California's cattle economy, which once thrived on the hide and tallow trade with New England and later on trade with the Far West's mining regions. Newly in control (California gained statehood in 1850), the Americans demanded that land ownership be verified. Thousands of ranchers, the so named *Californios,* in possession of often extensive Spanish and Mexican land grants, were smothered in an avalanche of costly legal battles. Ranchers who had gotten rich during the years when beef sold at a premium in the gold camps suddenly found themselves high and dry when gold production declined. From still another quarter, ranchers were assaulted by competing stockmen, who brought better breeds of cattle from New Mexico, Texas, and even Missouri. Severe floods in 1861–62, followed by draught during the next several years, practically swept grazing lands clean. Then, as the first round of wheat farmers gained a foothold, cattle ranchers were forced to compete with them for land. With the no-fence law, in 1872, which made stockmen liable for crops damaged by wandering cattle, the legislature acknowledged the accomplished fact: The supremacy of cattle ranching had come and gone (Cleland 1951; also Pisani 1984, on the various constraints that made stock raising a viable option).

4. A good overview of the ethnic division of labor in California truck gardening from the Gold Rush to the turn of the century may be found in Sucheng Chan (1986).

5. Extensive crops, defined by the U.S. Census and U.S.D.A. Statistical Bulletins, were hay, forage, and cereals—corn, wheat, oats, barley, rye, buckwheat. Intensive crops were vegetables, fruits, nuts, cotton, hops (see Taylor and Vasey 1936: 286).

6. Citrus crops and sugar crops were the fastest expanding crop sectors in the United States during the first decade of the twentieth century (Barger and Landsberg 1942).

7. Carey McWilliams's devastating account of California farm labor, *Factories in the Field* (1939), provides a useful summary of the development and importance of the sugar beet industry. (See Chan [1986], for a skeptical critique.) Far and away the most bullish mover and shaker in the industry was Claus Spreckels, a millionaire and then some, who moved his cane sugar operations out of Hawaii on the eve of annexation. Once in California, he switched to sugar beets and soon came under the hermetic protection of the Dingley Tariff Act in 1897. A few years later, he bought out his major competitor, the American Sugar Refining Company, and established the Sugar Trust, an oligopolistic consortium of companies with Spreckels at the fore. He promptly built the world's largest sugar beet factory in Salinas, an eponymous company town to staff it, and his own railroad line to combat the Southern Pacific monopoly. Initially, he avoided the costs of directly engaging the company in the production of sugar beets by contracting with small farmers in the area. Before long, these growers were out of business, many becoming tenants to Spreckels, who basically controlled sugar beet prices. By 1911, land concentration under direct ownership or control by the domineering Spreckels interest—the company having been turned over to Claus's son John—characterized the industry.

Sugar beets were an especially labor-intensive crop, labor that was retained under factory-like, wage-labor conditions. Claus's other son, the disgruntled Claus A., who had returned to Hawaii to make his fortune in sugar cane, testified to this fact and to the particular social relations that had evolved under the tariff. "The fact that foreign labor is employed almost exclusively both in the fields and factories is carefully concealed by the sugar-beet people and the excessive profits made possible by our high sugar tariff are obtained by promoters in the refineries and not by farmers in cultivating sugar beets" (quoted in McWilliams 1939: 86). The Sugar Trust had locked into battle the remaining smaller growers of sugar beets and the large industrial concern of the Trust. It was in the refinery portion of this vertically integrated and monopolistic business that the importance of controlling prices fell, because it was this end of the production process that had to remain competitive with the few other producers of the finished product. With competitive prices at this end, other costs, labor in particular, were suppressed. A combination of white and non-white labor was the solution settled upon. Of the 10% of the labor which worked the refinery, most were white. The remaining 90% worked the fields. In northern California, these workers were almost entirely Japanese, and in Southern California, 20% were Japanese and 80% were Mexican. These field workers were paid less than the white field workers who had been employed earlier. So marked was the labor intensiveness of sugar beets that "for every man who formerly got work in the wheat fields, 41½ men were needed in the cultivation, harvesting, and processing of sugar beets" (88). By 1917, McWilliams writes, California sugar beets brought the greatest per acre profits and paid the lowest production costs per acre in the country.

8. I do not want to imply that labor was *the* determining factor for the location of crop production, for the salient fact about seasonal labor was that it was migratory. But I do follow McWilliams (1939), Liebman (1983), and Daniel (1982) in asserting that such labor was essential to California agriculture developing at all. For a thorough overview of patterns of crop production that takes account of mutually entraining factors, other than labor (e.g., soil, climate, crop varieties), see Crawford and Hurd (1941).

9. According to the 1890 census of agriculture, "Nearly 75 per cent of the truck produced in the United States comes from a belt of country along the Atlantic coast lying east of a line drawn from Augusta, Me., to Macon, Ga.; from southern Georgia, Alabama, and Florida; along the lines of railroad in the Mississippi valley from the Gulf of Mexico to Chicago, St. Louis, and Kansas city, and from the celery districts of Michigan and Ohio" (U.S. Department of Commerce, Bureau of the Census, Agriculture 1890: 602).

10. Unless otherwise noted, I am particularly indebted to the work of Donald Pisani (1984) for my overview of irrigation development.

11. Among the more strident publicists of the future West as irrigated empire was William Smythe, editor (1891–95) of *The Irrigation Age* and a columnist on irrigation for the popular regional magazine *Out West*. In 1899, he assembled his ideas into the impassioned, lengthy polemic *The Conquest of Arid America*. In this book, Smythe welded his vision of an irrigated empire to his vision of social change. He asserted that irrigation, as a cooperative undertaking, would erode the isolation and individualism of America society and, with the backing of federal investments in arid land reclamation, give rise to a friendly capitalism that would be far more democratic, far more equitable in doling out land, water, and profits, than that in place at the time (in addition to Pisani 1984, see Pisani 1983; Smythe 1905; Taylor 1970).

12. The leading irrigation counties in 1878 were Los Angeles (37,000 acres), Merced (37,000 acres), San Bernardino (20,000), Tulare (18,000), San Joaquin (2,000 acres), Yolo (12,250) (Pisani 1984).

13. About the only recognition of the fact that agriculture absolutely depended on steady and artificially contrived water inputs was the first-ever comprehensive survey of water resources, begun in the late 1870s by California's state engineer, William Hammond Hall. This survey was authorized only after Californians finally recognized that droughts came at least as frequently as floods, that hydraulic mining was choking streams with sediments and causing floods, and that a knot of unresolved water-rights claims was threatening to log jam the courts.

14. In point of fact, Miller and Lux continued to fight in the courts against appropriative rights into the twentieth century (Miller 1985).

15. Again, developments in irrigation should not be seen in isolation. If capital was now allowed to be moved from municipal coffers, this movement can be viewed in terms of the systematic circulation of capital in and out of the primary, secondary, and tertiary circuits, elaborated by David Harvey in *The Urban Experience* (1989b) and elsewhere. In the case of the bond purchases by public entities, capital was freed up in the tertiary circuit for absorption in the crisis-ridden secondary circuit.

16. Note that *racial discourse shifts along the agribusiness commodity chain*. The *Pacific Rural Press* proudly emphasizes that the large wholesalers in the produce exchange are white Americans, whereas the small-scale vendors are not. In the following chapter, we will note the reverse in California's agricultural areas: The strenuous rhetorical (and on-the-ground) efforts to keep a place for struggling white Americans on the small-scale farm.

17. Mapping the flows of money capital is notoriously difficult, not just for want of data but for the very fact that money does not tend to stay put. Nonetheless, there are good methodological examples of how such mappings might be done. Urban geographer Michael Conzen (1977) reconstructed bank correspondent accounts—that is, deposits that banks were required to keep in other banks beginning in the nineteenth century. From this effort, Conzen was able to model the changing hierarchy of urban regions and hinterlands. More recently, William Cronon (1992) has mapped capital flows centered on nineteenth-century Chicago, using bankruptcy records. He thus could reconstruct a picture of *direct* investments (often made by parties other than banks) that bank correspondent data do not reveal. But as Conzen points out, "the banking system directly or indirectly handled the bulk of the nation's liquid capital needs" (90). In California, the Bank Commissioners published data on where the bulk of the banks' capital was tied up. Though these data are provided only for the county level, they can be used to reliably reconstruct for particular moments just where capital went. See main text. Other examples of studies of capital flows in California are Doti (1995) and Odell (1992).

18. Because San Francisco was very much the dominant partner in financing the San Joaquin Valley, and Sacramento capital was virtually absent south of the Tehachapis, I have not made much of Sacramento's role in financing California's rural economies.

## Chapter 2

1. See also Friedmann (1978a, 1978b, 1980).

2. Capital that circulates in the form of credit, however, often has repercussions for class relationships. For such a discussion, see Roemer (1982, especially chapter 3). Roemer argues that credit markets function on the basis of surplus values extraction no less than labor markets. Controversially for Marxist economics, he argues that the "fundamental feature of capitalist exploitation is not what happens in the labor process, but the differential ownership of productive assets." When pushed on the point, however, he admits that his is not an either-or proposition. Credit markets may well depend upon some form of "labor enforcement," for if the debtor "simply consumes the loan, the creditor loses" (Roemer 1982: 95, footnote 1).

3. California was not alone in this. Allan Bogue provides ample evidence of the disciplinary force of the credit system in his outstanding studies of the Midwest (Bogue 1955 and 1963).

4. Bogue argues that the takeoff period in the farm-credit "industry" dates to early in the nineteenth century when the federal government demanded that sales of public land be on a cash basis, thus forcing many farmers to turn to private sources of financing: "Until 1820 the purchaser of government land could spread his payments over four years. So abused were the credit provisions of the land code that Congress approved the Revision Act of 1820, allowing cash sales only and a minimum price of $1.25 per acre. The implications of this congressional decision were far reaching. Now the pioneer farmer must depend solely on private enterprise for aid in meeting the cost of land." Such "aid," while difficult to track, increasingly came in the form of credit (Bogue 1963: 170).

5. Paul Rhode argues that capital accumulation and cheaper credit, rather than the spread of irrigation or the inability of wheat producers to compete globally, are the real key to the transition to intensive agriculture. Wheat producers began to get out of

wheat even while grain prices were rising, because of declining yields on exhausted soils. And the growth of fruit acreage expanded ahead of irrigated acreage. "The key points are that the interest rate was an important determinant of the relative profitability of fruit versus alternative land uses and the falling interest rates almost undoubtedly expanded the range of conditions in which fruit cultivation was competitive. Given the capital intensity of fruit growing, the interest rate also had a major impact on production costs" (Rhode 1995: 793).

6. During the 1914–21 upswing, there was a growing presence of individuals, both former farm owners and large landowners, and land-colonization companies as holders of farm mortgages (i.e., as sellers of credit to farmers). The high land prices of the period kept land sales exceptionally active and drove credit sales toward the roof. Shrewd landowners took the opportunity to sell out, taking mortgages as part of the payment of their land (Chenowith 1923: 41). Individuals also sold first mortgages in some cases, especially in Southern California, where land values were high (Agricultural Economics Staff 1930: 44).

7. One reason that the irrigation district bond market was slow to build, and a possible reason for its limited geographic development, is that the bonds could not legally be bought wholesale—that is, below par. Therefore, they held limited attraction to large bond buyers. There was a solution, widely practiced, through which the law was evaded. Typically, an arrangement was made among a large bond buyer, a construction company, and the irrigation district issuing the bonds whereby the construction company would bid 125% of the actual cost of an irrigation project and pass on the extra 25% to the bond buyer, who in that way would receive the desired discount on the bond purchase (Commonwealth Club 1911: 566–67).

8. That credit was a disciplined and disciplining social relation was also insisted upon by farmland developers, who sold mortgages on their small-farm subdivisions. "A simple contract will not be sufficient. Some details for consideration are determination as to payment dates of interest and principal; limit of delinquency allowed; conditions effecting termination; crop mortgage security for advances and overhead delinquency; use of insurance money; developments required, such as ditching, clearing, etc., and extent to which seller should control and guide farming operations, planting of shade trees, locating of improvements and managing of irrigation and drainage" (Mendenhall 1924: 286).

9. While wage labor on California farms has been a very distinctive feature of the state's agriculture, it is by no means an isolated phenomenon. The Midwest, that region of the family farm, bar none (supposedly), relied significantly on the waged worker. See Gates (1957) and Bogue (1963, especially 182–87).

## Chapter 3

1. Connections to gender were for many decades implicit: Men dominated field labor through the 1920s. (My concern in this chapter is primarily with field labor.) Women gained entry into packing shed and cannery labor much more easily, however, and their unpaid domestic labor was also key to the reproduction of field labor, especially for particular groups of field workers, such as Mexican and Japanese Californians. It is my understanding that women were more present in the fields by the 1930s. That said, for a discussion of women field workers, the work of historian Margo McBane is essential. See McBane (1995, 1976, and 1983). For examples of studies on the gendering of agricultural work, focusing on the 1930s and after, see Weber (1994), Ruiz (1987), Zavella (1987), and Thomas (1985).

2. See Taft (1968), Kazin (1987), and Cornford (1987) on the autonomy of the California State Federation of Labor from the AFL and the California organization's generally more progressive politics.

3. As a point of emphasis, it ought to be said that the *Press*'s bourgeois stance developed over time. Just what processes were involved would make an interesting story. For now, we might just draw out a contrast. During the late nineteenth century, in the heat of populist politics, the *Press* maintained a regular section as a clearinghouse of information for the California Grange, including news from local Granges, Grange meeting times, and numerous articles on the rights of labor and alternative arrangements of capital and labor on the farm. To give one example:

> A system by which all who are employed should be part-owners and joint-sharers in proceeds whenever practicable, would give a new stimulus to industry and remove all that selfishness on the part of proprietors and that jealously on the part of employes [sic] which cause so much trouble between the two classes. Laborers in a manufactory would no longer find an apparent enemy in labor-saving machinery, since their own work would be lessened and they would all share in the increased profits. Laborers on a farm of many square miles in extent owned by themselves in approximately equal shares, would toil with more zeal and more contentedly when knowing that they are to obtain the entire benefits of their care and industry, whether resulting from sales of products and stock or from the increased value of the land with its improvements. Such laborers would have no desire to destroy steam threshers and patent reapers and mowers, as all would derive increased profit from their use. All would be interested in employing the best methods of agriculture administered by a thoroughly competent directory. Every means of profiting by cooperation would be encouraged. There would be no antagonism between capital and labor, nor any display of the disposition on the part of one to pay as little wages, and of the other to do as little as possible. There would be a steady and profitable accumulation of capital which would cause no jealousy, envy or discontent, since all would share in it. (Moore, "Safe Accumulations," 1889: 597)

4. There is a larger issue raised by the *Pacific Rural Press*'s comments in defense of Japanese labor, which is whether or not race mattered to capital and, if so, in what ways? There is no easy or once-and-for-all answer. The *Press*'s and Adams's view was one kind—that is, what matters is whether workers are doing the work they are supposed to do and whether the employer has free reign to buy the labor power desired at an agreeable price. Another view, more complex, was expressed when members of the bourgeoisie made discriminations that seemed to afford them no advantage, at least in terms of their capital. Statements made in the Bank of Italy's employee magazine, *Bankitaly Life*, are a case in point. In the summer of 1919, the magazine ran an article with a view not unlike the *Press*'s and Adams's. "Banks, having among their depositors many foreigners, do not always realize the important part they may play in bettering the condition of these people . . . [The foreigner's already demonstrated] thrift instinct which leads him to a bank can ofttimes be made to serve as a stepping stone to high ideals . . . [Bankers] should remember that all advice given these strangers ignorant of our language and customs, makes for better citizenship by helping to inculcate in them a love for our country and its institutions, as a direct result of which our banks will enjoy the confidence of our adopted citizens and share in the material advantages of their success" (Clavere 1919: 5). Here, the bank is clearly doing what it ought to be doing: seeking out money where it is to be found. By 1923, however, the magazine had rethought this policy when it came to California's Asian people. It came out in support of the restricted immigration on the grounds that the "hordes" were unassimilable and threatened to water down the "American" population, which was not reproducing fast enough to keep pace. The fear was that the "predominating race on the Pacific coast will be the yellow race" (9). Why should a bank care about such a prospect? *Bankitaly Life* did not go so far as to suggest that they were unable to get many Asian depositors, though it seems fair to guess that had they had many depositers

from the ranks of the newly emigrated, they might have felt otherwise. At any rate, the hypocrisy of the matter is illuminated by the fact that when the Bank of Italy itself first "emigrated" to the Los Angeles area, where the Anglo presence was much stronger than in its San Francisco stomping grounds, the bank (heavily staffed by Italian Americans) was rebuffed (Nash 1992: 46). There is nothing *automatic* about the geography of capital.

5. Requa and Cory's allusion to the czar is an interesting one. Around the same time, William Ellsworth Smythe, a well-known champion of small-scale agriculture, was scheming about how to make family farming work without hiring wage workers. He likened his attitude about Little Landers to the ideas of the Narodni Socialists in Russia, who were researching what unit of land might be workable by a single family only. Smythe's motto during his years stumping for the Little Landers was "big farms bigger, small farms smaller." The issue for him was not whether there were large farms hiring wage workers. Indeed, he saw this as an inexorable tendency of capitalist agriculture. The issue was whether there would be a way for wage or salary workers to make a living for themselves. See the journal *Little Lands in America,* especially Smythe, "Land Revolution in Russia," 1917: 168–69 and "The Land and the Multitude," 1916: 166–69.

6. Occidental's articles of incorporation reveal the founders' high ambitions as much more than land developers. The purposes of the company were

> to buy, sell and deal in fruits and vegetables of all kinds and to manufacture, introduce, sell and deal in concentrated fruits and fruit products . . . to buy, sell and deal in agricultural lands and real estate of all kinds on commission or otherwise; to plant gardens, orchards and vineyards, and to contract for, buy, sell, and deal in the products thereof, either concentrated, fresh or cured; to locate, buy, sell, lease or otherwise acquire water and water rights; to construct, and maintain dams, canals, ditches and flumes and to sell and distribute water for manufacturing business or other purposes; to apply for and secure patent and patent rights, trademarks and copyrights in this or foreign countires, upon the machinery, processes or products of this corporation or otherwise; and to buy, sell, and deal in the same or [?] secured by any other party or parties whomsoever; to buy, sell, and deal in machinery and appliances, merchandise, and supplies of any description, useful or necessary in carrying on the business of the corporation; to borrow money and to issue bonds or other certificates of indebtedness, and to mortgage or hypothecate real and personal property to secure the payment of the same with interest and to acquire and invest in the securities of other corporations; to do a general mercantile, manufacturing, and commission business, and generally to do and transact any business for which individuals may lawfully associate themselves. (Occidental 1904)

Occidental's real business, it would seem, was simply the business of California.

7. Histories of the ideologies of work and the languages of class in the United States may be found in Glickstein (1991) and Kulikoff (1992).

## Part Two, Introduction

1. Chapter 5 explains how southern California became "Southern California." For the sake of consistency, I am using the "S" throughout this work.

2. Readers may wish to consider this development a kind of reprise of what capitalist development had already done. Quite a few of the novels I will be examining delve into the obliteration of the rancho economy that dominated before the Anglo takeover. The classic California novel treating this theme is Helen Hunt Jackson's *Ramona*.

3. Wyatt's premise is precisely one that I wish to dispute: "In the literature of the West, and of California in particular, the energies that had been concentrated into convenant theology or the rationalization of southern history are displaced into an *unmediated encounter with landscape*. In California the history of these encounters usurps the function of ideology" (xvi, italics added).

4. By *production of nature*, I mean the transformation of nature under the forces of agricultural change (dam building, ditch digging, seed sowing, orchard planting, appropriation of labor power, etc.), the mechanisms for accomplishing that transformation (financial circuits, technological knowledge, and labor market development), and, quite critically, the emergence of a socially made "second nature" (e.g., rifts between urban and rural). "Second nature" is a constitutive *and* produced landscape, akin to what Marx called the second form of differential rent, the landscape of human-produced geographical differences produced through processes of capitalist uneven development (*Capital*, Vol. 3; see also Smith 1985, Lefebvre 1991).

5. I am outlining these two rhetorics not for the purpose of overtly categorizing in those terms the novels discussed in part two, but to suggest two constitutive features of rural realism in the California novel. It is appropriate, too, to suggest here that rural realism speaks to agrarianisms in American cultural history. In the form of agrarianism that Henry Nash Smith describes lay the hope (in the minds of a stream of politicians and literati) that American society would be vitalized by the continued availability of cheap arable land and the employ of westward-moving masses in an agriculture that they controlled (Smith 1978). In fact, many historians of California have charted the distinctive failure of social ideals that seem to have had more life elsewhere in the American countryside (e.g., Taylor 1945; McWilliams 1939; Daniel 1982; Jones 1970; Chan 1986). But the "erosion of agrarian idealism," as Cletus Daniel puts it, captures only part of what was happening in California, for a further point can be made. Americans never did have in mind a unified idea of what agrarianism was all about. Agrarianism had always been a flexible and changing set of ideas and practices over time and space. For example, just as antebellum southerners and northerners held wildly different plans for agro-economic expansion into the western territories, midwestern and southern Populists clashed over their different goals for rural reform in the 1880s and '90s (Markusen 1987; Shannon 1945). Within western households, Anglo-European men and women struggled over what their collective rural future ought to look like (Kolodny 1984). And the "agrarian" goals of Chinese farmers in California were distinct and variable in their own right (Chan 1986). "Agrarianism," if it must have a single definition, would better refer to a discourse comprised of the variation of claims on the purposes agriculture was to serve and the institutions thought necessary to agriculture's survival. It is the field in which and through which agriculture is represented.

Nor is agrarianism only a farmer's domain. As the pace of industrialization increased after the Civil War and gave birth to "agrarian" Populist or city-based countryside nostalgia, agriculture remained a source of tremendous wealth to farm-related economies—that is, the economies of real estate dealers and developers, bankers, implement manufacturers, food processors, and the rest. The circulation of capital was making new geographies in which the interface between nature and capital remained flexible (Mann 1990). Agrarianism, in the sense defined just above (and of which we could say that rural realism was a permutation), was therefore constructed and reconstructed in the representations of a gamut of interested parties, farmers, land developers, bankers, and so forth, included.

## Chapter 4

1. For example, here is John Muir's observation of the Tulare Lake area in 1874: "cheerless shanties sifted through and through with dry winds, are being displaced by true homes embowered in trees and lovingly bordered with flowers; and content-

ment, which in California is perhaps the very rarest of the virtues, is now beginning to take root" (cited in Preston 1981: 159). Muir's was an often heard statement on the push toward domesticity, which was a strong theme in middle-class American and frontier culture. The ideology of domesticity is strongly represented in the Mussel Slough novels treated in this chapter.

2. See, for example, Rice et al., *The Elusive Eden* (1988). This book contains an excellent and thorough account of the Mussel Slough incident by Richard Orsi, a co-author of the text. I have drawn on Orsi's definitive reconstruction extensively.

3. This concern with abstraction comprises an entire cultural history in itself. For example, on the subject of the printing of paper money and the problems it created for the representation of value in late-nineteenth-century America, see Michaels (1987).

4. Although the Department of the Interior acknowledged the route change, it halted the sale of uninhabited public land along the route until the railroad came into full ownership. How this happened was rather complicated. In 1868, under political pressure from coastal counties and from a national consortium of land speculators with an eye on the valley, the Department of the Interior decided to prevent the grant of land to the railroad. Their reasoning was based on the fact that the Central Pacific's originally proposed southern route, the one stated in its approved charter, had been different. The Central Pacific subsequently purchased the Southern Pacific (which would soon absorb its parent company) and in 1870, with support of valley residents, convinced Congress and the California legislature to approve the "new" route. Four years later, patents for sections of railroad that were complete—San José to Tres Pinos and Goshen to Bakersfield—began to be issued to the company. "For nearly three years in the late 1860s, however, the legal status of the Southern Pacific's grant had been in limbo. Enough uncertainty remained to lead some to take the chance that the railroad's land titles would one day be overturned" (Rice et al. 1988: 220; see also Showalter 1969).

5. The Southern Pacific developed a strategy to ensure that its land would not revert back to the public domain if it could not sell it within the time allotted. McAllister reports that on April 1, 1875,

> the southern Pacific Railroad Company conveyed all of its lands lying in California then unsold to D. O. Mills and Lloyd Tevis to hold in trust as security for mortgage bonds [to raise capital for construction costs above the revenue generated by land sales], which it issued to the amount of $46,000,000. Since the Supreme Court had ruled that a mortgage was a disposal that complied with the provisions in the land-grant acts the company had in that sense disposed of its lands. After such a mortgage disposal, the lands were not subject to government suits for returning them to the public domain for non-compliance with the three-year disposal provision in the land-grant act of March 3, 1871. (McAllister 1939: 283–84)

6. For an alternate rendering of these, see Wyatt, *The Fall into Eden* (1986). Wyatt emphasizes the images of verticality in *The Octopus,* seeing these moments as attempts to evolve past the base and beastly motives of the railroad. I am arguing that, at least for Presley, verticality—Presley's fantasy of an infinite gaze—is a figure *for* the railroad and capital's conquests of time and space.

7. I am indebted to Don Mitchell for having made a very similar observation about the representation of the American Western landscape in a quite different context.

8. It should be noted that Magnus and Behrman are actually victims of their own capitalist drives. (According to the argument that follows in the main text, they are figures for what overaccumulating capital does to capital's circulation.)

> Magnus remained the Forty-niner . . . willing to . . . hazard a fortune on the chance of winning a million. . . . It was in this frame of mind that Magnus and the multitude of other ranchers . . . farmed their ranches. They had no love for their land. They were not attached to the soil. They worked their ranches as a

> quarter of a century before they had worked their mines. . . . When, at last, the land . . . would refuse to yield, they would invest their money in something else; by then, they would all have made fortunes. (298–99)

The ranches are revealed here as just another permutation of invested capital, of the logic of capital motivating the ranchers and extracting life from the state's body. The intimation, however, is that capital will reach a critical juncture when it must pull out of the very landscape it creates and move on. Toward the end of the novel, a harvester, a new steam-powered model used by S. Behrman, is called a "brute," a "monster," and it is operated by an "engineer" (615–16). These terms are the same nomenclature applied to the railroad and similar to the ones the author uses to describe nature. The new thresher, an integral component of ranch operations, *shares* in railroad-capital logic: it is not that logic's opposite. They are party to the contradictions that enmesh them.

9. See Sundquist (1982), Sundquist, ed. (1982), Michaels (1987), and Orvell (1989) for excellent discussions of late-nineteenth-century concerns with the demise of authenticity.

## Chapter 5

1. Another guidebook of the period corroborates Widney and Lindley's definition. "The valley of the San Joaquin, like San Luis Obispo County, though in the Southern half of California, is not now included in the term 'Southern California' as it is generally used here" (Van Dyke 1886: 220). The popularity of Southern California inflamed the jealousy of the north. In 1885, for example, the *San Jose Times-Mercury* mockingly noted that the "average Eastern mind conceives of California as a small tract of country situated in and about Los Angeles. . . . The result shows the pecuniary value of cheek" (quoted in Dumke 1944: 40). Before long, Southern California had acquired such a winning reputation for its productivity, its climate, its aesthetic qualities as a "land of homes" that writers of guidebooks had to remind readers of other portions of the state.

> The beautiful southern counties enjoy a fame wholly out of proportion to geographical area, which is greatly to their credit, and which is due to their success in putting water upon the land far more than to any other single factor. But it is the region north of the Pass of Tehachapi which was endowed by nature with the greatest valleys of fertile soil and the most abundant supplies of water available for irrigation. The climate, too, is fully equal to that of the south in productive capacity. Indeed, the earliest fruit of every kind, including oranges is grown hundreds of miles north of Los Angeles. (Daniels, ed. 1909: 26–27)

By 1916, the economic influence of Southern California had grown to such an extent that boundaries between north and south began once again to blur. "No longer does the line of the Tehachapi Mountains mark the extreme northern limit of the territory which is trade tributary to Southern California. The mountains have been crossed and the dividing line has been pushed back a couple of tiers of counties. Southern California now holds San Luis Obispo and Tulare and Kern County as part of itself by right of conquest and mutual advantage" (*Touring Topics*, April 1916: 12, quoted in Lillard 1966: 161). Particularly enabled by the rise of automotive trucking, Southern California's influence leapfrogged into the southern San Joaquin Valley (beating out San Francisco) and into the Imperial Valley (beating out San Diego). Investments, branch banking, and traffic patterns all bear this out (Lillard 1966).

2. In fact, Widney could not see how California would remain one state for long, so deep-rooted were climatic, topographic, and economic differences between north and south. He argued that northern Californians knew less about Southern Califor-

nians than did people on the eastern seaboard and that people streaming into Southern California knew nothing about northern California. The sectional differences were causing an estrangement between north and south and generally retarding the state's progress. Widney was striking a historically rich but sensitive vein. As early as the Spanish period, the Franciscans had urged a north-south demarcation of the Mission system at the Tehachapis. Under Mexican rule, a cleavage at the same boundary was put forward at the inaugural session of the legislature. The rift continued after 1850. The south felt that it was contributing to northern coffers way out of proportion to its population. For example, in 1852, the six "Cow Counties" had 6,000 people. The counties in the north had 120,000 people. The south paid $42,000 in property taxes, the north, $21,000 (McWilliams 1973).

3. San Diego, aided by its natural harbor, was an outlying node of the "sub-Tehachapi" transformation, but I am placing emphasis on the Los Angeles region because of its dominance (see Dumke 1944).

4. The county of Los Angeles paid out 5% of its assessed value in 1872, about $527,720, while the city contributed $75,000 worth of Los Angeles and San Pedro railroad stocks and 60 acres of land for a depot (Parker 1937: 117).

5. Although he does not include the 1860s purchases, California historian W. W. Robinson argues that real estate sales in California have followed a cyclical pattern, with peaks about every twenty years on average: 1855, 1875, 1887, 1906, 1923, 1946 (Robinson 1948: 209). Also see Robinson (1939).

6. Contrast with San Diego County: Real estate valuation, 1880–90, grew from $1.3 million to $20 million and improvements grew from $340,000 to $4 million (Hinton 1891: 87).

7. Dumke stresses the difference between urban- and rural-based mortgages. Strictly according to the numbers, the contrast is admittedly striking. But acre for acre, urban lots were more costly. Viewing the figures in this light, the trading in rural acreage can be appreciated as very substantial and extensive.

8. Railroad expansion, land subdivision, and irrigation in the 1870s and '80s bequeathed to the following generation of developers a distended urban-rural framework. For example, Henry Edwards Huntington, a nephew of Southern Pacific president Collis P. Huntington and President of the Pacific Electric railway company, "would link his trolleys with underdeveloped areas he had invested in as the principal in one or another real estate syndicate . . . He and his associates would then sell the land, whose value skyrocketed once it became accessible to downtown Los Angeles." Harrison Gray Otis, with his own dollars sunk in real estate, would then promote the tracts in his paper (Starr 1985: 70). What Huntington and his consorts accomplished was largely a filling in of the framework begun by the Southern Pacific Railroad and the agricultural colonies and was advanced by the rapid developments following the Santa Fe Railroad connection with Los Angeles.

9. For a time during the 1870s, Mexican ranchers and farmers resisted giving up their work. As they lost their property or their jobs on the ranchos, many were able to find part-time or seasonal work as vaqueros or sheep shearers. Others attempted to farm on a subsistence basis. Until the time when these practices proved fruitless, the wage-labor market was filled largely by Chinese workers, who had replaced the declining numbers of Native Americans. Camarillo notes that

> Chinatowns were located adjacent to the barrios in Los Angeles and Santa Barbara. . . . The Chinese—like the Chicanos—experienced racist hostility from Anglo society. In fact, a racist xenophobia, together with economic and political harassment, eventually drove most of the Chinese from southern California cities during the last two decades of the century. The decline in the Chinese population and the increasing impoverishment of Chicano workers, who could no longer support families on income from seasonal, pastoral-related employ-

ment, provided the impetus to push Chicanos into the labor market by the late 1870s and early 1880s. (Camarillo 1979: 136)

10. See Griswold del Castillo (1980) for a perceptive study of the Mexican and Anglo co-construction of Southern California's "fantasy heritage." Griswold del Castillo's discussion also takes to task the idea that Mexican Californians were financially inept.

11. The backgrounds of many of these authors are touched upon in Walker (1950).

## Chapter 6

1. Western American water history has been composed through a number of different analytics. For a treatment that lays particular emphasis on the evolution of a water-management bureaucracy, see Marc Reisner, *Cadillac Desert: The American West and Its Disappearing Water* (1986). For a refutation of Worster's portrait of a monolithic water empire and support for the view that water development is driven by popular demand, see Norris Hundley, Jr., *The Great Thirst: Californians and Water, 1770s–1990s* (1992). John Walton's *Western Times and Water Wars* (1992) employs theories of the state and popular resistance in a detailed study of California's Owens Valley. Robert Gottlieb and Margaret FitzSimmons in *Thirst for Growth: Water Agencies as Hidden Government* (1990) argue specifically that capitalist dynamics drive water development (more my own view). Worster approaches this argument in his recounting of water development during the era of the "capitalist state" but argues strongly for the hydraulic society as a set of semi-autonomous processes. As for literary production surrounding water development, Worster, Webb, and Walton all draw upon novels (and film), but none offers a sustained critical reading of them, such as I am attempting here.

2. In 1902, during a power struggle in the California Development Company, Chaffey was ousted from the company. He immediately set forth on other irrigation and land-development ventures. These included the irrigation and subdivision of 12,000 acres of citrus land in La Habra Valley (about twenty miles east of Los Angeles) and the purchase of water rights to several Sierran streams in the Owens Valley, which he sold in 1905 to Los Angeles interests that were intent on importing water to the city (McWilliams 1983). Chaffey's banking interests extended far afield from Imperial. Following his departure from the Valley, he teamed up again with his son and returned to Ontario, where they organized the First National Bank of Ontario in 1902. In 1903, they formed the American Savings Bank of Los Angeles, and two years later the First National Bank of Upland. In 1905, they also began acquiring interest in country banks throughout San Bernardino and Los Angeles counties. In the 1920s, they began to merge a number of their Southern California banking interests into a holding company, the California Group, whose combined assets were valued at $120 million (Alexander 1928). Chaffey's life is a plain illustration of the regionalization, through continual reinvestment, of capital and the making of place in Southern California and the Imperial Valley.

3. On the relationship between irrigation and social reform, see William Ellsworth Smythe (1905, repr. 1969) and Pisani (1984).

4. Los Angeles was crucial to the Valley's economy before and after the flood. Several examples: In 1910, the North American Dredging Company of Los Angeles built a dredger for use in the canals, which were in regular need of being cleaned of silt deposits. The dredger was basically a duplicate of the one that had been built for dredging Los Angeles's San Pedro Harbor (Cory 1915). Also, Los Angeles capitalists were drawn to the Imperial Valley to add to their fortunes. Many of the Valley's town and agricultural real estate developers had careers as developers, merchants, or bankers elsewhere in Southern California before arriving in the Valley (Howe and Hall 1910).

Other Los Angeles businessmen, such as H. W. Blaisdell, a principal stockholder in the California Development Company, were absentee investors in the Valley (Cory 1915). After the Imperial Valley Irrigation District was formed, Los Angeles–based real estate consortium the Imperial Valley Farm Lands Association purchased a 47,000-acre tract from the Southern Pacific, which it began selling off in portions of any size desired by buyers (Imperial Valley Farm Lands Assoc. c. 1920). Imperial Valley boosters were fully aware of these regional ties, including Imperial's role in supplying products to the coast as Southern California's urban expansion ate into its agricultural periphery. "It is Imperial Valley," two of them ventured, "which is making a city of a million inhabitants of Los Angeles" (Howe and Hall 1910).

5. On this subject, see Henry Nash Smith's *Virgin Land* (1978); also Leo Marx, *The Machine in the Garden* (1964). Marx writes that "[s]ince Jefferson's time the forces of industrialism have been the chief threat to the bucolic image of America" (26). My emphasis is on how the bucolic image was reworked and reproduced by the incorporation of those very forces.

6. All was not as simple, in rhetorical terms, as it seemed. The Southern Pacific liked burning the candle at both ends. To wit, it promoted the Imperial Valley nationally as a new agriculture in a new environment, claiming in one of its brochures that the arid West could provide homes for the thousands of failed tenant farmers in New England and the Midwest who needed them. Yet, quoting Frederick Newell, the head of the U.S. Reclamation Service, Southern Pacific asserted that "[t]he irrigated countries are no place for the poor farmer" (Wells 1910: 11).

7. See John G. Cawelti, *Adventure, Mystery, and Romance: Formula Stories as Art and Popular Culture* (1976).

8. That labor is a potentially leveling force is a dangerous idea, however. Clearly, Wright did not want to imply that all people were equals. There had to be some rationale, other than labor, for social distance in the work-ethic society. That something was race, or rather the belief that race "naturally" conferred position. From "dark Pablo," Wright notes, ". . . still far down on the ladder of the world's upward climb" to the "self-hidden financier" Jefferson Worth, each "stood for a vital element in the combination of human forces that was working out for the race the reclamation of the land" (289–290).

9. An excellent review of gender theory in western American history, which makes a case for the *social process* of gender that is sympathetic (I hope) to the line of argument employed here, may be found in Susan Lee Johnson (1996).

10. For an analysis similar to the one I am developing here, only in the Latin American case of how "eroticism and nationalism become figures for each other," see Doris Sommer, *Foundational Fictions: The National Romances of Latin America* (1991: 31).

11. See also Vera Norwood and Janice Monk, eds., *The Desert Is No Lady: Southwestern Landscapes in Women's Writing and Art* (1987).

12. Jan Cohn ascribes to romance a set of gender relations similar to those of Gilman's sex market and asserts that heroines gain power by gaining wealthy and handsome suitors. Romance thus serves to redistribute power between the sexes. My reading of *The Winning of Barbara Worth*, a novel that she does not refer to, differs in that the redistribution of power is not real but is read into landscape. See Jan Cohn, *Romance and the Erotics of Property* (1988).

13. Over the next couple of decades, Imperial Valley farm employers became increasingly aware of the cost of inadequate working conditions. On the migrant worker strikes of 1928, 1930, and 1933–34, see Daniel (1982) and Mitchell (1996).

## Chapter 7

1. For details on Mary Austin's career, see Armitage (1990), Langlois (1990), Lanigan (1989), and Austin (1932).

2. The Los Angeles–Owens Valley story has been told frequently. Unless otherwise noted, this account relies on Reisner (1986), Kahrl (1982), and Walton (1992).

3. In his original plans, Mulholland expected that the Owens and San Fernando Valleys could share use of the water more or less equitably. But agricultural growth in the latter surpassed by far his projections. Moreover, whereas he expected that the San Fernando would increasingly turn to orchard crops, "large sections of the valley in the war years were given over to the water-intensive production of beans, potatoes, and truck garden crops. As a result, during periods of peak irrigation demand, the consumption of water in the valley equaled the entire flow of the aqueduct and at times exceeded the total mean flow of the Owens River itself" (Kahrl 1982: 228).

# References

## A Note on Biographical Sources for California Novelists

Most of the novelists that have been treated in this book have not had the pleasure of a large critical following, of the sort that leads to the writing of book-length biographies that are widely accessible. Nonetheless, biographical notes on several of these novelists, including Stewart Edward White, Frederick Sanford, Horace Annesley Vachell, Theodore S. Van Dyke, and Harold Bell Wright, may be easily tracked down in popular histories of California literature and culture—for example, Kevin Starr (1981, 1985), Franklin Walker (1950), and Lawrence Clark Powell (1971, 1974). Russel Nye (1970) is also helpful. Unless otherwise noted in the main text, I have drawn upon biographical sources for the remainder of the authors as follows: William Chambers Morrow is treated in Burk and Howe (1972), Marquis (1900), Stewart (1951), and Hinkel (1942). He also earned a brief biographical essay in the *Overland Monthly* 41 (1883): 257. Entries on Frank Lewis Nason are to be found in Marquis (1900), Stewart (1951), Spence (1970), and *Who's Who* (1921). Burke and Howe (1972), Marquis (1900), Stewart (1951), and Hinkel (1942) include coverage of Joseph Allan Dunn. Ednah Aiken is discussed in Burke and Howe (1972) and is the subject of a short sketch in the *Overland Monthly* 81 (1923): 27.

## Novels Treated in Part Two

### *San Joaquin Valley*

Morrow, William Chambers. 1882. *Blood-Money.* San Francisco: F. J. Walker and Co.
Norris, Frank. 1901. *The Octopus: A Story of California.* Reprint ed., New York: Penguin Books, 1986.

### *Southern California*

Nason, Frank Lewis. 1905. *The Vision of Elijah Berl*. Boston: Little, Brown, and Co.
Sanford, Frederick R. 1889. *The Bursting of a Boom*. Philadelphia: J. B. Lippincott Co.
Vachell, Horace Annesley. 1899. *The Procession of Life*. New York: D. Appleton and Co.
Van Dyke, Theodore S. 1890. *Millionaires of a Day: An Inside History of the Great Southern California Land 'Boom.'* New York: Fords, Howard and Hulbert.
White, Stewart Edward. 1920. *The Rose Dawn*. Garden City, N.Y.: Doubleday, Page, and Co.

### *Imperial Valley*

Aiken, Ednah. 1914. *The River*. Indianapolis: Bobbs-Merrill Co.
Wright, Harold Bell. 1911. *The Winning of Barbara Worth*. Chicago: Book Supply Co.

### *San Francisco and Los Angeles*

Austin, Mary. 1917. *The Ford*. Boston: Houghton Mifflin Co.
Dunn, Joseph Allan. 1924. *The Water-Bearer*. New York: Dodd, Mead and Co.

### All Other Sources

Adams, Frank. 1905. "The Distribution and Use of Water in Modesto and Turlock Irrigation Districts, California." In United States Department of Agriculture, "Annual Report of Irrigation and Drainage Investigations, 1904." *Office of Experiment Stations, Bulletin No. 158:* 93–139. Washington, D.C.: Government Printing Office.
Adams, R. L. 1921. *Farm Management: A Text-Book for Student, Investigator, and Investor*. New York: McGraw-Hill Book Co.
Adams, R. L., and Bedford, W. W. 1921. *The Marvel of Irrigation: A Record of a Quarter Century in the Turlock and Modesto Irrigation Districts—California*. San Francisco: Bond Department, Anglo and London Paris National Bank.
Agricultural Economics Staff. 1930. "Economic Problems of California Agriculture." *California Agricultural Experiment Station, Bulletin 504*. n.p.
Aiken, Charles S. 1908. "The Surprise of the Desert." *Sunset* 21.5 (September): 375–98.
Alexander, J. A. 1928. *The Life of George Chaffey: A Story of Irrigation Beginnings in California and Australia*. Melbourne: Macmillan and Co.
Almaguer, Tomás. 1994. *Racial Fault Lines: The Historical Origins of White Supremacy in California*. Berkeley: University of California Press.
Armitage, Shelley. 1990. *Wind's Trail: A Biography of Mary Austin*. Santa Fe: Museum of New Mexico Press.
*Associated Grower*. 1922. July 1: 19.
Austin, Mary. 1932. *Earth Horizon*. Boston: Houghton Mifflin.
Azuma, Eiichiro. 1994. "Japanese Immigrant Farmers and California Alien Land Laws." *California History* Spring: 14–29.
Baker, Howard. 1931. *Orange Valley*. New York: Coward-McCann.
Bakhtin, Mikhail. 1981. *The Dialogic Imagination: Four Essays*. Trans. by Caryl Emerson and Michael Holquist. Austin: University of Texas Press.
Bancroft, Hubert Howe. 1888. *California Pastoral, 1769–1849*. San Francisco: A. L. Bancroft.
Barger, H., and Landsberg, H. H. 1942. *American Agriculture, 1899–1939: A Study of Output, Employment and Productivity*. New York: National Bureau of Economic Research.

Barnes, Dwight H. 1987. *The Greening of Paradise Valley: Where the Land Owns the Water and the Power.* Modesto, Calif.: Modesto Irrigation District.

Bassett, C. E., and Moomlaw, Clarence W. 1915. "Cooperative Marketing, and Financing of Marketing Associations." *Yearbook of the United States Department of Agriculture, 1914:* 185–210. Washington, D.C.: Government Printing Office.

Beach, Frank L. 1963. "The Transformation of California 1900–1920: The Effects of the Westward Movement on California's Growth and Development in the Progressive Period." Ph.D. dissertation, Department of History, University of California, Berkeley.

Bean, Walton. 1968. *California: An Interpretive History.* San Francisco: McGraw-Hill Book Co.

Beck, Warren A., and Williams, David A. 1972. *California: A History of the Golden State.* New York: Doubleday and Co.

Blackford, Mansel. 1977. *The Politics of Business in California, 1890–1920.* Columbus: Ohio State University Press.

Bloom, Khaled. 1983. "Pioneer Land Speculation in California's San Joaquin Valley." *Agricultural History* 57.3 (July): 297–307.

Blum, Joseph A. 1984. "South San Francisco: The Making of an Industrial City." *California History* 63.2 (Spring): 114–34.

Bogue, Allan. 1963. *From Prairie to Corn Belt: Farming on the Illinois and Iowa Prairies in the Nineteenth Century.* Chicago: University of Chicago Press.

———. 1955. *Money at Interest: The Farm Mortgage on the Middle Border.* Ithaca: Cornell University Press.

Bonadio, Felice A. 1994. *A. P. Giannini: Banker of America.* Berkeley: University of California Press.

Borus, Daniel. 1989. *Writing Realism: Howells, James, and Norris in the Mass Market.* Chapel Hill: University of North Carolina Press.

Bradbury, Malcolm, and MacFarlane, James. 1976. *Modernism: A Guide to European Literature, 1890–1930.* New York: Penguin Books.

Brodhead, Richard. 1993. *Cultures of Letters: Scenes of Reading and Writing in Nineteenth-Century America.* Chicago: University of Chicago Press.

———. 1988. "Sparing the Rod: Discipline and Fiction in Antebellum in America." *Representations* 21: 67–96.

Burke, W. J., and Howe, W. D. 1972. *American Authors and Books: 1640 to the Present Day.* New York: Crown Publishers.

California Board of Bank Commissioners. (Superseded by Superintendent of Banks in 1908.) 1878–1924. *Annual Report.* Sacramento: California Board of Bank Commissioners.

California Commission of Immigration and Housing. 1919. *A Report on Large Landholdings in Southern California.* Sacramento: California State Printing Office.

California Development Association. 1924. *Report on Problems of Agricultural Development in California.* State Chamber of Commerce.

California Orchard Company. 1921. "You Can Make BIG Money." *Associated Grower* 2 (February): 26–27.

Camarillo, Albert. 1979. *Chicanos in a Changing Society: From Mexican Pueblos to American Barrios in Santa Barbara and Southern California, 1848–1930.* Cambridge: Harvard University Press.

Cawelti, John G. 1976. *Adventure, Mystery, and Romance: Formula Stories as Art and Popular Culture.* Chicago: University of Chicago Press.

Chan, Sucheng. 1986. *This Bittersweet Soil: The Chinese in California Agriculture, 1860–1910.* Berkeley: University of California Press.

Chenowith, Clyde Garfield. 1923. "Long Term Agricultural Credit in California." Master's thesis, Department of Economics, University of California, Berkeley.

Chipman, N. P. 1896. "Have We Reached the Limit of Profitable Fruit Growing in California?" *Pacific Rural Press* 52 (December 12): 372–73.

Ciriacy-Wantrup, S.V. 1947. "Major Economic Forces Affecting Agriculture, with Particular Reference to California." *Hilgardia* 18.1 (December): 1–76.

Clark, Alfred. 1970. "The San Gabriel River, a Century of Dividing the Waters." *Southern California Quarterly* 52.2 (June): 155–69.

Clavere, Felix H. 1919. "Assisting Our Foreign Brethren." *Bankitaly Life* 3.8 (August): 5.

Clawson, Marion. 1945. "What It Means to Be a Californian." *California Historical Society Quarterly* 24.2 (June): 139–61.

Cleland, Robert Glass. 1951. *The Cattle on a Thousand Hills: Southern California 1850–1880.* San Marino, Calif.: Huntington Library.

Cleland, Robert Glass., and Hardy, Osgood. 1929. *March of Industry.* Los Angeles: Powell Publishing Company.

Clements, Kendrick A. 1979. "Politics and the Park: San Francisco's Fight for Hetch Hetchy, 1908–1913." *Pacific Historical Review* 48: 185–215.

Clements, Roger V. 1953. "British-controlled Enterprise in the West Between 1870 and 1900, and Some Agrarian Reactions." *Agricultural History* 27.4 (October): 132–41.

Cochrane, W. W. 1979. *The Development of American Agriculture: A Historical Analysis.* Minneapolis: University of Minnesota Press.

Cohn, Jan. 1988. *Romance and the Erotics of Property.* Durham, N.C.: Duke University Press.

Commonwealth Club of California. 1921. "Land Tenancy in California." *Transactions of the Commonwealth Club* 17.10. San Francisco.

———. 1916. "Land Settlement in California." *Transactions of the Commonwealth Club* 11.8 (December): 369–96.

———. 1911. "Marketing Irrigation Bonds." *Transactions of the Commonwealth Club* 6.8 (December): 515–83.

Conzen, Michael P. 1977. "The Maturing Urban System in the United States, 1840–1910." *Annals of the Association of American Geographers* 67(1): 88–108.

Cooper, Edwin. 1968. *Aqueduct Empire: A Guide to Water in California.* Glendale: Arthur H. Clark Co.

Cornford, Daniel. 1987. *Workers and Dissent in the Redwood Empire.* Philadelphia: Temple University Press.

Cory, H. T. 1915. *The Imperial Valley and the Salton Sink.* San Francisco: John J. Newbegin.

Crawford, L. A., and Hurd, Edgar. 1941. "Types of Farming in California Analyzed by Enterprises." *Agricultural Experiment Station, Bulletin 654.* Berkeley: University of California, College of Agriculture.

Cronon, William. 1991. *Nature's Metropolis: Chicago and the Great West.* New York: W. W. Norton and Co.

Cross, Ira. 1927. *Financing an Empire: History of Banking in California.* 4 vols. San Francisco: S. J. Clarke Publishing Co.

Cumberland, W. W. 1917. *Cooperative Marketing: Its Advantages as Exemplified in the California Fruit Growers Exchange.* Princeton: Princeton University Press.

Dana, Julian. 1947. *A. P. Giannini: Giant in the West.* New York: Prentice-Hall.

Dana, Richard Henry. 1840. *Two Years Before the Mast.* New York: Harper.

Daniel, Cletus. 1982. *Bitter Harvest: A History of California Farmworkers 1870–1941.* Berkeley: University of California Press.

Daniels, Stephen. 1987. "Marxism, Culture and the Duplicity of Landscape." In Richard Peet and Nigel Thrift, eds., *New Models in Geography,* vol. 2. London: Unwin Hyman, 196–220.

Daniels, T. G., ed. 1909. *California: Its Products, Resources, Industries, and Attractions.* Sacramento: California Alaska-Yukon Exposition Commission.

Davis, John Emmeus. 1980. "Capitalist Agricultural Development and the Exploitation of the Propertied Laborer." In F. Buttel and H. Newby, eds., *The Rural Sociology of the Advanced Societies.* Montclair, N.J.: Allanheld, Osmun, 133–53.

Davis, Mike. 1990. *City of Quartz: Excavating the Future in Los Angeles.* London: Verso.
Deverell, William. 1994. *Railroad Crossing: Californians and the Railroad, 1850–1910.* Berkeley: University of California Press.
Dickason, James F. 1983. *The Newhall Land and Farming Company.* New York: Newcomen Society of the United States.
Doti, Lynne Pierson. 1995. *Banking in an Unregulated Environment: California, 1878–1905.* New York: Garland Publishing.
Dowrie, George W. 1930. "History of the Bank of Italy." *Journal of Economic and Business History* 2: 271–98.
Dumke, Glenn S. 1944. *The Boom of the Eighties in Southern California.* San Marino: Huntington Library.
Duxbury, Norman. 1913. "Alien Land Bill and the Workers." *Labor Clarion* 12.19 (June 20): 13.
*Economic Trends in California, 1929–1934.* San Francisco: Division of Research and Surveys, California Emergency Relief Administration.
"Editorial." 1921. *Pacific Rural Press* 102 (July 30): 109.
Edson, George T. c. 1927. "Mexican Labor in Imperial Valley." Typewritten manuscript, Bancroft Library. Berkeley, California.
"Farmers Need Ready Money." 1921. *Pacific Rural Press* 102 (July 9): 28–29.
Ferrari, Louis. 1923. "Immigration Laws." *Bankitaly Life* 7.2 (February): 7–9.
Fisher, Lloyd H. 1953. *The Harvest Labor Market in California.* Cambridge: Harvard University Press.
FitzSimmons, M. 1986. "The New Industrial Agriculture: The Regional Integration of Specialty Crop Production." *Economic Geography* 62: 334–53.
Foucault, Michel. 1986. "Of Other Spaces." *Diacritics* 16: 22–27.
Frank, Alvin H., and Co. 1925. *California Irrigation and the Investor.* Los Angeles: Alvin H. Frank and Co.
Friedland, W. H. 1984. "Commodity Systems Analysis: An Approach to the Sociology of Agriculture." *Research in Rural Sociology and Development* 1: 221–35.
Friedmann, Harriet. 1980. "Household Production and the National Economy: Concepts for the Analysis of Agrarian Formations." *Journal of Peasant Studies* 7:158–84.
———. 1978a. "Simple Commodity Production and Wage Labour in the American Plains." *Journal of Peasant Studies* 6:71–100.
———. 1978b. "World Market, State, and the Family Farm: Social Bases of Household Production in the Era of Wage Labor." *Comparative Studies in Society and History* 20: 545–86.
Gates, Paul. 1957. "Frontier Estate Builders and Farm Laborers." In Walker D. Wyman and Clifton B. Kroeber, eds., *The Frontier in Perspective.* Madison: University of Wisconsin Press, 144–63.
George, Henry. 1879. *Progress and Poverty.* Reprint ed. New York: Robert Schalkenbach Foundation, 1940.
Gilman, Charlotte Perkins. 1906. "Passing of Matrimony." *Harper's Bazaar* (June): 496.
———. 1898. *Women and Economics.* Reprint ed., New York: Harper and Row, 1966.
Glasscock, C. B. 1933. *Lucky Baldwin: The Story of an Unconventional Success.* Chicago: A. L. Burt Co.
Glazener, Nancy. 1997. *Reading for Realism.* Durham, N.C.: Duke University Press.
Glickstein, Jonathan. 1991. *Concepts of Free Labor in Antebellum America.* New Haven: Yale University Press.
González, Gilbert G. 1994. *Labor and Community: Mexican Citrus Worker Villages in a Southern California County, 1900–1950.* Chicago: University of Illinois Press.
Goodman, D. et al. 1987. *From Farming to Bio-Technology: A Theory of Agro-industrial Development.* Oxford: Basil Blackwell.
Gottlieb, Robert, and FitzSimmons, Margaret. 1990. *Thirst for Growth: Water Agencies as Hidden Government.* Tucson: University of Arizona Press.
Gregory, Derek. 1994. *Geographical Imaginations.* Cambridge, Mass.: Basil Blackwell.

Griswold del Castillo, Richard. 1980. "The del Valle Family and the Fantasy Heritage." *California History* 59.1: 3–15.

———. 1980. *The Los Angeles Barrio, 1850–1890: A Social History.* Berkeley: University of California Press.

Guerin-Gonzales, Camille. 1994. *Mexican Workers and the American Dreams: Immigration, Repatriation, and California Farm Labor, 1900–1939.* New Brunswick, N.J.: Rutgers University Press.

Guinn, J. M. 1915–16. "The Passing of the Rancho." *Annual Publications of the Historical Society of Southern California* 10.1–2: 46–53.

Hahn, S., and Prude, J. 1985. *The Countryside in the Age of Capitalist Transformation: Essays in the Social History of Rural America.* Chapel Hill: University of North Carolina Press.

Harding, S. T. 1960. *Water in California.* Palo Alto: N-P Publications.

Hardy, Osgood. 1927. "Some Economic Aspects of the Gold Age in California." *Proceedings of the Pacific Coast Branch of the American Historical Association.*

Hart, James. 1950. *The Popular Book.* Berkeley: University of California Press.

Harvey, David. 1989a. *The Condition of Postmodernity.* New York: Basil Blackwell.

———. 1989b. *The Urban Experience.* Baltimore: Johns Hopkins University Press.

———. 1982. *The Limits to Capital.* Chicago: University of Chicago Press.

Haug, W. F. 1986. *Critique of Commodity Aesthetics: Appearance, Sexuality and Advertising in Capitalist Society.* Trans. by Robert Bock. Minneapolis: University of Minnesota Press.

Hazzard, Lucy Lockwood. 1927. *The Frontier in American Literature.* New York: Thomas Y. Crowell Co.

Heber, A. H. 1904. "Address of Hon. A. H. Heber, President of the California Development Company to the Settlers of the Imperial Valley in Support of the Water and Property Rights Owned by the Company on the Colorado River at Imperial, California, July 25, 1904." Collection of the Bancroft Library. Berkeley, California.

Heizer, Robert F., and Almquist, Alan J. 1971. *The Other Californians: Prejudice and Discrimination Under Spain, Mexico, and the United States to 1920.* Berkeley: University of California Press.

Henderson, George. 1994a. "Race and Real Estate: The Cultural Anatomy of a Western Land Boom." Paper presented at the Annual Meetings of the Association of American Geographers, April 1994, San Francisco.

———. 1994. "Romancing the Sand: Constructions of Capital and Nature in Arid America." *Ecumene: A Journal of Environment, Culture, Meaning* 1.3 (July): 235–56.

"Hindu Labor." 1913. *Labor Clarion* 12.32 (September): 8.

Hinkel, E. J. 1942. *Biographies of California Authors.* 2 vols. Oakland, Calif.

Hinton, Richard J. 1891. *Progress Report on Irrigation in the United States. Part 1.* (51st Congress, 2nd Session. Ex. Doc. No. 53.) Washington, D.C.: Government Printing Office.

Hittell, J. S. 1874. *The Resources of California,* 6th ed. San Francisco: A. Roman and Co.

Hodges, R. E. 1921. "Colonizing Lands with No Failures." *Pacific Rural Press* 102 (December 24): 659.

Holt, L. M. 1907. *The Unfriendly Attitude of the United States Government Towards the Imperial Valley.* Imperial, Calif.: Imperial Daily Standard Print.

Holt, William F. 1942. *Memoirs of a Missourian.* Holtville, Calif.: Tribune Printing.

Horsman, Reginald. 1981. *Race and Manifest Destiny: The Origins of American Racial Anglo-Saxonism.* Cambridge: Harvard University Press.

Horton, Donald C., et al. 1942. "Farm-Mortgage Credit Facilities in the United States." *USDA Miscellaneous Publication No. 478.* Washington, D.C.: USDA.

Howe, Edgar, and Hall, Wilbur J. 1910. *The Story of the First Decade in Imperial Valley, California.* Imperial: Edgar F. Howe and Sons.

Hundley, Norris Jr. 1992. *The Great Thirst: Californians and Water, 1770s-1990s.* Berkeley: University of California Press.

Hunter, James J. 1950. *Partners in Progress, 1864–1950: A Brief History of The Bank of California, N.A., and of the Region It Has Served for 85 Years.* New York: Newcomen Society in North America.

Hutchins, Wells A. 1931. "Irrigation Districts, Their Organization, Operation and Financing." *Technical Bulletin, No. 254.* Washington, D.C.: United States Department of Agriculture.

———. 1930. "Commercial Irrigation Companies." *Technical Bulletin, No. 177.* Washington, D.C.: United States Department of Agriculture.

———. 1923. "Irrigation District Operation and Finance." *Bulletin No. 1177.* Washington, D.C.: United States Department of Agriculture.

Hyde, Anne Farrar. 1996. "Culture Filters: The Significance of Perception." In Clyde A. Milner II, ed., *A New Significance: Re-Envisioning the History of the American West.* New York: Oxford University Press, 175–201.

———. 1990. *An American Vision: Far Western Landscape and National Culture, 1820–1920.* New York: New York University Press.

"Immigration." 1913. *Labor Clarion* 12.43 (December 5): 5.

Imperial Land Company. 1904. *Imperial Valley Catechism*, 12th ed., revised. Los Angeles: Imperial Land Co.

———. 1902a. *An Album of the Imperial Settlements, San Diego County, California.* Los Angeles: Times-Mirror Printing and Binding House.

———. 1902b. *From Desert to Garden, From Worthlessness to Wealth. As Illustrated in the Imperial Settlements, San Diego County, Southern California.* Los Angeles: Times-Mirror Printing and Binding House.

Imperial Valley Farm Lands Association. c. 1920. "Imperial Valley Lands: A 47,000 Acre Tract, a Million-dollar Irrigation System." Los Angeles: Imperial Valley Farm Lands Assoc.

Iser, Wolfgang. 1974. *The Implied Reader.* Baltimore: Johns Hopkins University Press.

Issel, William, and Cherny, Robert W. 1986. *San Francisco, 1865–1932: Politics, Power, and Urban Development.* Berkeley: University of California Press.

Jackson, Helen Hunt. 1884. *Ramona.* Boston: Roberts Brothers.

James, Marquis, and James, Bessie Rowland. 1954. *Biography of a Bank: The Story of Bank of America N.T. & S.A.* New York: Harper and Brothers.

Jelinek, Lawrence J. 1982. *Harvest Empire: A History of California Agriculture*, 2d ed. San Francisco: Boyd and Fraser Publishing Co.

Johnson, Susan Lee, 1996, "'A Memory Sweet to Soldiers': The Significance of Gender." In Clyde A. Milner II, ed., *A New Significance: Re-Envisioning the History of the American West.* New York: Oxford University Press, 255–78.

Jones, Holway R. 1965. *John Muir and the Sierra Club: The Battle for Yosemite.* San Francisco: The Sierra Club.

Jones, Lamar B. 1970. "Labor and Management in California Agriculture, 1864–1964." *Labor History* 11: 23–40.

Kahrl, William. 1982. *Water and Power: The Conflict over Los Angeles' Water Supply in the Owens Valley.* Berkeley: University of California Press.

Kaplan, Amy. 1988. *The Social Construction of American Realism.* Chicago: University of Chicago Press.

Kazin, Michael. 1987. *Barons of Labor: The San Francisco Building Trades and Union Power in the Progressive Era.* Urbana: University of Illinois Press.

Kershner, Frederick D., Jr. 1953. "George Chaffey and the Irrigation Frontier." *Agricultural History* 27.4 (October): 115–22.

Kidner, Frank L. 1946. *California Business Cycles.* Berkeley: University of California Press.

Kluger, James. 1970. "Elwood Mead: Irrigation Engineer and Social Planner." Ph.D. dissertation, University of Arizona. Tucson.

Kniffen, Fred. 1931–32. "The Natural Landscape of the Colorado Delta." *University of California Publications in Geography* 5: 149–244.

Kolodny, Annette. 1984. *The Land Before Her: Fantasy and Experience of the American Frontiers, 1630–1860*. Chapel Hill: University of North Carolina Press.

Kulikoff, Allan. 1992. *The Agrarian Origins of American Capitalism*. Charlottesville: University Press of Virginia.

"Labor and Immigration." 1913. *Labor Clarion* 12.11 (April 25): 8.

Langlois, Karen. 1990. "A Fresh Voice from the West: Mary Austin, California, and American Literary Magazines." *California History* 69.1 (Spring): 22–35.

Lanigan, Esther. 1989. *Mary Austin: Song of a Maverick*. New Haven: Yale University Press.

Lavender, David. 1981. *Nothing Seemed Impossible: William C. Ralston and Early San Francisco*. Palo Alto, Calif.: American West Publishing Co.

Lears, T. J. Jackson. 1983. *No Place of Grace: Antimodernism and the Transformation of American Culture, 1880–1920*. Chicago: University of Chicago Press.

Lefebvre, Henri. 1991. *The Production of Space*. Trans. by Donald Nicholson-Smith. New York: Basil Blackwell.

Leonard, Karen. 1997. "Finding One's Own Place: Asian Landscapes Re-visioned in Rural California." In Akhil Gupta and James Ferguson, eds., *Culture, Power, Place: Explorations in Critical Anthropology*. Durham, N.C.: Duke University Press, 118–36.

Leyshon, Andrew, and Thrift, Nigel. 1997. *Money/Space: Geographies of Monetary Transformation*. New York: Routledge.

Liebman, Ellen. 1983. *California Farmland: A History of Large Agricultural Landholdings*. Totowa, N.J.: Rowman and Allanheld.

Lillard, Richard G. 1966. *Eden in Jeopardy, Man's Prodigal Meddling with His Environment: The Southern California Experience*. New York: Alfred A. Knopf.

Limerick, Patricia Nelson. 1987. *The Legacy of Conquest: The Unbroken Past of the American West*. New York: W. W. Norton.

Lindley, Walter, and Widney, J. P. 1888. *California of the South: Its Physical Geography, Climate, Resources, Routes of Travel, and Health-Resorts*. New York: D. Appleton and Co.

Lister, Roger C. 1993. *Bank Behavior, Regulation, and Economic Development: California, 1860–1910*. New York: Garland Publishing.

"Livermore." 1920. *Bankitaly Life* 3.8 (August): 17.

London, Jack. 1913. *The Valley of the Moon*. New York: Macmillan.

Maass, A., and Anderson, R. L. 1978. *. . . and the Desert Shall Rejoice: Conflict, Growth, and Justice in Arid Environments*. Cambridge, Mass.: MIT Press.

Madison, James, H. 1990. "Taking the Country Barefooted: The Indiana Colony in Southern California." *California History* 69.3 (Fall): 236–49.

Mann, Susan A. 1990. *Agrarian Capitalism in Theory and Practice*. Chapel Hill: University of North Carolina Press.

Mann, Susan A., and Dickinson, James M. 1978. "Obstacles to the Development of a Capitalist Agriculture." *Journal of Peasant Studies* 5(4): 466–81.

Marchand, Roland. 1985. *Advertising the American Dream: Making Way for Modernity, 1920–1940*. Berkeley: University of California Press.

Markusen, Ann. 1987. *Regions: The Economics and Politics of Territory*. Totowa, N.J.: Rowman and Littlefield Publishers.

Marquis, A. N., ed. 1900– . *Who's Who in America*. Chicago: Marquis Who's Who.

Marx, Karl. 1867. *Capital*. Vol. 1. New York: International Publishers, 1967.

———. 1885. *Capital*. Vol. 2. New York: International Publishers, 1967.

———. 1894. *Capital*. Vol. 3. New York: Penguin Books, 1981.

Marx, Leo. 1964. *The Machine in the Garden*. New York: Oxford University Press.

Matthaei, Julie A. 1982. *An Economic History of Women in America: Women's Work, the Sexual Division of Labor, and the Development of Capitalism*. New York: Schocken Books.

Matthews, Glenna. 1987. *"Just a Housewife": The Rise and Fall of Domesticity in America.* New York: Oxford University Press.

McAfee, Ward M. 1968. "A Constitutional History of Railroad Rate Regulation in California, 1879–1911." *Pacific Historical Review* 37.3 (August): 265–79.

———. 1968. "Local Interests and Railroad Regulation in California During the Granger Decade." *Pacific Historical Review* 37.1 (February): 51–66.

McAllister, W. A. 1939. "A Study of Railroad Land Grant Disposals in California." Ph.D. dissertation, Department of History, University of Southern California. Los Angeles.

McBane, Margo. 1995. "The Role of Gender in Citrus Employment: A Case Study of Recruitment, Labor, and Housing Patterns at the Limoneira Company, 1893 to 1940." *California History* 74.1: 68–81.

———. 1983. "The Role of Women in Determining the California Farm Labor Structure: A Case Study of the Women's Land Army of America During World War I." M.A. Thesis, Department of History, University of California, Davis.

———. 1976. *The History of California Agriculture: Focus on Women Farmworkers.* Prepared by Margo McBane for the United Farmworkers of America and the Coalition of Labor Union Women of Santa Clara County Retail Store Employees Local 428, in Cooperation with the Youth Project, San Francisco, California.

McKee, I. 1948. "Notable Memorials to Mussel Slough." *Pacific Historical Review* 17: 19–27.

McMichael, Philip. 1987. "Bringing Circulation Back into Agricultural Political Economy: Analyzing the Antebellum Plantation in its World Market Context." *Rural Sociology* 52(2): 242–63.

McWilliams, Carey. 1946. *Southern California: An Island on the Land.* Reprint ed., Salt Lake City: Gibbs M. Smith. 1983.

———. 1949. *California: The Great Exception.* Reprint ed., Santa Barbara: Peregrine Smith. 1979.

———. 1939. *Factories in the Field: The Story of Migratory Farm Labor in California.* Reprint ed., New York: Archon Books, 1969.

Mendenhall, J. V. 1924. "Colonization." *Realty Blue Book of California.* Los Angeles: Keystone Publishing.

Michaels, W. B. 1987. *The Gold Standard and the Logic of Naturalism.* Berkeley: University of California Press.

Miller, M. Catherine. 1985. "Riparian Rights and the Control of Water in California, 1879–1928: The Relationship Between an Agricultural Enterprise and Legal Change." *Agricultural History* 59.1 (January): 1–24.

Mitchell, Don. 1996. *The Lie of the Land: Migrant Workers and the California Landscape.* Minneapolis: University of Minnesota Press.

Mooney, Patrick. 1987. "Desperately Seeking: One-Dimensional Mann and Dickinson." *Rural Sociology* 52(2): 286–95.

———. 1986. "The Political Economy of Credit in American Agriculture." *Rural Sociology* 51(4): 449–70.

———. 1982. "Labor Time, Production Time and Capitalist Development in Agriculture: A Reconsideration of the Mann-Dickinson Thesis." *Sociologia Ruralis* 22(3/4): 279–91.

Moore, J. C. 1889. "Safe Accumulations." *Pacific Rural Press* 38.26 (December 28): 597.

Moses, Herman Vincent. 1994. "The Flying Wedge of Cooperation: G. Harold Powell, California Orange Growers, and the Corporate Reconstruction of American Agriculture." Ph.D. dissertation, Department of History, University of California, Riverside.

Muir, John. 1894. *The Mountains of California.* Reprint ed., Garden City, N.Y.: Doubleday and Co, 1961.

Myres, Sandra L. 1982. *Westering Women and the Frontier Experience 1800–1915.* Albuquerque: University of New Mexico Press.

Nance, J. W. "The Irrigator: Information on the Stability of Californian Irrigation Enterprises." *Pacific Rural Press* 42.1 (July 4): 3.

Nash, Gerald D. 1992. *A. P. Giannini and the Bank of America.* Norman: University of Oklahoma Press.

———. 1964. *State Government and Economic Development: A History of Administrative Policies in California, 1849–1933.* Berkeley: Institute of Governmental Studies.

Nash, Roderick. 1982. *Wilderness and the American Mind.* 3d ed. New Haven: Yale University Press.

Nelson, Howard J. 1959. "The Spread of an Artificial Landscape Over Southern California." *Annals of the Association of American Geographers* 49.3, Part 2: 80–99.

Netz, Joseph. 1915–16. "The Great Los Angeles Real Estate Boom of 1887." *Annual Publications of the Historical Society of Southern California* 10.1–2: 54–68.

Niklason, C. R. 1930. *Commercial Survey of the Pacific Southwest.* Domestic Commerce Series No. 37. U.S. Department of Commerce. Washington, D.C.: Government Printing Office.

Nordhoff, Charles. 1875. *California for Travelers and Settlers.* New York: Harper and Brothers.

———. 1874. *California: For Health, Pleasure, and Residence.* New York: Harper and Brothers.

Norris, Frank. 1903. "The Frontier Gone at Last." In Frank Norris, ed., *The Responsibilities of the Novelist.* Reprint ed., New York: Haskell House Publishers. 1969.

———. 1899. *McTeague.* Reprint ed. New York: New American Library, 1981.

Norwood, Vera, and Monk, Janice, eds. 1987. *The Desert Is No Lady: Southwestern Landscapes in Women's Writing and Art.* New Haven: Yale University Press.

Nye, Russel. 1970. *The Unembarrassed Muse: The Popular Arts in America.* New York: Dial Press.

O'Malley, Michael. 1994. "Specie and Species: Race and the Money Question in Nineteenth-Century America." *American Historical Review* 99.2 (April): 369–95.

Occidental [Concentrated] Fruit Company. 1904. Articles of Incorporation. California State Archives. Sacramento, California.

Odell, Kerry A. 1992. *Capital Mobilization and Regional Financial Markets: The Pacific Coast States, 1850–1920.* New York: Garland Publishing.

Olney, Warren. 1909. "Water Supply for the Cities About the Bay of San Francisco." *Out West* 31.1 (July): 599–605.

Omi, Michel, and Winant, Howard. 1986. *Racial Formation in the United States: From the 1960s to the 1980s.* New York: Routledge and Kegan Paul.

Orr, N. M. 1874. *Stockton and San Joaquin Basin.* Stockton, Calif.: Stockton Board of Trade.

Orsi, Richard J. 1975. "*The Octopus* Reconsidered: The Southern Pacific and Agricultural Modernization in California, 1865–1915." *California Historical Quarterly* 54(3): 197–220.

———. 1974. *A List of References for the History of Agriculture in California.* Davis: Agricultural History Center, University of California.

———. 1973. "Selling the Golden State: A Study of Boosterism in Nineteenth-Century California." Ph.D. dissertation, University of Wisconsin, Madison.

Orvell, Miles. 1989. *The Real Thing: Imitation and Authenticity in American Culture, 1880–1940.* Chapel Hill: University of North Carolina Press.

*Pacific Rural Press.* 1921. 102: 52.

"Pacific-Southwestern Banks Form Merger." 1922. *Associated Grower* 3 (July): 18–19.

Page, B., and Walker, R. A. 1991. "From Settlement to Fordism: The Agro-Industrial Revolution in the American Midwest." *Economic Geography* 67.4 (October) 67.4: 281–315.

Parker, Carleton H. 1920. *The Casual Laborer and Other Essays.* New York: Harcourt, Brace, and Howe.

Parker, Edna Monch. 1937. "The Southern Pacific Railroad and Settlement in Southern California." *The Pacific Historical Review* 6.2 (June): 103–19.

Parsons, E. T. 1909. "Proposed Destruction of Hetch-Hetchy." *Out West* 31.1 (July): 607–27.

Passenger Department, Southern Pacific Company. 1908. *Imperial Valley, California*. San Francisco: Passenger Department, Southern Pacific Co.

Paul, Rodman. 1973. "The Beginnings of Agriculture in California: Innovation vs. Continuity." In Knoles, ed., *Essays and Assays: California History Reappraised*. San Francisco: California Historical Society in conjunction with the Ward Ritchie Press.

———. 1958. "The Wheat Trade Between California and the United Kingdom." *Mississippi Valley Historical Review* 45 (December): 391–412.

———. 1947. *California Gold: The Beginning of Mining in the Far West*. Lincoln: University of Nebraska Press.

Perkins, David. 1992. *Is Literary History Possible?* Baltimore: Johns Hopkins University Press.

Pisani, Donald. 1984. *From the Family Farm to Agribusiness: The Irrigation Crusade in California and the West, 1850–1931*. Berkeley: University of California Press.

———. 1983. "Reclamation and Social Engineering in the Progressive Era." *Agricultural History* 57.1 (January): 46–63.

Pomeroy, Earl. 1965. *The Pacific Slope: A History of California, Oregon, Washington, Idaho, Utah, and Nevada*. New York: Alfred A. Knopf.

Post, Charles. 1982. "The American Road to Capitalism." *New Left Review* 133: 30–51.

Powell, Lawrence Clark. 1974. *Southwest Classics*. Pasadena, Calif: Ward Ritchie Press.

———. 1971. *California Classics*. Santa Barbara, Calif.: Capra Press.

Pred, Allan, and Watts, Michael. 1992. *Reworking Modernity: Capitalisms and Symbolic Discontent*. New Brunswick, N.J.: Rutgers University Press.

Preston, W. L. 1981. *Vanishing Landscapes: Land and Life in the Tulare Lake Basin*. Berkeley: University of California Press.

Pudup, M. 1987. "From Farm to Factory: Structuring and Location of the U.S. Farm Machinery Industry." *Economic Geography* 63: 203–22.

Ralmo, Mabel MacCurdy. 1925. *The History of the California Fruit Growers Exchange*. Los Angeles: n.p.

Raub, Patricia. 1994. "A New Woman or an Old-Fashioned Girl? The Portrayal of the Heroine in Popular Women's Novels of the Twenties." *American Studies* 35.1: 109–30.

Reis, Elizabeth. 1985. "Cannery Row: The AFL, the IWW, and Bay Area Italian Cannery Workers." *California History* 64.3 (Summer): 175–91.

Reisner, Marc. 1986. *Cadillac Desert: The American West and Its Disappearing Water*. New York: Penguin.

*Report of the Commission on Land Colonization and Rural Credits of the State of California*. 1916. Sacramento, Calif.

Requa, M. L., and Cory, H. T. 1919. *The California Irrigated Farm Problem*. Washington, D.C.

Rhode, Paul. 1995. "Learning, Capital Accumulation, and the Transformation of California Agriculture." *Journal of Economic History* 55(4): 773–800.

Rhodes, Benjamin Franklin. 1943. "Thirsty land: The Modesto Irrigation District, a Case Study of Irrigation Under the Wright Law." Ph.D. dissertation, Department of History, University of California, Berkeley.

Rice, R., Bullough, W., Orsi, R. 1988. *The Elusive Eden: A New History of California*. New York: Alfred A. Knopf.

Richardson, Elmo R. 1959. "The Struggle for the Valley: California's Hetch Hetchy Controversy, 1905–1913." *California Historical Society Quarterly* 38: 249–58.

"Right Use of Money." 1921. *Pacific Rural Press* 102 (September 3): 228.

Robbins, William. 1994. *Colony and Empire: The Capitalist Transformation of the American West*. Lawrence: University Press of Kansas.

Robinson, W. W. 1948. *Land in California*. Berkeley: University of California Press.

———. 1939. *Ranchos Become Cities*. Pasadena, Calif.: San Pasqual Press.

Rockwood, C. R. 1909. *Born of the Desert.* Calexico, Calif.: Calexico Chronicle.
Roemer, John. 1982. *A General Theory of Exploitation and Class.* Cambridge, Mass.: Harvard University Press.
Romo, Ricardo. 1983. *East Los Angeles: A History of a Barrio.* Austin: University of Texas Press.
Rothstein, Morton. 1982. "Frank Norris and Popular Perceptions of the Market." *Agricultural History* 56.1: 50–66.
———. 1963. "A British Firm on the American West Coast, 1869–1914." *Business History Review* 37.4: 392–415.
Ruiz, Vicky. 1987. *Cannery Women, Cannery Lives: Mexican Women, Unionization and the California Food Processing Industry, 1930–1950.* Albuquerque: University of New Mexico Press.
Sakolski, A. M. 1932. *The Great American Land Bubble.* New York: Harper and Brothers Publishers.
Sartori, J. F. 1923. *Departmental and Branch Banking in California.* Los Angeles: Security Trust and Savings Bank.
Saxton, Alexander. 1990. *The Rise and Fall of the White Republic: Class Politics and Mass Culture in Nineteenth-Century America.* New York: Verso.
Schudson, Michael. 1984. *Advertising, the Uneasy Persuasion: Its Dubious Impact on Society.* New York: Basic Books.
Selvin, David F. 1966. *Sky Full of Storm: A Brief History of California Labor.* Berkeley: Center for Labor Research and Education, Institute of Industrial Relations, University of California.
Shannon, F. A. 1945. *The Farmer's Last Frontier: Agriculture, 1860–1897.* New York: Reinhart and Co.
Shaw, Jr., John Andrew. 1969. "Commercialization in an Agricultural Economy: Fresno County, California 1856–1900." Ph.D. dissertation, Department of Economics, Purdue University. Westville, IN.
Showalter, J. 1969. "A Reappraisal of Mussel Slough." M.A. thesis, Chico State College. Chico, Calif.
Singer, Edward, et al. 1983. "The Mann-Dickinson Thesis: Reject or Revise?" *Sociologia Ruralis* 23(3/4): 276–87.
Smith, Henry Nash. 1978. *Virgin Land: The American West As Symbol and Myth.* Cambridge: Harvard University Press.
Smith, Neil. 1984. *Uneven Development: Nature, Capital and the Production of Space.* New York: Basil Blackwell.
Smith, Wallace. 1939. *Garden of the Sun.* Los Angeles: Lymanhouse.
Smythe, William E. 1917. "Land Revolution in Russia." *Little Lands in America* 4 (November): 168–69.
———. 1916. "The Land and the Multitude." *Little Lands in America* 2 (November): 166–69.
———. 1909. "The Triumph of Irrigation." In Daniels, ed., *California: Its Products, Resources, Industries, and Attractions.* Sacramento: California Alaska-Yukon Exposition Commission.
———. 1905. *The Conquest of Arid America.* Reprint ed. Seattle: University of Washington Press, 1969.
Sommer, Doris. 1991. *Foundational Fictions: The National Romances of Latin America.* Berkeley: University of California Press.
Spence, Clark. 1970. *Mining Engineers and the American West: The Lace-Boot Brigade, 1849–1933.* New Haven: Yale University Press.
Spring Valley Water Company. 1912. *The Future Water Supply of San Francisco: A Report to the Honorable Secretary of the Interior and the Advisory Board of Engineers of the United States Army.* San Francisco: Rincon Publishing Co.
Starr, Kevin. 1990. *Material Dreams: Southern California Through the 1920s.* New York: Oxford University Press.

———. 1985. *Inventing the Dream: California Through the Progressive Era.* New York: Oxford University Press.

———. 1981. *Americans and the California Dream.* Santa Barbara: Peregrine Smith.

Stauber, B. R. 1933. "The Farm Real Estate Situation, 1931–32." *USDA Circular No. 261.* Washington, D.C.: USDA.

Stewart, Wallace W. 1951. *Dictionary of North American Authors Deceased before 1950.* Toronto: Ryerson Press.

Stone, George G. 1967. "Financing the Orange Industry in California, Part Two." *Pomona Valley Historian* 3(1): 31–46.

———. 1966. "Financing the Orange Industry in California, Part One." *Pomona Valley Historian* 2(4): 159–74.

Storper, Michael, and Walker, Richard. 1989. *The Capitalist Imperative: Territory, Technology, and Industrial Growth.* New York: Basil Blackwell.

———. 1984. "The Spatial Division of Labor: Labor and the Location of Industries." In W. Tabb and L. Sawyers, eds., *Sunbelt/Snowbelt.* New York: Oxford University Press.

Sundquist, Eric. 1982. "The Country of the Blue." In Sundquist, ed. (1982).

———, ed. 1982. *American Realism: New Essays.* Baltimore: Johns Hopkins University Press.

Taft, Philip. 1968. *Labor Politics American Style: The California State Federation of Labor.* Cambridge: Harvard University Press.

Taylor, Paul. 1970. "Reclamation: The Rise and Fall of an American Idea." *American West* 7.4 (July): 27–63.

———. 1945. "Foundations of California Rural Society." *California Historical Society Quarterly* 24.3 (September): 193–228.

Taylor, Paul S., and Rowell, Edward J. 1938. "Patterns of Agricultural Labor Migration within California." *Monthly Labor Review* 47.5 (November): 980–90.

Taylor, Paul S., and Vasey, Tom. 1936. "Historical Background of California Farm Labor." *Rural Sociology* 1.3 (September): 281–95.

Taylor, Ray W. 1926. *Hetch Hetchy: The Story of San Francisco's Struggle to Provide a Water Supply for Her Future Needs.* San Francisco: Ricardo J. Orozco.

Taylor, Walter Fuller. 1942. *The Economic Novel in America.* Chapel Hill: University of North Carolina Press.

Teague, Charles. 1944. *Fifty Years a Rancher.* Los Angeles: Ward Ritchie Press.

Ten Broeck, A. 1891a. "A Bright Idea and What Became of It." San Francisco: Occidental Fruit Co.

———. 1891b. "How They Did It." San Francisco: Occidental Fruit Co.

———. 1891c. "Over a Late Cigar." San Francisco: Occidental Fruit Co.

Thickens, Virginia. 1946. "Pioneer Agricultural Colonies of Fresno County." *California Historical Society Quarterly* 25(1): 17–38; 25(2): 169–76.

Thomas, Brook. 1991. *The New Historicism and Other Old-fashioned Topics.* Princeton: Princeton University Press.

Thomas, Robert. 1985. *Citizenship, Gender, and Work: Social Organization of Industrial Agriculture.* Berkeley: University of California Press.

Thompson, C. W. 1916. "Costs and Sources of Farm Mortgage Loans in the United States." *USDA Bulletin No. 384.* Washington, D.C.: USDA.

Tout, Otis B. 1931. *The First Thirty Years in Imperial Valley, California.* San Diego: Otis B. Tout, Publisher.

Trava, Jose. 1987. "Sharing Water with the Colossus of the North." In High Country News, ed., *Western Water Made Simple.* Washington, D. C.: Island Press.

Turner, Frederick Jackson. 1894. "The Significance of the Frontier in American History." *Annual Report for 1893.* Washington, D.C.: American Historical Association.

U.S. Department of Agriculture. 1924. *Agricultural Yearbook.* Washington, D.C.: Government Printing Office.

U.S. Department of Commerce, Bureau of the Census. 1932. *Fifteenth Census of the United States: Irrigation of Agricultural Lands, 1930.* Washington, D.C.: Government Printing Office.

———. 1922. *Fourteenth Census of the United States: Irrigation and Drainage, 1920.* Washington, D.C.: Government Printing Office.

———. 1913. *Thirteenth Census of the United States: Abstract of the Census, 1910.* (With supplement for California.) Washington, D.C.: Government Printing Office.

———. 1902. *Twelfth Census of the United States: Agriculture, 1900.* Part 1. Washington, D.C.: Government Printing Office.

———. 1895. *Eleventh Census of the United States: Statistics of Agriculture, 1890.* Part 3. Washington, D.C.: Government Printing Office.

Valgren, V. N., and Engelbert, Elmer E. 1922. "Bank Loans to Farmers on Personal and Collateral Security." *Bulletin No. 1048.* Washington, D.C.: USDA.

———. 1921. "Farm Mortgage Loans by Banks, Insurance Companies, and Other Agencies." *Bulletin No. 1047.* Washington, D.C.: USDA

Vance, James E., Jr. 1964. *Geography and Urban Evolution in the San Francisco Bay Area.* Berkeley, Calif.: Institute of Governmental Studies.

Van Dyke, Theodore S. 1886. *Southern California: Its Valleys, Hills, and Streams; Its Animals, Birds, and Fishes; Its Gardens, Farms, and Climate.* New York: Fords, Howard, and Hulbert.

Vaught, David. 1995. "'An Orchardist's Point of View': Harvest Labor Relations on a California Almond Ranch, 1892–1921." *Agricultural History* 69.4: 563–92.

Veblen, Thorstein. 1921. *The Engineers and the Price System.* New York: B. W. Huebsch.

Veeser, H. Aram, ed. 1989. *The New Historicism.* New York: Routledge.

Walker, Franklin. 1950. *A Literary History of Southern California.* Berkeley: University of California Press.

Walton, John. 1992. *Western Times and Water Wars: State, Culture, and Rebellion in California.* Berkeley: University of California Press.

Wangenheim, Julius. 1956. "Julius Wangenheim, An Autobiography." *California Historical Society Quarterly* 35(2): 119–44; 34(3): 253–74.

Warner, Charles Dudley. 1904. *Our Italy.* Hartford: American Publishing Co.

Waters, Frank. 1946. *The Colorado.* New York: Rinehart and Co.

Weaver, Mrs. Wiley M., with Board of Supervisors of Imperial County, California. 1915. *Imperial Valley 1901–1915.* Los Angeles: Kingsley, Mason, and Collins Co.

Webb, Walter Prescott. 1931. *The Great Plains.* Boston: Ginn.

Weber, Devra. 1994. *Dark Sweat, White Gold: California Farm Workers, Cotton and the New Deal.* Berkeley: University of California Press.

Weeks, Edward. 1934. "The Best Sellers Since 1875." *Publishers Weekly* 125: 1503–6.

Wells, A. J. 1910. *Government Irrigation and the Settler.* San Francisco: Passenger Department, Southern Pacific.

Wells, Miriam J. 1996. *Strawberry Fields: Politics, Class, and Work in California Agriculture.* Ithaca: Cornell University Press.

West, Charles H. 1929. "The Use, Value, and Cost of Credit in Agriculture." *California Agricultural Experiment Station, Bulletin 480.* Berkeley: Giannini Foundation of Agricultural Economics, University of California.

White, Richard. 1991. *"It's Your Misfortune and None of My Own": A New History of the American West.* Norman: University of Oklahoma Press.

Whitney, D. J. 1921. "Great Los Angeles Wholesale Markets Complete." *Pacific Rural Press* 102 (December 31): 679.

*Who's Who Among North American Authors.* 1921. Los Angeles: Golden Syndicate Pub. Co.

"Why Not More Native Laborers?" 1921. *Pacific Rural Press* 102 (August 13): 148.

Wickens, David L. 1932. "Farm-Mortgage Credit." *Technical Bulletin No. 288.* Washington, D.C.: USDA.

"A Wider Reach of Rural Credit." 1921. *Pacific Rural Press* 102 (September 10): 252.

Williams, H. C. 1913. "Our Feudal Principalities." *Labor Clarion* 12.40 (November 14): 3.

Williams, Raymond. 1973. *The Country and the City.* New York: Oxford University Press.

Winther, Oscar Osburn. 1953. "The Colony System of Southern California." *Agricultural History* 27.3 (July): 94–103.

Woirol, Gregory. 1992. *In the Floating Army: F. C. Mills on Itinerant Life in California, 1914.* Urbana: University of Illinois Press.

Wood, Gordon S. 1994. "Inventing American Capitalism." *The New York Review of Books* 41 (June 9): 44–49.

Wood, Will C. 1929. "California Banks in Development of Real Estate." *Real Estate Handbook of California.* Los Angeles: Real Estate Publishing Co.

Worster, Donald. 1985. *Rivers of Empire: Water, Aridity and the Growth of the American West.* New York: Pantheon Books.

Wright, Benjamin C. 1980. *Banking in California, 1849–1910.* New York: Arno Press.

Wyatt, David. 1986. *The Fall into Eden: Landscape and Imagination in California.* New York: Cambridge University Press.

Zavella, Pat. 1987. *Women's Work and Chicano Families: Cannery Workers of the Santa Clara Valley.* Ithaca: Cornell University Press.

[Zonlight] Cooper, Margaret Aseman. 1979. *Land, Water and Settlement in Kern County, California, 1850–1890.* New York: Arno Press.

# Index